Crosswordese

Crosswordese

A Guide to the Weird
and Wonderful Language
of Crossword Puzzles

David Bukszpan

CHRONICLE BOOKS

SAN FRANCISCO

The Roz Chast cartoon on page 245 ("Answers to Last
Week's Puzzle: 'A Toughie'") appears with permission.

All emojis designed by OpenMoji—the open-source emoji
and icon project. License: CC BY-SA 4.0

Library of Congress Cataloging-in-Publication Data

Names: Bukszpan, David, author.
Title: Crosswordese : a guide to the weird and wonderful language of
   crossword puzzles / David Bukszpan.
Description: San Francisco : Chronicle Books, [2023]
Identifiers: LCCN 2023022742 | ISBN 9781797203027 (hardcover)
Subjects: LCSH: Crossword puzzles. | Crossword puzzles--History.
Classification: LCC GV1507.C7 B728 2023 | DDC 793.73/2--dc23/eng/20230530
LC record available at https://lccn.loc.gov/2023022742

Manufactured in China.

Design by Liam ibn Terry Flanagan.

10 9 8 7 6 5 4 3 2 1

Chronicle books and gifts are available at special quantity
discounts to corporations, professional associations, literacy
programs, and other organizations. For details and discount
information, please contact our premiums department at
corporatesales@chroniclebooks.com or at 1-800-759-0190.

Chronicle Books LLC
680 Second Street
San Francisco, California 94107
www.chroniclebooks.com

Introduction and How to Use This BOOK: [Something to read] First

Before the FUN of [Crosswords, say]

Gathered here are crosswords' most useful, curious, conspicuous, and vexing answers, paired with their most guiling and beguiling clues.

As when solving a crossword, approach this book however you like: Follow its path from beginning to end, or jump in and out, skip around, and explore different sections. The important thing is to have **FUN**—after all, as we'll see, that was the [First word in the first crossword].

It may be useful to keep a pencil handy, as each chapter closes with an original crossword puzzle. Like daily crosswords in any paper, these puzzles will contain answers not covered in this book. And they'll get slightly harder as the book progresses, as most newspapers' puzzles do over the course of the week. Answer keys are in the back, but in a way they're on every other page along the way too.

So whether you're reading the chapters [Explaining] answers or [Putting letters into boxes?] at each chapter's end, happy **SOLVING**!

[Fashion] Forward
A STYLE Guide to How Clues and Answers
Are Presented in These Pages

You'll notice the typography of the text is unusual. Conforming to the conventions generally used when writing about crosswords, **ANSWERS** are indicated in blue, bold, and all-caps.

CLUES associated with an answer—like [This and others], [You're looking at them]—are indicated by brackets and found contextualized near the answer, over in the **SIDEBAR**, or both here and ["Over ___"] **THERE**. (One caveat: From time to time, a chart will list many clues for the same answer, in which case the brackets will be omitted.)

Clues for each answer have been chosen because they're used **MORE** frequently than others, present some beguiling fact or [Extra] bit of trickery, or highlight a surprising point. Necessarily, a far [Greater number] of clues for each answer are absent, lest the book become [Never ending?].

As evident in that last case, clues may conclude with a **QUESTIONMARK**, which is worth marking, as it often signals there's [Something uncertain] going on. In the "cruciverse"—a word I'll use for the world of crosswords—a [Crossword clue with a question mark, frequently] is a **PUN**: a [Groaner?] serving as the [Crux of some riddles] that are a [Cruciverbalist's specialty]. **CRUCIVERBALISTS**—a term for [Crossword creators] or crossword solvers like [You and others]—can read that last clue in the preceding paragraph as referring to how "more" can be an ending for "never" in "**NEVERMORE.**"

Note how important a question mark can be by comparing two clues. A [Stumper] might bespeak an **ENIGMA**, but a [Stumper?] could take to the box as an **ORATOR**. Harder puzzles may omit question marks from clues, leaving solvers to potentially miss [One making a delivery] as their minds go to the wrong sort of address.

Underlined answers like this <u>**ONE**</u> may prove most helpful. The underline can be viewed as a sort of <u>**APB**</u> ("all points bulletin") for

STYLE [Vogue], [Hairdo], [Bob or weave], [Do], [Approach]

ANSWERS [No one has all of them]

CLUES ["Jeopardy!" boardful], [What are you looking at?]

SIDEBAR [Court conference], [Hearing at a hearing?], [Digression, of sorts], [Article accompanier]

THERE [Voilà!], [Pointed remark?]

MORE [Oliver Twist's request], ["Utopia" author], [Else], [Seconds], [Another request?], [Not less], [Sometimes less]

PUN ["Ba dum tss" prompter], [Full-groan wordplay], [Wit's end?], [The Beatles, e.g.], ["The lowest form of humor," per Samuel Johnson], ["The lowest form of humor—when you don't think of it first": Oscar Levant]

NEVERMORE [Raven's remark], [Croak the raven]

ENIGMA [Knot], [It's not clear], [Puzzling situation], [Puzzling person]

ORATOR [Figure of speech?], [One who gets paid to wax?], [Loud speaker]

ONE [A], [Half and half?], [Next to nothing?], [What I might be?], [Number within "loneliest"]

APB [Black-and-white broadcast?], [Catchy communication, for short?]

TOME [A-B or C-D, e.g.], [Volume], *or as "to me" in* ["It's Greek __!"]

ERI [Form of the Italian "to be"] *(See also chapter 6)*

WAS [Is past?], [Has been?], [Existed], [Saw around?]

OFT [Frequently], [What's frequently used by poets?]

the most important entries in this **TOME**. Or, at least that's ["The way I see it..."].

Some answers are underscored because they are particularly unfamiliar words, names, or constructions, like <u>ERI</u>. Others may be the most familiar word there ever **WAS**, yet <u>OFT</u> appear in ways that cloak them eerily. So whether naturally [Way out of the public eye] or made [Hard to grasp] by clues, these underlined answers are frequently **OBSCURE**.

Infamous answers that once abounded in crosswords but have since been cast out of circulation, like ESNE, a [Feudal serf]—which we'll dig into later—are not in boldface.

On rare occasions, answers appear in similar typeface to indicate that they are being discussed in a way disassociated from their clues: for example, if <u>OFT</u> was brought up again here. The same typeface will also be used for imaginary or invented answers, such as those constructor Rebecca Goldstein created for a puzzle featuring ad hoc answers like HONEYMOONBADGER, clued as a [Nagging newlywed?], by combining "honeymoon" and "honey badger" in whole-ly matrimony.

Finally, note that crosswords sometimes put clues in brackets themselves to indicate a sound or emotion. As this book uses brackets to show something is a clue, a clue for **ALAS** rendered in this book as [[Sigh]] illustrates that in an actual puzzle, it would appear as [Sigh]. ["So it goes."], I guess. Still, ["I wish it weren't so"] and ["Woe is me"] for any confusion it causes.

INTRODUCTION AND HOW TO USE THIS BOOK

SEEDS of Doubt and [Sources] of Pleasure
Whence the Clues

EVERY clue found in the text and sidebars of these pages is taken from a published puzzle, most from the countless fantastic crosswords presented regularly by the likes of the *Atlantic*, the *Los Angeles Times*, *Newsday*, the *New Yorker*, the Universal Crossword, *USA Today*, the *Wall Street Journal*, the *Washington Post*'s Sunday paper, and of course the *New York Times* (also referred to here as the *Times*).

Clues have also been compiled from erstwhile sources of terrific crosswords, like the *Chronicle of Higher Education* and the *New York Sun*. Many of the most amusing and outrageous clues ran first in the *Onion*, AV Club Xwords, the *Chicago Reader*/Inkwell, and CrosSynergy.

Countless other American and foreign papers also include crosswords, most syndicating the **LAT**, **NYT**, or Universal puzzle. For instance, the *Washington Post* publishes the *Los Angeles Times*'s weekday puzzles, the *Ottawa Citizen* provides its readers with the *New York Times*'s puzzle, and the *Toronto Star* and the *Boston Globe* offer Universal's.

While clues have been culled from all the sources named above, an especially large number come from the *New York Times*, due in part to the wealth of data available about its puzzles, their popularity, and prestige. Unless otherwise stated, data about the frequency of answers and clues will refer to appearances in the **TIMES**, which tends to track with their [Occasions] in other leading puzzles.

Fortunately, this is a golden [Era] of crosswords: Whether clues come from a puzzle in a [New York or Los Angeles paper] or anywhere else, [They may be good and hard]. So let's dive in and find out [What "x" might mean].

SEEDS [Gets things growing], [They can be the pits]

EVERY [Part of EGBDF], [Opposite of no]

LAT [Big California paper] *(See also chapter 3)*

NYT [WSJ competitor], [Will Shortz's paper, for short]

TIMES [Life partner?] *(See also the [Sort of table] or [___Square] in chapter 1)*

PART ONE

[What the ___] HECK
Is Crosswordese?

Crosswordese:
What It Is,
Why It's Important,
ANDHOW to
Master It ["You
said a mouthful!"]

Good NEWS That's
[Front page fill]
You're Smarter Than You Thought

Whether you're a veteran solver breezing through several puzzles a day or someone who's just crossword curious, this probably won't come as **NEWS**: Crosswords have a funny way of making solvers question their own [Intelligence].

The wide range of [Information] solvers think they possess can suddenly seem rather [Skinny] when faced with empty boxes. And even if solvers can [Kind of stand] being stumped by some [Word] or [Facts], the truth is [It gets old quickly]. No wonder then that many people's initial forays into the cruciverse are [Kind of brief]. For a pastime that's supposed to be a fun escape, clearly [None of this is good].

News [___ flash]: [What's going on] rarely reflects gaps in one's intellect or learning, but an unfamiliarity with a relatively small set of short, oft-repeated answers.

Novices might at first rejoice to discover that most crossword answers are only three or four letters long. But those short answers include an impressive collection of [Extra stuff?] like rare words, dusty names, aberrant abbreviations, archaic contractions, unmoored prefixes and suffixes, and foreign imports.

Nevertheless, I bring good [Tidings]: It's natural for any or all of this regular [Morning paper fare] to be [Something you didn't know]. Just as it's natural to have a few choice four-letter words of your own in response to first encountering them.

Here's the [Headline material]: These [Noteworthy items] are called "crosswordese."

OPINIONS [They're just what you think]

OPINIONS differ on just which answers qualify as "**CROSS-WORDESE**" and why. When the term once appeared as an answer in a *Times* puzzle, the clue eschewed defining it, preferring to cite two prime examples and the typical response to them: [Etui or oast (tsk-tsk!)]. That echoes the vague consensus, at least. In an inter-

BOOK [Leaf collection?], [It may be thrown at you], [Something bound to sell?]

view for this **BOOK**, David Steinberg, the crossword constructor and editor of the Universal Crossword, said:

> Crosswordese words are typically short (three to five letters long) and full of common letters such as vowels. Personally, I have no problem with crosswordese words that I consider widely known, such as **OREO**, **ERIE**, and **ODE**, though I try to avoid crosswordese words that I only know from solving puzzles, such as **OAST**, **ALEE**, and **ERNE**.

Jeff Chen—the crossword constructor who also co-runs the indispensable crossword blog *XWord Info* with its founder, Jim Horne—concurred, saying:

> "Crosswordese" is a vague term, covering everything from esoteric terminology like **ADIT** that virtually no one knows, to vocab that's seen in crosswords disproportionately compared to real life, like **ONO**. I'm fine with the latter, but the former is

terrible. No one should have to wade through a mire of **ESNE**, **ETUI**, *and* **ORLE** *to achieve their victorious finish.*

Both Steinberg and Chen sort crosswordese into two groups, something like the "terrible" and the "tolerable." And Chen also charts a useful track by using the words "from" and "to," suggesting a range of answers between the likes of **ADIT** and <u>ONO</u>.

For our purposes, let's think of crosswordese as answers that seem to appear more frequently in crossword puzzles than in our daily lives, and that exist across a spectrum.

On the one end might be <u>OREO</u> and <u>ODE</u>, widely familiar answers that nevertheless recur with outsize frequency in crosswords. At the other end might be **ORLE** and **OAST**, which turn up rarely in crosswords—and practically never in popular discourse.

This book will draw from the entire swath but focus on the most useful or interesting examples. But as a rule, I'll reserve the term "crosswordese" for the true oddball answers encountered least **IRL** ("in real life"), applying it to any such linguistic **IMP** individually or for the [Small handful] of them collectively. While grids have become increasingly successful at ridding themselves of these most obscure and obnoxious cases, typically at least a couple are still bound to rear their heads in any puzzle, causing a [Little pain in the you-know-where].

Together, this collection of answers might form a sort of **KEY-RING** solvers can attach to their belts. The jangly, jagged little keys at first seem indistinguishable, their uses enigmatic. But once recognized, they represent the difference between gaining access to all the delights of crosswords and feeling locked out in the cold.

I'll **TEND** to celebrate crosswordese as a set, though not necessarily everything in it. Here and there, I'll pick a few examples whose reputations I'll try to burnish and others I believe crosswords should banish. But in **GENERAL**, I'll leave such value judgments to the **READER**.

IRL [Unvirtually], [Offline, online]

IMP [Recurring pain?], [Pain to a pediatrician], [No little angel]

KEYRING [Remote place?]

TEND [Lean], [Mind], [Gravitate], [Shepherd], [Serve behind bars?], [Focus on the goal?]

GENERAL [Blanket], [One with star potential?]

READER [One involved in a plot?]

TOR de Force

Clearing Up Misconceptions on the [Rocky rise] Toward [Peak] Puzzling

Before diving into crosswordese, let's address a few ideas that can trip up solvers straight out of the blocks.

False Impression #1: Clues test what you know

While many clues do ask for specific information, a surprising number **ARE** up to something else. And though crosswords are **WORD** games, that doesn't mean success hinges on knowing a lot of fancy language.

ARE [Modern art?], [Is for more than one?], [Is for you?], [Were present?]

WORD [This is one], [News], ["Amen!"]

Thinking of crosswords as exercises in trivia and vocabulary belies the fact that many clues need be "solved," not simply answered. And that's a shame, because solving is a lot more fun than just plain answering.

For example, solvers confronted with an [Air port?] that's a [Plane part] might take a second to land on the truth: that the answer's as plain as the **NOSE** on their face—or the ["-", in :-)]. Thus, even when the answer alludes to something a solver knows, a clue can still elicit the equivalent of ["Dunno," in Spanish] (as in *no sé*). Yeah, they can really do a [Kind of job] on you!

NOSE [Blow it?], [A hook might give it a hook], [Breather?], [Bridge locale], [What smells?]

Therefore, it might be more accurate—and helpful—to think of crosswords not as word games but "wordage" games. Or even **MIND** games. Which is to say, they're **PUZZLES.**

MIND [Tend], [Matter topper?], [Reading material for psychics?], [Matter master]

PUZZLES [Stumps]

Ultimately, solving crosswords is in large part a creative endeavor, less testing what solvers know than challenging how they think about what they know.

False Impression #2: A Sunday puzzle is as good a place to start as any

Though crosswords are increasingly solved digitally, many solvers' first attempts still involve a pencil and paper. And often that attempt is on a Sunday, or whatever **DAY** the mood strikes them to give it a go.

DAY [It's constantly breaking around the world], [Break time?], [Word after field or before dreams], [Time for light work?], [One revolution]

But all days' puzzles are not made equal. Sunday crosswords are generally about twice the size of the usual 15 × 15 weekday grid,

THEMES and Revealers: [Crossword features, usually]

Not only are Friday and Saturday puzzles typically the toughest, they're also usually "themeless." The rest of the week, puzzles almost always have "themes," usually sets of four or five long answers (or several more on Sundays) sometimes called "themers," which share some hidden trait. (You'll find a themed crossword concluding each chapter of this book except for the last, which will offer a taste of the themeless variety.)

The best **THEMES** are like [Some bars returned to again and again?]: Solvers can find themselves in the dark. They rely on an answer colloquially called a "revealer" to offer an often punny explanation. Themes rarely display any connection to the day a puzzle runs, though they're apt to celebrate some holidays or heed an anniversary or major event.

For example, a puzzle appearing on December 31 might include themers like:

- ☐ **IFIVESAIDITONCE** [Start of a broken record?],
- ☐ **TIMESOFOURLIVES** [When we have the most fun?],
- ☐ **YOURBREATHREEKS** ["Have a mint"],
- ☐ **CARTOONNETWORK** [Animation station].

Though experienced solvers will likely see where this is going, others might need the help of the revealer:

- ☐ **ONE** [The last thing many people will say tonight, following words hidden in several answers to this puzzle]

---

and puzzles tend to grow more challenging over the course of the week. The easiest puzzles appear on Mondays, and the bar rises through Saturday. Sundays typically are on a **PAR** with a tough **WED** or an easy **THU**. Starting with a Sunday puzzle means a solver is already on pretty rocky terrain, while venturing off on an extralong journey.

Novice solvers are wise then to lace up their solving boots on a Monday. Fortunately, publishers like the *New York Times* often provide access to any past puzzle on any day, so beginners can spend the whole week practicing Mondays. The *New Yorker* flips the **SCRIPT**: Their online crosswords **WAX** easier as the week wanes, so beginners who subscribe have reason to exclaim **TGIF**.

PAR [Round number?], [Course average?], *(See even more in chapter 7)*

WED [Not single], [Do the rite thing?], [Ring up?], [Take for life?], *(Re-engage with this answer in chapter 2)*

THU [Fifth of seven: Abbr.], [July 4, 1776, for one: Abbr.]

SCRIPT [Picture book?]

WAX [Grow, in a way], [Put a coat on?]

TGIF ["I've waited all week for this!"], ["Friyay!"], ["Thank God it's___!": Homer Simpson]

False Impression #3: Crosswordese makes puzzles harder to solve

TOR [The Blue Jays, on score boards], [AL East squad], [Craggy hill], [Prominence], [Lonely lookout], [Windswept spot], [Big publisher in science fiction]

Novice solvers quickly learn the value of scanning puzzles for easy clues, using those answers to gain toeholds in the grid like mountaineers scaling a **TOR**, or [Rocky peak]—(an answer which, when used for the [Major Can. city], works in two respects for [Raptors' home: Abbr.]). To a beginner, a three-letter answer for [Crag] may not provide much purchase, but it's used so often in puzzles that, for experienced solvers, answering such a clue is the [Height] of simplicity. Indeed, it can bring a grin to a [Mountain climber's face].

APEX [It's all downhill from here]

Hardly **APEX** [___ predators], crosswordese answers can often provide an entry [Point], so tackling them should be a [Top] priority. It takes time to learn them, but with each puzzle, what once seemed an insurmountable [Windswept spot] will look increasingly like a mere [Hilltop]. With practice, any dedicated solver can reach the [Peak] that is crosswords' [Crowning achievement]: the [Summit] of Mt. Saturdaywithoutlookingstuffup.

ESE [Amarillo-to-Dallas dir.], [Vane direction], [Suffix in language names], [Suffix for "Japan"], [Suffix with official], [Legal conclusion?], [-speak], [-talk], [Chemical suffix], [Journal ender], [Tip of a tongue?], [Compass point], [Needle point?]

The last word on how crosswordese can make things easier must go to **ESE**, the [Linguistic suffix], which, thanks to "crosswordese," is a [Crossword finisher?]. Despite being something of an eyesore, the answer contains such useful letters that it ranks among crosswords' 40 most-frequent answers. It's also the [Direction opposite WNW], which roughly corresponds to the route many solvers take through a grid, moving from the top left corner to the bottom right. No wonder it's [Crossword's conclusion].

ETUI
An Exemplary If Exceptional [Crossword case]

ETUI [A case of pins and needles?], [Case of the seamstress?]

ETUI, the word for a small case used to hold sewing supplies, is a notorious example of crosswordese and a good case in point for examining crosswordese as a whole.

Of the roughly 370 occasions **ETUI** has appeared in *New York Times* puzzles, the word "case" was part of the clue nearly 80 percent of the time. Two clues alone—[Small case] and [Needle case]—were used over 40 percent of the time. That's characteristic of the sort of crosswordese that exists on the less familiar side of the spectrum: Clues often rely on the same threadbare language. Interesting details and wordplay are rarely woven in.

Etuis are small, portable, often oblong kits containing the sort of accoutrements useful for mending clothes on the run: needles, **PINS**, [Spare pieces?] of thread, small scissors, a **THIMBLE** or two. Larger models might contain a [Long hairpin], or **BODKIN**, a term once used for any sharp object, like [Hamlet's knife]. Despite their practical purpose, etuis were often pretty **FANCY**, and many are now museum pieces. [Imagine] that!

Popular and rather necessary from the 18th century into the early 1900s, the **ITSY** kits have been made largely obsolete by cheap clothes, though new ones can be found on the **ETAIL** ("e-tail") site **ETSY**.

The French use "**ETUI**" (as *étui*) more generally. It can be a glasses case, a folding-style cell phone case, or as a [French CD holder]—a jewel case. But just because it's a **WEE** word, don't dismiss "etui" as **TWEE** (itself a word dating back over a century, from the [Too cute] way a child might say "sweet"): *Étui* is also a French "holster."

That usage hints at the word's former life of crime, including **PRIORS** when "etui" was used in English as a "sheath" and its time as "prison." Some etymologists trace its French root—*estuier*, "to keep"—back to the Latin *studere*, "to be diligent," in which case its past is present in any "student" of English.

On one notable occasion, the crossword constructor Greg Johnson plucked **ETUI** from the dictionary—where it's frequently the entry just above "etymology"—and clued it as the [Word in the etymology of "tweezers"].

Johnson's fascinating, unorthodox clue appeared in *Newsday*'s justly named "Saturday Stumper," edited by Stanley Newman. Confident their audience would be familiar with **ETUI** as an answer, Johnson and Newman could present a fresh clue and provide what solvers relish most: an **AHA** moment.

PINS [Stickers], [They're taken out in alleys]

THIMBLE [Grannies often give it the finger]

FANCY [Quite like]

ITSY [Minute, informally], [Teeny] *(See also an answer spelled only a [Wee] bit differently, ITTY, in chapter 9)*

ETAIL [Amazon area], [Net sales]

ETSY [Crafty site], [Creative outlet?]

WEE [Baby], [Minute], [Like some hours]

TWEE [Overly precious], [Sentimental], [A bit too-too, to a Brit]

PRIORS [Rap sheet entries]

AHA [Sound of a lightbulb going on], [Response when something hits you]

OER [Shortened again], [Opposite of 'neath]

TIME [Hourglass figure?], [Show of hands], [Hard thing to do?]

REALLY ["Is that right?"]

JOB [Robbery]

ETHER [A real knockout?], [Old number?] *(as it was an old method of numbing)*

SIL [Part of RSVP], [Meaning of an embossed "S," maybe], [Start of a pleasing expression?]

ERE [Poetic contraction], a [Poet's "before"], ["Ended, __ it begun" (Emily Dickinson poem)]

INN [Hostel work environment?], [Overnight letter], [Halfway house?]

Even a straightforward clue repeated **OER** and o'er for **ETUI** like [Decorative sewing case] is likely to stump most novices most of the **TIME**. But puzzles' crosswordese clue-recycling program helps beginners learn crosswordese. Decidedly uninspired clues can even be read as a modest apology: "I know it stinks to have this unknown thing in here," they seem to intimate, "so the least I can do is give it to you straight."

Regrettably, this **REALLY** is the least they can do. Yes, an etui holds needles, we get it. But solvers may still wonder: What *is* it?

True, answering that question is not quite crosswords' **JOB**—nor that of the [Puzzle maker, e.g.]. But without a mental image of an etui, the connection between the actual object and what it's called gets replaced by one merely associating clue and answer. It's as if the soul of the word "etui" is gone—the case with needles in it vanished into the **ETHER**, leaving behind just the letters that spell it.

Sometimes crosswords seem only able to laugh at this conundrum. Back in 1992, **ETUI** reached the pinnacle (or nadir) of crosswordese when it was clued in the *Times* as a [Crosswordese case]. The two defining characteristics of the etui were its being "crosswordese" and a "case." The *raison d'être d'étui*, **SIL** *vous plaît*, was to hold together not sewing supplies, but a crossword.

[Plain __] JANE?
More Like "Jane, Yeah!" The Puzzle as Eyre B&B

Conversely, one of puzzles' greatest gifts is their capacity to surprise solvers with references to something beloved: a novel, a lyric, a place. **ERE** finishing a puzzle, a Charlotte Brontë reader may swoon at a clue like [Literary Jane who says, "No net ensnares me; I am a free human being with an independent will"], especially as it might hint that the constructor's an **EYRE** fan too.

The grid is more than a field of interlocking letters: It's a sort of ephemeral **INN** where parts of different worlds can materialize and cross paths in curious and serendipitous ways. It can ignite the imagination. But to be a [Suite spot], answers must have meaning for solvers outside of the grid.

Bereft of answers or clues offering such connections, solvers might ask, **ALA** ("à la") Jane Eyre, "Do you think I am an automaton?—a machine without feelings?" And the poor crosswordese answer might itself pick up her remonstrance, "Do you think, because I am poor, obscure, plain, and little, I am soulless and heartless? You think wrong!"

ALA [Like], [After], *(or, as "Ala.")*[A near-Miss. state?]

In short, like an **AIRBNB** host leaving a review, puzzles would do well to describe their guests in more than a couple of vague words.

AIRBNB [Site with many home pages?]

BTW, Charlotte Brontë made her own folding wallet-style etui, which can be seen at the Brontë Personage Museum in Haworth, England. While "etui" can't be found [Incidentally, in a text] of any of Brontë's novels, in Paris her books can be found in *étuis*, as the French also use the word for a slipcover.

Et Tu, ETTU?
Crosswordese as [Dying words?]

Puzzles' approach to the problem of the most disliked crosswordese has largely been to eradicate it. For instance, ETUI showed up in seven *New York Times* puzzles in 2000 but just once from 2020 to 2021. Its numbers have declined fast in the **WSJ** and **WAPO** as well, though less quickly in the *Los Angeles Times*.

WSJ [Mark Shenk is its puzzle editor]

WAPO [DC daily, for short]

But as the frequency of an answer like ETUI diminishes, so does solvers' ability to recognize it, meaning puzzles grow even more dependent on the old, recognizable, direct, tired clues.

Imagine what would happen if puzzles embraced an answer like ETUI, making it more of a frequent answer. On Mondays and Tuesdays, it might be clued as "It holds needed needles," "Thing for string," or "Previously popular purse string holder." Having laid the groundwork with descriptive clues, more difficult puzzles could provide more playful ones:

No doubt, it's too late for **ETUI**. Trying to bring it back into the fold would be a slow process sure to annoy many solvers who'd dismiss it as a [Case for trivia]. While I've made a [Special case] for it, this isn't a [Vanity case]: The point is that rather than junking an answer, perhaps it's worth junking old clues.

The more answers available to constructors, the easier it is for them to **SEW** a puzzle together. And as ETUI disappears, puzzles need to rely more on some stunt-doubles like **ELOI**, **ELHI**, **EREI**, **ETAL**, [And others] that may be overused already. And I'm looking at you too, **ETTU**.

Fortunately, crosswords don't need to rely only on other old answers to pick up the slack: An influx of brand names, slang, and pop culture references have lent a hand. Meanwhile, puzzle-building software has enormously assisted constructors in their efforts to **FILL** [___-in-the-blank] spaces in grids with less noxious "fill," the term for [Non-theme entries, to crossword constructors].

SEW [Be in a bee?]

ELOI ["The Time Machine" race]

ELHI [Precollege, briefly] *(See chapter 7)*

EREI *("Ere I")* ["...___ saw Elba"]

ETTU ["And you," to Caesar] *(See chapter 1)*

PERIODIC Tables
Why [Intermittent] Crosswordese
Helps [On a regular basis]

ERA [Period] *(See chapter 7)*

ERA has been the most common answer in the *New York Times* since November 21, 1993. That's an important date in the cruciverse: It marks the beginning of the current [Age] in crosswords, a [Span of time] widely known as the "Shortz Era."

The **LABEL** speaks to both the impressive length of Will Shortz's tenure as the *Times* puzzle editor and the profound impact he's had on crosswords.

From the start of his term in 1993 through 2021, Shortz oversaw the publication of about 10,000 puzzles, composed by a total of roughly 1,000 constructors. About 800,000 total answers appeared, relying on about 116,000 discrete answers, which we can think of as constituting crosswords' lexicon. In other words, each of those 116,000 entries has been used at least once as one of the 800,000 answers in the *Times*'s 10,000 crosswords since late 1993.

Drawing on that data, the following charts demonstrate why this book focuses on short answers: 1. Crosswords use short answers frequently. 2. Crosswords rely on relatively few discrete short answers.

Warning: The following pages contain **GRAPHS** and **MATH**. (Note: The following graphs represent only answers 15 letters long or shorter, accounting for 99.7 percent of all answers.)

The first graph (see Fig. 1) distributes the 800,000 answers by length. Roughly half—48 percent—have been three or four letters long.

LABEL [Motown, for one], [Where the price is fixed]

GRAPHS [Plots, in a way]

MATH [Field with bases], [Work with planes, maybe], ["You do the ___!"]

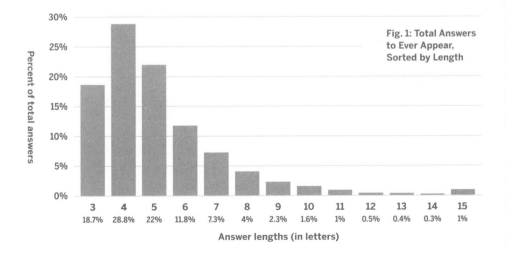

Fig. 1: Total Answers to Ever Appear, Sorted by Length

Percent of total answers

| 3 | 4 | 5 | 6 | 7 | 8 | 9 | 10 | 11 | 12 | 13 | 14 | 15 |
| 18.7% | 28.8% | 22% | 11.8% | 7.3% | 4% | 2.3% | 1.6% | 1% | 0.5% | 0.4% | 0.3% | 1% |

Answer lengths (in letters)

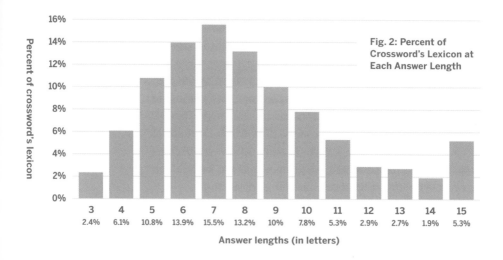

Fig. 2: Percent of Crossword's Lexicon at Each Answer Length

Answer lengths (in letters)												
3	4	5	6	7	8	9	10	11	12	13	14	15
2.4%	6.1%	10.8%	13.9%	15.5%	13.2%	10%	7.8%	5.3%	2.9%	2.7%	1.9%	5.3%

The second graph (see Fig. 2) sorts the 116,000 discrete answers by length. Answers that have appeared 25 times, say, are counted the same as those that have been used once. It reveals that only 2 percent of the answers in the crossword lexicon are three letters long; only 8 percent are under five letters long. Taking the first graph's data into account, this means that 48 percent of crossword answers are drawn from just 8 percent of its lexicon. And just 2 percent of answers—about 2,700—have answered about a fifth of the 800,000 total clues in Shortz Era puzzles.

Notice that small bump at 15-letter answers? The undeniably thrilling way they span the grid makes them a favorite of constructors and solvers alike.

The third graph (see Fig. 3) reveals the stunning consequences: Each of those 2,700 three-letter words has appeared an average of 56 times.

To put this in perspective, the most common 13-letter answer during the Shortz Era turns out to be—aptly enough—**PERIODIC-TABLE** ("periodic table"), which appeared six times. Meanwhile, ERA has appeared in over 600 puzzles during that span.

PERIODICTABLE [Place for I, O, or U]

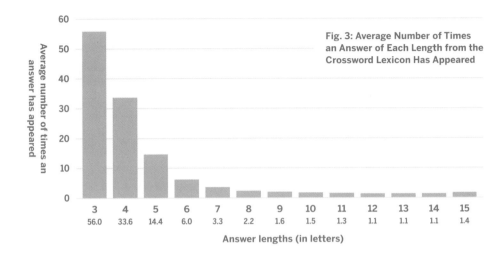

Fig. 3: Average Number of Times an Answer of Each Length from the Crossword Lexicon Has Appeared

3	4	5	6	7	8	9	10	11	12	13	14	15
56.0	33.6	14.4	6.0	3.3	2.2	1.6	1.5	1.3	1.1	1.1	1.1	1.4

Answer lengths (in letters)

ERA is an extreme example. But hundreds of other three-letter answers have been used over 150 times. That's about once every two months, or about as often per **ANNUM** as PERIODICTABLE has in total since 1993.

ANNUM [Year: Lat.], [Revolution for Caesar?]

A little back-of-the-**NAPKIN** math reveals that, on average, each of crosswords' three-letter answers appears about 10 times as often as any other answer.

NAPKIN [Laptop accessory?]

With short answers in such high demand in grids, and unfamiliar (like ETUI) or dubious (like ESE) answers in low demand for solvers, puzzles turn to familiar answers, doing whatever they **CAN** to de-familiarize them [Behind] tricky clues to keep [John] Q. Solver on his toes.

CAN [Know how], [Let go], [Preserve], [Fire], [Sack], [Ax], [86], [Rear], [Kicker's target], [Jail, slangily], [Lock up], [Pen]

So it turns out the cruciverse is really a **SMALL** world after all. One could even say it's ["Fun-size"].

SMALL [Kind of potatoes], [Peanuts, in a manner of speaking], [Back part]

[Fill in] the Blanks:
A BRIEF History
of Crosswords
and Crosswordese

INTHE ["___beginning..."]
There Was the Word-Cross

Arthur Wynne Invents
Crosswords (and Crosswordese)

INTHE [___dark (clueless)],
[Words with clear or way]

TOY [Bit of kiddy litter?],
[First car, for many?],
[Miniature]

BOX [Cuff], [Check point?],
[Present location?]

CORRECT ["Yes"], ["That's
right!"], [OK], [PC part?]

Wanting to give his readers a special gift one Christmas, Arthur Wynne, the editor of the "Fun" section of the *New York Sunday World*, devised a new sort of **TOY**. In the December 21, 1913, issue he presented what he called "Fun's Word-Cross Puzzle": a numbered grid above a set of clues. Readers were instructed to "Fill in the small squares with words which agree with the following definitions."

Wynne's puzzle differs from modern crosswords in a few key ways. For starters, it arrived with an answer already filled in, and the grid was shaped like a diamond. (Maybe a **BOX** containing a diamond would have suited the season better than a diamond containing boxes, but it sparkled nonetheless.) Also atypical were its hollow center, its numbering system noting answers' first and last squares, and the four "unchecked" or "uncrossed" squares at the grid's corners. As each of those squares contained a letter that's part of only one answer, there was no way to "check" if its contents were **CORRECT**.

2–3. What bargain hunters enjoy.
4–5. A written acknowledgment.
6–7. Such and nothing more.
10–11. A bird.
14–15. Opposed to less.
18–19. What this puzzle is.
22–23. An animal of prey.
26–27. The close of a day.
28–29. To elude.
30–31. The plural of is.
8–9. To cultivate.
12–13. A bar of wood or iron.
16–17. What artists learn to do.
20–21. Fastened.
24–25. Found on the seashore.

10–18. The fibre of the gomuti palm.
6–22. What we all should be.
4–26. A day dream.
2–11. A talon.
19–28. A pigeon.
F–7. Part of your head.
23–30. A river in Russia.
1–32. To govern.
33–34. An aromatic plant.
N–8. A fist.
24–31. To agree with.
3–12. Part of a ship.
20–29. One.
5–27. Exchanging.
9–25. To sink in mud.
13–21. A boy.

DOVE [Went off the deep end?], [One likely to vote against a strike?]

COO [Sweet talk], [Cote call], [Co. bigwig]

COTE [Pigeon's coop]. [Bird house], [Ewe's shelter], [Ram home?], [It's for the birds]

TODAY [Now], [Procrastinator's least favorite time?]

SALES [Commissioned work?], [Pitching staff?], [Concern of the force?]

FACE [Feature presentation?], [Mirror image?], [Thing to save]

RULE [Draw the line?], [Gag follow-up?], [Be awesome]

DOH ["Dumb. dumb, dumb!"], [[Head slap]], [Exclamation added to the OED in 2001], [Simpson trial outburst?], [Line from Homer], [FOX cry?], [Play conclusion?] *(If the last clue's a stretch, think of the gunk)*

WOE [Blue state?], [Job experience?], [What "vey" of "Oy, vey!" translates to]

HOMER ["D'oh!" nut?], [Reason for a diamond jubilee?], [Reason for National pride?]

ONER [Remarkable thing, in slang], [Unique individual], [Doozy], [British pound, informally], [Lollapalooza]

SERE [Saharan], [Ungreen], [Wizened up]

ARID [Desertlike], [Unused to showering?]

Also unlike crosswords made today, the grid housed the same answer twice: Two clues—[A bird] and [A pigeon]—each called for a **DOVE**, making the puzzle **COO** a bit like a **COTE**. Today, even if one clue referred to a homograph (i.e., [Went under]), nesting the same answer twice doesn't fly.

Grids of crisscrossing words were hardly new; one was even found during the excavation of Pompei. Wynne would later modestly attest, "All I did was to take an idea as old as language and modernize it by the introduction of black squares." Yet the crossword craze that ensued—and to some extent continues **TODAY**— so clearly began with the publication of Wynne's puzzle that his diamond Word-Cross is roundly considered the first crossword.

I'll go a step further. Along with **SALES**, **FACE**, and **RULE**, Wynne also called for solvers to come up with **DOH** for [The fibre of the gomuti palm], which I believe qualifies him as the creator of crosswordese.

Who knows how Wynne knew "doh," though he may have pulled it from one of the countless word-based puzzles he'd solved as a boy in England.

But **WOE** to the *World* readers who hadn't spent their youth the same way. Not knowing **DOH** was [The fibre of the gomuti palm] would hardly justify a [Verbal facepalm] or cries of ["Silly me!"]. Truly, in those ancient days before **HOMER**, [It's a long shot] anyone would've known it. But that's how solvers discovered the genius of Wynne's creation: By crossing words, they could be a [Diamond big shot] even if their vocabulary didn't [Go deep].

And **DOH** was hardly Wynne's only onerous **ONER**. He also included rarities like the Scottish **NEIF**, [A fist], and **TANE**, [One]. Only slightly better is **NARD**, [An aromatic plant] mentioned in the Bible, which remarkably cropped up in three *Times* puzzles 2008– 2009. No doubt solvers will raise a stink if it ever does again.

Wynne also seeded a couple of tough answers that, while rare, are still called on in crosswords. The **NEVA**, [St. Petersburg's river], flows into the occasional puzzle, and **SERE**, which he clued through its obsolete usage as [A talon], continues to claw its way into grids, most often as [Withered] or [Bone-dry]—clues also aired for **ARID**.

Springing Episodically from SPRINGFIELD
(That's [Homer's city], Not the ["Father Knows Best" setting])

ABE Simpson

- Simpson who said: "Grass today is sharper than when I was a boy"
- "The Simpsons" character who says, "The metric system is the tool of the devil! My car gets 40 rods to the hogshead and that's the way I likes it"

See chapter 1 for the even older [Springfield sobriquet]

APU Nahasapeemapetilon

- "The Simpsons" character who claims he can recite pi to 40,000 places
- 1998 Outstanding Voice-Over Performance Emmy role
- "Much ___ About Nothing" ("The Simpsons" episode)
- "The Problem with ___" (2017 documentary)

MOE Szyslak

- Yellow beer server
- "Simpsons" barman who says "I've been called ugly, pug ugly, fugly, pug fugly, but never ugly ugly"

See chapter 8 for mo' on the other [Stooge of TV]

NED Flanders

- Leftorium owner on "The Simpsons"
- Homer frequently borrows from him
- Whom Homer once referred to as "stupid sexy Flanders"

See chapter 9 for others with the [Nickname for Benedict or Edgar]

OTTO Mann

- Pot-smoking bus driver
- "Simpsons" character who said, "Real songs are about deals with the devil, far-off lands, and where you'd find smoke in relation to water."
- "Simpsons" character whose last name was supposed to be Mechanic
- Good name for a mechanic

*See chapter 9 for more **OTTO** men you oughta know*

Disco **STU**

- Afro-sporting character on "The Simpsons"
- Discus ___ ("The Simpsons" character in an episode inspired by "The Odyssey")

*See chapter 10 for more to **STU** on*

COAL [Frosty material?], [Rock around the Christmas tree?]

RECEIPT [Slip on a new piece of clothing?]

SPAR [Exercise one's rights?], [Go a round with?], [Work on a canvas]

TRADING [Thing done by those in the pits?]

DRAW [Appeal], [Pick a card, any card?], [No-win situation?], [Make a face?], [Take lots?], [Work on one's figure?], [20-20, e.g.], [Engage in sketchy behavior?]

TIED [Even], [Having no loose ends?], [Leaderless?], [Pulled some strings?], [Knotted up, say], [20-20, e.g.]

MIRED [Bogged down]

SAND [Ocean liner], [Beach blanket?], [Bank deposit?], [Take the edge off?], [Soft rock?]

HARD [Unlike a picnic?], [Herculean], [Like a Saturday crossword], [Knotty]

KIND [Class], [Like some souls or words], [Generous cousin?]

GOOF [Err], [Idle, with "off"]

IRKED [Cross], [Got the goat of], [Put out]

With 6 of its 31 answers being so uncommon, one can imagine Wynne's Christmas gift—despite its diamond shape—going over like a stocking filled with **COAL**.

Yet the response was overwhelmingly positive. Perhaps by presenting the literally **FUN**-filled puzzle, Wynn provided solvers not only a practical boost but a psychological one. Though solvers may have responded to something more subtle: the puzzle's humorous tone. For instance, **FUN** is crossed by **RULE**, an intersection of forces still at play in crosswords.

As solvers progressed, other pairs of linked or juxtaposed answers might have tickled them: **SALES** arrives right before **RECEIPT**. **SPAR** goes toe-to-toe with **TRADING**. **DRAW** and **TIED** are **MIRED** together, which Wynne planted firmly in the **SAND**. Speaking of paired answers: Smiles must have lit up the faces of solvers who noticed that this Christmastime puzzle contained a [Gift on the second day]: that pair of **DOVES**.

Solvers who felt mired themselves would have appreciated that [What this puzzle is] proved to be **HARD**, ironically making it perhaps the puzzle's easiest answer.

The next week, Wynne's second Word-Cross was accompanied by a note: "The great interest shown in 'Fun's' word-cross puzzle has prompted the puzzle editor to submit another of the same **KIND**."

A week later, a slight but significant change to the instructions directed readers to "Find the Missing Cross Words." The linguistic cross-up has been attributed to a typographical **GOOF**, but the flip-flop hardly proved a flop. The fourth puzzle was rebranded "Fun's Cross-Word Puzzle."

So it could be said that crosswordese predates even the word "crossword." I like to imagine some poor schlub, **IRKED** but determinedly solving those early puzzles, deriding Wynne for using wordcrossese.

"Play . . . D'oh!!!"

ACROSS

1 Grampa Simpson
4 Homer Simpson's middle name—and middle initial
7 Type of shooter or coat
8 Stringed instrument popularized in Hawaii, but actually from Portugal, for short
9 "Do the___," song based on the alter-ego of a Springfield boy, which topped the U.K. pop charts for 3 weeks in 1991
11 Ad___(improvise)
12 Last name of the proprietor of Moe's Tavern
16 Lao Tzu's "___ Te Ching"
17 Lead-in to a Pen used by nurses
18 It might air "Simpsons" reruns
19 Added value?

DOWN

1 "Calling all cars!"
2 "There are way too many numbers. The world would___ better place if we lost half of them": Homer
3 In the beginning stages
4 Popular newspaper puzzles
5 Alias, for short
6 Japanese currency
10 "Yes, indeedy," old style
12 Springfield resident whose last name is Discoteque
13 Sound of a mosquito being fried
14 Kwik-E-Mart owner who's also chief of Springfield Volunteer Fire Department
15 Kardashian or Cattrall

What's Farrar Is FAIR

Margaret Farrar Says ["You've got a point"] and Makes Things Square

FAIR [Clear], [OK], [C-worthy], [50-50, say], ["Eh"], [Just], [Light], [Objective], [Rural event], [Liable to get burned?], [Light-headed?]

NEE [Born], [At birth], [Formerly], [Born this way?]

SMITH [One of about 2,400,000 in the United States], [Expert on forgery?], [Heavy metal fan?]

HIREE [Enlisted person?], [Fresh blood]

NIT [Cavil], [Young bug], [Lousy egg?], [Critic's pick?], [Tiny carp?], [Kind of wit]

BUT [Still], [Start of a protest], [Save], [Waffle introducer?], [Exceptional word?], ["I'd tell you, ___ then I'd have I'd have to kill you"]

ADO [Bother], [Hubbub], [Kerfuffle], [Carrying-on], [Foofaraw], [Flurry]

IRE [Spleen], [Pique condition?], [Madness?], [Burning sensation?], [Mountin' pique?], [Bring to a boil?], [Red state]

In 1921, the editor of *Sunday World*, John O'Hara Cosgrave, on the recommendation of his stepdaughter, Elsie Finch, hired Margaret Farrar (**NEE** Petherbridge), Elsie's roommate at **SMITH**, to help with the burgeoning Sunday section. Wynne didn't mind that the **HIREE**, just two years out of college, neither cared nor knew anything about crosswords; her job was simply to handle all the mail the puzzle's popularity had generated and make a [Firm selection] from the submitted puzzles.

The flood of complaints and submissions established the model that's remained crossword editors' "in-box-filler" ever since. Regrettably, Petherbridge discharged her duties just as Wynne had: dismissing any critique as a **NIT** from a [Fool] and sending submissions to print without fact-checking, a practice which doubtless became—like this clue from Juliet Corless—a [Cause of some headscratching] among solvers.

To make things worse, Petherbridge picked puzzles not by the merits of their content **BUT** the visual appeal of their shapes. [On the other hand], it would have been impossible for her to do otherwise, having never tried solving a single crossword.

Petherbridge dismissed even the weekly Monday-morning harangues of her colleague, the esteemed columnist Franklin Pierce Adams, who'd report the many shortcomings of the previous day's puzzle. "To avoid the moronish feeling that usually followed such a lecture," she'd later write, she tried solving the upcoming puzzle. She found that errors, "hideously warped definitions" and words unfairly "dragged out of their native obscurity" added such [Confusion] and [Difficulty] that Adams's weekly **ADO** was no petty, [Foolish fussing]. In fact, so directly did the crossword's shortcomings [Provoke] her **IRE** that "Then and there," she'd write, "with my left hand reposing on a dictionary and my right raised in air, I took an oath to edit the cross words to the essence of perfection."

That proved just the start. Petherbridge, who would succeed Wynne at the *World*, also set to standardizing puzzles, establishing guidelines still in use today: Grids would be **SQUARE**, display rotational symmetry, and have a limited number of black boxes; clues would be numbered simply and divided by their answers' orientation; answers would be at least three letters long. And every box's contents would be "checked" or "crossed" by two answers.

SQUARE [Even], [9 to 3], [Pay off], [Times in New York, e.g.]

In 1924, Petherbridge edited the first book **EVER** published by Simon & Schuster, a collection of crosswords that, in a sign of the crossword fad then gripping the nation, sold out in 24 hours.

EVER [What's before after, at the end?]

Two years later, Petherbridge married the publisher John Farrar, then quit the *World* to focus on her family. But she continued to **EDIT** crossword books, one terrifically popular edition after another. Investing the royalties, she used the compiled income to help bankroll her husband's new publishing house, Farrar & Rinehart, paving the way for his co-founding of another house, the eventual Farrar, Straus and Giroux. (She'd [Revise] many authors' manuscripts at both houses.) Thus two of the world's premier publishing houses, S&S and FSG owe a debt to her ability to [Fix text] and [Prepare a crossword for publishing].

EDIT [Add or subtract, say], [Deal with issues at work?], [Make amends?], [Sub text, maybe]

YET it's for her 27-year **POST** as the first crossword editor of the *New York Times*—from editing its first grids in 1942 to establishing it as the nation's preeminent puzzle—that Margaret Farrar is best remembered. Assessing her half-century career in crosswords, many would still agree with the *New Yorker*'s 1959 appraisal: Despite Wynne's achievement, it's Farrar **WHO** is "probably the most important person in the world of the crossword puzzle."

YET [Still], ["Everyone likes me,___ nobody understands me": Einstein]

POST [One feeling pier pressure?], [Place to get hitched?], [Miss Behavior?] *(as in Emily)*

WHO [Personal question?], [Which one?], [First person in a routine?], [The English Doctor?], [Nameless one]

That *New Yorker* article also offered Farrar's succinct **TAKE** on the answers now known as crosswordese: "We avoid as much as possible obsolete words, variants, obscure words, and clichés—words like 'gnu' and 'emu' and 'proa.' Their odd letter structures make them awfully useful in filling difficult spots, but they're a bore by now."

TAKE [Cut], [Net], [Haul], [Stomach]

And that was way back in 1959!

AINT [Misbehaving]: Rebus Puzzles
Rare Times You [Aren't wrong] Wondering
If Something [Isn't amiss?] with the Grid

The "rules" governing crosswords turn out to be less rigid than the punctilious arrangement the grid might suggest. Some puzzles will blithely transgress a norm. They may use a grid that's not square, feature answers with fewer than three letters, or contain unchecked squares. More often, the **TRICK** is how answers are filled in: Letters may be skipped or rearranged, and answers may change direction. Much of the pleasure seasoned solvers [Take in] solving crosswords can arise from encountering and conquering some brand new [Ruse]. And constructors take pride in creating puzzles that seem to say, as Peter Gordon once put it, you'll have to [Think "a wile" to get this].

Crosswords' most wily [Visual puzzle] is the **REBUS**. The very term can be an [Image problem?] to novices since it's used outside crosswords for the kind of [Puzzle that might express love using a picture of an eyeball, a heart, and a female sheep] or use ["TTTTTT" for "sixty," e.g.]. In the cruciverse, a rebus refers to a crossword that violates the basic "one letter per box" rule, requiring the entry of multiple letters—or even a number or symbol—into a single square.

For instance, back in 1993, the very first clue in the first crossword Will Shortz edited for the *Times* was for a four-letter answer to [Site of the Shandog Peninsula]. The answer was **YELLOWSEA**, requiring solvers to squeeze (or color) "yellow" into the first box. Solvers would also have to find three-letter solutions to ["Let's Stay Together" singer"]—**AL(GREEN)**—and [Bit]—**SH(RED)**. For solvers used to the *Times* puzzle's staid ways, the crossword was a tough—too tough, many agreed—bold departure (and one constructed, incidentally, by the same Peter Gordon mentioned above).

Aside from the occasional Sunday, rebuses almost always appear on Thursdays, so solvers can better expect to be punked. Certainly they won't run on a Monday or Tuesday. And even in rebus puzzles, only a small fraction of the answers will be **AWRY** in some way. So if there is a general rule for beginner solvers, it's this: If an answer doesn't fit without being [Distorted], chances are it's not the grid that's [Not quite right].

Predictable [Predicaments]
Crosswords' PROBLEMS Are Nothing New

Actually, we can find similar grumbling way back in 1924. Just six months after Farrar's first book of crosswords debuted, the *New York Times* ran an editorial that pivoted swiftly from applauding crosswords' educational potential to drolly browbeating their stubborn reliance on certain odd little answers.

Titled "Words, Down and Across," the **OPED** opened happily enough: "Teachers of English, in their struggles with the vocabulary of the undergraduate, have found a welcome ally. It is the crossword puzzle." Heralding "new pedagogical possibilities," it suggested that through crosswords, "new horizons open up." But there the valentine abruptly gave way to a lighthearted—though still high-minded and earnest—plaint:

> To be sure, they are not limitless horizons. After a while the cross-worder finds himself in a world curiously standardized and restricted . . . Egypt made her place in history secure by developing a bird named **IBIS** and a goddess named **ISIS** . . . Japan almost dominates with **YEN** and her immortal broad sash, the **OBI**.
>
> Natural selection operating in the zoological realm favors immensely the survival of the three-lettered animal. The lion and elephant are dethroned and in their place rule the **EMU**, the **GNU**, and the **EEL**. If Coleridge's Mariner were living in this cross-world of ours, he would not be carrying an albatross around his neck. He would be proudly sporting an **AUK**. Cross-worders puzzling on the origin of life differ as to whether the auk came before the **OVUM**, or the ovum before the auk.

Reading between the **LINES**, it's clear that, gripes notwithstanding, the author really did enjoy crosswords. A century later, it's striking that so little has changed. Those same answers still permeate puzzles. And curmudgeonly grousing about them and other

OPED *("op-ed")* [Piece with a view], [Slanted lines], [Take in the paper]

LINES [Stage set?], ["Breadthless lengths," per Euclid], ["Your place or mine?" and others]

crosswordese still resounds, though now on blogs and Twitter, typed by folks whose **YEN** for puzzles endures despite their objections.

That said, these answers would be considered "tolerable" crosswordese by most solvers today. Even if emus and gnus don't appear in most solvers' daily lives, they're familiar enough, likely in part due to the very peculiarity of their names. Equally important, they benefit from an assortment of amiable clues. When **EMU** is a [Fast food source?] or **GNU** is heard as [A new homophone?], who's going to raise a ruckus? In fact, the latter has remained such a paragon of common crosswordese that Michelle Arnot titled her fantastic book on the history of crosswords *What's Gnu?* (For an answer to that question, and more emu musings, see chapter 8.)

The article also bemoaned examples of the sort of crosswordese the cruciverse still almost unanimously considers "terrible." Many of the most egregious cases—like **TAEL**, a [Chinese weight]—would persist until at last the *Times* decided to deal with them itself, in its own **PAGES**, seventy years later.

YEN [Craving], [Long], [¥], [Currency whose name means, literally, "round"]

PAGES [Beeps], [Leaves], [Leafs], [House aides]

Good WILL Hunting
Shortz's [Plans to]
[Resolve] the Crosswordese Issue

Even as a boy, Will **SHORTZ** may have had a clue he'd become an [Overseer of "Times" squares]. At age 12, he titled a homework assignment on what he hoped to do when he grew up, "Puzzles as a Profession." In it he wrote about Dmitri Borgmann, author of *Language on Vacation*, a bestseller on logology (the study of recreational linguistics, from the Ancient Greek word for "word," **LOGOS**). The precocious student even wrote to Borgmann soliciting career advice. The author's response, according to Shortz, amounted to "Don't do it, it's impossible, you won't survive."

Of course, Shortz did more than survive. In college, he devised his own major, enigmatology, the study of puzzles. After 15 years working at *Games* magazine, he was the **NATURAL** answer when the *New York Times* searched to fill their opening for a new crossword

LOGOS [Stationery objects?], [Firm symbols], [Divine word]

NATURAL [Artless], [Quick learner], [Initial dice throw of 7 or 11], [Seven, for one]

puzzle editor in 1993. (Since then, he's also answered to "puzzle-master" as the [Co-host of NPR's Sunday Puzzle].)

Shortz was really ahead of the *Times* when editing *Games*. Along with Stanley Newman and other editors who became known as the "New Wave" in crosswords, he was already plotting ways to improve puzzles. Dislodging crosswordese hovered near the top of their **TODO** (to-do) list.

Interviewed when he took the helm at the *Times*, it was the big *Games* guy **QUA** big game hunter: "I'll put the **ANOA** out to pasture," he promised, setting his crosshairs on the [Celebes ox] (a clue using an old name for the Indonesian island of Sulawesi). He also drove out **ESNE**, an Anglo-Saxon [Feudal laborer] who was doubtless thrilled to roam free after years bound to the grid, toiling away, earning only solvers' scorn in return. Another cast from its **ANCHORAGE** was **PROA**, the swift [Singapore ship] with a sail and a supporting outrigger. By dint of its spelling, **ESNE** was by far the most common answer of the trio, even if it was the most uncommon word—which is saying something considering how few Americans would know an anoa from a proa.

These changes may seem of little note now, but they represented something of a sea change. Shortz's predecessor at the *Times* was Eugene Maleska, a former Latin teacher and school superintendent often seen as the standard-bearer of crosswords' old guard. A few years before retiring, Maleska offered his thoughts about crosswords' reliance on obscure answers, zeroing in on **ESNE**: "Only somebody who does crossword puzzles would know that word. It's what I call crossword-ese. It crops up all the time in puzzles. Who cares about that word? Nobody, but it's easy to fit in the grid." Though the insinuation that he coined "crossword-ese" is misleading—the term had been circulating for at least a decade by then—it's likely many editors and constructors would have agreed with his sentiments. But then, with casual resignation, he **ADDED** a rhetorical question which would amount to a challenge to the New Wavers: "What can you do?"

Well, something. **ESNE** last appeared as an answer in the *Times* in 2015, when it was clued—winkingly—as [A slave to crosswords?]. The answer's last occurrence in any major crossword was a 2016

TODO [Not yet completed], [Brouhaha], [Big fuss], [Stir]

QUA [Sine ___ non], [In the capacity of], [Acting as], [As]

ANCHORAGE *(as "anchorage")* [Berth place] *(or as "Anchorage")* [Iditarod start]

ADDED [Put on], [Threw in]

Wall Street Journal grid, where it was tagged as [Lowly laborer in the crossword business]. Both those instances were in Saturday puzzles, where the **SOLVER** would likely be in on the joke. Ever since then, it's been **IXNAY** on the ESNE.

TAEL's tale is also telling. The Chinese government took the [Bygone Chinese money] out of circulation back in 1933, but puzzles kept filling their pockets with it, seemingly skeptical of adopting the **YUAN**. TAEL retained its crosswords currency—appearing in 11 *Times* puzzles from 1991 through 1993—**TIL** Shortz took **OVER**: TAEL came up just 11 times over the next 22 years before finally disappearing into crosswords' seat cushions in 2015. Constructors and puzzle building software certainly deserve much credit for junking such answers, but editors like Shortz clearly deserve big **UPS** too. While representing a few of crosswords' most frequent answers over the years, a comparison of how often PROA, ESNE, ANOA, TAEL, and GNU have appeared in the *Times* since the paper started running a daily puzzle in 1950 helps illustrate the extent of the changes since Shortz took charge (see Fig. 4).

SOLVER [You, evidently]

IXNAY [Slangy refusal], ["Nope"], ["No way"], ["Forget it!"], ["Cut that out!"], ["Over my dead body!"]

YUAN [Chinese cabbage?]

TIL [Up to], ['Fore]

OVER [Past], [During], [Again], [Above], [Through], [Extra], [Not loving anymore], [Turn the page]

UPS [Big__(praise, slangily)], [Big box company?], [Delivery company nicknamed "Big Brown"], [Raises], [Boon times], [Santa's helper]

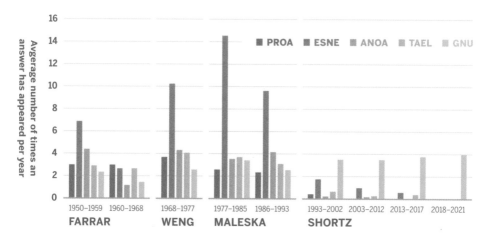

Fig. 4: Average Number of Appearances Per Year of PROA, ESNE, ANOA, TAEL, and GNU

Note: Data are segmented to illustrate averages between and across periods

A few takeaways:

1. Comparing the two halves of Farrar's term, editors seem capable of limiting certain answers. (Recall Farrar's 1959 interview with the *New Yorker*, in which she spoke of trying to avoid **GNU** and **PROA**.)
2. Shortz has proven effective in eradicating much of this crosswordese, even if it's been a gradual process.
3. Conversely, Shortz has grown increasingly indulgent of **GNU**, perhaps indicating that he considers it in a different class than the other four answers, or that it has become more useful as other answers were struck.
4. These five answers combined to answer about 25 clues per year during the first half of Maleska's term. Presently, they combine to show up just four times per annum. So other answers must be stepping in.

The Flip Side to Crosswordese
OREO as a [Cookie with a twist?]

Shortz has described his job editing puzzles as primarily curatorial: selecting not just which puzzles run, but which words, phrases, names, and so on are worthy of use, and how frequently. Passing up **PASSE** ("passé") answers was just half the plan. For Maleska, ridding puzzles of their **CANT**, or [Jargon], was ["Not doable"]. Fortunately for Shortz, puzzle-building software has helped constructors find more elegant solutions. But Shortz simultaneously pursued an even more useful—if not always more elegant—solution, replacing crosswords' [Argot] with [Lingo] from other milieux. To do so, he'd [Lean] into areas of language his predecessor had considered ["Out of the question"]: pop culture, slang, and product names.

Perhaps no answer better illustrates the pronounced shift than **OREO**. Debuting in the grid in 1952, it would make over a hundred appearances—about 2.5 times per year—in the years leading up to

PASSE [So last year], [Out]

OREO [New "biscuit" of 1912], [Cookie that has been deemed kosher since 1997], [Snack item with approximately 53 calories], [It has 12 flowers on each side], [Treat thought to be stamped with symbols of the Knights Templar], [It's nearly impossible to split its cream equally between both wafers, per research from MIT], [Little dipper in a milky way?], [After-dinner sandwich?], [Filling treat?], [One twisted cookie]

the Shortz Era. Over 99 percent of the time, it arose from one of two clues: [Mountain: Comb. form] or [Mountain: Prefix]. Say what?

The answer those clues reached out for didn't represent the [Subject of Weird Al's "The White Stuff"] but the prefix "oreo-," from *óros* (the Ancient Greek for "mountain"), a cognate of the Latin that led to "**ORIGIN**."

ORIGIN [Roots], [Etymology, for one]

The prefix helps form "oreography" (or "orography"), the study of mountains, and "orogeny," the process by which orogen, a layer of the earth's crust, rises into mountains when compressed. (Fun fact: "Orogeny" helped form the topography of **OREGON**, but not its name. The area also happened to be a home of an extinct camellike mammal whose name means "mountain teeth," the oreodont.)

OREGON [Salem's home], [Home to the deepest lake and river gorge in the US], [The Snake borders it], [Snake's place, partly]

Clearly, it should have been an "oreo-**DONT**" to clue <u>OREO</u> as "oreo-," which is evidence of how strongly puzzles once preferred even such a supremely rare linguistic <u>ORT</u> to a brand name. (Fortunately, the alternative form of the prefix, <u>ORO</u>, could and continues to be mined more easily as [Spanish gold].)

DONT [Word of warning], [Terse bit of advice], [Faux pas], [[Stern glare]]

ORT [Food scrap], [Crumb], [Leftover morsel]

ORO [Conquistador's loot]

Despite being a [Cookie that's one year older than crosswords], the *Times* treated solvers only once in over forty years to the **OREO** they actually wanted—and then that once only in the most begrudging way: finally acknowledging it as a [Mountainous cookie?].

Imagine solvers' delight in 1994 at finally seeing the actual [Cream-filled cookie], as Shortz served it the first time he used the answer. Over the next 28 years, the *Times* gorged on the answer 335 times—that's about once a month, on average—referring to the cookie each time.

Maybe it's only fitting that the **OREO**, the [Best-selling cookie brand in America] has become the [Most common commercial name in "New York Times" crosswords], easily ranking among the top 10 most-frequent four-letter answers.

Crosswords also find it befitting that the [Treat with a 71%–29% cookie-to-cream ratio] has a strikingly similar vowel-to-consonant ratio: With their sweet tooth for vowels, it's a [Filling treat] for grids. In fact, in the cruciverse, its very letters make it a [Snack item that's partly foreordained?]. (See how that clue's last word makes a [Cookie sandwich]?)

But it's not always [Everyone's favorite snack in crosswords?]. Some decry the "brandification" of the grid, while others have simply had their fill: They couldn't give a [Fig Newton rival] if they never saw the [Stale cookie of crosswords?] again. Perhaps they have a point: Who wants to be served **OREO** [___ O's breakfast cereal]?

That's **OREOOS** ("Oreo O's"), a [Former chocolaty Post cereal], whose third "o" refers to their shape.

Much more appealingly, constructors Lucy Howard and Ross Trudeau pulled apart what may have been **OREOS**'s surprising start (and middle and end): [Their name has the "re" of "cream" and the two o's from "chocolate"]. (That's just a theory, though. Another suggests a connection to the Ancient Greek.)

Nevertheless, clues like Howard and Trudeau's show crosswords at their best, illustrating how creative, thought-provoking, or revealing clues for common answers like **OREO** can rebrand a [Treat older than sliced bread] as a [Black-and-white treat].

It's also a reminder that in clues, **INFO** solvers don't know can double as **STUF** they can figure out.

Even [Dessert item that was clued as "Mountain: Comb. form" in old crosswords] can be sussed out. The only mountain to climb is remembering crosswords' favorite four-letter "dessert item" is an **OREO**. Which is another reason it's a true [Black-and-white classic].

INFO [411], [Deets], [Dope], [Lowdown]

STUF [Mega___(Oreo variety)], [Oreo morpheme]

[It's berry tasty!] to Crosswords

Get Lost, Gumati, the ACAI Is the New Palm in Town

The most common clue during the Shortz Era has been [Jai ___], for **ALAI**. As a sport, jai alai might not mean much to many Americans, but **ALAI** alone means nothing. The same could be said of the clue that reaches for the obscure [Asia's Trans ___ mountains].

Of its 18 appearances between 2014 and 2021, **ALAI** arrived via [Jai ___] 16 times. Meanwhile, **JAIALAI** has all but vanished from

ALAI [Half-court game?], [End of a game?], [Half a game name that rhymes]

VIBE [Mood], [Feeling], [Vague sense]

ACAI [Kind of palm], [Fruit with a cedilla in its name], [Flavoring in Cedilla liqueur], [Superfood sometimes called "purple gold"], [Bowl berry], [__ oil, extract obtained from the Amazon rainforest], [Fruit with as many syllables as vowels]

BERRY [Preserves something]

SUPER [Extra], [Capital], [Crack], [Start of something big?]

ALOE [Natural healer] (see chapter 5)

VIP [Popular pass]

SETH [Brother of Cain and Abel], [Adam's boy], [Fifth person], [Fourth man], [Adam's third], [Abel successor?], [Member of the first family?], [Clockmaker Thomas]

most Americans' radar, leaving ever fewer solvers aware that the [Handball relative] is a [Lightning-fast Basque game] whose name is [Literally, "merry festival"]. So even a clue for **ALAI** like [Jai ___ (fast-moving sport)] is of little more help than [Jai ___], except to raise awareness for the next time a clue says [Jai ___]. So puzzles mostly rely on [Jai ___], reducing **ALAI** to crosswords' [Jai follower] (the answer's second most-popular clue, by the by). Fortunately, due to both the sport's growing obsolescence and the inability to find a better clue, the answer only alights about once a year. At least that limits the clue-and-answer duo's ability to perpetuate crosswords' old, lamentable, you-have-to-know-the-secret-password-to-enter-the-clubhouse **VIBE**.

Fortunately, help came in 2010, shaped like an [Exotic berry in some fruit juices]: **ACAI**. Skyrocketing in frequency, by 2021 its 20 appearances ranked it 12th among all answers. Clearly this is one [Popular berry]. And of those 20 appearances, clues found a new way to dish the **BERRY** 17 times. Between the versatility of its clues, its relative freshness to the grid, the berry's cultural cachet, and its short, vowel-heavy name, the "superfruit" might qualify as **SUPER**-crosswordese.

While **ACAI** hangs out with other A-listers of the cruciverse like smooth-skinned **ALOE** over at the **VIP** table, there's not much for **ALAI** to do. Except maybe dream of one day regaining relevance by pairing up with **SETH** Rogen to star in a stoner flick called "High ___."

But that dream is partly a revenge fantasy, as the rapid rise of **ACAI** clearly hastened **ALAI**'s precipitous fall. Notice the huge "C"-change: Previously, with only **ALAI** to work with, a constructor might have needed to use an unappealing answer like **LAVE**, (clued as [Wash up]); having **ACAI** opens the door to **CAVE** (clued as [Give in]).

Yet this cuts both ways. There are times when a grid would work better with an "L" than a "C": Why use **CAVA**, as in [Vena ___ (passage to the heart)] when there's [Hot stuff] like **LAVA**? And every time **ACAI** shows up, it becomes less an [Exotic berry] and more a [Ubiquitous berry, nowadays].

Geoffrey Chaucer's idea that familiarity breeds contempt is only half the story in the cruciverse. Both unfamiliarity (as in **ALAI**) and overfamiliarity (as in **ACAI**) breed solvers' contempt.

Ideally, the two answers would better balance each other out. A movie like *High Alai*, even if it stunk, would be a boon for crosswords. (Not to mention that puzzles would repay the favor through lots of free publicity in clues.)

Such a film might even refurnish puzzles with answers that have fallen from the lexicon, like **PELOTA**, a [Jai alai ball]; **CESTA**, a [Jai alai basket]; and **FRONTON**, a [Jai alai arena], which in turn could be a ["High Alai" theater?].

Obviously, this scenario is just an example of how answers interact. The movie, in so many words, is just a pipe dream. (Right, Seth?)

Can You DIGIT?

Trying to [Figure] Out Crosswordiness

As we've seen, "crosswordese" can stem from a perceived imbalance between an answer's frequency in puzzles and its usage outside them. So is that measurable? If so, could we determine at long last which answers really are crosswordese and see how well the grid actually reflects language outside it?

DATA visualization specialist Noah Veltman thought this was possible. He took a calculated approach, devising a formula comparing answers' frequencies in *Times* puzzles from 1996 through 2012 against [Figures] from Google Books counting how often those words appeared in print outside of puzzles over the same period. The formula took in the [Stuff to crunch] and pumped out [Statistical numbers] for each answer, which Veltman labeled as each answer's "crosswordiness," which commendably rolls **OFF** the tongue more easily than "crosswordese-iness."

According to his math, the dubious honor of "crosswordiest" answer went to . . . **DRUMROLLPLEASE** . . . ["Wait for it"] . . .

ASEA. So, umm, yeah, okay, not exactly the cruciverse's most ogrish, inscrutable answer, but an undeniably frequent one, ranking

DIGIT [Finger or toe], [Two or three], ["Far out, man!"]

DATA [Cloud contents], [It can be mined], [It may be roaming overseas]

OFF [Incorrect], [Switch position], [Canceled], [Repellent choice?], [Broadway opening?], [Season opener?], [Running partner?], [Ice, so to speak], [Position with no power?], [Sour], [A little peculiar]

ASEA [On the briny], [Cruising], [Between ports], [Topside, perhaps], [Making a crossing], [Lost], [Befuddled], [Washed out?], [Using clippers?], [In the Black?], [In the Red?]

MAIN [Ocean], [Cardinal], [Key], [Common street name], [It might cross 1st, 2nd, or 3rd], [Big drag?]

SMEE [Hook's helper], [Right-hand man for a man with no right hand], [Hook hanger-on]

HOOK [Disarmed captain?], [Golf goof], [Selling point], [Left or right, say]

SMEW [Old World duck], [Duck in the Eurasian taiga], [Cousin of a goldeneye], [Duck that nests in tree hollows], [Duck with a large white crest]

URSA [Major animal], [Major or Minor?], [Connect-the-dots bear?]

SNEE [Snick and___]

TEXTS [Avoids talking, in a way], [Cell exchanges], [Comments from ones who are all thumbs?], [Thread count?]

AERO [Prefix with space], [Flying start?], [Designed to minimize drag]

ENOL [Hydroxyl compound], [Carbon compound], [C+C (OH) compound]

in the top hundred. It's certainly more than capable of leaving solvers [Clueless]—which [On the main] happens to those [Not well grounded] with "the main" part of that clue. Generally a literary and archaic term for the open seas, it's been floated in enough clues that in crosswords, it's important for solvers to remember the **MAIN**. You could even call it a [Major water line].

The second crosswordiest answer—taking the silver medal as a good pirate should—is a character who was often asea: [Hook's henchman], Mr. **SMEE**, the ["Man who stabbed, so to speak, without offence," in a 1911 novel]. He's the four-letter ["Peter Pan" pirate] and [Barrie baddie] whom every seasoned solver at least once took a stab at but mistook for **HOOK**. **SMEE** seems less than handy in one pointedly zen koan–like clue that's hard to shake: [Hook's right hand]. Puzzles used to mishandle **SMEE** by identifying it as a [Diving duck] or [Eurasian duck]; crosswords now identify that bird as a **SMEW**.

Also placing sky high, **URSA**, the [Celestial bear] that's a [Major in astronomy?], ranked third. Not bad for an answer which, as Samuel A. Donaldson and Tracy Gray spotted it, is a [Bear that's up all night?].

In fourth was **SNEE**, an obsolete word for an [Old dagger] or the use of one. If heard at all anymore, it's as part of the idiom "snick and snee," a similarly archaic bit of English meaning "to stab, as in a knife fight." The good news is **SNEE** can only snick, or nick, solvers, as puzzles wield it about only once a year.

Even if each of those answers is likely overused in puzzles, it's doubtful even the least familiar, SNEE, would rank atop many solvers' most unwanted lists. Veltman has pointed to several factors that might have skewed the results: chiefly, that for various reasons he excluded proper nouns, phrases, abbreviations, and foreign words. Consider, too, how many **TEXTS** are published on academic topics. That could account for why his algorithm didn't decry answers like **AERO** and the abysmal **ENOL**, which escapes the lab to terrorize the gridsfolk about once a year.

But perhaps the results suggest that the worst crosswordese just doesn't appear in grids very often. Or that what's unfamiliar may still be quite pertinent.

Regardless, the results posted at noahveltman.com are worth exploring, especially as each answer links to ranked lists of clues and keywords. It shows, for example, that **ALEE**—ranking seventh on Veltman's list and high on David Steinberg's too—was most frequently clued as [Away from the wind], while the words most often appearing in its clues were "sheltered," "wind," and "side." Recognizing such "clue-answer word pairs," as Veltman calls them, is a critical skill in solving puzzles.

ALEE [On the quiet side?], [Toward shelter], [Stern command?] *(See chapter 4)*

Looking AHEAD
What's Coming [Up] for Crosswordese, in Puzzles and These Pages

Evidence suggests that more people are trying their skills at constructing puzzles than ever before. In 2021, 25 percent of *Times* puzzles were debuts by new constructors, up from 18 percent in 2020 and 9 percent for the five years before that. By late 2021, so many submissions were flowing into the *Times*—up to 200 per week, suggesting an acceptance rate of about 4 percent—that despite expanding its puzzle staff, the paper temporarily stopped accepting new crosswords. Again, the availability of crossword construction software has helped. So too has an apparent renewed enthusiasm for solving puzzles, buoyed by anytime-access to crosswords and the increased ease of solving by **APP**. (No doubt, the surge of interest in hobbies during the Covid pandemic introduced a huge new citizenry to the cruciverse.) Meanwhile, the number of magazines and websites featuring their own crosswords is steadily on the rise.

AHEAD [In the first place?], [Best way to leave Las Vegas?], [Each]

APP [Many a time suck], [Thing involved in a phone tap?], [Intro course?]

All this likely spells good news for crosswords and **BAD** news for crosswordese—which itself is likely [Good in some cases]. Inevitably, some answers in this book will soon join **ESNE** and **ANOA**, ousted from the grid. Maybe this is bye-bye, **ALAI**.

BAD ["Tsk! Tsk!"], [Turned], [Counterfeit]

What follows then is a snapshot of the state of play as it now stands: part resource for solving crosswords, part celebration of puzzles' pleasures, and part romp through their language, surveying its cluttered collection of curiosities and appraising their capacity to bemuse, amuse, and amaze.

["There's this thing called Google..."]: Revelatory Anagrams, Whether to LOOKITUP, and Profitable Pointers

ANAGRAMS are a [Letterman's favorite activity]. So when the opportunity arises to use one in a grid, solvers can usually count on constructors to bring their **AGAME**: a [Good thing to bring to the field] of crosswords.

Impressive **ANAGRAM** Clue List
(Aren't you [Eager to agree, say?])

Hated to death?
Plane to Nepal?
Tokyo for Kyoto?
Breadth to the Bard
Asked for a desk, say
Antes up for peanuts?
Anemone, to name one
Substitute for butt tissue?
Sport shoes for hoopsters, e.g.
Get Meg Ryan out of Germany?
Nerd's epithet to the president?
African lions, vis-à-vis Californians
Chemical agent for climate change
Schoolmaster for the classroom, e.g.

It's even hard to say which is [Canniest, for instance]: [An insect, for instance] or [Ancients, for instance]?

While it's hard enough for solvers to see these clues and realize they represent an **ANAGRAM**, perhaps the most demanding is the aptly minimalistic [Eno, for one], capitalizing on the name of the great [Minimalist musician] of crosswords, Brian **ENO**. *(See chapter 6.)*

[Cheaters, for teachers] is an especially popular clue for **ANAGRAM**. Perhaps the cheaters-teachers dynamic strikes a chord, as it seems to echo one of the great quandaries of the cruciverse: *Is it OK to cheat and look something up? Am I cheating myself? Or teaching myself?* These are questions that solvers can answer only for themselves.

Of course, for solvers who want to look those answers up, here it is: Look up anything you want. Anytime. Until you don't want to anymore.

Looking something up not only helps solvers find the answer; they also learn about the answer. Eventually, solvers who look things up become solvers who don't need to. Besides, it's undoubtedly better to look something up and continue solving than call it quits. The name of the game is pressing on. As in pressing "on" the Google search button.

Here are a few other tips:

1. Use a pencil (or the "pencil" option in solving software)—but really use it. Don't be afraid to write a wrong answer. Sometimes the wrong answer contains a right letter. If after many efforts not a single crossing answer fits, no matter how right it seems, erase and reconsider it.

2. Remember that there really is no opponent, particularly not the puzzle. Though it may feel adversarial, a puzzle exists to be solved. And it employs its army of clues not against solvers but in solvers' service.

   "**PSST**, ["Over here!"]," says each **CLUE**, "I'm trying to tell you something. Listen to [This, e.g.]: You may think I'm an [Answer's opposite], but it's more accurate and [Helpful] to see me as an [Answer guide?]. And when I'm a [Mystery item], my pals around me, especially those cluing answers passing through mine, will often be a bit easier on purpose, and maybe even give you a [Sign] as a [Tip-off]."

3. Notice such signs within clues. They're not always present, but the earlier in the week, the more likely they will be. Clearest of all, as noted earlier, are question marks, indicating wordplay. But here are some others:

☐ Abbreviations: Instead of using "Abbr." or "for short," a clue will often employ an actual abbreviation, so **MPH** might be [Inits. on the road], [Ticket fig.], or [Hwy. speed, maybe].

☐ Foreign words, locations, and names: These indicate an answer is connected to a language. **TIA** might be [Acapulco aunt], [Su padre's hermana], [Jose's aunt].

☐ "S" and "D" (plurals and tense): Clues will consistently reflect grammatical distinctions of their answers. Even if a solver has no idea what a four-letter [Cleric's closetful] could be, the second word suggests the answer is a plural noun, so it's worth guessing the answer's last letter is an "s." Go ahead and fill it in. That can lead to another answer, and so on, helping to iron out **ALBS**, [Vestments] we'll revisit in chapter 2.

"Puzzle Power!"

ACROSS

1 A jack, or a jerk
4 Muscle pains
10 The NCAA's Seminoles
13 Author Tolstoy
14 Entertain, as with a story
15 Hoopsters may hang from it
16 Phone no. addition
17 Spotted wildcat
18 Greeting in Rio
19 Part I of quote
22 "Entertainment Tonight" cohost John
23 School cupcake sellers: Abbr.
24 "___ girl!" (encouraging cry)
26 Like "dough" for "dollars"
28 Its icon is an envelope
29 Part II of quote
34 "Smooches!"
35 Part III of quote
41 Takes part in a virtual meeting, say
42 Morning ringer
44 Golden Fleece vessel
45 The most popular key of music played on Spotify: Abbr.
49 [HHHAAAAHaaahhh-HAhahaaa!]
50 Mass seating
51 Large ecosystems
53 Looker
54 End of quote
57 Speaker of quote, and first "New York Times" editor of the quote's last word
61 Against
62 Gothamite, briefly
63 Coke, but not weed
64 They're kept in books or towers
65 Capital of Norway
66 What to get into before bed

DOWN

1 The "A" in IPA
2 A little December attire that's big in October?
3 In other words
4 Gator's cousin
5 Post-game synopsis
6 In sports, a free one may be expensive
7 Mediterranean island site of a WWII conference
8 Makes some points in math class?
9 Rogen of "Knocked Up"
10 "Full___with Samantha Bee"
11 Collared shirt accessory
12 Actress Thurman
20 [Let me pretend to actually consider that]
21 Metrical foot, in poetry
22 Chinese menu general
25 Roker and Gore
27 Squawkers at the shore
28 Tropical fruit
30 Fish eggs
31 They often get turned on without being touched
32 Car company whose name inspired the "Can't Fight This Feeling" band
33 Olive who doesn't cook her man's spinach
35 Donned
36 School with lots of spelling tests?
37 "As I see it," seen in texts
38 Under the weather
39 Make it well-known a well-known is known well?
40 Med school students spend their nights looking at his Anatomy?
41 Kill a bug, in a way
43 Springfield barkeep
45 "Buon ___!" (Italian greeting)
46 Ambles (along), as a cowboy
47 Green-bottled beer brand
48 Hairstyle it takes chutzpah to pick out?
51 Womenswear item that sounds like a synonym for "dude"
52 "___ horse walks into a bar..."

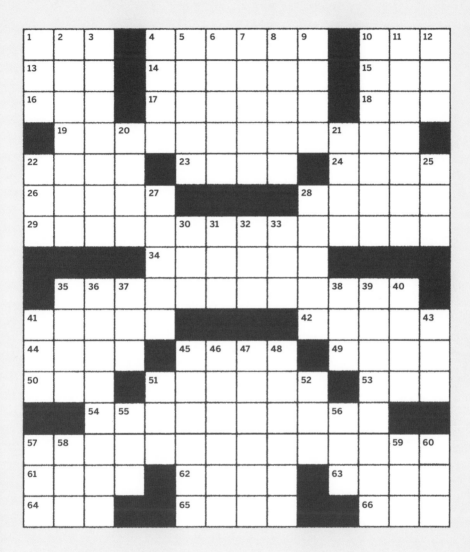

PART TWO

CROSSWORDESE:
[Puzzle lingo]

Chapter 1

ALPHA [___-Bits]
English, Part of Greek, and a Little Latin

When a quick brown fox jumps over the lazy dog, she's not just performing **ABIT** to show off her **SLY** acrobatics; she's also a **PANGRAM**, a [Sentence containing all 26 letters]. Also called holoalphabetic sentences, pangrams were once used to teach penmanship and test typewriters.

> **ABIT** ("a bit") [Not much], [Sort of], [Somewhat], ["Isn't that ___ much?"]
>
> **SLY** [Foxy], [Kind of dog], [Not straight], [Vulpine], [Having designs], [Artful], [Apt letters missing from "_tea_th_"]

Within the cruciverse, though, a **PANGRAM** describes a different sort of [Wordsmith's feat]: a puzzle that uses every letter at least once. It's rarer than you might expect. Only about 3 percent of puzzles manage it.

More often, puzzles invoke the alphabet directly by using names of letters as answers.

Though the alphabet would seem as [Easy as ___] **ABC**, even that [First string?] can be anything but the [Epitome of simplicity] thanks to a sly clue like [FOX rival].

> **ABC** [It's a start], [Block letters?], ["Lost" letters?], [2 phone letters?]

After getting a read on some of the odd ways crosswords present the 26—or 27?—English letters, we'll fraternize with the 24 letters of the Greek alphabet. Then we'll cross the Ionian Sea and brush up on some Latin. By the end, we should be able to solve a crossword in **TROY** or **ROME**.

> **TROY** and **ROME** [New York city] (See chapters 3 and 2, respectively)

Now You'll Know Your ABCS
[Initial lessons?] in Letters

Even the **ABCS** are hardly [Kid stuff?] when it comes to crosswords, as puzzles have some neat tricks to [Block letters?] from coming to mind.

Here are some answers, ordered **ATOZ**, exemplifying the [Full range] of what might turn up for letter-based clues, even if it's far from [Entirely] [Exhaustive].

A **AAA**: This [Small battery] of the letter "A" can also be plugged in as [Motorists' org], a [Good rating for a bond], or a [Minor-league classification].

Sometimes the grid requires a different-size **CELL**, like **AAS** or a really [Tiny battery] like an **AAAA**. Word nerd alert: The plural of the letter "a" is "aes," as in "There are two aes in Adlai." But even puzzles don't go that far, reserving **AES** for the [1950s political inits.] belonging to Adlai Ewing Stevenson.

B The **BBB** ("Better Business Bureau") is composed of three **BEES**, and, as it happens, the Salt Lake Bees are the AAA affiliate of the **LAA** ("Los Angeles Angels").

BBS, too, are [Stingers, of a sort], but as [Shot of minors?]—the "minors" refers to kids, not ballplayers yet to reach the majors.

C **CEES** refer to the letter in clues like [Broccoli bits] and [Hitchcock triple feature?]. (See that couple of curly florets in broccoli, or the three seeded in Hitchcock?)

FDR established the Civilian Conservation Corps, alternately known as the **CCC** or C's, which sent men to improve the parks system from sea to shining sea. **CCC** is also the [Roman 300], or, less heroically a [Junk bond rating]. Note that it's the Roman numeral that sets the value of a **CNOTE**.

ATOZ *("A to Z")* [Complete], [The works]

AAA [Remote starter?], [Grp. that might give you a hand on the shoulder?], [Popular tower?]

CELL [Sentence structure?], [Theater turn-off?]

AAS *(as "AAs")* [Smallish batteries], [Remote cells?], [Small juice containers?], *(as "A as")* ["___ in apple"]

BBB [Consumer protection org.]

BEES [Makers of fine combs], [Some queens], [Socials], [Humbugs?] *(See also chapter 9)*

LAA [A.L. West team, on scoreboards]

BBS [Cheap shot?]

CEES [Middling grades], [Six L's], [XXX x X]

FDR [New Deal inits.], [He said "Be sincere; be brief; be seated"]

CCC [New Deal program], [Old tree-planting org.], [XXX x X], [Six L's]

CNOTE *("C-note")* [Benjamin], [Franklin's bill?], [Jackson five?], [Where to find Independence Hall?]

[A "perfect" one uses all 26 letters once each, as seen in four answers in this puzzle]: The PANGRAM

In 2013, a *Times* puzzle by Raymond C. Young managed to achieve the crossword pangram **FOUR** times over, permitting him the rare chance to clue what otherwise might be [More than a crowd?] or [Number before H?] as [Minimum number of times each letter of the alphabet appears in this puzzle's solution].

Three years later, David C. Duncan Dekker raised the bar, managing to meet the **FIVEFOLD** mark (a word he clued in that crossword as [Like 100 vis-à-vis 20]). It's too bad that the term **PENTAGRAM** is already taken, but that puzzle deserves a [Five-pointed star] all the same.

The **HOLY** grail in non-puzzle pangrams, though, is the [Not just good] but "perfect pangram," a term reserved for a holoalphabetic sentence that uses each letter exactly once while eschewing obscure language. "Mr. Jock, TV Quiz **PHD**, bags few lynx," shows a [High degree] of effort toward that linguistic [Field goal, for some].

But as the clue for PANGRAM in the title of this box suggests, one puzzle sought to marry the two pursuits, and presented a fresh set of perfect pangram contenders. In 2020, Evan Birnholz, who writes the *Washington Post*'s Sunday puzzle, stretched the grid's width to 26 boxes to squeeze in this odd quartet, displayed here with added punctuation to aid reading:

☐ LGBTQ VJ NIXED SCHWARZKOPF? YUM!
   [A non-straight '90s MTV personality canceled general Norman? Delish!]

☐ WORD UP! SCHMALTZY QB VEXING JFK
   [Yo, dude! A sappy NFL passer is annoying everyone at a New York airport.]

☐ MERV, FX OWNS KLUTZY PDQ BACH JIG
   [Mr. Griffin, the "Atlanta" network holds the rights to that clumsy dance tune by the fictional composer of "A Little Nightmare Music."]

☐ BJ, FAX QVC MY KID'S HERTZ PLUG NOW
   [Mr. Novak, please send that home shopping network a copy of Junior's car rental ad immediately.]

D **DEES** aren't just [Poor grades] [Sandra and Ruby] might earn, but letters that are [Middle's middle], [Two of diamonds], and an [Odd couple?]. See **DEM DERE** [In dat place] in de mi<u>dd</u>le? By the same formal logic, they take the cake as a [Wedding centerpiece?].

DDS ("doctor of dental surgery") fills in cavities in crosswords demanding a [Crown molding expert: Abbr.]. Similar gags abound for **ADA**, the "American Dental Association" [Tube inits.]. (Squeeze more out of this answer in chapter 4.)

While most straitlaced puzzles won't contain **DDD** as [Like some huge chests], **CCUP** and **BCUP** provide a [Measure of support?]. When **ACUP** isn't a [Lingerie specification], it fills in what's raised by Robert Burns's "Auld Lang Syne" lyric, ["We'll tak' ___ o' kindness yet"]. Of course, a **BRA** is like kindness: [It may give one a lift].

DEM [Dose guys], [Blue person, for short?], [Boxer from Calif., for instance?]

DDS [Drill specialist, for short?], [Dr. with a lot of pull?], [Deg. for a bridge builder?]

BRA [It may be wireless], [Cup holder?], [It might make the torso seem moreso], [Car protector], [Support system?], [Flammable garment?]

E **EEE** is the largest [Wide shoe spec] on that classic foot-size measuring tool, the Brannock Device—"D" being the average width. Charles Brannock's invention landed him in the National Inventors Hall of Fame, alongside **EES** ([English letters] standing here for "electrical engineers") like the inventor of the graphing calculator, Edith Clarke. Befitting the first woman to be employed as an EE, ees being the **LIM** at each end of <u>E</u>dith Clark<u>e</u>.

Either **EEO** ("equal employment opportunity") or **EOE** ("equal-opportunity employer") can fill openings for [Want ad abbr.] and [Fair-hiring inits.]. And they're employed equally to do so.

Even worse, **ECG** and **EKG**, (both short for "electrocardiography") and **EEG** ("electroencephalogram") are all ordered as a [Hosp. test]. But as **EEG** is by far the most common of the three, guessing it might make you feel like a [Mind reader?].

EEE [Evidence of big foot?], [A foot wide], [Oxford letters], [Spec for a roomy flat?].

EES [Many MIT grads], [Some Tesla employees, in brief], [Wide shoe widths], [Boot ending], [Ending for "employ" or "honor"]

LIM [Boundary: Abbr.], [Calculus abbr.]

ECG and EKG [Change-of-heart indicator?], [Tape with beats?], [Lines coming from the heart, briefly?], [Ticker tape?]

EEG [Brain test, for short], [Headlines, for short], [Lines on "ER"], [Thinking graphically?]

F **FFF** ("*fff*," short for *fortississimo*, read as "triple forte") means [Extremely loud, in music scores], while *ff* stands for *fortissimo* ("very loud"). And while **EFS** can be [G.P.A. killers], in crosswords they can spell trouble through clues like [Daffy duo?] and [Affluent couple?]. Only in crosswords' math could [40% of fifty?] get you the same answer as [2 of fifty]! It's enough to make statisticians wonder if fractions aren't their **FORTE**.

FFF [Very loud, to Verdi], [Musical climax letters], [Loud, when scoring]

EFS [Right side of a cliff?], [Puff pieces], [Lead film festival character]

FORTE [Loud], [Strength], [Strong suit], [F in music class?]

G **GEE** is a [Plowman's command] meaning [Go the right]. And ["Fancy that!"]: It only takes a gee to spell **AGEE**, which can mean [Askew] or [Atilt].

But more often clues go straight for the [American author/ critic/screenwriter James] **AGEE**. He's best remembered for winning a posthumous Pulitzer for his autobiographical novel *A Death in the Family* and for his monumental collaboration with the photographer Walker Evans documenting the lives of Alabama tenant farmers, *Let Us Now Praise Famous Men*.

As the most common author answer in crosswords, **AGEE** is so ubiquitous that the seemingly opaque clue [Writer James] has been used in Monday puzzles.

The [1958 Pulitzer-winning James] **AGEE** shares his name with the [1969 World Series hero Tommie], and the ["Palindromania!" writer Jon], a professional "palindromist" whose books include *Go Hang a Salami! I'm a Lasagna Hog!* and *So Many Dynamos!* (That latter title seems apt for the Agees across the **AGES**.)

H **HHH** is the [Vice-presidential monogram] of Hubert Horatio Humphrey Jr., the [1968 loser to RMN] after serving **LBJ** as **VEEP**. Besides Humphrey and **SPIRO AGNEW**, crosswords rarely call on **VPS** to be write-in candidates unless they've been **PREZ** (also spelled **PRES**).

I **III** is a [Name tag?] when it comes after the name of a [Junior's junior], like HHH's son Hubert Horatio "Skip" Humprey III. And as a [Sequel's sequel] it might be viewed as a [Trailer for "Rocky" or "Rambo"?]. If you picture [Three on a clock], you can see how it's [Right on time?]. Oddly enough, it's the number of the [1969 Super Bowl], even though that was the [First Super Bowl to be called "Super Bowl"].

J **JAY** joins the fray as the name of the letter that's a [Jump start?], a [Late-night name] for the old [Rival of Dave], or the [Raucous bird] signifying a [Toronto baseballer], referring to the Blue **JAYS**.

GEE [Go the right way?], [$1K], [Thou], [Word of wonder]

AGEE ["The African Queen" co-screenwriter], ["Permit Me Voyage" author James], [Contemporary author-illustrator Jon] *(See chapter 7 for the [1966 AL Rookie of the Year Tommie])*

AGES [Many moons], [Gets on], [Seasons], [Passes the time?]

HHH [LBJ's veep]

LBJ [Great society inits], [JFK's VP]

VEEP [#2], [Sharer of a winning ticket?]

SPIRO [Dick's first second], ["Dum___Spero" (SC motto, which means "While I breathe I hope")]

AGNEW [One of Nixon's vices?]

VPS [Corp. officers], [FDR had three]

PREZ and **PRES** [W, for one], [Big cheese], [Univ. bigwig], [U VIP], [Cabinet maker?: Abbr.], [US 1?]

PRES *(as pres.)* [Certain tense], *(as près)* [Near: Fr.]

III [:15 number], [Richard___], [Grandson, maybe], [Three, of a kind], [Roman triumvirate?], [A crowd for Caesar?], [I and II], [IX minus VI], [Words for an egoist]

JAY [Conan slayer?], [Kind of walk?], [Mr. Gatsby], [Yank rival], [Homer Simpson's middle name]

JAYS [Ones with caws for alarm?]

K   **KAY** is the surprise answer for [Capital of Korea?]. While the incredulity that clue might cause is **OKAY**, it's decidedly [Not great] to have to think about the KKK, so they're typically personae non gratae in the grid.

Yet Ben Tausing, who was the grand wizard—**ERR**, ["Umm…"], j/k—make that impressive genius behind the delightfully irreverent (now sadly defunct) Inkwell crosswords in the *Chicago Reader*—**OKED** its usage, but only when the KKK was the butt of a joke. For example, he "hoodwinked" at the answer via clues like:

- [Grp. whose parades often draw more protesters than participants]
- [Org. that suggests Obama's success is attributable to his being half-white]
- [Super uncool org. despite having Wizards and Knights]

While calling on that answer can **KAYO** a solver with its ugly associations, the [Numbing blow] of each of Tausig's clues may illustrate how [It's a bout done?] best.

L   **ELL** needs to be thought of as [Kay's follower] to see why it's the [Logical conclusion?] for [Third of July?]. The letter's shape lends itself to usage for things with a [90° bend], like a [Building wing] or a [Pipe joint].

The letter's name is alternatively spelled with half the **ELS**, which also is "elevated" in grids as [Overhead trains, for short]. For more of what **ELS** tees up, like [Golfer Ernie] Els, see chapter 7.

The letter has also been indelibly stamped by **OGDEN NASH**, whose poem "The Lama" starts with "The one-l lama / He's a priest. / The two-l llama / He's a beast."

Thanks to these **DROLL** lines, **LAMA** might be summoned as [Nash's priest] and **LLAMA** can be herded as [Nash's "two-l" beast]. **LOL**.

ONEL ("one L") appears sometimes as [Like Nash's lama], though it's more often the legalese for a [First-year law student], used in *One L*, the classic 1977 [Scott Turow book about his law school experience] at Harvard. **SCOTTTUROW** is himself an alphabetical anomaly, being the only triple-T answer to have appeared in multiple *Times* puzzles.

Going one better, the constructor William S. Cotter once built a puzzle around answers with quadrupled letters: A [Fisherman's catch] was THREEEELS, [Phone a rock group?] was BUZZZZTOP, and [Cases for a zoo vet?] were ILLLLAMAS.

M **MMM** and **YUM** answer many identical clues and both end in **EMS**, letters that themselves are a [Common pair]. Fortunately, **EMS** ("emergency medical services") is most often [Ambulance letters] and **EMT** ("emergency medical technician") tends to be [CPR pro], but both answer the call for [911 responder, for short].

In such critical situations in crosswords, there's little to do but make [A musing sound] like **HMM**, which constructors Jay Kaskel and Daniel Kantor amusingly thought an ideal answer for [Not an ideal answer to "Do these jeans make me look fat?"].

N **ENS**, like **EMS**, are [Type units] refering to [Dash lengths] the widths of the uppercase letters they're named for, making **ENDASH** [–] and **EMDASH** [—]. (Yeah, it works better if the font is consistent!) Hyphens connect words like "40-yard dash," en dashes work like "to" in "France–England match" or "2–1," and em dashes connect sentence parts—in case you were wondering.

Representing **NORTH**, "ens" help denote **NNW**, **NNE**, **WNW**, and **ENE**.

ENS and ENE joined ASEA as the most frequent answers in the *Times* in 1967. None of these three ranked in the top 250 answers of 2021, but each still arrives fairly frequently as an **ANS**. So too does **ANSE**, an answer perennially extant as William Faulkner's ["As I Lay Dying" father].

ONEL [Student taking Contracts, maybe]

SCOTTTUROW [Legal thriller author who wrote "Presumed Innocent"], [Best-selling novelist whom *Time* called "Bard of the Litigious Age"]

MMM ["Dee-lish!"], [Bop preceder?]

YUM [Comment while putting something away] *(See chapter 8)*

EMS [What moms have that dads don't?], [Four characters in "A Midsummer Night's Dream"], [Mammal's head and heart]

EMT [One rushing to work?], ["Let me think…"]

HMM [Sound of wheels turning?]

ENS [Half of none?], [Half of nine?], [Pair of nines?]

NORTH [Needle point?], [0°]

NNW [Hitchcockian dir.?]

NNE [Uptown in NYC]

WNW [U-turn from ESE]

ENE [Memphis-to-Nashville dir.], [67°30'], [Chemical suffix], [Benz back?], [Epic ending?]

ANS [T or F, e.g.: Abbr.], [Key part: Abbr.]

OOO [One thousand minus one?], [Grand finale?], [Xer's downfall]

OHS [17 of them are sung before "my gosh" in a 2010 #1 Usher hit]

OXO [Big brand in kitchenware], ["Good Grips" brand], [Kitchen brand whose name is an ambigram]

LOGO [Target's target, e.g.], [Apple's apple, e.g.], [Jordan is found on one]

OMNI [Luxury hotel brand], [Old Dodge], [Present opener?]

OPP [Antonym: Abbr.], [Vs.], [Long, for short: Abbr.]

PEE [Start to push?], [Top finisher?], [What makes ale pale?], [Cue preceder]

PIANO [Soft], [Roll player?], [One grand?], [One of the Baldwins?]

PPS [Second addendum to a letter, for short], [Letter ender?], [Letters that further extend letters]

OXY [Moronic beginning?], [Popular acne medication], [Prefix with acetylene]

PSS [Ltr. addenda]. [They're not part of the body: Abbr.]

EDS [Salon workers, for short?], [People people, for short], [Mr. and McMahon]

STET [Latin for "let it stand"], ["Leave in," to a copy editor], [Editorial override], [Put back in], [[Do not delete]]

MSS [Ed.'s stack], [Orig. texts]

CUE [Signal], [Shark's stick], [Game room poker?], [Banking instrument]

HAM [___ it up] (*See chapter 2 for a second helping*)

O | **OOO** are traditionally [Valentine's Day hugs] in letters—in letters. When [Away from work, in emails] (short for "out-of-office"), they may be fooling around as a [Naughty threesome?]—a clue capitalizing on how capital "oes" (the plural of the letter) resemble zeros, or "naughts."

Such cluing is bound to elicit **OHS**—be they [Cries of surprise], [Raised-eyebrow remarks], [Neutral responses], or [Clicking sounds] (as made when an answer "clicks").

Of course, instead of playing hooky, **OOO** may be playing for a [Tic-tac-toe victory]. More ticky-tacky answers like **OOX**, **XXO**, **OXX**, and **XOO** fill in for a [Losing line], though **XOX** checks in as an [Affectionate sign-off], and **OXO** is handy as the [Palindromic kitchen brand] whose **LOGO** is legible **OMNI**-directionally.

P | **PPP** ("*ppp*," short for *pianissimo*, and read as "triple piano") means [Very, very soft, in music], making it the **OPP** of *fff*.

PS: While the avant-garde composer György Ligeti was known to pile up one **PEE** after another to produce a pin-like *pppppppp*, the most **PIANO** answer to appear in the *Times* is **PPPPPP**, the [Rare dynamic marking seen in Tchaikovsky's Sixth Symphony].

PPS: **PSP** is the palindromic [Handheld Sony gadget] produced 2004–2014, the aptly petite form of the otherwise **OXY**-moronic "PlayStation Portable."

PPPS: This [Afterthought #3: Abbr.] pops up less often than either the odd plural for "postscripts," **PSS**, or the stuff that **EDS** ("editors") edit, perhaps with the word **STET**: **MSS** ("manuscripts").

Q | The [Letter after ar] can be spelled **KUE** or **CUE**, but the latter typically queues up the sort of schtick seen in [Stick that breaks?]. It's also a [Line to follow?], where the "line" isn't a queue but an actor's prompt. Patrick Berry, a constructor always well-equipped with an equivoque (a fancy term for "pun," which, like "equivocal," combines the Latin for "equal" and "to call"), quipped that **CUE** was a [Ham helper].

Solvers finding Berry's wry serving of **HAM** dicey will find a cure by seeing it as a [Scene stealer].

It's also easy to get snookered by clues for **MASSE**, a [Curving shot in billiards], which is truly another [Cue shot with a curve] when it looks like a [Shot for those who mastered English?]. Here **ENGLISH** is used in its billiards sense, for [Spin].

R | **ARS** can be [Three in school] thanks to **RRR**, themselves [Elementary letters] easily confused with **ABC**, causing some solvers to **GRR**, a [Chow line?]. That's **CHOWS** as in the [Dogs with dark tongues]—though it could just as well apply to the breakfast chow line, "They're Gr-r-reat!"

BRR is a similar [Icy response?], but a sort heard more often in winter by folks at **RRS** exhaling [Short lines?] of icy breath.

S | **ESSES** assemble in **SSS**, which refers to the Selective Service System in clues like [Lottery letters], [Draft org.], and [Draft inits.], all of which also work for **NBA**, **NFL**, or **NHL**—answers we'll pick up again later.

Like **SSS**, another [Org. that's got your number?] is the **SSA** ("Social Security Administration"), which issues a person's **SSN** ("Social Security number").

One group decidedly against the draft was the **SDS** ("Students for a Democratic Society"), the [1960s radical grp.] and [New Left org.]—though they did draft and ratify the Port Huron Statement, which helped popularize the term "participatory democracy."

T | **TEE** tends to take up golf puns like [Ball point?], [Course requirement?], [Ball holder], and even [Athletic supporter]. It's also a [Kind of time] for golfers, a [Timeout sign] for other athletes, and the [Beginning of time?] for spellers—and football players, who see it as a [Kickoff point].

As demonstrated by the clues [World's smallest elevator?] and [Elevator in a country club], constructors get a rise out of **TEE**. The letter so often suits grids that a "**TEE**"-chart suits it **TOAT**.

MASSE [En___], [Pool stroke]

ARS [Trio of horrors?], [Mexicans roll them], [Some seen in mirrors?], [Things often dropped in Harvard Yard?], [___ Technica (tech review site)]

RRR [Ed. basics], [Trio in elem. school]

GRR ["Don't touch my squeaky toy!"], [Lab warning?], ["Stay away," in Maltese?]

BRR [Cold call?], [Zero reaction?]

RRS [Monopoly quartet: Abbr.], [Things with x-ings]

ESSES [Trouble for Sylvester the Cat], [Pair of shoes]

SSS [Sibilant sound], [Snake's warning], [Sound of a leak]

SSA [Govt. org. since 1946], [65-year-old agency?]

SSN [It never starts with 666: Abbr.], [Until June 25, 2011, its first three digits had geographical significance: Abbr.], [Lifelong assignment, briefly?]

TOAT ("to a T") [Perfectly], [Just so]

TEE [___ time]: How Puzzles TEE [___ off]		
Golf Related	**Letter Related**	**Other**
Hole opener	It starts tomorrow?	Start to giggle
Begin, with "off"	Capital of Texas?	Top choice
Ball-bearing gadget	Stylized Tesla logo	Simple top
Place to drive from?	Certain intersection	Pipe joint
Swing site	What's big in Texas?	Polo alternative
Fore sight?	First of three?	5K souvenir
It may be hit by a driver	Fight back?	It may have a ring collar
It can give drivers a lift	Split end?	Football supporter
Driving holdup?	Talking head?	Kick stand?
Driving need	End of August?	Tick (off)
	20th of 26	

U UES, New Yorkers' abbreviation for the Upper East Side, is usually considered too local for puzzles, yet the [Brooklynese pronoun] **YOUSE** gets used. The plural of the letter "u" isn't "us" but "ues." A pair of doubled "ues" outfits **MUUMUU**, the [Oahu attire] from the Hawaiian for "cut-off," as it traditionally lacks a **YOKE**, the upper part of a shirt or skirt supporting a looser section below.

YOKE [Join], [Ox-cessory?], [It keeps a team together]

V **VEE** makes another sartorial yoke as a [Neckline shape], while the **VEES** seen in [Pair of skivvies?] make a sartorial joke.

VEE [Flashed hand signal], [Dove's sign]

W The [Internet start-up] **WWW** is the start of a **URL**, the [Brief address] short for Uniform Resource Locator.

URL [Bit of modern history?], [Dotted line?], [Address that can't receive packages], [Surfer's destination?]

X **XXX** is rare, but can be clued as [Really dirty], [Love letters?], [Moonshine marking], [Turkey, to a bowler], or—as Peter A. Collins cleverly drew it up in a football-themed puzzle—[Pigskin stitching].

Solve for [X]: How Puzzles MARKTHESPOT

While X on a treasure map denotes the destination, in puzzles it's often only the starting point. A few crosswords have even crossed up solvers by repeatedly using the minimalistic clue [X] for different answers in the same grid. In 1995, constructor Rich Norris showed that [X] could equal an **UNKNOWNQUANTITY**, a **TICTACTOESYMBOL**, and ironically enough, an **INCORRECTANSWER**.

Here are **TEN** other solutions for [X] (plus a few other clues for each answer):

[X] =

CHI	[Ill. city], [Tai___], and many more in the [Greek letter] section to follow
DELETE	[Go back on one's word?], [One way to kill characters?], [Takeout order?]
MARK	[Former German capital], [Luke preceder], [A or B], [Twain who called Washington, DC, "the grand old benevolent National Asylum for the helpless"]
KISS	[Smack in the face?], [Meet face to face?], [Tell's partner], [Pay lip service to?], [French connection?], [Band whose makeup has stayed the same over the years?], [Peck]
PECK	[Lot of trouble], [Eat off the floor], [Work for chicken feed], [Hit with the bill], [Eight quarts], [Kiss]
PLACE	[Come in second], [Silver]
TEN	[Pin number?], [Perfect figure?], [Number of prime ministers on Downing Street?] *(Revisited as the [Till bill])*
TICK	[Pet peeve?], [Time piece?], [Watch word?]
TIMES	[Periods], [V and X, on a sundial]. *(See the introduction for other [Instances] when [They may "try one's soul"].)*
TIREIRON	Clued as such in a Thursday puzzle by Daniel A. Finan that also included [J] for **FISHHOOK**, [O] for **HULAHOOP**, [U] for **HORSESHOE** and [Y] for **WISHBONE**. No doubt, until they solved those last two answers, many solvers must have felt out of luck.

WYES [Yesterday's beginning and end?], [Yucky couple?], [Followers of exes]

NYY [The Bronx Bombers, on scoreboards]

YOGI [Lawrence Peter Berra, familiarly], [Poser?], [One bending over backward], ["It ain't over till it's over" author], ["You observe a lot by watching" speaker], [It's said that he said, "I never said most of the things I said"]

ZEES [A lot of pizzazz?], [Jazz duet?], [Puzzle pieces?]

JAZZ [Meaningless talk, in slang], [What makes cats happy?], [Holiday music?]

RAZZ [Tease], [Ride]

ZEE [One in a zillion?], [1/4 of zero?], [A fifth of booze?], [Capital of Zimbabwe?], [Intro to zoology?], [Last thing learned in kindergarten?]

ZZZ [Sound of sawing wood?], [Only three-letter word in Scrabble that requires both blank tiles]

ZED [End of the alphabet, in Canada], [Part of Queen Elizabeth's makeup], [One of two parts of a British puzzle], [What many Brits don't spell "realize" with]

AMPERSAND [Q&A part?], [Character in "Thelma & Louise"?]

SUE [Try to have tried?], [Go after], [Bit of lawyerly advice]

DET [Pistons or Lions, on scoreboards]

IVE ["___ been had!"], ["___ seen worse,"], [Act ender?], [It may be added to impress?], ["Now ___ seen everything!"]

Y Two **WYES** appear in **NYY**, whose longtime catcher, outfielder, and manager **YOGI** Berra was such a [Wise guy] that he's seen in puzzles as a [Quotable catcher].

By coincidence, **YOGI**'s three roles with the Yankees made him a [Person holding many positions], and his squatting behind the plate made him [One in an awkward position].

But when Hanna-Barbera claimed that the name they chose for their [Toon bruin], Yogi Bear, just happened to sound like one of America's most loved and amusing athletes, the production company was the one maintaining an awkward, twisted position.

Z **ZEES** are required to give **JAZZ** like Hanna-Barbera's claim its proper response: a **RAZZ**. The term for a [Bronx cheer] is taken from "raspberry," slang dating at least to the 1890s for another off-putting thing in the air, itself a vestige of the original bawdy rhyming euphemism: "raspberry tart."

A single **ZEE** might sound like a [Bit of a snore?] as a [Sleep unit] referring to part of **ZZZ**—the [Last entry in the "Random House Unabridged Dictionary"]—but overseas it sounds like **ZED**.

& Once considered the 27th letter, the **AMPERSAND** now takes eight letters to spell and is seen in connection with a different number, since [It's paired with 7] on a keyboard.

Clues [Go a-courting?]
SUE [Grafton of mystery] Books

DET, is unlikely to be easily apprehended by a novice [Clue analyzer] as a [Gumshoe] nowadays. Worse, the dated term **TEC**, an indefatigable bit of crosswordese first used by 19th-century scofflaws, is another term for a [Private eye, briefly]. But it helps to know that of the two answers, **TEC** is the [One taking the lead?] by appearing more often.

DET and **TEC** are both taken from "detective." In a surprise twist, with what's left, **IVE** ["___ noticed..."] a [Secret ending].

Readers wondering how sharp the **DET** or **TEC** at the center of Sue Grafton's famous "Alphabet" mystery novels is need not skip to the last page; sufficient evidence for conviction can be found in Kinsey Millhone's last name.

One hardly needs to be as keen as Det. Millhone to see why Grafton's "Alphabet" books—whose titles follow the model of *"A" is for Alibi*, *"B" is for Burglar*, *"C" is for Corpse*, etc.—**ABET** constructors who need some clue to [Lend a helping hand, in a bad way] for ungainly answers like **IIS**, as in "I is" ["___ for Innocent" (Grafton novel)].

Some answers don't need Grafton's help. **BIS** has meanings connected to twos. **CIS** connects with its Latin roots meaning [On this side: Prefix] as the [Gender prefix], or can be "C is" in a way "that's good enough for me." And **DIS** can be [Put down] as a [Burn].

EIS just manages to skate by as [Frozen Wasser] in Germany, and **FIS** drops by after first saying [Hi-___]. **GIS** and **HIS** each have a more air-tight **ALIBI** for being in the grid.

But Grafton's titles can serve as a useful **ALIAS** for answers like **AIS**. Grafton's **AIS** ["___ for Alibi"] was published in 1982, but—in a plot point perhaps the reader sees coming—wasn't called in for questioning until the Shortz Era. Before Grafton, the usual suspects for cross-examination for **AIS** were ais, [Sloths]—specifically [Three-toed sloths]. And what did the sloth say when interrogated by the sleuth? "Ai didn't do it!"

In her 2015 follow-up to **WIS** ["___ for Wasted"], Grafton broke from the "x-letter is for x-word" model, and simply titled it *X*. "I've checked the penal codes in most states and xylophone isn't a crime," she said, "so I'm stuck." The decision must have surprised the *Los Angeles Times*, which earlier that year clued **XIS** as [Expected 26th Sue Grafton title starter]. Happily, the Greek alphabet provides the cruciverse "xis," as described in the next section.

Grafton returned to form with *"Y" is for Yesterday* but passed away before completing the cycle with *"Z" is for Zero*. Posting on Facebook, Grafton's daughter told fans that since her mother "Would never allow a ghost writer to write in her name . . . As far as we in the family are concerned the alphabet now ends at Y."

DET and **TEC** [P.I., e.g.], [Gumshoe], [Sam Spade, e.g.], [Sleuth], [Dick], [Mystery title: Abbr.], [Shamus]

ABET [Help badly?], [Help hold up?], [Help lift something, maybe?], [Back up on a job?], [Help wanted?]

BIS [Dumbbell curls build them, for short], [Twice, in music], ["Encore!"], [One's sexually flexible, for short] *(Mentioned briefly [Again!] in chapter 3)*

CIS [Lead-in to gender], [Opposite of trans, in gender studies], ["___ for Cookie" ("Sesame Street" song)]

EIS [Autobahn hazard], [Rocks on the Rhein?], [Sue Grafton's "___ for Evidence"]

GIS [Grunts], [Bill and Joe?], [Ones on base?], [Yanks]

HIS [Short waves?], [Her match?], [Dad's alternative?], [What a flat "b" palm facing a nearby fellow stands for, in A.S.L.]

ALIBI [Cover story], [Hearing aid?], [Out lines?], [Suspect story?], [Pretext], [Out]

ALIAS [Smith, sometimes]

AIS [Start of an alphabet book], [Some game-playing computers] (as A.I.s, "artificial intelligences")

WIS [Ill. neighbor], [Badgers' home: Abbr.], [Superior home?: Abbr.]

Common Alpha BETS
How a Puzzle [Sees, in a way]
Greek Letters and [Makes it interesting]

BETS [Doesn't check, say], [Gets into the pool], [Book deals?], [Pot growers?]

FRAT [Rush home?], [School house?]

HAZE [Break a pledge?], [The night before, to a hard partier?]

Greek letter names litter grids like so many red cups on a **FRAT** house lawn. Indeed, their clues are often identical: **PHI**, **CHI**, and **PSI** can all be a [Sorority letter], [Letter from Greece], or [Character in the Iliad?]. Such hijinks can **HAZE** any solver.

Note the appearance of the letters: [Θ] can take shape for **THETA**, while [α] and [A] are each a literal (*letter*-al?) description of **ALPHA**.

ALPHA	A α	A for Aristotle A Greek letter? First of the Greeks? Homer's first letter #1 of 24	Letter opener? Leading character Leader of Athens Leading man? Socially dominant
BETA	B β	B in Greek Philosophy? Byzantine capital? Phi follower?	Kind of blocker Test stage Early stage for some bugs?
GAMMA	Γ γ	Gallows-shaped letter	Type of ray
DELTA	Δ δ	Symbol of change Greek airline?	A river runs through it Runoff at the mouth?
EPSILON	E ε	Greek E	Elasticity symbol, in economics
ZETA	Z ζ	Zeus's beginning? Z abroad	Letter that's only 25% of the way through the Greek alphabet, surprisingly
ETA	H η	H Homer's H Athenian vowel	When you might land GPS display JFK stat

ETA (cont.)	H η	Letter in the classical spelling of "Athena"	Due time
		H as in Athens	Best guess?
		I ___ Pi (punny fraternity name)	Down-to-earth fig.
		Z follower	Touchdown info?
			Info for waiters?
THETA	Θ θ	Letter found between two vowels in the alphabet	Eighth letter
		Second letter in the Greek for "Athens"	Thucydides had one
			Trig angle symbol
IOTA	I ι	I	Little bit of Greek
		Jot	Ithacan's capital?
		Tiny bit	Small Greek character?
		Smidgen	Cyclops's I?
KAPPA	K κ	Phi Beta ___	Key letter
		Beta follower?	Letter for a scholar?
		Honor society letter	Capital of Crete?
LAMBDA	Λ λ	Upside-down V	Leader of Lesbos
		Letter that looks like a flipped "y"	Kind of particle in physics
Mu (MUS)	M μ	Greek M's	Juilliard sub.
		M&M?	R&B and C&W: Abbr.
		M M M	Field of note?: Abbr.
Nu (NUS)	N ν	N N N	Xi preceders
		N's in Athens	Two letters from "Santorini"
		Lowercase letters resembling v's	Antigone is spelled with two
Xi (XIS)	Ξ ξ	Omicron's predecessors	They follow the nus
OMICRON	O o	O	First letter given to Odysseus
		Head of Olympus?	Original opening to Homer's "Odyssey"?
		Greek for "little O"	

Pi (PIS)	Π π	Letters before rhos	Gumshoes
		Circle ratios	Dicks
		Brief case handlers?	Tecs
RHO	P ρ	Plato's P	Chi-___ (religious symbol)
		P pronounced like an R	Letter seen in a Christogram
		Hector's end?	Fraternity letter that's a homophone of where fraternities might be found
		Serving after pi?	
		Pi + 1?	
SIGMA	Σ σ/ς	Greek "S"	Calculus symbol
		Summation symbol, in math	Start for Sophocles
TAU	T τ	Leader of ancient Troy?	Cross shape
		Symbol for torque	Greek letter that once symbolized life and resurrection
		___ particle	
UPSILON	Y υ	Y lookalike	Greek vowel
PHI	Φ φ	___ Beta Kappa	Golden ratio symbol
		Key letter	The Eagles, on scoreboards
		Letter voiced by a Greek giant?	N.L. East team
CHI	X χ	Greek cross?	Bears' home, briefly
		Greek antepenultimate	Spiritual energy
		Windy City, for short	Life force, in China
PSI	Ψ ψ	Trident-shaped letter	Greek letter spelled out at the start of a Beatles title?
		Tire gauge meas.	Beginning to love you?
		Inflationary fig.	
OMEGA	Ω ω	Ohm symbol	Literally, "great O"
		Sign of resistance	Last word in watches?
		Symbol for the resistance?	Series finale
		___-3	The end

Caesar SALAD
An [Introductory course?]
on How Latin Gets Tossed into the Mix

Puzzles may **SIC** (formerly usually spelled "sick") a dialectical variation of Latin on solvers, even if the Latin *sic*—meaning "thus," an [Error indicator in a quotation]—is unrelated to its English homonym meaning ["Get 'em!"].

IDES abides as that [Fateful day in 44 BCE] [When "et tu" was spoken]. It was a particularly [Bad day for Caesar], but ides were a regular [Midmonth occasion] associated with the full moon and generally considered a [Date sacred to Jupiter], the god of the sky. They were observed on [A 15th] during March, May, July, and October; they otherwise always fall on the 13th, as in January—rising as such in the tricky clues [One 13th?] and [February 13, e.g.].

CASCA was the [First to stab Caesar], but of course **ETTU** ["___, Brute?"] was Caesar's [Question for Brutus].

The [Famed "fiddler"] **NERO** was an [Emperor who, in actuality, played the lyre, not the violin]. Regardless, his name gets plucked by puzzles so often that it's been joked that solvers must think him the only Roman emperor. But it doesn't take the Nero who's [Detective Wolfe] of Rex Stout's mystery novels to see that when a [Cruel Roman emperor] calls for eight boxes, it's **CALIGULA**. It's horse feathers that [He made his horse a senator], so that clue should be put out to pasture.

[Mass Confusion]
Learning to Love and even Conquer
Confusing LATIN Trios

Caesar's less final words echo through grids as well: **VENI**, **VIDI**, **VICI**, any of which can be [One of a Latin trio] or [Part of an old boast], though the first of the triad is by far the most common. And you can add **ETTU** to those three for four-letter answers that can arrive via [Caesarean section?].

SALAD [Greek ___], [One getting dressed for lunch?], [Leaves undressed, perhaps], [Leaves for dinner?], [Leaves on the side?], [Bar food?], [Food that gets tossed?], [Course]

SIC [Attack order], [Set (on)], [[Someone else's error]], [[Not my mistake]]

IDES [13th or 15th], [10/15, e.g.], [Killing time], [Middle March?], [Caesar's last date?]

ETTU *("et tu")* [And you: Lat.], [Latin rebuke], ["Traitor!"], ["You too?!"], ["Really? Is *nobody* on my side now?"] [Caesarean rebuke], [Cutting remark?], [Comment to a backstabber?], [March line?], [Brute question?] *(See also part one for the role it could play in a proposed plot to kill off another of puzzledom's [Famous last words])*

NERO [Claudius's successor], ["I, Claudius" role], [Fiery fiddler?], [Emperor who pulled strings?], [Roman emperor who said before dying "What an artist the world is losing in me!"], [Stout fellow?]

LATIN [Pig language?], [Vulgar language], [Mass medium], [Like salsa], [Homo sapiens, e.g.]

AMOR [Latin love], [Roman god of love], [Caesar's love], [Another name for Cupid], [Cupid, or his concern], [Lover boy?], [Spanish love], [Love of mythology], [Latin lover's love], [Love child?]

AMO ["Te __"], ["Just __" ("Be right with you")], [Latin trio leader]

AMAS [You love, to Livy], [Reddit Q&A's] *(short for "Ask Me Anything")*

AMAT [Latin loves?], [Word for a Latin lover?]

WOO [Court], [Romance], [Try to win], [Go after]

HIC [Minute Maid brand], [Sot's sound], [Sound after a shot?], [What this would be to Caesar?]

HAEC [Hic, __, hoc], [Caesar's "these"]

ADHOC [Like some committees], [Improvised], [Having limited focus]

LIB [A little freedom?], [Women's __], [Lefty], [Ad trailer?], [Justin Trudeau's party: Abbr.], [A little freedom?], [Left-winger]

ADLIB [It comes off the top of one's head], [Fashion lines?], [Go off line?]

REM *(rapid eye movement)* [Sleep inits.], [Kind of cycle], [Out sign?], ["Stand" band, 1989]

REP [One of 435 in DC], [Seat occupier, for short], [One push-up, say], [Gym unit], [Cred], [Standing on the street?], [Part of a gym set?], [Short salesman?], [Pitcher?]

ADREP [Person of account, informally?]

A less violent vanquishment appears through a clue seen for **AMOR**—["Omnia vincit __" ("Love conquers all": Lat.)], as well as ["__ vincit insomnia" (Christopher Fry quip)].

The Latin verb, *amare*, "to love," is among the first that students learn to conjugate. Its simple present tenses sound like a Roman version of the Gershwins' "He Loves and She Loves": *amo, amas, amat* ("I love," "you love," "he/she/it loves").

Puzzles pay conjugal visits to **AMO** as [I love, in Latin]; **AMAS** as [Amo follower]; and **AMAT** as [Third in a Latin series]. And each [Latin lover's word?] could be [Part of a loving threesome?].

On dates when those three answers—like **VENI, VIDI, VICI**— fill in as [Part of a Latin trio] or [Latin 101 word], solvers might wish puzzles would show them a little more love.

Another common Latin trinity crosswords pitch the **WOO** to is "**HIC, HAEC, HOC**," the three forms of "this" or "these."

But **HIC** is usually a [Sound from a drunk] or, as "Hi-C," the [Juice brand] that's drunk. And while **HOC** may be hard to spot as an [Ad follower], it fills in on the spot for [Ad __ committee]—and well it should, as **ADHOC** ("ad hoc," "for this") means "when necessary" or "created for this specific purpose."

Patience may be needed, though, as **HOC** isn't the only member of the committee convened to decide on [Ad __] and [Ad's conclusion]. Others called on for input:

- **LIB** is free to jump in, as in **ADLIB** ("ad lib," short for *ad libitum*, literally, "according to pleasure"), meaning to [Wing it].
- **REM**, when not in a [Dreamy state?], can flutter in as part of **ADREM** ("ad rem," literally, "to the matter") meaning [To the point].
- Okay, so **REP** is not Latin, but Latinx, perhaps, as [A.O.C., e.g.], though also, amazingly, it works as [Dem.'s opposite]. But to the point: It's a party to **ADREP** (as in an "ad rep," as in "advertising representative"), a [Spot seller, in brief] akin to an **ADMAN**, a [Madison Avenue worker].

[It's a state] Motto [Entity]
BEING (and Seeming to Be) in Latin and Late Night

ESTO means [This, in Spanish], but what's ["This" to Tomás] is also a form of the Latin verb *sum* ("to be") to Tiberius. While crosswords let it be perpetually clued as Spanish, it can periodically prove pesky as the [Idaho motto opener] (*Esto perpetua* or "Let it be perpetual") and the [End of Missouri's motto] (*Salus populi suprema lax esto*, or "The welfare of the people shall be the supreme law").

The Latin **SUM** solves the question of what ["I am," to Descartes], as in [Cogito ergo ___]. Three other forms of *sum*, **ERAT**, **ESSE**, and **EST**, also pose existential questions for solvers. Since each of these is yet another possible answer to the clue [Latin 101 verb], those trying to solve would be wise to **COGITATE**, "I [Think], therefore I am not sure."

ERAT is most often clued as [Part of Q.E.D.] because it's [The "E" of Q.E.D.], as in *quod erat demonstrandum* ("what was to be shown"). There, **QED**, ["That proves it!"].

Oh, I almost forgot to add: **ERAT** also fills in [Quod ___ faciendum], another proof-ender meaning "what was to be done."

The verb's present infinitive, **ESSE**, is hardly [Ab ___ (absent, in Latin)] in English: It's the essence of its cognate, "essence." It's also an essential word to Tarheels, being that it's in the [North Carolina motto opener]: *Esse quam videri* ("To be, rather than to seem").

The proud **PALMETTO** State native, Stephen **COLBERT**, managed to **FLIP** the phrase in a [Cheeky] way, modifying his northern neighbors' **MAXIM** to fit his old show, *The Colbert Report*, [Saying] "*Videri quam esse*" ("To seem to be, rather than to be").

If you ever looked at a [Much-abbreviated Latin text], [Namely], "i.e.," and wondered what [That is], here are some [Words of explanation]: It's **IDEST**. [In other words], [That is to say] *id est* is ["i.e." spelled out].

[Id's partner] here is not the **EGO**. Instead, [The "e" in i.e.] is **EST**—the answer that literally [Is: Lat.]. But *est* [Is: Fr.] too, and a lot else:

ERAT [It was: Lat.], [Form of the Latin "sum"], [Latin 101 word]

ESSE [To be, to Brutus], [To be in ancient Rome?]

QED [Proof ending letters], [Logical conclusion], [Relative of "Voilà!"], [Triumphant end], [Ending letters], [Last thing seen by a proof reader], [The end of mathematics?]

PALMETTO [South Carolina flag feature]

COLBERT [Comedian who was the only man on the "Maxim" 2012 Hot 100 list]

MAXIM [Proverb], [Saw], [Words to live by], [Axiom], [Adage], ["Look before you leap," e.g.], ["He who hesitates is lost," e.g.]

EGO ["I" problem?], [Big head], [Id checker?], [It may be inflated], [Conceit], [Star quality?], [Maniacal leader?], [Vanity case?], [Mind's I?], [Trip taken in vain?]

[And so on: Abbr.]

Et Al., Ibid., Op Cit, ETCETC

What EST Is, or Might Be: [It's anybody's guess: Abbr.]		
Word/form	**Meaning**	**Clues**
est	[Third-person form of "être"] in French and [Form of Latin "to be"]	[Is in Paris?], ["C'___ la vie!"], [Is in the Vatican], [Is from Ancient Rome]
est	"East" in French and Italian	[E, on a French map], [90° from Nord], [A direction in Roma]
EST	"Eastern Standard Time"	[A New York minute?], [Winter hrs. in Miami], [DE Dec. setting], [Jersey time]
Est.	[Abbr. on a cornerstone]	[Abbr. before 1895 on the "Cheers" bar sign]
Est.	[Approximate fig.]	[Body shop fig.], [Part of ETA], [Stab: Abbr.], [It's in the neighborhood: Abbr.], [It's just a guess: Abbr.], [Ballpark figure: Abbr.], *oddly, also a* [Crowd no., often]
Est.	Estonia	[A neighbor of Lat.]
-est	[Superlative suffix], [Beyond -er], ["To the max" suffix]	[What means the most at the end?], [Guinness suffix], [Record finish?], [Great ending?], [Weird ending?], [Wild finish?], [Maximum ending?], [Suffix for "winning"], [Suffix for "tough"]

While **ETC** (short for et cetera, literally, "other things") is used as a [List-shortening abbr.] for things, **ETAL** (et al., literally, [And others, for short]) is used specifically for names (not necessarily **ALS**).

Usually an **ABBR** for the neuter "et **ALIA**," et al. can also stand for "et **ALII**" (masc.)—or "*et aliae*" (fem.), which doesn't appear in puzzles. In other words, both **ALIA** and **ALII** are four-letter answers for clues like [Et ___] and [Others, to Ovid]. But only **ALIA** finishes [Inter ___ (among other things)].

IBID is a [Footnote abbr.] short for *ibīdem* (literally, "the same place"), used in lieu of a title named in an immediately preceding citation. Crosswords capitalize on its meaning to create confusing clues like [See above] or [Same source as before].

Another [Footnote abbr.], **OPCIT** (*op. cit.*, short for *opus citatum*, or "the work cited") is also used in place of a title mentioned earlier, but only when not referring to the immediately preceding citation, making it an [Ibid. relative].

Either half of **NOTA BENE** (literally, "mark well" or "take note") appears apart as [Part of NB]. **NOTA** can be ["___ problem"] at all, but **BENE** is also the [Italian well]—that's "well" as the adverb, not the noun—so only a hole in the grid awaits those seeking a hole in the ground for an [Old Roman well?], just as a steep levee awaits any failing to heed an [Italian fine?].

ETC [Series finale?], [+, briefly], [Yada, yada, yada], ["Stuff like that"], [It can reduce a sentence], [End of the line?], ["...you get the idea"]

ETAL [List-ending abbr.], [Abbr. used by a name-dropper]

ALS [Green and Gore], [Gore and more], [Ice Bucket Challenge cause, for short]

ABBR [OH or HI], [E.g., e.g.], [Short, for short], [This answer, for one]

ALIA and **ALII** [Et ___ (citation words)]

ALIA ["Search Party" actress Shawkat]

[Cultural pursuits]
Latin ARTS, Gods, and Goddesses

Besides potentially making a cute [Married couple?], **ARS** can also represent [Ancient art?], reflecting the Latin *ars* ("skill" or "craft"), as in *ars poetica* (the "art of poetry," specifically referring to a meditation on poetry). For instance, in his epistle "Ars Poetica," Horace wrote that poetry ought to delight and inform its audience—suggesting that Horace might have liked crosswords too.

ARS is also [Art of MGM], referring to the studio's motto, *Ars gratia artis* ("art for art's sake"). **MGM** ("Metro-Goldwyn-Mayer") is the [Co. whose films have roaring starts] since it's the [Co. whose

MGM [Bond-issuing company?], [Grand opening?], [Leo's den?]

LEO [It's a sign] *(See also chapter 2)*

CHIMERA [Fire-breathing monster of myth], [Mythical hybrid], [Impossible dream], [Vain, foolish, or incongruous fancy]

DOSO *(do so)* ["Get on it"], [Obey]

OVO [Egg: prefix], [Lacto-___ vegetarian], [In___(embryonic)], [Egg head?]

RES [Hi-___], ["Hi" follower], [Pixelatedness, for short], [Like some telephone nos.], [Followers of dos]

LEDA [Mother of Castor and Pollux], [Spartan queen], [Queen who fell for Zeus's swan song?]

HELEN [Abductee of myth], [Paris attraction], [Ship launcher?], [Hunt for a film?]

OVUM [Bank asset that's frozen?], [Breakfast for Caesar?], [Part of a preconception?]

OVA [Caesar salad ingredients], [One in the sac?], [Eggs Florentine, once?], [Donations for life?]

DEUS [Jupiter or Mars], ["___vobiscum" ("God be with you")]

logo includes Leo the Lion]. **LEO** seems a natural choice for the [MGM roarer] as the [Zodiac sign whose name is Latin for "lion"] and for sharing letters with the last name of the studio's founder, Marcus Loew. A **LION** also starts (and ends) other pieces of fiction, as it's the [Front part of a chimera] and the [Rear half of a griffin].

MGM's slogan—a word-for-word translation of the 19th-century French motto *l'art pour l'art*—is also something of a **CHIMERA** as the fabricated Latin is a pile of bull, grammatically.

Speaking of artistic goofs, an aphorism attributed to Hippocrates, *ars longa, vita brevis*, is often rendered as "Art is long, life is short," to suggest "Art, unlike life, lasts." But a less artful, more accurate translation might read more like, "It takes a long time to master a craft (like practicing medicine), but life offers only a short time to **DOSO**." It's true: ["One can only ___ much!"]

The text of Horace's "Ars Poetica" provides the first use of two other common Latin phrases: *ab* **OVO** ("from the start") and *in medias* **RES** ("in the middle of things"). *Res* is also the start of a [Law "thing"], *res* as in [___ ipsa loquitur] (literally, "the matter speaks for itself"), a [Matter in court] suggesting that the unlikely nature of an incident implies the defendant's guilt.

Speaking of responsible parties, *ab ovo* traces its own beginning to the story of Zeus and **LEDA**, leading to the birth of **HELEN** from an **OVUM**: that [Egg] was the [Start of something big]. Similar cracks are made for the plural of "ovum," **OVA**, those [Monthly travelers?] that are [Eggs, pluribus?].

Despite what we've just done, Horace used *ab ovo* to suggest that—like tracing the Trojan War back to Helen's birth—a poet need not go back too far.

But this is puzzledom, not poetics, so let's at least mention how [God in Latin], **DEUS**, resembles "Zeus" since both likely descend from the ancient root *dyew-*, meaning "sky" or "heaven." The same heavenly origin is found in "Jupiter," "Tyr," "deity," and even "meridian." **DEUS** can still be seen in [___ ex machina] (*deus ex machina*, literally, "god from the machine"), used to describe another storytelling concern: the introduction of an unlikely plot-saving device.

Deus ends ["Ditat ___" (Arizona's motto)] (*ditat deus*, meaning "God enriches,") and—**PLOTTWIST**—joins with *ama* to form **AMADEUS**.

The plural of *deus*, **DEI**, usually manifests via fill-in-the-blank clues like [Opus ___] Dei ("Work of God," the Catholic organization) and [Agnus ___] *dei* ("lamb of God"), though some are only able to hit on the [Verbum ___ (word of God)] *dei* [___ gratia] ("by the grace of God").

The surname of the ["L.A. Law" actress] Susan **DEY** has more earthly origins. Back in the day, a "dey" was a female servant, particularly a "dairymaid," a word whose first syllable may contain an ounce of the old "dey."

DEY is also an [Old Ottoman title] or [Pasha of the past], a usage that may have evolved from a mispronunciation of **BEY**, an [Old Turkish title] for an [Ottoman bigwig].

Thanks to Beyoncé, **BEY** has received a fierce makeover, becoming [Queen ___ (nickname in pop music)]. The clue can be tricky, as Jay-Z's **BAE**—[Hon, modern style] is also "Queen Bee." Do **BEA** ["___ dear"] and don't confuse it with the Bea who's the [Arthur with a Tony].

Queen Bey, by the by, appeared at the 2017 Grammys bedecked and bejeweled like a **GODDESS**. The Grammys are sort of a "*Dies IRAE*," or Judgment Day. (Losers might see it as the more literal, traditional translation: "Day of wrath.") But "Dies Irae" typically refers specifically to the title of a Medieval Latin poem sung in a Requiem Mass and heard in many classical pieces, including Mozart's *Requiem*, featured on the Grammy-winning soundtrack to the 1984 film *Amadeus*.

A more quotidian form of *diēs*, **DIEM**, gets repaid regularly in puzzles as [Per ___] or seized upon in [Carpe ___].

PLOTTWIST [It was all a dream, maybe]

AMADEUS [Famous middle name that means "love of God"]

DEI [Latin gods], [Mater ___ (title for Mary)]

BAE [Sweetie], [Modern love?], [Boo]

BEA [Actress Arthur of "Maude"]

GODDESS [Nike, for one], [Venus, say], [Flora or Fauna]

IRAE [Dies ___], ["Of wrath," in a hymn title], [Wrath, in a hymn]

[It can be funny or easy]
Some Latin [Coinage] That's on the MONEY

MONEY [Evil's root, it's said], [Green], [Dough], [Composition of some rolls], [Exchanged notes?], ["___often costs too much": Emerson]

UNUM [One, on a bill], [Part of a coined phrase?], [One for the money?], [One word?]

OBS [Delivery people?], [Labor day VIPS], [No longer used, in a dict.]

OBVI ["Duh," in modern slang]

ROMAN [Not italic], [Type type], [Like Jupiter, but not Zeus], [Like M, L, or XL, but not S], [I, for one!], [Like DC and MI]

ANNO [Part of AD], [Word used in dating?], [Year of Latin], [Year abroad]

ANNI [Years in old Rome], [MMIV and MMV, e.g.], [Italian for years], [Years in Italy]

CASH [Bills, e.g.], [Green], [Plastic alternative], [Change into something green?]

PENNYWISE [Saving, in a small way], ["It" baddie]

ABE [#16, familiarly], [Five Georges], [Half a Hamilton], [Familiar face to a cashier], [Cent gent], [Tad's dad], [Japanese PM Shinzo___]

FIN [Half a sawbuck], [End of a French film], [Bass part], [Cod piece?]

TEN [One followed by nothing?], [Something to take or hang], [X amount], [Beauty mark?], [Pin number?], [It looks like two in binary]

LINCOLN [Center of New York]

E pluribus **UNUM** appears on the reverse—as opposed to the front, or "obverse"—side of a single dollar bill. The Latin *ob-* means "toward," and pairs with *via* ("way") to form "obvious." It also combines with *stō* ("to stand") to bear those who "stand before" women in labor: obstetricians, or **OBS**, **OBVI**.

ROMAN numerals on a single's reverse side spell out 1776, observing the important **ANNO** (Latin and Italian for "year," whose plural is **ANNI**). While they're hardly Latin, other answers about American **CASH** are linguistic relics and [Hard stuff] nonetheless.

PENNYWISE, **ABE** qualifies as a [Copper head?], but the ['60s White House name] is used specifically as slang for a [Fiver], or in more dated slang, a [Fin], making the [First bearded prez] [The fin man?]. **FIN** likely originated as slang for an [Abe] or [Five-spot] because of its proximity to "five" in Yiddish (*finf*) and German (*fünf*)—not because the [Perch part] might be mistaken for something supported by [Five bones].

You can exchange [Two fins] for a **TEN** or a [Sawbuck], the latter via a visual metaphor: A "sawbuck," or sawhorse, is a stand to support wood for sawing. As each pair of its outer legs is traditionally crossed to form an [X], the structure's name has come to be synonymous with the [Bill] reflecting the Roman numeral.

Curiously, a number often associated with **LINCOLN** is found in a clue for **TEN**: [Perfect score... or half of one].

Bono Goes PRO
[Ace] Clues Containing "Pro"

Seeing as we're already mentioning a [Point in favor] of certain clues, **PRO**, the Latin for [For], beyond being one of crosswords' most frequent and [Crackerjack] answers, returns the favor with its [Support] for Latin clues.

QUID, as in [___ pro quo] (*quid pro quo*, literally, "something for something"), is Latin for "what." "Quid" became a term for the [British pound, informally], because a [Bath buck] was the "something" given or taken in payment.

A clue like [Pro ___] might seem a big **TIP**, but like [President pro ___] it could warrant **TEM**. Short for *pro tempore*, "pro tem" means "for the time being."

RATA (as "rat-a") can be a [Sound that comes before two tats?]— as in rat-a-[___-tat-tat], but more often clues use it for *rata*, another [Pro accompanier?] or [Pro tailer?], as in [Pro ___] (*pro rata*, literally, "for [the] determined," referring to a proportional distribution), comparable to the English "prorated."

Finally, it's no [Pro ___] **FORMA** (*"pro forma"*: "perfunctory") point that another four-letter [Pro ___] answer available to take the stage is **BONO** (as in *pro bono publico*, literally, "for the good of the public"). Fittingly, the [U2 frontman] and [Popular singer born Paul David Hewson], who rechristened himself using the Latin for "good," habitually works for nothing as the [Singer at the Live Aid concert].

In 1994 and 1996, "pro Bono" votes in the **PALM** Springs area of **CALI**—[It has its faults]—elected the city's former mayor Salvatore Phillip "Sonny" Bono to Congress.

Yet it's the former romantic and vocal [Partner of Sonny] whom crosswords prefer to nominate. Her career as a [Singing star since the '60s] and a [One-named Oscar winner] combine to make [The Goddess of Pop] such an ideal candidate for perennial reelection that it's clear: The cruciverse is decidedly pro **CHER**.

PRO [All for], [Whiz], [Old hand], [Person who plays for work], [Golf club VIP], [What an athlete may turn?], [One for the money?], [One giving you the aye?], [Anti-anti?], [Angel or Saint, e.g.], [Lion, Tiger, or Bear, e.g.], [Active leader?], [Tour leader?], [Bono's opener?]

TIP [Reward for waiting], [Not stiff?], [Scratch on the table?], [Q follower?]

TEM [Pro follower], [Judge pro___], [President pro__ (senator presiding over the Senate in the absence of the vice president)]

BONO [One-named rock star], [Good for Caesar?], [Cher's son Chaz]

PALM [Where to get a date?], [Reading matter?], [Provider of a lifeline]

CALI [Only place in the US to host both the Summer and Winter Olympics, informally], [Colombian metropolis], [City WSW of Bogotá]

CHER [Dear: Fr.], [One-named pop diva], ["Clueless" protagonist]

Chapter 1 Puzzle: "Super Salad"

ACROSS

1 "My precious!" speaker
7 Utah town named for a Biblical kingdom
11 Candy that pops out of a neck
14 "Break Free" singer Grande
15 "Frozen" princess
16 Be in the red
17 Clear
18 Bright light
19 Understand
20 Just looking at these recipes, a reader QUITE SLOBBERS...
23 "Night" author Wiesel
24 Sister in a habit
25 Get together
28 Christmas mo.
29 ...but those who dislike shellfish might want to REWORD CONCH...
32 Place for Joe
33 Oldies group __ Na Na
34 Apt noise made at a Lions game
35 One opening a can of worms?
38 Inclines
40 Additional
41 Really move
44 Something left at a bar
45 ...and as there's NO CHEF IN, NOR a line cook...

48 Member of the fam
51 Strike it before it's hot
52 Eggs in a lab
53 Sea bird
54 ...DO CHECK ONLINE (or consult these clues) to prepare them yourself
58 Play-__ (toy originally invented to clean walls)
60 Don't screw up?
61 Cloak oneself?
62 "__ sera, sera"
63 Cookie that's two cookies
64 Zigzagged
65 Confess it
66 Ooze
67 With 1-Across: (from) A-to-Z

DOWN

1 Really annoyed
2 Orange flyer
3 Brain system largely in charge of emotions
4 Expire
5 Foot, pound, or stone
6 Created
7 Knots on top?
8 About 2.5 centimeters
9 Years in Mexico
10 "Macbeth" ghost
11 Neptune, to Greeks
12 Barnyard mother
13 Capital of Zaire?

21 Time off from the Army, for short
22 Open a gift
26 Suckled part of a 12-Down
27 Goes off course
29 Helpful hint
30 "Queen of All Media"
31 Must
32 Hold tightly
35 Alarm clock toggle
36 "You've Got Mail" director Ephron
37 Woman's name derived from Margaret
39 Civil Rights Memorial designer Maya
42 Chewbacca, e.g.
43 Surround completely
46 Casual slacks
47 Fleming or McKellen
48 9x9 numeric puzzle
49 "Yeah, right!"
50 Runs, as a color
53 Wimbledon winner Ivanisevic
55 Give a toot
56 Fit snugly inside
57 Anne Sexton's palindrome-inspired poem "Rats Live __ Evil Star"
58 Blizzard sellers, briefly
59 Overseas agreement?

Chapter 2

ARCHITECTURE, Religion, Fashion, and Brands
Tips for [Building style] and Grace

Answering any clue is a small [Leap of ___] **FAITH**. And especially considering how grids often look, reading the first clue of any crossword can feel like ["Taking the first step even when you don't see the whole staircase," per MLK]. But here's [Something to keep] in mind: You can have [Confidence] that some logical solution exists. One could even approach clues as ["The evidence of things not seen"].

Historically, crosswords have drawn heavily from Christianity, demonstrating a [Conviction] that solvers would recognize [One of "these three," in Corinthians], for example. To be sure, there's nothing inherently wrong with thinking of **FAITH** as the [Hope and charity partner]. But what might be seen as catering to solvers' spheres of familiarity nevertheless offers a revelation: Puzzles' tendency to favor those who typically made and edited them has come at the expense of inclusivity.

FAR [Where overachievers go?]

CROSS [Angry], [Betray], [Hybrid], [Sign of the times?], [Go from side to side?], [Vampire repellent]

SMALLC ("small-c") [__conservative (one who doesn't identify with a party)]

CATHOLIC as "Catholic" [Like Madonna, and much of her imagery], *but as "catholic"* [Broad in tastes], [Wide-ranging], [Comprehensive], [Universal]

HEAVEN [The Big Rock Candy Mountain, to hobos], [Angels' playing field], [Good resting place?]

The good news is that crosswords' worldview is widening, in part thanks to concerted efforts to present puzzles by constructors and editors with diverse voices. References to religions and **FAITH** [__ No More] are [Something to keep] cluing without more consistently drawing on [Islam or Buddhism], [Zoroastrianism, e.g.], or a [Kwanzaa principle]. (Even skeptics can find it as the [Hill in Nashville], referring to the country music star.)

While it's a step too **FAR** to believe the collection of answers that **CROSS** themselves in the **TIERED** grid can ever refrain from being slightly [Stacked] one way or other, if compiled in a **SMALLC CATHOLIC**—that is, [All-embracing] and [Of interest to all]—way, they could still construct a kind of stairway to **HEAVEN**—a place that, as surely as it might be [St. Peter's domain], could be a [Hindu's Devaloka].

KEEP Column and Carry On
Old Architecture Terms That [Persist in] Puzzles

KEEP [Start to KISS, as a matter of principle?], [It's earned], [Castle stronghold]

AGORA [Ancient gathering place], [Lead in to phobia], [Pythagorean square?], [Early mall?]

ATRIA [Lobbies for light galleries?], [Openings in the hotel business], [Parts of hearts], [Two of hearts?], [Pair of hearts?]

IONIC [Architectural order], [Column order], [Kind of chemical bond in salts], [Kind of bond created when opposites attract?]

With so many open spaces filled with old Greek and Roman words, a crossword grid can resemble an **AGORA**, the lively [Ancient Greek marketplace] that was a [Grecian hub]. That sounds sort of lively, but overloading a grid with antiquated language risks transforming it into an [Old Greek square].

Here are a few classic terms from classical architecture capable of holding up a solver's progress:

Architecturally, **ATRIA** (sing.: atrium, from the identical Latin, meaning "entry hall") are [Central courtyards] that still serve as [Features of many malls]. Anatomically, they're [Heart chambers].

Similarly, **OCULI** (sing.: oculus) is Latin for [Eyes], but this term for [Caesar's peepers] can also be seen as [Round windows], especially [Dome openings, in architecture].

The **IONIC** [Column style] is the ancient Greek architectural [Order with scrolls on the capital], or top part. So it was made to order as the [Jefferson Memorial column type] honoring the bibliophilic president in his nation's capital. As its name suggests, the form originated in **IONIA**, the [Ancient region of Asia Minor], which one clue suggested was a [Slice of old Turkey?].

DORIC columns, [Like the columns of the Lincoln Memorial], fit the 16th president, as they're a bit more austere, being a [Column with a simple capital]. Like tourists visiting a Greek temple, solvers might wonder which five-letter [Kind of column]—**DORIC** or **IONIC**—they're looking at in clues like [Architectural order] or [Corinthian alternative]. But as **IONIC** bonds better with other answers, it's more frequent and is a well-grounded guess.

Here's a tip for realtors: If prospective buyers point to an [S-shaped molding] or [Double-curved molding] known as an **OGEE** and say, "[Oh gosh, a molding?]," don't dismiss them as an [Arch type]. Rather, recognize them for the inveterate crossword solvers they evidently are.

Here's some additional [Classified information?]: It would be **APT** to also highlight the [Felicitous] breakfast nook ("[Well-suited] for a cup of coffee and a puzzle!"), the checkered kitchen tiles ("Isn't there something [Fitting] about a grid design?"), and how [On point] it is that the building superintendent provides free pencil-sharpening services. ("He's just downstairs in **ONEA**, the [Super's apartment, often]!")

Initially, **SRO** stood for "Single Room Occupancy," a [Fleabag hotel, for short] or a room in a similar sort of boardinghouse, often found near Broadway in New York. Now it's seen more as another sort of ["Rent" sign] or [B'way sign] that's a [Sign of success], referring to the [Sellout abbr.], "Standing Room Only."

It must have been SRO sometimes at the **STOA**, an [Ancient sheltered promenade] or [Greek colonnade]—often specifically the [Site of Zeno's teaching]. That stoa served not only as the school for **ZENO** of Citium (c. 334–c. 262 BCE), the [Founder of stoicism], but also as the stony foundation of the very word "**STOIC**."

ZENO the [First Stoic] ought not be confused with his forerunner, the [Paradoxical fellow] Zeno of Elea (c. 490–c. 430 BCE). Yet, paradoxically, solvers could think of the wrong [Greek philosopher] and still be correct. **ELEA**, [Where Zeno taught]—no, the other Zeno—was so populated by Greeks that the area, located in present-day

IONIA [Ancient Aegean land], [Birthplace of Pythagoras]

DORIC [That's an order], [Like the Parthenon], [Classical style]

APT [Well-put], [Inclined], [Prone], [Quick on the uptake], [Address abbr.], [A little flat?], [Letters that complete this word: _P_ROPRIA_E], [Like the anagram "I'll make a wise phrase" of "William Shakespeare"]

ONEA ("one-A") [Seat for a priority boarder, maybe], [Draft classification], [Suited to serve], [Ready for service?], [What the word "draft" has?]

SRO [Smash letters?], [Packed letters?], [Sign of being full?], [Hit sign?], [Standing invitation?]

STOIC [Stone-faced], [Impassive], [Epictetus, e.g.], [Zenophile?]

southwestern Italy, had the somewhat paradoxical name of *Magna Graecia* ("Great Greece" in Latin).

The Ancient Greek for "foreign," *xénos*, gives English both the [Foreign: prefix] **XENO** and the element **XENON**, a [Member of a noble family]. Whether or not that clue made solvers exclaim "[It's a gas]" might have to do with how foreign it was to them, although [It's often in the spotlight].

The old Greek for "new," **NEON**, may seem an [Illuminating subject?] to avoid when it's exposed as a [Broadway flasher?]—especially if [Its gas gets attention]. The name of the [TV princess] **XENA** is neither new nor paradoxical as a [Lawless role]: Lucy Lawless's former character wasn't afraid to break a few rules in her fight for justice.

Erector <u>SET</u>

Three Contemporary Architects
and Their [Collected works]

The [First name in architecture] belonging to Finnish-American **EERO** Saarinen (1910–61) makes him a natural grid girder. Meaning [Eric, in Finland], it's especially apt as a standard answer for a drawer of blueprints, as it means "eternal ruler."

EERO Saarinen was drawn to the catenary curve, the bend seen in a chord suspended from both ends. The shape inspired his most famous structure, St. Louis's Gateway Arch, and makes the [Finnish architect Saarinen] an [Arch-itect]. He is also [A Saarinen], as his father was the famous architect **ELIEL** Saarinen—whose name has thus been labeled [Eero pop?].

The younger Saarinen designed the **TWA** Flight Center at Terminal 5 in **JFK**. The Flight Center was repurposed in part in 2019 to form the TWA Hotel, where visitors can rest their arches while lounging in a "Tulip Chair," a curvy [Kind of chair] Saarinen co-designed with [Chair-maker Charles] **EAMES**.

IMPEI ("I. M. Pei," short for Ieoh Ming Pei, 1917–2019) is another [JFK terminal architect]. His project, Terminal 6, was demolished in 2011. The Chinese-American [Louvre Pyramid architect] was known

---

XENO [Strange start?], [Alien introduction?]

NEON [It's a gas], [Kind of sign], [Sign of nightlife?]

TWA [Bygone carrier], [Major airline until 2001], [Former American rival], [This does not fly]

JFK [Place for an N.Y.C. touchdown?], [Stone work], [His Secret Service name was Lancer]

for incorporating open spaces and natural environments. Clues note his work designing the JFK Presidential Library, the Bank of China **TOWER**, and the Rock and Roll Hall of Fame in **CLE**— letters that also unlock the [Key to "la cité?"] with the French *clé*.

PEI ("PEI," "Prince Edward Island") also muscles its way in as [Canada's smallest prov.]. **IEOH** Ming Pei erected the 57-story Commerce Court West building in Toronto, but he never pieced anything together in the provincial PEI.

MING might go over some solvers' heads as the [Center of Houston?], but that's the right place for the high-rising former Houston Rockets player, **YAO** Ming.

Another former Rocket, Jeremy **LIN**, shares a name with another great crossword "constructor": the architect Maya **LIN**, who was named the [Vietnam Memorial designer] at just 21. She's gone on to develop works including the Civil Rights Memorial in Alabama, the Museum of African Art in New York, and a series of art installations along the Columbia River called the Confluence Project. Like Saarinen, Lin has a first name befitting her line of work, as the **MAYA** were [Ancient pyramid builders].

Here Is the STEEPLE

Puzzles a-[Spire] to an a-[Pealing place] and Make Weddings a [High point of church?]

Puzzled souls seeking answers might be saved by visiting a church. If that sounds a little **ARCH**, just consider how many of its [Principal] parts can offer support.

The **NAVE** is the long, central [Pew area] of a church [Where parishioners sit]. Exiting the nave, parishioners might [Cross] under a **ROOD**, a large [Crucifix] that's a [Big cross] word.

Letters on the rood often form **INRI**, the [Cross inscription] representing *Iesus Nazarenus, Rex Iudaeorum* ("Jesus of Nazareth, King of the Jews"). **INRE** ("in re," from the Latin, literally, "in regard to") those words, a passage from the book of John reports that the phrase

TOWER [Soar], [Truck with a tailgater?]

CLE [Cavs, on a scoreboard], [A.L. Central team], [Browns, in brief], [French key]

PEI [Who might say "I'm I.M."], [I. M. sent to a construction site], [Shar-___ (wrinkly dog)]

IEOH [I.M. Pei's "I"] *(though the name is pronounced "yoh")*

MING [Vase style], [Dish dynasty]

YAO [Big Chinese import?], [Rocket from China?]

LIN [Jeremy ___, first Asian-American NBA champion], [___-Manuel Miranda], [The "L" in the Broadway monogram "LMM"], [Mao colleague ___ Bao]

MAYA [Belize native], [Yucatan native], [Chichén Itzá people], [Angelou who said, "Nothing will work unless you do"], [Rudolph with a parody of Kamala Harris on "SNL"], [___ Harris, sister and campaign chair of Kamala]

ARCH [St. Louis landmark], [Mischievous], [Clever in a bent way?], [Sole support?], [Enemy leader?]

NAVE [Place for the masses?], [Place for a flock]

INRI [Calvary inscription], [Cross reference?], [Sign of the cross], [Letters for Jesus]

INRE [About], [Concerning], [Memo opener], [First words from a dictator?]

was inscribed on Jesus's cross not only in Latin, but also in Greek and Hebrew.

Beyond the rood is the chancel, which often includes a **LOFT** for the **CHOIR**. The chancel, perchance, might end in an **APSE**, an [Area with a half dome] or [Semicircular recess] at the very front of the church.

In the chancel you may see a [Promising site]: the **ALTAR**, a [Shrine] in puzzles consecrated to knavery, hallowed ground not for taking a knee but for getting in knee-slappers.

Putting the ALTAR in [The rite place]

Hitching post?	Last place to be single?	Union station?
One raised in church?	Train stop?	Site for many kisses

The [Word] **VOW** might answer [One of two at a wedding], but such a [Veiled statement?] could also be **IDO** ("I do"). These latter [Words with a ring to them?] are hardly monogamous, as they can consort with all sorts of partners. Puzzles also resound with **IDOS** ("I do's"), another [Pair at the altar] echoing clues similar to those below.

IDO: The [Short sentence?] That's a [Life Sentence]

Mating call	Words from an altar ego?	Bachelor's last words?
Swear words		
Prelude to a kiss	Words that leave you in a bind?	Conclusion of a singles match?
Famous last words	Altar-ed speech	"Sign me up!"
Prenuptial agreement?	The rite answer	Bridal line?
	Chapel line	Solemn promise

Jokes aside, when couples **WED**, it's best to [Take seriously?] each party's desire to [Trade rings] and [Become a union member?], even if they might [Have an "altar-cation"] and find that their [Espoused] arrangement lasts only a single [Hump day: Abbr.].

Wise In-VESTMENTS
Priestly [Attire] Cloaked in Puzzles

Like a bishop before a **SER** ("ser.," for "sermon") grabbing a **MITER** from the **VESTRY**—the [Church room] [Where robes are kept]—crosswords are in the [Habit] of donning clerical **GARB**.

SER [Sun. talk], [To be, in Spanish], [Spanish 101 verb]

MITER [Bishop's hat], [High hat], [Top of the Catholic church]

GARB [Duds], [Togs], [Threads]

A **STOLE** is a long, narrow, heavily ornamented [Clerical scarf]. Imagine a priest, [Made hot?] that his flock [Took the wrong way?] his sermon about [Cold shoulder treatment?], [Ripped off] his [Shoulder warmer], declared [It's a wrap], [Went quietly] out the back door, [Walked off with] plans to [Scarf] down a [Poached] egg, and from then on [Did a bank job]. (Hey, it could happen.)

Far more likely (in the real world and puzzles) is **ALB**, [Priestly attire] which may be an [Item from a surplice store?], as a surplice is another sort of [Vestment]. When not referring to a white robe that's [Father's wear] and [Clothing for the masses], it may refer to the Canadian [Neighbor of BC], Alberta—itself often covered in a white layer—or the European [Neighbor of Gr.], Albania. The latter's [Largely Muslim capital city] might appear as either **TIRANA** or **TIRANE**.

But the crowning achievement of clerical wear is the **PAPAL TIARA**, also known as the triregnum or triple crown. Or at least it was: Paul VI ended its use in 1964.

PAPAL [Vatican-related], [Like some bulls]

TIARA [Coronet], [It's fit for a queen], [Rock band], [Plastique___ ("RuPaul's Drag Race" constestant)]

Speaking of tops for [Pops] with [Pop], one of crosswords' finest **DAD** [___ jokes] was popped out by constructor Molly Young: [Having a baby makes one]. You can almost hear the pitter [Pater] of little pink pencil erasers, drubbing away in ap-[Parent] perplexity.

DAD [Little league coach, often], [Old man?], [June honorary], [___bod], [X or Y supplier], [Paw], [He's your father]

[See people] in the Puzzle
POPES Form a [Long line in Rome]

Instead of white smoke, puzzles might announce that they've chosen a **POPE** by floating a clue like [Word before or after Alexander], referring to Pope Alexander and the [English poet Alexander] Pope. While the first might require penance for a mistake, the latter would

POPE [Cardinals' manager?], [Urban, e.g.], [Innocent, e.g.], [John or Paul, but not Ringo], [See figure 1?]

POP [Short report?], [Art opening?], [Weasel word?], [Crush, e.g.], [Old man]

LEO ["Seinfeld" uncle], [Bill Clinton, to the stars?], [Sign up in July?], [Constellation whose brightest star is Regulus], [The Lion] *(See also chapter 1)*

ATTILA [Fifth-century invader], [The Scourge of God]

HUN [Vandal], [Horde member], [Enemy in "Mulan"]

ROME [The Eternal City], [Seven Hills city], [End of all roads?], [Multi-day building project?], [Apple variety], [New York city], [Erie Canal city]

FIT [Suit], [Hale], [A toddler might throw one], [Working out well?]

ECO [Green prefix], [Prefix with tourism], [Friendly introduction?], [System starter?], [Logical start?], [Italian author Umberto], ["The Name of the Rose" author]

POPEMOBILE [Mass transportation?], [Holy roller?]

FORD [Cross], [First assemblyman?], [Focus group?]

FOCUS [Make it really clear?]

JOHNS [Bordello patrons], [Cans], [Long___]

HBO [World's first channel to be transmitted via satellite]

likely be quicker to forgive, being the [Writer who popularized the saying "To err is human, to forgive divine"]. Popes who **POP** up regularly don't always [Jump off the page]:

- The [Papal name] **LEO** doubles as the [Sign of summer]. This [Sort who's a natural leader, supposedly], includes no less an [August one?] than [Bill Clinton or Barack Obama].

  [Thirteen popes] were **LEOS**, but they weren't the ones constructor John Lieb conceived of when he trickily treated solvers to the idea that [They may be conceived around Halloween].

- **LEOI** ("Leo I"), the [Fifth-century pope], was the [First pope to be called "The Great"], and the first of five popes to become a **STLEO**, now also a [Tampa suburb named after a pope]. He's "the Great" in part for meeting with **ATTILA** the **HUN**, whom he dissuaded from attacking **ROME**.

- [Any of 12 popes] could be called **PIUS**, from the word giving English "pious." Similarly, the Latin **PRIOR** is a direct [Antecedent] of the English word also used for a [Monastic officer].

  Meanings of the Latin *prior* like "first" and "superior" probably informed Toyota's name for their [Green car], the **PRIUS**. The neologism built on the old root manages to sound futuristic, making it a good **FIT** for the **ECO**-friendly model.

  While some thought Pope Francis would pick a Prius for his **POPEMOBILE**, he opted for a **FORD FOCUS**.

- **JOHN**, the [Most common papal name], is also the one treated least piously in puzzles: He's often (dis)regarded as a [Loo] or [Lav], even if honored as the [Place to solve a crossword, maybe]. As the [Name of 23 popes], many a [Dear guy?] had the same label as a certain [Legend of pop music]. That's a lot of **JOHNS** who wound up [Going places?] in life.

No need to spring for **HBO**; clues of that sort make crosswords a game of thrones.

[Place to go in London] Where the [English head]: <u>LOO</u>		
☐ John, to Ringo	☐ English facilities	☐ Head across the
☐ Elton's john	☐ Head of Hogwarts	Atlantic?
☐ John of York	☐ Head of Parliament?	☐ What might charge a
☐ Brit's closet	☐ Seat at Wimbledon	going rate?
☐ British can	☐ Can of Prince Albert?	☐ Throne room at
☐ British throne?	☐ Can of Newcastle	Buckingham Palace

"What HATH God Wrought?"
Answers the Puzzle [Possesses, biblically]

Even the doctrine of papal infallibility doesn't preclude popes from erring in crosswords. Luckily, a mere **LAIC**—a nonordained member of the church—can be more than a **LAYMAN** at solving clues after the briefest bit of bible study.

LAIC [Secular], [Of the flock], [Not of the cloth], [Like some church matters], [Nonclerical]

LAYMAN [Congregation member], [Nonexpert]

LEV (short for "Leviticus," literally, "of the Levites") is the [Book after Exod.], but there's also the book [Chaim Potok's "My Name Is Asher ___"] Lev, a novel of an artist's coming of age. Both Trotsky and Tolstoy could say, "My name is also Lev," since it was Leon [Trotsky's real first name] and Leo [Tolstoy's first name, in Russia]. And actor **LIEV** [Schreiber of "Ray Donovan"], whose mother was a big fan of the Russian realist novelist, can say, "My name is almost Lev."

LEV is also a [Bulgarian coin] equal to [100 stotinki]. North of the Bulgarian border, in **LIEU** of the lev, use **LEU**—[Romania's currency] and [Moldovan money]—whose plural is **LEI** (though that answer, which we'll loop back to in chapter 4, is usually laid out as the [Luau garland]).

LIEU [Place], [Stead]

[Balkan capital] could also refer to [Bulgaria's capital], **SOFIA**, or the previously **TROD** terrain of **TIRANE** (a.k.a. **TIRANA**), where they use the [Albanian currency], the **LEK**.

SOFIA [A Coppola], [Vergara of "Modern Family"]

TROD [Stepped], [Walked], [Put one's shoes on?]

EZRA [Metrical Pound], [Pound of letters?]

TORAH [Literally, "law"], [Numbers place]

ARC [Bow], [C, for one], [Parabolic path], [Tangent starter?], [Homer's path], ["The___of the moral universe is long, but it bends toward justice": MLK]

MORSE [Dotty inventor], [Dashing fellow?], [Code name], [- - - - - .- .....]

NUM [Book before Deut.], [O.T. book], [Fig.]

HATH [Owneth], [Had in old form?]

The titular [Biblical prophet] **EZRA** the Scribe of the [Book before II Chronicles] is remembered for returning the Jews to Jerusalem from Babylon. Historians believe he may have helped determine the contents of the first **TORAH**. Ironically, the scribe shares his name with the poet Ezra Pound, famous for modernist verse and infamous for his virulent fascism and antisemitism. The poet who delicately likened "The apparition of these faces in the crowd" to "Petals on a wet, black bough" also equated Hitler to "Jeanne d'**ARC**, a saint."

EZRA [Cornell of Cornell University] is yet a third Ezra of letters: no less through his 30,000 personal correspondences than for co-founding Western Union. Today, on the campus bearing Ezra Cornell's name, much clothing bears the name of Ezra [Fitch of Abercrombie & Fitch].

Ezra Cornell addressed many of his letters to his funder, Samuel **MORSE**, who quoted from **NUM** ("Num.," for "Numbers") in the first telegraphic message: "What **HATH** God wrought?" (A question perhaps no one could answer better than Ezra the Scribe.)

ADAM and Eve, Exposed
You Wouldn't Be the [First one]
to [Not know from ___]

THO [Howe'er], [However briefly?], [Short while?], [Vietnam's Le Duc___]

FIG [Brief leaf?], [Newton fruit], [Newton's tree?], [Worthless amount], [Abbr. next to a chart]

GOETH [Doth proceed], [Biblical leaves?]

DOEST [Performs, biblically], [Perform, à la Shakespeare], [Acts of the Apostles?]

THO Adam and Eve got the heave-ho from **EDEN**, they'll forever find little squared-off plots in crosswords, where [Paradise lost] is repeatedly found. Judging by the ways they offer **ADAM** and **EVE** cover and make **EDEN** hard to find, constructors clearly don't give a **FIG** if they lead innocent solvers astray.

Crosswords even manage to see the [Ending of the Bible] either as **ETH** (which is also an [Ordinal suffix], as in "twentieth") or **EST** (discussed at length in chapter 1), capitalizing on the forms of the [Biblical verb ending] seen in words like **GOETH** and **DOEST**, respectively.

ADAM		
First of all?	#1 dad?	Unborn person?
First mate?	Fall guy?	One with a first-person narrative?
First name?	Noted exile	
First person?	Cain raiser?	Man with an apple named after him?
First to arrive?	Race starter?	
First husband?	Leading man?	Apple consumer with an unhappy story to tell?
First lady's man?	Garden party?	Name that derives from the Hebrew word for "earth"
First bone donor?	Bachelor No. 1?	
First family member?	Being number one?	Driver around a lot?
Party of the first part?	Early fruit sampler?	West of Hollywood

EVE		
First mate?	Fall starter?	Before time
First lady?	Fall guy's partner?	Predate?
First offender?	Second name?	Threshold
Spare rib?	Second person?	12/31, for one
Prime rib?	Snake charmee?	1/2 vis-à-vis 1/3, say
Result of a ribbing?	Serpent's mark?	Gift-wrapping time
Apple user?	Serpent's pigeon?	Time that's the same forward and backward?
Apple picker	Wife without in-laws?	
Adam's apple?		Wall-E's love in "Wall-E"
Apple pioneer?	"Life" in Hebrew	There's a film all about her?

EDEN		
Utopia	Elysium	Opening day site?
Fall scene	Xanadu	Hebrew for "delight"
Fall setting?	It's perfect	Garden for early birds?
Fall garden?	Dreamland	Adam's apple location?
Biblical plot?	Shang-ri La	Garden spot in Sweden?
Plot of Genesis?	Ideal world?	Where Adam spared a rib?
Tempting spot	Starting place?	Two-person starter home?
First place?	Heaven on Earth	1950s British P.M. Anthony ___
First base?	Depeopled area?	Not the best place for apple-testing
First nudist colony?	Home and garden?	
First family's address	Nod neighbor	Place whose population was 1, then 2, then 0

[With the greatest of ___] EASE
Enoch, Enos, Esau, Edom, Elam, and Edam

EASE [Relaxation], [Let up], [Facility]

ELEARNING [University of Phoenix specialty]

ENOW [Adequate, old-style], [Sufficient, for Shakespeare]

CAIN [First born?], [Third person], [Brother of Seth], [Number one son], [First offer?], [Something that might be raised in a fight], ["Double Indemnity" author]

NOD [Affirmative action], [Drop (off)], [Head down?], [Bean dip?]

NOAH [Rain man], [Man famous for doing a double take?], [Webster's first?]

ENOS [First grandchild?], [Biblical figure born to a 105-year-old father], [Slaughter in Cooperstown?]

ANOS [Yucatan years], [Years abroad], [Mayo containers?]

SPACE [Elbow room], [#, to a proofreader], [What " " contains], ["The breath of art," per Frank Lloyd Wright], [Character from a bar?]

BANDNAME [U2, e.g.], [Of Montreal or Berlin, e.g.]

APE [Mimic], [Copy], [Bruiser], [Big galoot], [Large copier?], [Bad way to go?], [Great one?]

HAM [Noah's second son], [Scenery chewer], [Cured cut?] *(See also chapter 1)*

LAPD [Sgt. Friday's force], [Hollywood blues?]

CBS [Ultimate "Survivor" winner?], [Some radios], [You might have a handle on these]

DUKE [Single fist?], [Noble]

"E" names from the Old Testament are rarely an **EAZYE** ("Eazy-E," the ["Straight Outta Compton" rapper] born Eric Wright), but a little **ELEARNING** (e-learning) will earn more than **EFOR** ("E for") [___ effort].

As if one wasn't **ENOW** ("enough"), two biblical forefathers were named **ENOCH**, meaning "dedicated":

CAIN was the [First son], making his own first son, **ENOCH**,the [Grandson of Adam]. [He was raised by Cain] in the Land of **NOD**, so he could tell you [Why isn't one done?] (because there's "no D").

The ensuing book of **ENOCH** tells of the next Enoch, [Methuselah's father], the great-great-grand-nephew of the first Enoch and the great-grandfather of **NOAH**.

There's also more than enough men (and even an ape) named **ENOS**:

The [First son of Seth], **ENOS** was another [Grandson of Adam], making him the cousin of the first Enoch, the great-great-grand-father of the second Enoch, and a direct [Ancestor of Methuselah] and Noah. Like others of his line, Enos lived a long time: A nonagenarian ten times over, he reached the ripe age of 905 **ANOS**, ["Years" in Spanish].

Despite becoming the [First and only chimpanzee to orbit Earth] in 1961, "**ENOS** the **SPACE** chimp" was preceded to [The heavens] by another great ape with a Biblical namesake, Ham the Astrochimp. (**BANDNAME**, anyone?)

The strange physics of the cruciverse provides space for **APE** to answer to [Parrot], and for **HAM** to be a [Stage hog] or a [Mugger?] looking to [Cutup] a [Broadway hot dog?].

Speaking of roles for hams, the [Hazzard County deputy] **ENOS** Strate joined the **LAPD** in the 1980–81 *Dukes of Hazzard* spin-off, *Enos*, but **CBS** soon sent him back to chasing Bo and Luke **DUKE** across Georgia.

The baseball player **ENOS** Slaughter spent a few years playing minor league ball in Georgia before joining the Cardinals. We'll revisit him at the other end of his long career when we reach Cooperstown in chapter 7.

Finally, the fifth **ENOS**—but only(!) the second from religious history—was the eponymous author of the [Fourth book of the Book of Mormon] and son of the Mormon prophet Jacob.

Okay, ["All right already!"], ["Uncle!"]. Between two Enochs and five Enoses—six if you count the book—["Eight Is ___"] **ENOUGH**!

That Mormon prophet, of course, was a different **JACOB** from the [Biblical twin] of **ESAU**, yet another four-letter [Genesis son] or [Biblical brother]. Remembered as the [Biblical birthright barterer], Esau traded his inheritance, the [Biblical country] of **EDOM**, for a bowl of stew.

Speaking of sneaky trades, **EDOM** can show up calling itself a [Biblical kingdom] or a [Land in Genesis], making it impossible to distinguish from **ELAM**.

But **ELAM** often is credited as [Jack of "Rio Lobo"] or [Oater actor Jack]. An **OATER** is a [Western film, in old slang], especially a low-grade [Cowboy flick], akin to a [Horse opera]. The [Oater actor Gulager] whose actual career in ways echoed the character Rick Dalton's in Gulager's last film—Quentin Tarantino's *Once Upon a Time in Hollywood*—had a name perfectly suited for puzzles. The [Actor Gulager whose name sounds like a crossword hint] answered to **CLU**.

A cheese you might want to pair with an **OAT** cracker as a [Meal starter?] is **EDAM**, the [Dutch export] seen in [Dutch wheels]. A coastal [Dutch town with a cheese named after it], Edam was established when locals dammed the local river—called the "E" or "Ee" or "IJe"—so they could charge shippers who needed to access it. As the Dutch for "dam" is *dam*, the town called itself "E dam," or Edam.

Over time, **EDAM** became famous for its [Mild cheese] now found in Babybels. Though some might think [It's cheesy] to point out that it's [Cheese that's made backward?] (as it's spelled E-D-A-M), there's no disputing that in crosswords it's the [Big cheese?].

JACOB [Man with a ladder?], [Genesis patriarch], [Third book of the Book of Mormon], [2018 and 2019 Cy Young winner deGrom]

ESAU [Isaac's eldest], [Biblical name meaning "hairy"], [Twin seen in a thesaurus?]

EDOM [Esau's other name], [Ancient kingdom in modern-day Jordan], [Biblical land whose name means "red" in Hebrew]

ELAM [Ancient rival of Assyria], [Kingdom east of Babylonia]

OAT [Horse's bit?], [Bit in a horse's mouth?], [Kind of milk], [Stable particle?]

I've How Many <u>IVES</u>?

Who's [...going to St. ___] Ives as a [Currier's partner], and Who's Not

<u>IVES</u> is another crosswordese name with enigmatic variations. The confusion begins with the seemingly simple nursery rhyme, "As I Was Going to St. Ives":

> *As I was going to St. Ives,*
> *I met a man with seven wives.*
> *Every wife had seven sacks,*
> *Every sack had seven cats,*
> *Every cat had seven kits.*
> *Kits, cats, sacks, and wives,*
> *How many were going to St. Ives?*

GOING [Auctioneer's word], [On the way]

HAVE [Eat], [Suffer from], [Moneyed one]

TWO [Tango requirement], [Jefferson's bill], [Snake eyes], [Double standard?], [Noah count?]

ZERO [Round number?], [One out of 10?], [Complete loser]

MATHS [British subject?]

The answer is often given as "one," as only the narrator is said to be "**GOING** to St. Ives"—the rest assumedly he would **HAVE** met as they traveled in the opposite direction. Or perhaps it's "**TWO**": the narrator and "the man with seven wives." Or it might be "2,802," if everyone's going to St. Ives—including all the **KITS** (which here are not [Hobby shop buys] but certain baby animals, such as [Little foxes]). Or, if the narrator is merely wondering "how many *of them* were going to St. Ives," and therefore excluding himself, the answer could be "**ZERO**."

MATHS aside, St. <u>**IVES**</u> is a common hagiotoponym, or place named after a saint. Perhaps the narrator means [St. ___ (Cornwall resort town)] on England's southwest shore, named after Saint Ia; or is it the St. Ives near Cambridge, named for Saint Ivo of Ramsey?

Such permutations might have challenged even **ENIAC**, the 8-foot high, 80-foot long, and 80-foot deep [Pioneering computer] known as the ["Giant Brain" that debuted in 1946], whose name is an [Old computing acronym] for Electronic Numerical Integrator and Computer.

Luckily, the most challenging calculation crosswords typically ask about the story is [One of four in "As I Was Going to St. Ives"], yielding **IAMB**, which merely appears to measure distance when seen as a [Metric foot]. Of course, whether a **POEM** is short or long, [It may be measured in both feet and meters].

But the **IVES** who's a [Saint in a children's rhyme] is just one of five Ives guys canonized in crosswords. The four others are all Americans:

There's the [Lithographer James] Merritt **IVES**, partner of Nathaniel Currier.

Then there's the ["Venus in Fur" playwright David] **IVES**. Known for his brilliant **ONEACT** plays like *Words, Words, Words*, Ives took his title's words right out of the mouth of **HAMLET, ACTII** ("Act II"), a little before [When Hamlet says, "The play's the thing"]. No great skills in subtraction are needed to know that happens well before the part in **ACTIV** ("Act IV") [When Rosencrantz and Guildenstern are last seen in "Hamlet"]. After that, it could be said that those two characters—like Hamlet most of the play—are **INACTIVE** in **ACTIV**.

That the **REST** is [Silence, in music] wouldn't have been news to [Modernist composer Charles] **IVES**. Often cited as the ["Central Park in the Dark" composer], this Ives probably lifted the title of his piece *The Unanswered Question* from classic literature too: "Thou art the unanswered question," wrote **RALPH WALDO** Emerson in his poem, "The **SPHINX**." If Charles Ives read the title's "thou" reflectively, then Ives indeed lives up to his name as "the unanswered question."

The [Folk singer Burl] **IVES** is remembered for his hit "A Little Bitty Tear," and his kid-friendly version of "Big Rock Candy Mountain." He gets cast as [Oscar winner Burl] for his role in the oater *The Big Country*, though he may be better remembered as the [Burl who narrated "Rudolph the Red-Nosed Reindeer"] and voiced Sam the Snowman. Six feet tall and 270 pounds, **IVES** lived up to his name: The [Burl of "Roots"] certainly was a [Burly Burl]. With such a storied career, **BURL** was many things, but certainly [Knot] a [Bump on a log].

IAMB [Poetic foot], [One foot, to a poet], [Shakespeare's foot?], [Pound foot?], ["To be," e.g.]

POEM [Work with feet?], [It's measured in feet, not inches], [Frost lines], [Pound piece], [Burns writing], [Pope piece], [Muhammad Ali's "Me! Whee!," e.g.], [Amanda Gorman's "The Hill We Climb," for one]

ONEACT *("one act")* [Kind of play], [Like Satre's "No Exit"], [Without a break], [A little drama?]

HAMLET [Tiny village], [Great Dane?]

INACTIVE [Out of commission], [Retired], [Passive]

REST [Sign not to play], [Time out?], [Staff break?], [Balance], [Others]

RALPH ["Me fail English? That's unpossible" speaker on "The Simpsons"]

WALDO [Face lost in the crowd], [Literary crowd member?]

SPHINX [Enigmatic one], [The riddler?]

YVES and Others
Making the Cut
From a [First name in Fashion] Wear
to Wetsuits and Woodshop

YVES [The "Y" of Y.S.L.], [Surrealist Tanguy]

YSL [Designer inits.], [Fashion monogram]

DIOR ["New Look" designer], [Christian of the cloth?], [Christian designer?], [Christian with a big house], [Christian name]

ALINE [Drop __ to (write)], [Something worn with flare?]

AFRAME [Home with a pointy roof], [Steep-roofed structure], [Ski lodge, often], [Chalet type]

IBAR and **IBEAM** [Letter-shaped support], [Girder type]

TNUT [Letter-shaped fastener], [Certain bolt holder]

THOM [Radiohead's lead singer Yorke]

IRR [Like the verb "to be": Abbr.], [Discount rack abbr.]

SIZE [Number of shoes?], [Economy for one]

COUNT [Matter], [Dracula's title], [3-2, e.g.], [Go from 0 to 60, e.g.?]

COUNTESS [Earl's wife]

BELT [Hit hard], [Big swig], [Big shot at a bar?], [Champion's accessory], [Holdup accessory?], [Middle manager?]

"Ives" is likely etymologically linked to the name of another Saint, **YVES**, as in [Fashion's ___ Saint Laurent]. The designer behind the [Fashionable initials] **YSL** was just 21 when he took over the house of Dior.

Saint Laurent's muses included the mononymous [Somali-born supermodel] **IMAN**, whose name, from the look of it, might make her seem monogamous. Indeed, after becoming [David Bowie's widow], she said she would never remarry, and that Bowie "is always going to be my husband."

[Designer Christian] **DIOR** created the **ALINE** [Dress style], which somehow has yet to be clued as an "indefinite article?" It pointedly shares its shape with another [Triangular construction], the **AFRAME** [House style], whose construction may call for an **IBAR** or **IBEAM** secured by a **TNUT**.

[Shoemaker Thom] **MCAN**'s small name is a [Big name in shoes] and puzzles. **THOM** the [Shoe man McAn] also slips easily into puzzles thanks to his equally short, **IRR** first name. (Few folks in the cruciverse are so lucky as to have two **SIZE** four names.)

ALDO [Gucci of fashion] shares his stylish first name with Canadian Albert "Aldo" Bensadoun, who turned his sobriquet into a label for his [Shoe brand that is also a man's name]. Another [First name in fashion] belonged to **OLEG** [Cassini of couture], the ['60s designer for Jackie] responsible for the "Jackie Look."

The son of a Russian **COUNT** and an Italian **COUNTESS**, Cassini went by his mother's surname, which his family traces to the 17th-century astronomer Giovanni **CASSINI**, namesake of a [Spacecraft that began orbiting Saturn in 2004] and a strip in Saturn's rings. Surely, that circular [Region] of debris is a [Cinch] for largest Cassini **BELT**.

[Fashion's Anna] **SUI** also traces her lineage to the 17th century, in her case to the Chinese poet Fang **BAO**. The designer's last name is pronounced "**SWEE**," but the Latin *sui* (pronounced "SOO-ee," meaning "himself"/"herself"/"itself"/"themselves") **SUITS** her work as part of the ensemble *"sui generis"*: "in a class by itself."

Sure, there's another **ANNA** of fashion who's so **CHIC** she's been [In vogue] literally for years, but Sui has her own **BOHO** Barbie doll. The four-letter description often trailed by [___-chic] is short for "bohemian." "Boho" fluffs up clues like [Boho boot brand], referring to the [Big name in boots] since 1978, **UGG**.

Like "Sui," the [Danish shoe brand] **ECCO** also has Latin ties, as the word on its tongue doubles as the [Italian "Behold!"], from the Latin "**ECCE**," a [Roman cry] that's ["Look!," to Livy]. Often seen following in the footsteps of *ecce* is [___ homo] (*"Ecce homo,"* "Behold, man!"—Pontius Pilate's declaration upon presenting Jesus with the crown of thorns). Also bouncing around puzzles is the [Urban brand] by the [Clothing designer Marc] **ECKO**. ECKŌ gets high marks as the [Clothing brand with a long vowel mark in its name], while its founder landed another long, high mark as [Fashion designer Marc who bought Barry Bonds's 756th home run ball and let the public vote to brand it with an asterisk].

Before a solver [Ties] Barry **BONDS** to the clue [Athlete who walked a lot] by realizing that **WALKS** are [Bases on balls], a picture might form of someone wearing a **SNEAKER** brand like **VANS** or **AVIA**, the [Walking shoe name] and [Shoe brand whose name is derived from the Latin word for "bird"].

During his career, Bonds, like crosswords, often sported **NIKES**, [Some sneaks] we'll catch up with in the next chapter.

But after retiring, he signed a deal with the [Sportswear company founded in Italy] in 1911 by brothers Ettore and Giansevero **FILA**. As their name is Italian for "line" and in English means [Threads, anatomically], it **BESPOKE** their destiny tied to a **CLOTHESLINE**.

SUI [___generis (unique)], [___juris (in one's own right)], [Olympics abbr. for Federer]

BAO [Chinese steamed bun], [Xiao long___ (soup dumplings)]

SWEE [___' Pea (Popeye's kid)] *(See chapter 9)*

SUITS [Befits], [Execs], [Deck quartet], [Poker set?]

ANNA ["Vogue" editor Wintour], ["I" in "The King and I"], [Siam visitor], [Sigmund's daughter], [___ Eleanor Roosevelt], [Ballerina Pavlova]

CHIC [Smart], [Tony], [In]

BOHO [Thrift-store fashion, informally], [Unconventional and hippielike, informally]

WALKS [Thoreau outings], [Takes steps], [Slugger's stat]

SNEAKER [Puma, e.g.], [Cat burglar, for one], [Converse pair?], [One of a tennis pair]

VANS [Shoes popular with skateboarders], [Warped Tour sponsor], [Touring bands' needs], [Circlers at airports]

AVIA [Running shoe brand], [Puma alternative]

NIKES [Some sneaks], [Air Force Ones, e.g.], [Low pair?]

BESPOKE [Indicated], [Custom-made]

CLOTHESLINE [Air dryer] *or as two words* [Tailor's profession]

[Mark] It Down!
Crosswords Stay on BRAND

Solvers can spend all day comparing brand names as they seek purchase in the puzzle. Enough household product names appear that despite its shape, the grid's rows and columns can look something like shopping aisles. Here's a sort of consumer report on what labels puzzles have in stock, and what sales pitches they might have in store for them.

AMANA has been an [Appliance brand since 1934], when it was founded in the Amana Colonies, a group of villages established in Iowa in the mid-19th century. The Amanians lived as a secluded religious sect: All meals were eaten communally, with no cooking done at home. Facing growing debts and desiring a more secular future, in the early 1930s they incorporated and established the non-profit Amana Corporation, a firm known first for freezers, then microwaves, and now all sorts of kitchen appliances. Today the company is owned by Whirlpool and based in Michigan.

TFAL ("T-fal") is a [Nonstick pan brand] founded in France in 1968, where it's known as "Tefal," combining **TEFLON** and a̲luminum to form a **PORTMANTEAU**, the sort of linguistic wedding that created ["Bridezilla," for instance]. ("Portmanteau" is an example itself, packing together the Middle French *porte*—meaning "carry"—and *manteau*—for "coat.") Tefal couldn't stick with their brand name in the United States as it was judged to conflict with "Teflon," which DuPont claimed after discovering the polymer in 1938.

As a [Name in kitchen foil], it's fitting that **ALCOA** ("Alcoa") is itself made of recycled parts: A̲luminum C̲o̲mpany of A̲merica.

OSTER is seen as a [Blender brand], but in the 1920s its rancher founder, John Oster, began with grooming products. There is no Blender Hall of Fame, but his electric clippers and latherers earned Oster entrance into the National Barber Museum and Hall of Fame.

Solvers can shave a few seconds off their time through sheer mastery of the [Gillette brand] **ATRA**, which in 1977 became the [First razor with a pivoting head], making the [Razor handle?] a

---

AMANA [Kitchen appliance brand], [Oven handle?]

TEFLON [Polytetrafluoroethylene, familiarly]

PORTMANTEAU [Large traveling bag], ["Frenemy" or "frankenfood"]

ALCOA [Major manufacturer of soda cans]

[Cutting edge product?]. A decade earlier, Gillette first used "Atra" as the code name standing for Australian Test Razor. Gillette never released that twin-blade prototype, yet its name nicks solvers to this day.

Mennen's aptly named aftershave lotion, **AFTA**, is an [Old Spice alternative]. Unfortunately, it doesn't provide much relief to solvers when clued as a [Shaving aisle brand], as it's just a razor's edge away from being the **OTRA** alternative, **ATRA**. (Of course, the real **OTRA** alternative is **OTRO**.)

OTRA [Other, in Oaxaca], [___vez (again, in Spanish)]

AVEENO is a [Big skin-care brand] that's truly an oat-based line: *avena* being Latin for "oat." Its competitor **AVON** is based in two sites in England: Its physical headquarters are in London, but nominally it's in [Shakespeare's stream].

OTRO [Other: Sp.], [Not esto or eso], [Overseas alternative?]

AVON [Door-to-door giant], [Company with a for-profit foundation?], [River through Bath], [Foundation maker], [Company calling?], [Call girl employer?]

The [1950s French president René] **COTY** was not related to the [Perfumer François] who founded the [Chanel rival] in 1904. But the [Big name in perfumery] became a big name in France too, as François Coty was one of its richest citizens and publisher of *Le* **FIGARO**, the Paris daily and namesake of the [Mozart title character].

COTY [De Gaulle's predecessor]

ESTEE ("Estée") Lauder became another [Big name in parfum] when Josephine Esther Mentzer rebranded herself with her childhood nickname and launched the company with her husband, Joseph Lauder, in 1946. She applied an accent (some e-liner?) to give it French airs. So Estée really is a [Makeup name?]. Its three "ees" make the [Name on Intuition perfume boxes] a popular answer to intuit as a perfume name for crossword boxes.

As for Mentzer's ability to produce perfumes, maybe she was born with it, given her given middle name, Esther, had the makeup for her line of work: **ESTER** (no relation, etymologically) is a [Fragrant compound] and [Perfume ingredient]—and even without multimillion-dollar ad campaigns, it outperforms **ESTEE** as a crossword ingredient.

ESSIE (branded as "essie") is the [Big name in nail polish] launched by the eponymous [Cosmetician Weingarten] and now owned by L'Oréal. Essie's esses and ees ensure it's no ordeal for grids to find room for it on its shelves.

ESSIE [L'Oréal nail polish brand], [Actress Davis of two "Matrix" movies], [Davis of "Miss Fisher's Murder Mysteries"]

But puzzles are far more obliging of its opposition, **OPI**, aided both by the puniness of its name and the punniness of its shades. Short for "Odontorium Products, Inc.," OPI is an odd name for a nail polish company, as **ODONTO** means [Teeth: Prefix]. The initials are a retainer from the firm's beginnings as a dental supply company whose **IPO** ("initial public offering"), so to speak, included tooth glues that became popular with manicurists for applying acrylic nails. Today, Coty owns OPI, which owns most of Kylie (Kylie Jenner's cosmetics brand): one brand polishing off another, at least in terms of **SOLE** proprietorship.

Kylie and OPI are among the options on sale at **ULTA**, along with alternatives like the following:

- **ALMAY**, the [Name in cosmetics since 1931] referring to its founders Alfred and Fanny May Woititz
- **NIVEA**, the [Brand whose name is derived from the Latin for "snow-white"]
- **OLAY**, founded in 1952 in South Africa as "Oil of Olay," which referred to its main ingredient, lanolin, a wax secreted by sheep and other wooly animals. The word "lanolin" was secreted by the Latin *lāna* ("wool") and *oleum* ("oil").
- **NAIR**, the [Brand once advertised with the jingle "We wear short shorts..."]
- **LOREAL** ("L'Oréal"), the [Company that started with the hair dye "Aureole"]

AUREOLE, a [Halo], rarely gets to shine in puzzles, but it's connected to the same "golden" Latin word, *aureus*, that often flies in crosswords via the common **ORIOLE**.

Another [Ring of color] might surprise, both for not being etymologically related and for how frequently it's flashed in puzzles: **AREOLA** (pl: areolas or areolae), from the Latin for "small open space" or "garden."

MASTODON sightings in puzzles are exceedingly rare, but its name is too surprising to skip. In 1817, Georges Cuvier, a French naturalist sometimes regarded as the "founding father of paleontology," coined "mastodon" by combining two Greek words to describe. The -odon comes from the same Ancient Greek for "tooth" seen in the "O" of OPI, but the front half of the word is much more surprising. As constructor Jill Singer pointed out two centuries later, Cuvier's curious construction makes **MASTODON** the [Extinct megafauna whose name derives from the Greek for "breast tooth"].

Perhaps someday a clue will dig up why Mastodon—which became another [Trendy social network] when **TWITTER** was purchased by **ELON MUSK**—chose to name its equivalent of a **TWEET** a **TOOT**.

TWITTER [Tizzy], [Where many people may follow you], [Feed supplier]

ELON [College town east of Greensboro], [University in a town of its own name], [Inventor Musk], ["___ Musk Debuts New Self-Parenting Child" (May 2020 headline in the Onion)]

MUSK [Secretion from a male deer, used in perfumery], [Cologne ingredient], [Pioneer in commercial spacecraft]

TWEET [Place for a #], [Message that might be sent in a storm?], [Birds do it], [give every1 a super quick update on what ur doing at the moment (w/ a lot of abbrs) because u only get 140 characters, and that's really not e]

TOOT [Spree], [Jag], [Blow], [It might mean "hello" or "goodbye" to a driver], [[Go! The light turned!]], [It's a blast]

Chapter 2 Puzzle: "A Real Kick in the Rear!"

ACROSS

1 Batting game for kids
6 "Enough already!"
9 Royal topper
14 Capital of Vietnam
15 Fistful of bills
16 Word on a face behind hands
17 Poultry purveyor open six days a week
19 "Akira" movie genre
20 Olympic gymnast Strug
21 Gourdgeous mo?
22 i lid?
25 American photographer who co-authoured "Let Us Now Praise Famous Men"
30 Fish symbol in Christianity
32 "Georgia on My Mind" singer Charles
33 Grassy field
34 ___ ghost (gets spooked)
35 Before, briefly
36 Comic Costello
37 "Let's revisit the fundamentals"
42 Calendario unit
43 Orange "Sesame Street" character
44 "Out ___" (Lemmon/ Matthau flick)
45 Shred
46 "Orange Is the New Black" actress Aduba

47 Musical composition often set to a poem
49 Nordic land
52 Born
53 Complimentary poem
54 Brand of wafers
56 Where you might meet your mensch
59 Uses the window for a door, say
63 Server's jot
64 "Delta of Venus" writer Anais
65 Smoke signal?
66 Lacks
67 Name of many popes
68 Kind of column

DOWN

1 Blunt letters
2 Exclamation of disgust
3 "Star Wars" nickname
4 Sure thing
5 "For instance?"
6 Shows off a skirt, perhaps
7 Zayn formerly of One Direction
8 Activist ___ B. Wells
9 Comedian Ullman
10 Network that began as Pax
11 "Thrilla in Manila" victor
12 Dream state
13 Chopper
18 Unravel
21 Colgate rival

22 Bans from practice
23 Vast
24 Hangout in a Barry Manilow hit
26 Border lake
27 Actress Janney of "The West Wing"
28 Early geologic period
29 Slice on a slice
31 Tongue-clucking sound.
35 Definite article
38 Harriet's TV hubby
39 Bugs, e.g.
40 Part of a smear campaign
41 "Help!" letters
46 Milk containers
47 L'Oréal competitor
48 Costa ___
50 Put down
51 She had a hard-knock life
55 Capital near Lillehammer
56 "The Problem with ___ Stewart"
57 Dr. who discovered Eminem
58 Summer cooler
59 Long-running NBC comedy show
60 Propel a boat
61 Paranormal showman Geller
62 Channel for cinephiles

Chapter 3

ANATOMY and Mythology

[Study every body?] in Heaven and on Earth

At times, constructors can seem to embody an [Almighty] **LORD** [___ of Darkness] themselves through their ingenious clues for some [Deity]. Even a smooth-talking [Lady's man] can be at a loss for words, except to exclaim ["Man..."], ["___ have mercy!"]. A solver may feel more like a futile peon than a [Feudal VIP] until the answer arrives with a [Surprised cry]. Then perhaps a **PAEAN**, a [Song of praise], might be in order.

So often do puzzles invoke classical deities that neither **ASGARD** nor **OLYMPUS** can challenge crosswords' claim as the true home of the most **GODS**. Similarly, grids can present such an assemblage of body parts that they beat **ANAT** class hands down and leave the **MORGUE DEAD** to rights. Gods willing, the answers in this section should help the average, earthly solver **ATAN** [___ impasse] feel less god-fearing and more body positive.

ASGARD [Home of the Norse gods], [Frigg's digs]

OLYMPUS [Zeus's mount], [Fuji alternative], [High point of Greek civilization?]

GODS [Olympians, e.g.] ["Ye___!"]

ANAT [Med school subj.], [Gray's subj.], [Art school subj.]

MORGUE [Body building?], [Place where people tend to show up late?]

DEAD [Out of juice], [Kaput], [Grateful follower?], [Free of charge?], [Giveaway description?]

ATAN ("at an") [Mussorgsky's "Pictures___Exhibition"], [Words before end or angle]

Ancient AESIR, Modern Marvels

The Edda-fying [Norse pantheon]:
[Odin, Thor, and company]

EDDA [13th-century literary work], [Icelandic epic], [Icelandic work that influenced Tolkien]

NORSE [Leif's language], [Language from which "reindeer" comes], [Danish ingredient?]

ODIN [Valhalla VIP], [God of war and magic], [God who gave an eye in his search for wisdom]

STEED [War horse], [Knight mare?], [Mount]

SLIP [Lose one's footing], [Faux pas], [Tongue trouble?]

HEL [Daughter of Loki], [Norse underworld queen]

RUSE [Dodge], [Trojan horse, e.g.], [Red herring], [Con]

RUNE [Old character], [Hard-to-read character], [Bit of ancient text], [It may be set in stone], [Letter to Odin?], [Enigmatic one in "The Hobbit"]

The **EDDA**, the [Poetic work with an account of Ragnarok] in Old **NORSE**, was written—or at least compiled—by Snorri Sturluson around 1220.

One of its heroes, **ODIN**, slips into English as the [Chief Norse god] [For whom Wednesday is named]. Doing so, Odin resembles his eight-legged **STEED** Sleipnir, which means "Sliding One" and is related to the English "**SLIP**."

The [Son of Odin] known in the German tradition as **TYR** more often travels through Bifröst to the grid as **THOR**. As the [Wielder of the hammer Mjölnir], he may look like a [Hammered superhero], and indeed, in the *Edda* he was renowned for his beer drinking ability. [The Norse thunder god], like his father, is a four-letter [Norse god of war]. And as sons follow fathers, it's logical that he's the [Thursday eponym].

[Thor's mischievous adoptive brother], **LOKI**, is the [Shapeshifting Norse trickster]. He's literally a [Hel raiser?] as the father of **HEL**, which is also the name of [Hades, in Norse myth].

Marvel fans know Hel as Hela, though the movies recast her as Odin's daughter. Still, that beats crosswords, which decades ago disowned HELA as too hellish a variant spelling. In the wake of the movies, though, HELA could well come back from the dead.

Speaking of shifty old characters, crosswords reuse the **RUSE** of referring to **RUNE**, an old [Anglo-Saxon writing symbol], as yet another four-letter [Old Norse character]. Or it can traverse universes altogether and be a [Tolkien character], as the author created and used his own system of runes to form a written language he called the Cirth.

ORDER Out of Chaos

Seeing the Greek and Roman Gods
as a [Group of families]

The classical gods must have been mad: eating their children, throwing apples, tipping the balance of wars. Solvers would be wise to remember their mythology, for the **SWAN** who swooped down to Leda (who later laid an egg or two) is the least of it: The gods are no less masters of disguise in crossword clues. But the following notes (and the chart on the following spread) should help prevent them from also driving solvers **NUTS**—which itself can shape-shift into [Bananas] or [Crackers].

For instance, **CIRCE** is an [Ancient Greek stockholder?] and the [First to show that men are pigs?] because [She turned Odysseus's men to swine]. So she hardly needed crosswords' help to make folks feel mad.

The Greek [Love child] **EROS** is [Love personified]. The same is said of his Roman analog, called both [Cupid] and **AMOR**. In Greek philosophy, *eros* (Ancient Greek for "love" or "desire," seen in the English "erotic") referred to passionate love, a sort of *theia mania* ("divine madness" or "madness from the gods").

A different sort of hunter seen at night is **ORION**, who stars as [Rigel's constellation]. Prone to big acts and big talk, Orion once [Belted one out there?], declaring that he would hunt down every animal on earth. Galled, Gaia interceded, turning Orion into the [Greek hero killed by a giant scorpion].

More pacifically, **PAX** is the [Goddess of peace]. The goddess is [Irene's Roman counterpart] and [Mars's opposite].

Pick up **STYX** for the goddess whose name is also the [River to Hades] that's the ferryman [Charon's domain], and a [Name on which ancient oaths were taken]. It should also stick in your head that the [River nobody remembers visiting] can be streamed on Spotify as the ["Come Sail Away" band, 1977] and the ["Mr. Roboto" band, 1983].

ORDER [Get to eat], [It's taken while waiting], [Law partner?]

SWAN [Kind of song], [Kind of dive], [Symbol of grace], [Adult cygnet], [Cob or pen], [Trumpeter in the park?]

CIRCE ["Odyssey" temptress], [Goddess of magic]

EROS [Lover boy], [One taking a bow?], [One who aims to hit singles?], [God who played with matches?], [Love of Greece?] *(See also AMOR in chapter 1)*

ORION [Heavenly hunter], [Betelgeuse's constellation]

PAX [Peace, to Pliny], [Roman peace], [Bellum's opposite]

STYX [River down under?], [Where Achilles took a dip?], [Dead waters?], [It goes to hell], [Final course?], [Where to catch the last ferry?]

URANUS *Gaea's son and husband, Roman counterpart: Caelus* [God of the heavens], [Father of the Titans]

CRONUS or KRONOS [Titan dethroned by his son Zeus], [Titan depicted with a scythe]

SATURN [God of agriculture], [Ring bearer] *Since* [Titan is its largest moon], [Titan's planet] *works in two ways*

RHEA [Greek "Mother of the Gods"], [Sister and wife of Cronus], [Second-largest moon of Saturn], [Emu cousin], [Actress Seehorn of "Better Call Saul"], [Perlman of "Cheers"]

OPS [Harvest goddess], [Goddess of plenty], ["Missions" for short]

ZEUS [Father of the gods], [Thunder achiever?], [Muses' father], [Top Olympian], [Hera's husband], [Helen's father]

JUPITER [Io circles it]

HERA [Goddess of marriage], [Goddess of childbirth], [Juno her name?]

JUNO [Queen of heaven], [Jupiter's sister], [Jupiter's wife], *and the aptly titled* [Film written by Diablo Cody]

HADES [Underworld god], [Greek underworld], [Land down under], [Charon's locale], [Pluto, to Plato], [Styx venue?]

PLUTO [Its moons include Charon and Styx]

POSEI-DON [God with a trident], [Father of Triton]

NEP-TUNE [Sea god], [Triton orbits it], [Last of eight]

LETO [Artemis's mom], [Apollo's mother], [Actor Jared]

APOLLO [Artemis's twin], [God of music], [God of poetry], [Greek sun god], [Harlem hotspot], [It had many missions]

ARTEMIS [Goddess of the hunt], [Moon goddess]

DIANA [Mythical hunter], [Supreme leader?], [1981 royal bride]

ATHENA [She sprang from Zeus's head], [Favorite child of Zeus], [Goddess of wisdom], [Goddess of war], [Greek Minerva], [Parthenon dedicatee]

CHAOS [Original state of the universe, in myth], [Most ancient of Greek gods], [Word from the Greek for "abyss"], [total zoo]

GAEA or GAIA [Mother (and wife!) of Uranus], [Greek earth goddess], [Mother of the Titans], [Mother Earth]

TERRA [Mother earth], [Rome's land?], [Land at an Italian airport?], [Earth], [Earth in Latin]

THEA *goddess of sight* [Sister and wife of Hyperion], [Woman's name meaning "goddess"], [Duke Ellington's "Take ___ Train"], [TV's "___ Team"]

HYPERION *the sun personified* [Father of Helios] [Moon of Saturn], [Unfinished poem by Keats]

CERES [Crop deity], [Goddess of agriculture], [Roman Demeter], [Closest dwarf planet], [First known asteroid]

HELIOS [Sun god]

SOL [Our sun], [Daily riser], [Spanish sun], [Sky light], [Space heater?], [Fa follower]

EOS ["Rosy-fingered" dawn goddess], [Goddess in a chariot], [Brand of camera or lip balm]

AURORA [Dawn of Roman civilization]

SELENE [Moon goddess], [Goddess in a chariot]

LUNA [Moon, personified], [Latin moon], [Large green moth]

ERIS [Greek goddess of strife], [Golden apple thrower], [Discordia's Greek counterpart], [The sun's "10th planet," once], [Largest dwarf planet]

ARES [God of war], [Helmeted deity], [Bellicose god], [Father of Eros], [Villain in the DC Universe]

MARS ["The Bringer of War"], ["The War of the Worlds" enemy], [Land of Opportunity?], [Where Vikings explored?]

Ares and Mars are the "Same dude, different name," points out the similarly named **OMAR** [Little, "The Wire" antihero], [Obama's favorite TV character of all time, who was based on Baltimore criminal Donnie Andrews]

NIKE [Certain sneak], [It started in 1964 as Blue Ribbon Sports], [Air Force 1 maker], [Puma rival]

The [Daughter of Styx], **NIKE** is the winged [Greek goddess of victory]. Founded by Phil Knight and his track coach at the University of Oregon, Bill Bowerman, the [Brand with a swoosh logo] was named after the [Trophy figure] whose Roman counterpart is Victoria.

MAY [Might], [Can alternative], [What "5" can mean], [Merry month?], [The shortest month?], [Time for a pole dance?]

The [Eldest of the Pleiades]—the seven sisters turned to stars—was the [Mother of Hermes], **MAIA**, the [Goddess of spring and rebirth]. If her name seems familiar, it **MAY** be because the [Period named for an earth goddess] sprang from it.

Are You Calliope a <u>LYRE</u>?
Muses and Four-Letter
[Old strings] to [Harp] On

If that's a lot to remember, consider praying to Mnemosyne, the goddess of memory and mother of the **MUSES**, or her daughter, **CLIO**,

MUSES [Ponders], [Nine daughters of Zeus], [Nonet of myth]

the [Muse of history]. Known as "the Proclaimer" and a celebrant of great accomplishments, Clio is the most commercially prized answer as the apt eponym of the [Advertising award].

ERATO [Muse of love poetry], [Muse of lyric poetry], [Odist's muse], [Goddess whose name means "lovely"]

ERATO, the [Sister of Clio and Calliope], is the [Muse of poetry] and a [Mythological figure often depicted holding a lyre]. The **LYRE** was also played by two of her sister Muses—Calliope (epic poetry) and Terpsichore (dance)—so clues for the [Zither relative] are liable to use any of the three sisters or Orpheus as a [Heavenly instrument] to lift [Apollo's plaything?].

A line above "lyre" in the dictionary is [Vega's constellation], **LYRA**, the [Harp-shaped constellation] that also gets plucked for [Heavenly strings]. Many clues for **LYRE** and **LYRA** can also be a part played by a **HARP**, but let's not [Dwell on that].

Delta FORCE

Egyptian Mythology That
[Might] [Make] Things Muddy

AMENRA, **AMONRA**, and even **AMUNRA** ("Amen-Ra," "Amun-Ra," or "Amun-Ra") are spellings of the [Supreme Egyptian deity] and [Sun god] often depicted holding an **ANKH**, the [Egyptian cross]. The dash in the god's name is telling: He created himself by fusing the [Egyptian deity] named **AMON** or **AMEN** (no relation to the word that's a [Mass conclusion]) with another god, named Ra. Then maybe he said, "**IMON**!" or ["Time for me to shine!"].

Another four-letter [Sacred symbol of ancient Egypt] is the **IBIS**, used for any of 28 species of [Long-legged wader]. The pronounced beak of the [Animal avatar of Thoth], the god of wisdom, is also capable of transforming it into a [Large bill holder].

Transform the second letter of "ibis" to make the [Egyptian fertility goddess] and [Egyptian goddess of life], **ISIS**. The [Mother of Horus] and [Wife of Osiris] is a [Goddess often depicted holding a staff of papyrus] and an ankh, with a solar disk framed by horns above her head.

And **SISI** ("sí, sí")—an answer that is becoming more of a **NONO** ("no-no") as it's a [Tsk-tsk elicitor] from some solvers who find it insensitively reductive—it's true: **ISIS** has also appeared as the [Sunni jihadist grp.], and as ["...what the meaning of the word ___" (Bill Clinton)]. Like the Clown in *Twelfth Night* who said ["That that ___": Shak.], we can imagine that if the former president came across his own quote in a puzzle—**FWIW**, he's a daily crossword solver—he'd know that that is "is is."

The benevolent [Husband and brother of Isis] is **OSIRIS**, the [Green-skinned god] and [Ruler of the afterlife]. Good old Osiris was [Good to go] until his brother, **SET**, the evil god of chaos and trickery, killed him and cut his body into pieces. (Isis gathered the [Collection] and [Fixed] them back [In place].) So Isis is Osiris's **SIS**, as is Nephthys, goddess of mourning and darkness. Their **BRO**, Horus, is the final **SIB** in the set of **KIN**.

ANKH [Looped cross], [Symbol of life], [Egyptian "key" of life]

AMEN ["You said it!"], ["Word"], [Word said just before opening the eyes], [Grace period?], [The final word], [Cry from the clock?], [Service line?]

IBIS [Nile bird], [Cousin of a spoonbill], [Wetlands denizen]

SISI [Emphatic Spanish assent], ["Absolutely, amigo"], [It's not a no-no], [Egyptian president Abdel Fattah el-___]

NONO [Taboo], [You shouldn't do this], [Double negative?], [Eating pizza with a fork and knife, to New Yorkers]

FWIW ["Just my opinion," in a tweet], [Qualification shorthand], [Texter's "methinks"]

SET [Decided], [6–3 or 7–6, e.g.], [Match maker?], [It begins with love?], [Place for an acting president?], [Take place?], [Quiet place?], [Word with over 400 definitions in the OED]

SIS [Member of the fam], ["___boom bah!"], [Start of a cheer], [Household name?]

BRO [Dude], ["Duuude"], ["My man"], [Short relative?], [Street address], [Man on the street?], [___ hug], [Family guy]

SIB [Short relative], [Little brother, maybe?], [Twin or quintuplet, for short]

KIN [Blood, so to speak], [Blood group?], [Relations], [People in a tree]

CLEO [Elizabeth Taylor role of '63], ["Pinocchio" goldfish]

ASP [Egyptian cobra], [African viper], [Curtains for Cleopatra?], Cleo's feller]

The [Queen of the Nile, informally], **CLEO**, styled herself after Isis, even copying her headgear. Cleopatra's [Exotic means of suicide] was the **ASP**, since [It was sacred to Isis], thus making the [Nile biter] [One with a bit part in "Cleopatra"].

[Brief missions?] to Saturn's Moons
Rhea, Atlas, OPS, and Optical Allusions

RHEA [Mother of Zeus]
(See also chapter 8)

The idea that "**RHEA**" might be grounded in the Ancient Greek "*éra*" ("earth" or "ground") was sufficient grounds for naming the [Grounded avian creature] so often grounded in the grid. But puzzles grant more [Photo-___] **OPS** (as "opportunities") to Rhea's Roman equivalent, Ops (or Opis), who appears—as her name means—"plenty."

OPS [Chances, briefly], [Coin-___], [Post-___(some hosp. patients)], [Some are performed in a theater, for short], [Photo finish?]

The Roman goddess's name shares a root with the **OPS** that are the covert parts of [Black-___] or [Special-___] "operations." Ironically, in Greek, *ops* is "eye," as seen in "optic," "ophthalmology," and "cyclops" (literally, "circle eye").

OPART (*"op art"*) [Abstract form prominent in the '60s], [Dizzying designs], [Eye-catching works], [Illusions in paint]

OPART can make solvers think they're seeing things. First, its clues often show [Some deceptive designs] like [Eyeball bender] or [Motion pictures?]. Failing to pass such an [Eye-cue test?], solvers may well wonder, "What's the O-part of 'O-PART'?!" Truly, [It can make you dizzy].

ALSORAN (*"also ran"*) [#2 or #3, say], [One who didn't even show?], [One out of the money], [Runner up], [Miss Congeniality, e.g.]

A similar experience can arise from a clue like [Candidate who lost]. Finding it hard to place who that could be, crosses could eventually reveal **ALSORAN**. "Al Soran?" Who was this famous, eminently forgettable [Concession speech giver]? It's enough to make the solver feel like an [Unsuccessful person].

Double Vision

Parts of the "**EYE**" with Multiple Meanings
Worth an [Attentive look]

The very answer **EYES** can make solvers think they're [Seeing things]. It can be hard enough to recall words first learned in school—that [Place for pupils] to learn with their [Peer group?] and [Buds]—without being sidetracked by clues like [Eight things that most spiders have] and [What a colon might denote].

A homophone for "eyes" is **IES** ("ies"), the spelling of the plural of the third vowel, but it's invariably clued as the [Plural attachment] "-ies."

So there are two "ies" in **IRIS** and an iris in each eye. The [Colored part of the eye] is named for the Greek [Rainbow goddess] and [Divine messenger] who linked gods and humans. Today, the name of the [Light-regulating eye part] still links humans to the goddess by serving as a synonym for [Rainbow].

IRIS is also the eponym of the [Showy bloomer] that's a [Blossom with a "beard"], or a [Flower girl's name?] that's an [Apt name for a botanist]—or an optometrist.

The iris controls the size of the **PUPIL**, the black hole in the eye's center, whose homonym makes it a [Student of optometry?]. Both meanings derive from the Latin *pupa*, meaning "little girl" or "doll." The connection is clear when looking into someone's eye and seeing one's own tiny reflection in the pupil. Besides becoming the English **PUPA**, *pupa* also morphed into "**PUPPY**" and "**PUPPET**."

The iris is part of the **UVEA**, another four-letter [Colored part of the eye], whose reddish-blue **HUE** is likely the cause of its name, as *uva* is Latin for "grape."

Blurrier still, a four-letter word for [Ophthalmologist's concern] could be **IRIS**, **UVEA**, **LENS**, or the common [Eye sore], **STYE** (not to be confused with another eye sore, **STY**).

EYE [Regard], [Spot], [Bedroom shutter?], [What cyclops has in common with a cyclone]

EYES [Focus group?], [Head set], [Bedroom shutters?], [Word with googly or goo-goo]

IES ["-y" pluralizer], [Suffix with pant or aunt], [Suffix with Moon]

IRIS [Pupil's place], [Eye opener?], [Part of eye makeup?], [Flower of one's eye?], [State flower of Tennessee], [Novelist Murdoch], [Body part that may be green], [Body part with a sphincter muscle]

PUPIL [It grows in the dark], [One who has class?], [It's in the eye of the beholder]

PUPA [Cocooned stage], [Stage between larva and imago], [Butterfly, once]

PUPPY [Young boxer?], [A little husky?], [Small part of a pound?]

PUPPET [Punch, e.g.], [Figurehead], [You might have a hand in it]

UVEA [Eye layer containing the iris], [Pacific island that's also the name of part of the body]

HUE [Shade], [Tint], [Tone], [Peach or plum], [Lemon or orange], [Chocolate or caramel]

LENS [Contact, say], [Focusing aid], [Zoom, e.g.]

STYE [Eye problem], [Lid bump], [Ocular woe], [Bad eye sight?]

STY [Digs on a farm?], [Hog heaven], [Oink pad?], [Where snorting isn't rude], [Place for mucking around], [It's a mess]

[Crunch time?]
How to WORKOUT Your Abs, Delts, and Pecs
(in Just a Few Clues a Day!)

Here's an amazing fact from crosswords: **MUSCLE** is the [Body part whose name comes from the Latin for "little mouse"], *mūsculus*. And yes, the next time you have a **MUSSEL**, feel free to tell your date that the [Paella piece] on your fork was born from a mouse too.

KAPUT [Shot], [Busted], [Finito]

The Latin *caput*, "head," didn't lead to **KAPUT** (which comes from *cappa*, like "cape"), but it did furnish English with **CAP**. It also helped build **BICEPS**, which are literally "two-headed" muscles. A muscle's "heads" are its points of origin, counted by the respective prefixes in biceps, triceps, and quadriceps. The bulging fibers between the heads are called a muscle's "belly." So when weightlifters get **SWOLE**, not only are they getting inflated heads, but plump bellies to boot.

CAP [Tube top], [Royal headpiece?], [Trade partner?]

BICEPS ["Guns"], [Curling target], [Mound of arms]

SWOLE [Very muscular, in slang], [Very buff], ["Jacked"]

Strictly speaking, "biceps" is both the singular and plural noun. ("Bicepses" is also grammatically correct, but that's a big lift for most folks.) Yet **BICEP**—technically an adjective, as in [___ curl]—is used so frequently for a singular [Arm muscle, informally] that it passes as an [Arm muscle] without qualification.

The further contraction of [Muscles used in pullups, informally] into **BIS** has no singular form in puzzles, as it would be only two letters. To isolate a muscle, try **TRI** for the [Numerical prefix] that's a [Muscle used in dip exercises, informally], a [Cycle starter], or the [TNT element?] that triggers "trinitrotoluene."

BIS ["Again!"] *(See chapter 1)*

TRI [Prefix for athlete], [Prefix with -mester], [One more than bi-], [Three in front?], [Head of state?]

Another [Muscle used in pull-ups, briefly] is the **LAT**, pulled from *latissimus dorsum* (literally, the "broadest of the back") in [Livy's lang.]. Also short for "latitude," it's the [GPS fig.] that's [Not long.].

LAT [Line on a map: Abbr.], [Small muscle?], [What doesn't go a long way?], ["Et alia" lang.], [50 degrees, say: Abbr.], [It's 34°, for LA] *(See the introduction for the paper covering that [Map. abbr.])*

Each **DEG** of latitude is divvied into [60 min.], then 60 seconds. Along the lat. line of 56°56'56" is the [Largest city in the Baltics], **RIGA**, [Latvia's capital]. Even tourists who don't want to stay in the [Capital on its own gulf] might look around and say ["Letts live here"].

DEG [U wish?], [BS, e.g.], [Bachelor's holding: Abbr.]

RIGA [Baltic seaport], [Baryshnikov's birthplace]

That clue cues a certain tune about [Latvians], also known as **LETTS**: ["Lithuanians and ___ do it" (Cole Porter lyric)].

But let's get back to the **BOD**—or rather to the front of it, where a **PEC** (*pectoralis major*, *pectus* meaning "breast") covers each pectoralis minor, so humans in fact have four **PECS**. And while a six-pack is cause for applause, humans technically have ten **ABS**.

The fibrous stuff that connects muscles and bone is **SINEW**, often clued by its metaphoric meaning, [Strength] or [Resilience]. In 2014, crossword constructor and editor Sam Ezersky really did make it tough when he asked solvers to untangle [Power cord?] before plugging it in.

BOD [Figure, briefly], [Shape, informally], [Beach___], [Dad___]

PEC [Chest muscle for short], [Muscle mag subject], [Prime spot for a tat], [___ deck (bodybuilder's machine)]

PECS [Bench targets, for short], [Nice pair of boxers?]

ABS [Things used during crunch time?], [Six-pack contents], [Fitness centers?], [Trunk supporters], [Core group?], [Focus of middle management?]

A Guide to Mount OSSA
Boning Up on [Bones] and the Classics

One of puzzles' most visited locations is the [Peak in Thessaly], Mt. **OSSA**. But as the plural of "os" (the scientific word for "bone," taken from the Latin), ossa are [Bones, anatomically]. The word for [Bone in Italian], **OSSO**, appears as the [Italian menu palindrome] that's usually served up as [___ buco] (literally, "bone with a hole").

OSSA [Greek peak], [Mount in Greek myth], ["Odyssey" high point]

The plural of the similar-looking Latin, *ōs* ("mouth"), is **ORA**, [Mouths: Lat], but today in Rome the word is equal to [60 minuti] and can be used for [Now, in Italy]. The Latin opening *ora* ([___ pro nobis] "pray for us," from the "Hail Mary") is still seen in **ORACLE** and one of crosswords' favorite recitations, **ORATE**.

ORACLE [Seer], [Forecast provider], [Futures analyst?]

ORATE [Speechify], [Pontificate], [Give one's address], [Speak highly?], [Stand and deliver]

The handiest bones in crosswords are **RADII**, but the **ULNA** is the [Radius's comrade-in-arms?], making the [Arm twister's need?] an [Almost handy bone?]. Its plural can have [Ones up in arms?], appearing as both **ULNAS** and **ULNAE**.

RADII [Forearm bones], [Spokes], [r's in geometry], [Circle lines], [Minute hands, essentially], [Spoke more than once?]

TARSI, the plural of "tarsus," are a group of [Ankle bones]. They include the actual [Ankle bone], called the **TALUS**, whose plural, **TALI**, is almost invariably clued as [Anklebones]. In a lucky break, the singular and plural forms of these answers are different lengths.

ULNAS and **ULNAE** [Hand holders?], [Arms runners?], [Arm twisters], [Latin for "elbows"], [Bones also called cubiti]

ILIA are the [Pelvic bones] that hip solvers will find as [Bones in a reptilian?]. Like another [Hip-related] answer, **ILIAC**, its root relates to the singular form, **ILIUM**, (pulled from the Latin *ile*, "groin"), more often exposed as the [Latin name of Troy]. So in a neat trick,

ILIAC [___crest (part of the pelvis)]

ILIUM [Hip place?], [Pelvic bone]

the city's mythological founders, King Ilion and his father, Tros, are credited as etymological forefathers of both the anatomical and historical sites. They can also claim naming rights to the upstate [New York city in Vonnegut novels]. So it goes.

Vonnegut's choice of "Ilium" was a clever contrivance, drawing on both the **TROY** that's a [Hudson River city] that some New York residents would consider a one-horse town, and the original [One-horse town?] that was the ["Iliad" setting]. Like those who'd previously failed to find the [Ancient city rediscovered in 1870], solvers might have trouble locating the ["Aeneid" city] [Where Paris took Helen] when it's cleverly clued as a five-letter [Home of Paris?]. A troy is also a [Type of weight] used for gems and precious metals, a term thought to derive from **TROYES**, the [City on the Seine upstream from Paris].

The Troy near Albany is the home of **RPI** ("Rensselaer Polytechnic Institute"). This [N.Y. engineering sch.] survives as the [Oldest technological univ. in America].

The **IVY SCH** (for "school") located nearby makes **ITHACA** not just [Cornell's home] but a place to read about [Ulysses's home].

The book, which clues might call an [Achilles spiel?], the **ILIAD** recounts a [Narrative set in the Bronze age]. Though the book begins decidedly later in the tale—cheers, Horace!—it could be said that the story that launched 16,000 lines of verse was set in motion when **ERIS**, the [Goddess of discord] and [Twin sister of Ares], threw her golden apple. The goddess's name endures as the [Dwarf planet larger than Pluto] discovered in 2005. Inspired by the quarrels over classifying it as a dwarf planet, "Eris" proved an even more apt name when that classification compelled the slightly less-massive **ORB**, **PLUTO**, named after the [Ruler of Hades], to be redesignated as the [Ninth planet no more].

Another [Troy story] is the [Source of the Trojan horse story]: Virgil's **AENEID**, which is the [Epic that opens "Of arms and the man I sing..."]. The Latin is **ARMA** ["___ virumque cano"]—and "the man" (*"virumque"*) is **AENEAS**, the [Trojan leader who survived the fall of Troy] to become the [Lover of Dido, in myth].

Aeneas's sudden abandonment of **DIDO**, the [Tragically heartbroken figure of myth], left her little reason to be a ["Thank You" singer].

DIDO's name has become synonymous with a [Mischievous trick], likely by virtue of the [Clever prank] the queen excuted to create her kingdom. The story goes that a suitor, King Iarbus, agreed to give her as much land as she could fit within the physical area of an oxhide. She executed a creative land grab by cutting the leather into such thin strips she encircled an entire hill.

The phrase "cut didoes" means to pull someone's **LEG**—an answer whose clues could describe Dido, since she was [One with a supporting role] for Aeneus during a [Part of a long journey]. And when she showed Iarbus the oxhide, he probably thought, "Well, [It's just over a foot]," having no idea that what she had afoot would turn out be a real [Kicker].

DIDO [Caper]. ["White Flag" singer, 2003], [Character with the aria "When I am laid in earth"], [Purcell's "___ and Aeneas"]

LEG [Trip part], [Stocking stuffer], [One of a piano trio], [Calf site], [Anchor, e.g.]

Chapter 3 Puzzle: "Is That 'Z' as in 'Zoos'?"

ACROSS

1 Say again?
5 Kweli of hip-hop
10 James or Jones of jazz
14 Ben Affleck film of 2012
15 Ohno of short-track speedskating
16 Tell a secret
17 NumbeR HEArd by many as "Heart and Soul"
19 ___ vu
20 First course of action
21 Yoko of music
23 Lost
26 Like thE ROSe Ball held anually in Monte Carlo
31 Woos
33 Autocrats
34 Easy throw
35 Art studio stand
38 White-tail, for one
39 Sweet cylinder often used to make squARES?
43 Commoner, for short
45 Progeny
46 Stick in the water?
49 Family of dogs
52 See 74-Across
54 Millionaire witH A DESk in the Kremlin, say
57 Bros
58 Sch. in East Lansing
59 Consumer activist Ralph
61 "Lion King" bird
64 Homes with a regal moNIKEr
69 Old Apple
70 Show the way
71 High-pitched wind
72 Artist Vincent van___
73 Prestigious Peach State campus
74 With 1-Across and 52-Across, "Huh???"

DOWN

1 WWII female flier
2 Royal title: Abbr.
3 Fourth word of the "Star Wars" opening text
4 Point made above the rest
5 "Toodle-oo!"
6 Copycat's activity
7 Eat___
8 Similar type
9 Buxom
10 Legendary city of gold
11 Cuffless shirt
12 ___ Mahal
13 Alias, for short
18 A.C. of "Saved by the Bell"
22 Neither's neighbor?
23 Commonly injured knee ligament, for short
24 Also
25 Secondary drop-down list on a computer
27 World book
28 Big club on the links
29 Western tribe
30 Cold War initials
32 Carrier with an Oslo hub
36 More bashful
37 Middle parts of a hammer?
40 Somewhat excessive
41 Him: Fr.
42 Mortgage provider
43 Angel dust, briefly
44 Clippers' crosstown rivals, on scoreboards
47 Citrus drink
48 Blog feed format
50 Uno y uno
51 Big name in contact lenses
53 David Ben-___, first Prime Minister of Israel
55 Dried pepper used in mole sauce
56 ___ tots
60 Fish voiced by Ellen DeGeneres in "Finding Nemo"
61 Veer one way
62 "Yo te___" (Spanish lover's phrase)
63 Veer the other way
65 Believer's suffix
66 Lawyers' grp.
67 Yves or Yvette, e.g.
68 Notice

Chapter 4

TRAVEL Agency
Ways to [Go places] and
a [Ride] Across America

Though crosswords provide a starting point and destination, it's up to solvers to find their ways from **ATOB** ("A to B"). Along the way, heading **ACROSS** and **DOWN** the clues, encountering a little gridlock is **NIGH** inevitable.

In fact, the celebrated constructor Merl Reagle once built a Sunday puzzle called "Gridlock," often cited as one of the greatest crosswords ever. The conceit lay at the center of its grid, where six 21-letter-long answers intersected, each a literal pile-up of cars stuck bumper-to-bumper. For instance, the answers for [Ford... Ford... Dodge... Dodge] (BRONCO-FUTURAARIESCOLT) and [Dodge... Ford... Buick... Chrysler] (OMNIPROBERIVIERAEAGLE) crossed with [Chrysler... Ford... Nissan] (CORDOBATAURUSINFINITY). Now that's the **STUFF** of a traffic **JAM**. *(More on Reagle in chapter 8.)*

ATOB [Tiny bit of progress?], [Narrow range], [Baby step?]

ACROSS [Over], [First word in puzzles?], [Down's opposite?]

DOWN [Blue], [Eat], [Fluff]

NIGH [Just about], [Practically], [Approaching], [Close], [Close to a poet?]

STUFF [Things], [This and that], [Work on pillows], [Thanksgiving day chore], [Jam]

JAM [Pickle], [Spot], [Fix], [Play with the band]

RTE [Hwy.], [Waze way: Abbr.], [Short way to go?], [1 is one]

UEY and UIE [180], [Reversal, of sorts], [Quick spin in a car?]

MAP [World view?], [Plot], [Site of a legend], [Paper route?]

AIR [Broadcast], [Inspired stuff], [Cause of inflation], [Basketball center?]

CAR [One for the road?], [Jam ingredient?], [Budget item?], [Idler?], [Tired runner?], [Coach for training?], [One staying in a lot?], [Lincoln or Ford]

Solvers unable to find a **RTE** to a particular answer can always skip ahead or fly clear across the puzzle, then pull a **UEY** (or **UIE**) and swing back around.

Let's **MAP** out what modes of transportation crosswords offer by **AIR** and sea, then we'll go **CAR** shopping. Finally, we'll hit the road in a 4 × 4—which, as far as crossword grids go, is even smaller than the [Mini, e.g.] crossword puzzle found on A-3 (that's the third page of the *New York Times*, not the popular highway name overseas). Then again, the best [Wheels] for a cross-country crossword [Ride] must be the Honda [Fit in a garage, e.g.].

AIRPLANE Mode
Airline Codes and Popular Destinations
a [Frequent flier] Should Know

Instead of looking up information on their phones, solvers stuck on a clue while stuck at a **GATE** may need only to look up to flight information boards for answers.

GATE [Scandal suffix], [Receipts], [Box office], [Ball-park figure]

STA [Training ctr.?: Abbr.], [Short stop?], [Stop: Abbr.]

TBD and TBA [Schedule abbr.], [Placeholder letters], [[No info yet]]

IFFY [Up in the air], [So-so], [????]

ETD [LAX posting], [JFK info], [Something rain might change, in brief]

FAA [Org. whose plans are up in the air?], [Org. concerned with traffic]

TSA [Screening grp.], [Org. into frisky business?], [Org. offering traveler's checks?], [Grp. concerned with body image?], [Org. concerned with air bags?]

Short for "arrival," **ARR** makes its descent as the [Flight board abbr.] that could be a [Pirate's exclamation] to news his ride won't be [In time?: Abbr.], but that's no [Short coming?]. As a [Sheet music abbr.], it's short for "arranged."

The time for a lift from the [RR stop] or **STA** ("station") might be left **TBD** ("to be determined") or **TBA** ("to be announced"). Things are a little less **IFFY** when it comes to **ETD** ("estimated time of departure") and **ETA** ("estimated time of arrival," an answer which arrived earlier as a Greek letter in chapter 1).

Alternatively, consulting an [Airport monitor?] for answers might mean seeking info from either [Air safety org.], the **FAA** or **TSA**, both of which can be a [Grp. concerned with JFK's safety?] or the [Org. that can't be lax about LAX?].

Despite how travelers might feel about the [Water bottle confiscators, for short], the **TSA** is popular in crosswords, no doubt thanks to its handy letters and its (overly?) familiar role at airports—even if it might require X-ray vision to identify the [Agcy. for Kennedy and Reagan].

But the [Grp. with a lot of baggage] also offers constructors the chance to try to sneak something funny aboard. Byron Walden got them down pat as [Wanders around LAX or JFK?] and the first-class constructor Brendan Emmett Quigley quipped, [Q: How many ___ agents does it take to change a lightbulb? A: Please remove your pants.]

Many airlines whose names or codes land in the grid are national **FLAG** carriers, so they enjoy privileged status in their countries and the cruciverse.

FLAG [Tire], [Standard], [One with a support staff]

EIRE [European Union member, to natives], [Isle named for a Gaelic goddess]

- Visitors to the [Emerald Isle]—which in the grid is more apt to be called **EIRE** or **ERIN** than [Ireland]—often opt for **AER** Lingus. The name of the nation's flag carrier is an anglicization of the Irish *aerloingeas*, meaning "air fleet," as *aer* is [What the Irish breathe]. "Eire," like the "Ire-" of Ireland, descends from the name Ériu, a goddess in Irish mythology.

  ERIN ["___go bragh!" ("Ireland forever!")], [Ireland, poetically], [Hibernia], [Green land], [Sportscaster Andrews]

  AER [___Lingus], [Gas: prefix], [Relative of atmo-]

  Another thing to come out of Irish mouths is **ERSE**, a term for either the [Old Irish tongue] (also called [Irish Gaelic]), or [Scots Gaelic]. **SCOTS** might appear to be negative when described as [Nae sayers], which is in accordance with puzzles' agreement to clue **NAE** as a [Dundee denial].

  ERSE [Highland tongue], [Limerick language], ["Whiskey" source], [Source of the word "trousers"], [Language that gave us "spunk" and "slogan"], [Language in which "Hello, how are you?" is "Halò, caimar a tha thu?"]

  A [Flat-top hat] atop a Scot is typically a **TAM**, short for tam [___-o'shanter]. The [Scottish cap] that's a [Pompom's place] takes its name from the eponymous, hard-drinking character in the Robert Burns poem.

  SCOTS [Glasgow natives], [Highlanders], [Language in which you might be greeted "Hullo, hoo are ye?"]

  NAE [Scot's not], ["Fat chance, laddie!"], ["Captain! The engines canna take ___ more!" (line from Scotty on "Star Trek")]

- The [Largest carrier in Japan], **ANA** ("All Nippon Airways"), is a much more popular option in puzzles than another [Carrier to Kyoto, briefly], **JAL** ("Japan Airlines").

  Solvers laid over in [Santa ___] **ANA**, California, the seat of Orange County, might consider driving to nearby Culver City, where they can pay $250 for a ["Wheel of Fortune" purchase] that either "Pat" or "Vanna" can provide: "an A." With it, they can solve the puzzle for [Santa ___ Winds], the hot, dry,

  ANA ["SNL" alum Gasteyer], [Actress de Armas of "Knives Out"], [CNN anchor Cabrera], [CNN commentator Navarro], [Finish of three state names], [Get ___ on (ace a test)], [What Alabama cheerleaders often request?], [Santa follower?], [Baptist leader?], [What makes men mean?]

SIERRA [GMC truck], [Letter after Romeo in the NATO alphabet], [S, in a phonetic alphabet], [Code word for "S"] *(It's the same [Rugged chain] also called the [___ Nevadas])*

CEL [Collectible animation frame], [Still at Disney World], [Image of Pluto, perhaps]

EDO [Tokyo's former name], [Pre-1868 Tokyo], [Shogunate capital]

TOKYO [City whose name means "eastern capital"], [1964 Olympics city], [Edo, today]

OSAKA [Tennis star Naomi], [Port near Kobe], [Honshu port]

KYOTO [Capital of Japan for more than a thousand years], [Japan's capital until 1868]

ETO [Ike's command], [WWII arena], [Domain of the Normandy campaign: Abbr.]

JAPAN [Black lacquer], [Go home?], [Finish, of a sort]

ELAL [Carrier to Ben-Gurion], [Airline since 1948], [Holy Land line], [Flight from Israel?]

autumnal gusts that blow westward down the **SIERRA** Nevada into the Los Angeles Basin. These frequent forest-fire fanners are also known as "devil winds." Indeed, it's been suggested that the original name might have been the Spanish *Caliente aliento de Satanás*: the "hot breath of Satan."

Such assorted info might be found in an **ANA**, a [Literary collection] of [Anecdotes], [Collected sayings], or other [Miscellany], typically about a person or place. It carries the same collection of meanings as "-ana," the [Suffix in the world of collectibles] seen in "Americana" and this clue for **CEL**: [Bit of Disneyana]. Drawn from the Latin *-anus* ("pertaining to"), it also pertains to how "mountain" and "Roman" were built.

Tokyo is more likely to show up in puzzles as **EDO**, literally "cove entry," referring to the city's location along Tokyo Bay. But if invited to enter a five-letter [Japanese metropolis], don't rush too quickly to **TOKYO**: It could be **OSAKA** or **KYOTO**, the [Noncapital city whose name means "capital city"].

ETO ("Eastern Theater of Operations") was [DDE's charge in WWII]. The "Eastern" doesn't refer to Japan: the zone was the [Pacific's counterpart in WWII: Abbr.], as [It once stretched from France to Russia: Abbr.]. Yet **JAPAN** is the source of the surname of Midori **ITO**, the [1992 Olympic figure skating silver medalist], and the 1995 [O. J. Simpson trial judge, Lance] Ito. With all these answers dating to the 20th century, younger solvers might wonder ["How was ___ know?"].

- The [Israeli flag carrier] **ELAL** ("El-Al," "To the skies" in Hebrew) is an [Airline with a flag in its logo] and the only commercial [Airline with missile defense systems]. The [Airline that doesn't schedule flights on Shabbat] is a paradox: It takes off by not taking off.

- **KAL** sometimes comes up as the initials of the [Asian carrier], "Korean Air Lines," the flag carrier for South Korea. It's also the first ingredient in Kal [___-Kan dog food]—the canine branch of Whiskas—and takes a lead role for Kal [Penn who plays Kumar in the "Harold & Kumar" films], who in 2009 went from White Castle to the White House when he joined the Obama administration.

While **PENN** might be [Teller's partner in magic], when crosswords crave the other side of Kal Penn's White Castle combo, they order up ["Star Trek" actor John] **CHO**, who reprised the [Classic George Takei role] of **SULU** in the 2009 movie reboot of the franchise.

- A popular [Carrier to Oslo] is **SAS**. Short for the seemingly interminable "Scandinavian Airlines System Denmark-Norway-Sweden," it's the flag carrier for all those nations, a [Finnair rival], and a [KLM competitor]. **KLM** is short for "Koninklijke Luchtvaart Maatschappij" (literally, the "Royal Aviation Company"), which, put plainly, is another long haul. (No **SASS** intended.)

[Now hear this!]
The SOUND of Science

In the past, a sound way to abbreviate a flight was to go by **SST** ("supersonic transport"), like the [Concorde, e.g., for short]. As the "e.g." suggests, the Concorde isn't the only such [Retired runway model]. The other commercial SST, the USSR's [Tupolev Tu-144, e.g.] was actually the first, beating the Concorde by two months, but was so problem-ridden it made only 55 flights before becoming an out-of-work [Old boomer].

The [Speed ratio] named for Austrian [Physicist Ernst] **MACH** uses the [Speed of sound]—767 **MPH** or 1,235 **KPH**—as a baseline. Capable of reaching Mach 2, the **SSTS** were a [Jet set?] that really flew—even if they were judged unsound.

Another [Russian jet] that's an [Acronymic aircraft name] is the **MIG** ("MiG," after its designers, Artem Mikoyan and Mikhail Gurevich). A current iteration, the MiG-25 Foxbat, is presently the fastest military **JET** in the world, capable of reaching at least Mach 3.2.

PENN [William with a state named after him], [Big name in tennis balls], [Brown alternative]

CHO [___ Chang, (Harry Potter's love interest)], [Comedian Margaret], ["I urge you all... to love each other without restraint. Unless you're into leather. Then by all means, use restraints" speaker Margaret]

SULU ["Mr." of "Star Trek"], [Enterprise crewman named after an Asian sea], [___ Sea, body of water between Borneo and the Philippines]

KLM [Airline with a crown in its logo], [Choice for people who go Dutch?], [Alphabetic trio for fliers]

SASS [Lip], [Cheek], [Fresh stuff], [Be wise to], [Smart comments], [Answers that may anger], [Reason for a grounding], [Fresh approach?]

SOUND [Healthy], [Ping or pong], [Wide inlet], [Dive suddenly, as a whale]

SST [Onetime JFK sight], [Noted "retiree" of '03], [Boomer that went bust, in brief]

MACH [Eponymous physicist Ernst], [Number associated with a boom], [Flight number?]

MPH [Dash letters], [Ticket fig.], [The going rate, briefly]

KPH [Eng. driver's concern], [Overseas rate: Abbr.]

JET [Runway model?], [Model with a nose in the air?], [Joe Namath was one], [It may have a wide body], [Means of getting high?], [Riff, e.g., in "West Side Story"], [Winnepeg NHLer] (so as either the singing gang or San Jose's team, a [Shark rival] or [Shark attack victim?])

ERG [Bit of work], [.0000001 joule], [Piece of work?], [Bit of energy], [Rowing machine, in fitness lingo]

OHM [Part of the resistance?], [Omega, in physics], [Big name in current research?], [Law man]

OMS [Yoga chants], [Sacred syllables]

An **ERG** (from the Ancient Greek *érgon* "work" or "task") is a [Unit of work] or [Unit of energy] that puzzles put to hard work. As a [Fraction of a joule], [It's not much work]—especially for a veteran solver. An **OHM** is a [Unit of electrical resistance] named for the German [Physicist Georg] Ohm. If a clue like [His law is represented as I = V/R] offers a [Bit of resistance] itself, don't get worked up.

Instead, try making [Meditation sounds] like **OMS**. Speaking of [Yogi's utterances], here's a wonderful one attributed to Yogi Berra that might be worth meditating on: "Make a game plan and stick to it. Unless it's not working." Perhaps that proves that [Some mantras] really are [Meditative retreats?].

[Crosswise, on a ship]
Shipshape Answers Offering
Landlubbers ABEAM of Light

ARGO [Golden Fleece ship], [Vessel that was 80 percent cargo?]

LAM [Bolt], [Cut and run], [Quick flight?]

ARGOT [Lingo], [Jargon], [Shoptalk], [Cant]

BEAM [Moon shine?], [4×4, e.g.], [Show one's teeth?], [Ship's width], [Widest part]

ABEAM [Perpendicular to the keel], [At right angles]

ABAFT [Sailor's behind?]

AFT [Back in the USS?], [Back on board?], [Back on the plane?], [Near the tail], [Early p.m.]

AFTER [À la], [Intro to math?], [Thought leader?], [Behind]

ALEE [Avoiding the draft?], [Ocean side?], [Avoiding blows?], [Out of wind] *(Mentioned also in part one, not long after the [Main course])*

The oceanic adventures of **JASON**—not [Momoa, who played Aquaman], but the [Argonauts' leader]—aboard the **ARGO**, along with his retrieval of the Golden Fleece, formed the plot of the supposed movie being filmed in the [Best Picture of 2012]. In the movie, the concocted subplot about the **FLEECE** was just a [Scam] to help the hostages go [On the ___] **LAM**, a word whose etymology continues to [Escape] consensus.

Nautical **ARGOT** can escape solvers, so clues often use a few words to guide the way like a lighthouse **BEAM**. For example, **ABEAM** can be [Crosswise, on deck] or [Crosswise to a ship's keel]. On tougher occasions, a clue omitting a [Nautical word] [Alongside] will challenge solvers to be more [Crosswise].

ABAFT, like **AFT**, is a sailor's [Sternward] word meaning [Back] or [To the rear, to a rear admiral]. As we're talking like sailors, a [Sailor's rear] is [Toward the poop]. Both "abaft" and "aft" are etymologically connected to "**AFTER**."

ALEE means [Sheltered], [Downwind], or [Sheltered from the wind]. So it's [On the safe side?] to assume that **LEE** is itself [One side of a ship], [Downwind], or the [Opposite of weather, on a ship].

Nevertheless, that sense has no bearing on the clue looking for a [Spike in direction]. Also blowing out of Hollywood is Lee [Majors in film], which is decidedly less of a breeze for younger solvers. But you don't need to have a [Gray head?] to recognize the [General at Appomattox].

The [Sailor's cry], **AVAST**, is a [Nautical "Stop!"] from the Dutch *houd vast* ("hold fast!").

A [Ship's front] is its **BOW** or **PROW**, which a clue deserving of a bow once described as [On-the-water front]. A **SCOW** is a [Flat-bottomed boat] that might be a [Garbage barge], but one man's [Craft with trash] was another man's pleasure boat when solvers were obliged to admit it as [Refuse transportation?].

As with "scow," it's possible that the name for the [Light racing boat] called a **SCULL** traces to the Middle English for [Oar], itself from Old Norse meaning to "wash." If so, "scull" could connect to **SCOUR**, or [Scrub]. But one would have to [Comb] and [Pore over] old texts to be sure.

The [Main part of a ship] is its **HULL**, which includes the **KEEL**, the [Bow-to-stern structure] that's the [Boat's backbone.] Either answer could be called up as a [Naval base?] or [Ocean bottom?].

To **LADE** is to [Fill with cargo] or [Put on]. Since [Put on] could also lead to the likes of **LOAD** or **HIRE** (both of which, like **LADE**, can also be [Bring aboard]), or **GAIN**, **WEAR**, **WORE**, **WORN**, and **HOAX**, it's a bit of a **PUTON** ("put-on"). The same Old English word, *hladan* ("to load") led to the English "lade," "load," and "**LADLE**."

[Use your scull]: Clues for OAR

It has a blade	Propeller	Big dipper?
Crew's control?	Galley item	Have a row?
Stroke, perhaps	Shell requisite	Dip stick?
Item put in a lock	Shell competitor	Stick in the water
Something a coxswain lacks	It may be used to get away from a bank	Stick in the dugout

BOW [Fiddle stick], [Yield], [Play's final act?], [Opposite of stern], [Salaam], [Be inclined?], [It'll do for the present]

SCULL [Shell that floats], [Boat, or the tool that moves it], [Certain oar]

HULL [Ship's framework], [Prow's place], [Oceanic body], [Body in the lake?], [Ship shape?]

KEEL [Fall (over)], [Ship stabilizer], [Balance beam?], [Frame from "Titanic"?]

LADE [Stow, as cargo], [Get on board], [Put weight on]

LOAD [Boatful], [Whites or colors, e.g.], [Washer/dryer unit]

HIRE [Engage], [What a limo may be for], [Get to work?]

GAIN [Put weight on], [Come by], [Appreciation], [Put on a spare tire?]

WEAR [Sport], [Don], [Slip into], [Fray, say]

WORE [Got old], [Became thin]

WORN [Dog-eared], [Used], [Weathered], [Frayed so?]

HOAX [Spoof], [Sham], [Fast one], [Sting, for instance]

PUTON [Sport], [Don], [Spoof], [Slip into], [Add, as weight], [Deception]

LADLE [Big dipper], [Soup scoop], [Transferrer of stock?]

SALT [Sea dog], [Tar], [A dash, maybe], [Preserve], [Put (away)], [Pepa's partner], [Main man?], [NaCl], [White on rice?]

SWAB [Stick in a cabinet, say], [Mop], [Deckhand], [Clean the decks], [Do a salt's job]

TAR [Gob], [Put on a black coat?], [Feather bed?], [Camel hazard?], [Besmirch], [2022 Cate Blanchett drama]

PITCH [Spiel], [Cast], [Hull sealer]

YAW [Go off course], [Pilot's problem], [Partner of pitch and roll]

JAG [Alternative to a Lambo], [Spree], [Toot], [Barb], [CBS legal drama], [Jacksonville pro]

PORT is often the product of pun-laden clues like [Left on board], [Left to the captain?], and [Left at sea]. One could imagine a clue like "Carry a trading hub's dessert wine left" yielding "PORT-PORTPORTPORT." Omitted from that reporting is the [Computer part] that's an [Opening in the computer business].

To **SALT** is to [Season], but a salt can also be a seasoned [Sailor]. A **SWAB** can fill in for [Salt] in a pinch, being another term for a [Sailor, informally], which could make "[Alcohol ___], swab" a demand for booze.

TAR, another nickname for a [Sailor] or [Bluejacket] (a sailor in the navy), outdoes itself with its clues: It can [Smear] with [Pitch]—if only to eventually have to [Swab] it with [Sea salt].

A ship or plane swaying horizontally is said to **PITCH**. If it sways from bow to stern it's said to **YAW**, a word possibly from the old German *jagen* (to "chase" or "hunt"), connecting it with "Jägermeister" (literally, "master hunter") and "**YACHT**" a [Vessel that's 1 percent full], or as constructor Colin Gale floated it, a [Blue blood vessel].

Though etymologically unrelated, another expensive ride is the Jaguar—puzzles always call it their **JAG**—a brand whose name originated in the Amazon as the Tupi term for the cat. A different "jag"

[There's something fishy about it]: The SEA

Main	Level area?	Kind of sick	Wet body
Host	School zone	Side front?	Dead body?
Multitude	Source of rays	Horse head?	Wide body?
Swell place?	Urchin's home	World leader?	Body in bed?
Deep space?	Waves home?	Start for bees or breeze	Pirate's body?
Irish, e.g.	Home to millions		What floats your boat?
Black, for one	Clippers arena?	Word before god or devil	Red thing that's really blue?
Yellow or White	Current location?	Lead-in to cow, horse, or dog	Where the floor is always wet?
China, for instance	Fisherman's lure?	Where gull meets buoy	Tranquility on the moon?
___-green	Where skates glide		

once meant a "load," as of hay or wood carried by a horse, which morphed into "as much liquor as a man can drink." In other words, a [Bender]. **LOADED** has become similarly loaded, meaning [Very rich... or drunk].

AYE, I could go for a fully loaded Jag myself.

LOADED [Flush], [Like some nachos and questions]

AYE [Swab's reply], [Word said in passing], [House call?]

SEMI Circle
The [Kind of truck] That [Kind of] Isn't

The [Half: Prefix] **SEMI** looks twice its size as [Circular opening?]. But that's not the [Half] of it, as the answer can have solvers unfamiliar with [Truck] terms spinning their wheels. So strap in, [It's a long ride].

SEMI [Formal introduction?], [Biographical opening?], [Big Mack?], [Before the final], [Big game?], [High roller?]

The front part of the truck is called the tractor-trailer. It pulls the back part (where the cargo goes), called a semi-trailer, a semi, or a trailer.

But by virtue of a synecdoche—a figure of speech where a part can be used for the whole—the entire truck is often referred to by any of the names of either part. So the entire truck—the "rig" or "18-wheeler"—can also be called a "tractor-trailer," a "semi-trailer," or a "semi."

Thus, **SEMI**, originally just the back half, doubles as a synonym for the entire [Rig], [18-wheeler], or [Tractor-trailer].

Consequently, a semi is part of a semi, which really seems to pull its weight as the [Large trailer puller] and the [Trailer]. It's [Kind of] a [Convoy vehicle] unto itself. No wonder [It can mean "not so"]! And to top it off, there's the clue referring to the prefix "semi-" as [Half up-front?]. We've indeed gone full circle.

Yes, such **SEMI**-circular reasoning is enough to make one [Quasi]-queasy. I think I'm starting to feel road sick myself—the [Colon variety].

Maybe I'm not the only one going half-loopy. Constructor Patti Varol called up **CBER** ("CBer," one using a CB radio, short for "Citizens' Band") as [One in a semi circle]. **ROGER** ["___ that!"].

CBER [Handle holder], [Semi conductor?], [Radioactive one?]

PARK It

Some Less [Common] Cars
Crosswords [Use a lot]

BAND [Tour group?], [Act in concert?], [Hot Chocolate or Vanilla Fudge], [Ring], [Yes, for example]

ANON [Shortly], [Coming up, to milady], [Mystery writer?], [Briefly unknown?]

ROMEO [Slayer of Tybalt], [Rival of Paris], [Lover of Shakespeare], [Casanova], [Play boy?]

HEMI [Powerful engine, informally], [Half: prefix], [Half-]

AVEO [Former Chevy subcompact], [2004 Chevy debut]

SONIC [Video game character that runs on many consoles]

GTO ['Vette alternative], ['60s song with "three deuces and a four-speed and a 389"], [1964 Ronny and the Daytonas hit]

CTRL [Key that's never used alone], [___-X (cut)], [___-C], [Lead in to P or C on a PC], [Part of many common shortcuts]

ALT [PC key], [Music genre prefix], [___-weekly (newspaper type)], [Computer key not pressed alone], [Delaware has the lowest mean one in the US: Abbr.]

DEL [Penn. neighbor], [First st.], [First of 50: Abbr.], [Diamond St.]

SZA [Singer with the 2017 #1 R&B album "Ctrl"]

[Santa Fe or Tucson]? [Aspen or Tahoe]? Considering that each of these clues gasses up an **SUV**, it's no wonder that crosswords enjoy taking car models for a spin. Before we visit the "used cars" lot, the only thing left to decide is [Boston or Chicago]? [Kansas or Alabama]? Which **BAND** should we listen to when we hit the road?

ALFA, as a ["Bravo" preceder], is a way to say [A, in communications]. As an [Italian sports car, briefly], it's acronymous for *Anonima Lombarda Fabbrica Automobili* ("Anonymous Lombard Automobile Factory"—the **ANON** part refers to its stockholders' names, which are kept private). An Alfa **ROMEO** may hum with a **HEMI**, named after its cylinder heads' hemispherical shape.

Despite being the [Car name that's Latin for "desire"], the **AVEO** must've sounded unappealing to buyers, as Chevrolet rebranded it the more familiar-sounding **SONIC**.

The **GTO**, an [Old Pontiac muscle car] produced from 1964 to 1974, took its [Sporty car initials] from the Ferrari 250 GTO. That's a speedy way to say *Gran Turismo Omologata*, or "Grand Touring Homologated" ("Grand Touring" referring to a class of limited-run road-racing cars sold to the public, and "Homologated" designating that the autos reached some technical specifications and sales). That it's rooted in the Greek *homologeo* (literally, "I say the same") is apt: Since there's only one three-letter answer to [Classic muscle car], it will always be homologous (having the same relation, position, or—in this case—structure) to **GTO**.

The four-letter [Classic muscle car] of crosswords is the [1980s Camaro] **IROC**. Chevy took the initials of what was initially a [Stock car competition from 1974 to 2006]—the International Race of Champions—and added a letter to form the car's full name: the IROC-Z. So while known familiarly as the **IROC**, gearheads who are sticklers probably prefer it clued as [___-Z] (a clue that seems certain to be tapped soon for **CTRL**, the abbreviation also associated with C, F, P, X, **ALT**, **DEL**, and **SZA**).

Like the IROC-Z, another [Classic Chevy], the **VETTE**, offered the [Sporty option] of a **TTOP**.

In the 1920s, the car designer Cecil Kimber named his now [Classic roadsters] **MGS** ("MGs") for Morris Garages, where he worked for the automaker William Morris. Like [Tiny dosage units: Abbr.], these [British two-seaters] are too small to park in puzzles without hitching an "S" on the back, so they're never seen solo in the grid. But seeing just one parked in a lot in 1962 was enough for keyboardist Booker Taliaferro Jones and [Booker T.'s backup group] to follow Kimber's lead and adopt the letters as their own. Later, when the company behind the [Bygone sports cars] refused to sponsor the band, the musicians decided the initials stood for "Memphis Group."

Adam **OPEL** founded his namesake company in 1862 to manufacture sewing machines but eventually changed his mind and started producing penny-farthings. (The coinage of the bicycle's name relates to the disparate sizes of the wheels: The tiny back one relative to the enormous front resembled the difference in the coins' sizes.) Opel died before his firm ever made an auto, so a clue like [German automaker] refers to the company, not the man.

The [1950s Ford flop] called the **EDSEL** was such a [Detroit debacle] that it's become an [Eponym for failure]. The infamous [Car bomb?] was released by Henry Ford II, who named it after his father, Edsel Ford, the [Son of Henry Ford].

To keep an **AUTO** from failing, consider using motor oil by **STP**, a [Big engine additive]. The [Letters on many a racecar] stand for "Scientifically Treated Petroleum."

Campers, **REV** your engines! **RVS** might be parked at a **KOA**— [Big inits. in camping] standing for "Kampgrounds of America"— but since many such sites offer **ATV** trails, an **RVER** with a **QUAD** can still get their motor running.

[What will happily sell its Soul?] **KIA**, of course, whose name arose from *ki* ("arise") and *a* (standing for "Asia"), roughly translating to "Rising from the East." Kia's compact **RIO** means "river" in Spanish, so it's an [Agua source] like the [Bravo, e.g.], or [El Misisipi, e.g.].

OPEL [German auto since 1899], [German car sold mainly in Europe], [Sister company of Peugeot], [Automaker sold by GM in 2017], [Car with a lightning bolt logo]

AUTO [Camera setting], [Road runner], [Wheels], [Self starter?], [Jam ingredient?]

STP [Canful at a gas station], [Indy 500 sponsor], [Indy inits.], [500 letters?]

REV [Title for MLK Jr.], [King, e.g.: Abbr.], [Father, familiarly], [Fire (up)], [Race], [Put one's foot down?], [Gun]

RVS ("RVs," "recreational vehicles") [Campers' campers, for short], [Park parkers, for short], [Road houses]

KOA [Campsite org.], [Place with RV hookups], [RV chain]

ATV ("all-terrain vehicle") [Off-road transport, for short], [4x4, e.g.]

RVER ("RVer") [Winnebago owner, briefly], [KOA customer]

QUAD [ATV], [Area of study?], [Brown rectangle?], [Brown green?], [Rice pad?]

KIA [Soul from Seoul], [Rio make], [Soul supplier]

RIO [Carnival city], [Grande preceder], [Ipanema locale]

RIVER [Missouri or Ohio], [Charles, e.g.], [Bank depositor?]

The source of *río* is the Latin *rivus,* which gives English **RIVER** and, more importantly for solvers, **RIA**, the cruciverse's [Narrow inlet]. Though this [Coastal feature] sounds foreign as a [Cousin of a fjord]—especially as it's [Spanish for "estuary"], American examples of this [Cove], [Narrow waterway], or [Inlet such as New York Harbor] include [Chesapeake Bay, e.g.].

[Ransom paid for cars?]
It's the Same <u>OLDS</u> Story

OLDS [Bygone GM car], [88 maker], [98, in the car world], [Part of REO], [Cutlass, e.g.], [Geezers, with "the"]

When Ransom Eli **OLDS** founded his Olds Motor Vehicle Company in 1897, he became a [Ford competitor]. Although his company no longer operates, the clue still applies in a way, as both he and **FORD** vie for the four-letter answer to [Assembly line pioneer].

REO [___ Speedwagon], [Ransom letters?], [Auto monogram], [Model T contemporary]

Olds left Olds—which became Oldsmobile—to establish the **REO** Motor Car Company. The [Auto co. whose name was its founder's initials] produced some wonderfully named models: the [Flying Cloud, for one], and the [Gold Comet, Raider, or Royale]. But it may be remembered best as the [Maker of the old Speed Wagon], a light truck.

That's thanks to the ["Can't Fight This Feeling" band ___ Speedwagon], who disregarded the fact that the company's name was pronounced as one word, like *"rio."* The discrepancy could be chalked up to the keyboardist, who first encountered **REO** on the blackboard in a History of Transportation class. Today, discerning solvers will pronounce the name of the band that sang "Keep Pushin'" differently from [The car in Thurber's 1933 story "The Car We Had to Push"].

Though the band still tours, the company's last incarnation, Oldsmobile, stopped cranking out numbers when the **ALERO**, the [Last Oldsmobile ever produced], rolled off the line in 2004. Like its predecessor, the **CIERA**, and the founder, it's an [Old Olds].

<u>VIA</u>-ble Options
Finding Routes [Through] a Crossword

GPS stands for "Global Positioning System," but as constructor Yacob Yonas pointed out, the acronym represents the [Bookend letters of "Google Maps," appropriately]. Solvers charting their own course through a puzzle benefit from knowing these thoroughfares.

GPS [Savior for lost souls, for short?], [Plot device, in brief], [Family docs]

Even a famous **AVE** can be disorienting when clued as [Park in N.Y.C.?], [Michigan, in Chicago: Abbr.], or [Constitution, in DC]. But when used as [Maria's intro?], the answer refers to the Latin *ave*, meaning ["Hail!"]. Thus it's a short way to say ["Greetings, Caesar"], or as Mark Feldman called it, ["Yo, Hadrian!"].

AVE [Michigan, e.g.: Abbr.], [Fifth, e.g.: Abbr.], [Ancient greeting], [Bird: Sp.]
(*See AVES in chapter 8 for more answers for the birds*)

VIA arrives in English [By way of] the Latin *via*, meaning "road," making it a Latin route with a Latin root. And when puzzles are solved [Using] clues like [___ Dolorosa (Christ's path to the cross)], the [Route word] is part of a "cross"-ward route. *Vía* is also "way" or "road" in Spanish, which explains Merl Reagle's roundabout clue, [Carlito's way?].

VIA [Itinerary word], [Direct word?], [Road that leads to Rome]

As it's also Italian for "street," when **VIA** surfaces [By] a clue like [Roman road], solvers can summon chariots or Fiats and still arrive at the answer. But when that road is a little longer, it's likely paving the way for the Latin **ITER**. Referring in Latin more often to a route or journey than a road, *iter* is more dutifully clued as a [Roman way]. In English, *iter* is an [Anatomical canal], particularly the midbrain passage called the cerebral aqueduct, and is the [Ancient route] found in English via "itinerary."

ITER [Way of old Rome], [Passage, in anatomy], [Path to Caesar]

The most famous Ancient Roman road was the **VIA** [___ Appia], built around 300 BCE to connect Rome and Brindisi. "Via Appia" is perhaps Western civilization's most famous **STREET** name, or odonym (alternatively, "hodonym"), itself rooted not in Latin but in the Ancient Greek "**WAY**" or "path," *hodós*.

STREET [A, B, or C, in Washington], [DC's D or C], [Side of a block], [Easy ___], [Way to go], [Part of many a grid]

WAY [Knack], [Modus operandi], [Ancient Rome's Appian ___], [Very, informally]

Perhaps it really is only the journey that matters, as *hodós* forgot its starting point and destination to become **ODO** ("odo-"), the [Lead-in to meter]. It's also seen in **EXODUS** (literally, a "way out of") and **EPISODE** ("the way into"). And it alights in **DIODE**, which—since this [Current path?] is [Part of L.E.D.]—means that, in a "way," it

EXODUS [Escapist reading?], [United flight?], [Moving experience?]

EPISODE [Pilot, for one], [Show piece?], [Serial number?]

DIODE [Electron tube with two elements], [Current director]

LED [Like some lights], [Was first], [Wasn't down], [Zeppelin leader?], [Opened], [Drove]

EMIT [Give off], [Radiate], [Put out], [Broadcast]

ODOR [Something fishy], [Secret target?], [Fragrance], [Kitchen drawer?], [Oxygen's lack], [Quality]

ANODE [+ terminal], [Battery part], [Cell division?]

ANTIPODE [Direct opposite], [The North Pole vis-à-vis the South Pole, e.g.]

CATHODE [Negative pole], [Where the juice comes out]

APLUS ("A-plus") [100],[Mark of distinction], [Super mark, it]

NONPLUS [Puzzle], [Bewilder]

FED [ATF agent, e.g.], [Ready for a toothpick?], [Broke a rule at the zoo?], [Grazed], [Fueled], [Flowed into], [Satiated], [Catered to?]

NSA [It checks for leaks, for short], [Group of crackers, for short?], [Intel processor?], ["The Puzzle Palace" org.]

CIA [Decoder ring, for short?], [Spooky org.?], [Virginia creepers?], ["The Company"]

DEA [Traffic cops?], [Initials of a crack team?], [Dealbreakers?: Abbr.], [Arm for taking needles, for short?]

ATF [Vice squad?: Abbr.], [Gangbusters, for short?]

FBI [Stingy group?], [Caseworkers' org.?], [D.N.A. testers, at times]

NFL [Ram's home?], [Texans are part of it, in brief]

even **LED** to L.E.D. ("Light-Emitting Diode"). (Of course, what crosswords themselves often **EMIT** is an **ODOR**—which isn't such [Bad nasal news] if it's just a [Hint] of newsprint.)

The same "odo" also powers **ANODE** and its **ANTIPODE, CATHODE**. Yet it's not connected to the **NODE** that's a [Connection point], [Lymph bump], or [Bump on a log, literally], which grew from the Latin *nodus*, for "knot."

Here's **APLUS** side to knowing this additional information: Batteries' sides are less likely to **NONPLUS** those who associate "anode" with the end that features "a node."

Changing the end of a Roman route transforms *iter* into another roadway: **ITEN** ("Interstate 10"), the [Major Calif.-to-Fla. route].

FED Up
Current and Alternating Acronyms
DC [Gave] to Crosswords

Puzzles revel in blurring the lines between federal agencies. A [Hush-hush grp.] or [Bug experts?: Abbr.] might be the **NSA** or the **CIA**. A [Raiders' grp.] might be the **DEA, ATF,** or **FBI**–let alone that [Patriots' org.] the **NFL**.

The **OSS** ("Office of Strategic Services"] was a [WWII spy org.]. Founded by FDR, the [CIA forerunner] is pretty obsolete but for pop culture references like [Org. in "Inglourious Basterds"] and [Where Wonder Woman first worked: Abbr.]. Yet it still crops up; it seems you just can't make crosswords without OSS.

GMAN and **TMAN** are antiquated too. Each an outmoded term for a [Fed] and [Gangbuster], the somewhat superhero-ish nicknames continue to save the day when constructors are in a tight spot.

GMAN ("G-man," a "government man") can refer to any [Fed. agent], but most often it is (was) used for an [FBI agent, in old slang]. **GMEN** are [Feds] or, when short for "Giants," [N.Y. footballers].

TMAN ("T-man" or "Treasury man," plural) might be used to tag a [Fake bill tracer] or [Catcher of counterfeiters, in old lingo], or any [IRS agent] or Treasury agent, like Eliot [Ness, notably].

Thanks in part to the [1997 Costner role], the ["Untouchable" Eliot] **NESS** remains a model of the combination of tenacity and incorruptibility he exhibited in his mission to [Loch ___] up Al Capone, essentially bringing Capone's life of crime to a [Bitter end].

CAPO, which means [Head, in Rome], is also used for a [Crime boss], making it a [Head among hoods]. A capo is unlikely to sing, but [It can change one's tune] and occasion a [Neck brace?] as a [Guitar clamp] used as a [Tool that raises a guitar's pitch].

NESS [Noted enforcer of Prohibition], [Name associated with a mobster or a monster], [Adjective-to-noun suffix], [Jonathan Van___, member of the "Queer Eye" cast]

CAPO [Head of the family?], [Family guy?], [Don], [Hit producer?], [Ukulele accessory], [String shortener], [Da___ ("from the beginning")]

["Anytown, ___"] USA
American Geography

When rushing through a crossword like a **RIG** heading cross-country, there often doesn't seem time to explore all the unfamiliar sights along the way. So let's visit some domestic destinations whose names—written so small and faint when plotted in an **ATLAS**—are far more pronounced in puzzle grids.

The largest and [Farthest of the Near Islands] of Alaska, **ATTU** is the [Westernmost island of the Aleutians] and a [US island occupied by Japan during WWII]. A [Dweller on the Bering Sea] is likely to be an **ALEUT**, which is also what's found to fill a five-box space for [Indigenous Alaskan] after a failed attempt to insert **INUIT** into it. Interchangeable as those two answers are, there's "**NOME**" mistaking the solution for ["There's no place like ___" (Alaskan's quip)].

The [Upper Midwest town with the world's tallest concrete gnome] is **AMES**. Surprisingly, [Iowa State's home] and [Big 12 college town] is the [Midwest city whose name is always spelled in Vietnamese?]. Founded as a stop along the Cedar Rapids and Missouri Railroad, it was named for Oakes Ames, the US congressman from **MASS** who was essential in establishing the Union Pacific line, though he was equally responsible for the Crédit Mobilier scandal. French masses discuss **AME** (as *âme*, [Soul: Fr]), which also represent [Letters in some church names] (as "A.M.E.," the African Methodist Episcopal Church).

USA [Today preceder], [Where to find MA and PA], [Home to about 75% of the world's tornadoes]

RIG [Fix], [Fix in a bad way?], [Outfit], [Semi], [Set sail]

ATLAS [Country album?], [World record?], [Book of legends?], [Book that comes with a set of keys], [Place holder?], [Holdup man?], [World-weary sort?]

NOME [Iditarod terminus], [Gold Rush town once called Anvil City], [US city connected to the outside only by airplane, boat and sled]

AMES [NASA's ___ Research Center] *(named for Oakes Ames's distant cousin, the physicist Joseph Sweetman Ames)*

MASS [It may be critical], [Father's concern?], [Large scale]

Oakes's uncle, Frederick L. **AMES**, footed the bill for the Ames [___ Building, Boston's first skyscraper]. A subsequent [Beantown skyscraper, with "the"], is "The **PRU**" ("The Prudential Center"), named for the [Aetna rival, informally].

IOWA [Corny state?], [Primary location?], [Geographical name that comes from the Sioux for "sleepy ones"]

Back in **IOWA**, 100 miles east of Ames, **COE** [College in Cedar Rapids, Iowa], shares its name with England's [Great miler] from the 1980s, [Runner Sebastian] Coe.

More than a [Kind of monster], the **GILA** is a [River of Phoenix] that feeds the Colorado. The latter river's headwaters are found at the resort town of **ESTES** [___ Park, Colo.], an answer which is also fed by references to the *90210* and ["Melrose Place" actor Rob].

Covering just two square miles, Minnesota's Lake **ITASCA** should be too small for crosswords to mention—and at six letters long, also too large. Yet it's significant as the [Lake that's the source of the Mississippi] (and three nicely spaced vowels). "Itasca" might seem Native American, but it's a **CON**: It's a concoction of the Latin *ver<u>itas</u>* ("truth") and *<u>cap</u>ut* ("head"). But there's no [Reason against] that, as Itasca is the "true head(waters)" of the river.

CON [Down side], [Take in], [Anti body?], [Kind of artist who's not very good?], [One in a big house?], [Pen pal?]

SOTO *("so to")* [Words before speak], [Words before bed?]

GOTO *("go to")* [Attend], [Words before sea, seed, or bed], *(or as "go-to")* [First choice], [Most-often-used]

OCALA, a [City between Gainesville and Orlando] near the eponymous [___ National Forest], does have old American Indian roots: The Spanish explorer [Hernando de ___] **SOTO** wrote of a large town there called Ocali, thought to mean "Big Hammock." It's unclear if De Soto ever did **GOTO** the settlement.

ALUM [Person involved in after-school activities?], [Rice gatherer?]

KING [Double-decker checker], [It may take a check], [Board member?]

The colonists who founded the [University of Maine town] of **ORONO** named it after the Algonquin chief Joseph Orono. Today, the school's most famous literary **ALUM** is Stephen **KING**.

ORNE [Author Sara___ Jewett], [French river to the English Channel], [Caen's river], [Birthplace of Camembert cheese]

ORLE [Heraldic border]

STATES [Conditions], [Union members?], [Their lines are often crossed]

During the late 19th century, Orono's most famous alum was Sarah **ORNE** Jewett, who wrote about Maine's southern shoreline. Orne is also a [French river or department] found along France's northwest coast. Either way, the answer is rare, as is its near twin, **ORLE**, which also has king and border connections as a heraldic design forming an inset [Shield border].

Back in the **STATES**, a straight shot down I-95 for five hours will reach **URI** ("University of Rhode Island"), the [Ocean State sch.]. That is, unless the [Mentalist Geller] psychically throws in some curves, or a constructor asks for [William Tell's canton]. The trick here is knowing that a "canton" is a political geographic subdivision, particularly used for a Swiss state. That's where Tell supposedly killed a [Town officer], or **REEVE**, also the name of [One of Chaucer's pilgrims], the [Teller of the third tale in "The Canterbury Tales"].

Wait, what happened? One second we're on I-95, the next we're back in Europe, in a canton on a Swiss **ALP** (near a French **ALPE**), and then in Canterbury! How'd we get . . . Geller!! Back in the car, everyone.

Our next stop is another college town, **IONA**, named after the [Inner Hebrides isle] [Where Macbeth is buried]. "Iona" seems to stem from the **YEW** tree, a [Plant in an English hedge] whose [Fine-grained wood] is [Wood for archery bows].

Also in **NYS** is **UTICA**, the [Upstate New York college] in the [Erie Canal city] named for the [Capital of the Roman province of Africa] from antiquity. Italians might be surprised to find that Utica, a [City 15 miles from Rome] and a [City east of Syracuse], is a [New York city]. It's just not *the* **NYC**.

Out west in **NEV**, **RENO** can look like two of a pair, as it seems like a long shot that the [Betting setting] is a [City near Virginia City], but Virginia City is another [Nevada locale]. And a suburb's name makes Reno a place where [Sparks can be seen at its edge], which is apt for an [Elopers' destination, often] considered a [Divorce mecca]. With so many games to play, no wonder crosswords ask solvers to come up with a [Better place?].

REEVE [Christopher of "Superman"], [Clark Kent off screen], ["The Canterbury Tales" pilgrim]

ALP [Finsteraarhorn, e.g.], [High point of "The Sound of Music"?]

ALPE [French peak], [Suisse peak], [Mont Blanc, par exemple]

IONA [College in New Rochelle, NY]

NYS [Buffalo's home], [Mets insignias]

NYC ["Annie" song with the lyric "Too busy / Too crazy / Too hot / Too cold / Too late / I'm sold"]

NEV [The Silver St.], [36th of 50: Abbr.]

[Superior's inferior]
ERIE Coincidences

Reno may be "The Biggest Little City in the World," but the biggest little city in the cruciverse is **ERIE**, the [Pennsylvania city] whose nicknames include [The Gem City, so-called because of its sparkling lake] and [The Flagship City], as it's the [Home of Oliver Hazard Perry's flagship Niagara].

The [Eponymous American Indian tribe], the **ERIE**, were a [Lake tribe] also known as the [Cat Nation people] or the "Panther Nation." Their full name was Erielhonan ("Long Tail"), thought to reference the Eastern cougar—which likely loomed large in their mythology—or to the racoon tails they wore. The [Tribe defeated by the Iroquois] and their [Language related to Wyandot] disappeared in the 18th century, and the Eastern cougar is presumed extinct.

Lake **ERIE** is the second smallest [One of the Greats?] by surface area, yet still the eleventh-largest lake in the world by that measure. In an **EERIE** twist—[Like a coincidence that makes you go "Hmm..."]—**ERIE** is also the second most popular four-letter answer in the history of the *New York Times* and ranks as around the 11th most popular word since Shortz took over. But it places fourth as [The "E" in HOMES] (a mnemonic device for the names of the Great Lakes).

EERIE [A little too quiet, perhaps], [À la King?] *(referring to the author)*

But the [Great Lakes canal name] that's the biggest drag for solvers is Michigan's **SOO** [___ Locks]. Solvers can thank their lucky Broadway stars for [Phillipa who played Eliza in the original cast of "Hamilton"]. The Tony nominee has started replacing clues like [Superior-Huron canals], which had left many solvers thinking ["Annnyway..."] ["An-n-nd?"] moving on to the next clue.

SOO [US/Canada's ___ Canals], [Jack of "Barney Miller"], ["Your point being...?"]

Getting [Hi in HI]
Saying ALOHA to Some Maui Wowies

It's right on the mark that **HAWAII** is the [State whose postal code is a greeting], as its famous greeting, **ALOHA**, is both a [Warm welcome?] and a way to say [Isle be seeing you?]. Solvers received a fine how-do-you-do when the always-welcome constructor Elizabeth C. Gorski saw it coming and going in another way, as the [Greeting that includes a Spanish greeting in reverse?].

ALOHA is also [HI goodbye], and a [Hilo hello] or [Hilo bye/yo]—the last two thanks to the [Big city on the Big Island], **HILO**.

HIHO ("Hi-ho!") is more of a [Jaunty greeting]. But clues for **ALOHA** like [Ho hi] and constructor Jeff Chen's pitch-perfect ["Hi, Ho!"] are jaunty greetings fine-tuned for the Aloha State: They refer to **DONHO** (Don Ho), the tiny-named [Hawaiian singer] behind the 1966 big hit "Tiny Bubbles."

Hawaii is home to perhaps the most easily confused pair of answers in the cruciverse. The Big Island's two volcanos are Mauna **KEA** (literally, "White Mountain") and Mauna **LOA** ("Long Mountain"). Since each has its own similarly named observatory, either **KEA** or **LOA** work for [Mauna ___], [Mauna ___ (Hawaiian volcano)], or [Mauna ___ Observatory].

Well over 90 percent of the time, a clue for **KEA** or **LOA** can be answered by either, and they arrive with similar frequency. But on rare occasions, clues can key a lone answer:

HAWAII [Only US state with two official languages], [One of two states with its own time zone]

ALOHA [Hello or goodbye], [Colorful kind of skirt], [Honolulu's ___ Stadium], [Greeting that means "presence of breath"]

HILO [Southernmost US city] *and as in "Omaha hi-lo"* a [Variety of stud poker, familiarly]

HIHO [Kermit the Frog's greeting], [Bygone cracker brand], [Onetime Ritz rival]

KEA	LOA
Hawaiian for "white"	"Long," in Hawaii
White in Waikiki	"Aloha nui ___" (Hawaiian sign-off meaning "lots of love")
Mauna ___ (dormant volcano)	"Mahalo nui ___" ("Thank you very much," in Hilo)
Mauna ___: Hawaii's highest peak	Mau ___ (forever, in Hawaii)
Brownish-green New Zealand parrot	Mauna ___ (macadamia nut brand)

Located in part along the western slope of Mauna Loa, the **KONA** Coast is the [Prime coffee-growing area in Hawaii] known for its [High-quality coffee variety] and as the [Ironman World Championship locale].

LANAI [Hawaii's ___ City, on an island of the same name], [Hawaiian island 98% owned by Larry Ellison]

LANAI, known as [The Pineapple Island], lends its name to the open-sided [Roofed patio] or [Island veranda]. In **FLA**, however, a lanai is a screened-in [Place for a pool, perhaps].

FLA [Key state geographically or electorally?: Abbr.], [Hollywood setting: Abbr.], [Jupiter's locale: Abbr.]

The [Second-largest of the Hawaiian Islands], **MAUI**, is the [So-called Valley Isle]. The [Island near Oahu] is named for the demigod Māui, who's said to have created the islands while fishing with his brothers. Snagging his hook on the sea floor, the [Trickster god in "Moana"] convinced his brothers to paddle with all their might, and together they pulled the islands up from the ocean.

The name of the [Disney title girl] **MOANA** was pulled from the word for "ocean" or "sea" in Hawaiian, Maori, and other Polynesian languages. Unsurprisingly, the name of Moana's pet chicken, Hei-hei, is Maori for "chicken."

The [Island known as "The Gathering Place"], **OAHU**, is [Honolulu's home] and the location of Pearl Harbor, Waikiki Beach, and the Iolani Palace, as well as [Obama's birthplace]. While some might look at that clue about **OBAMA**, [#44], and wonder how to squeeze **HAWAII**, [#50], into its meager four boxes, it's harder to sympathize with those trying to enter **KENYA**. (Can ya imagine, instead of a **BIRTH** certificate, a crossword answer certifying an [Inaugural event?])

KENYA [Its capital is Nairobi], [Mombasa's country], ["Born Free" setting]

BIRTH [Product of one's labor?], [Special delivery?], [It brings out the kid in you]

LEI It on Me
"Web" Words and [Polynesian present] in Puzzles

BASSO [Low man], [Low down singer?], [Operatic villain, frequently], [___ profundo]

SOLI [Most arias], [Star turns], [Numbers for one?], [Met expectations?] (See chapter 9 for the singular)

Nicknamed "The Garden Isle," the [Island NW of Oahu], **KAUAI**, was the first visited by Captain Cook. It was also the filming location of *South Pacific*, starring the Italian opera singer **EZIO** [Pinza of opera], easily the biggest **BASSO** to solo in crosswords.

Though not sung by Pinza, one of the hit **SOLI** in *South Pacific* is a chart topper in crosswords too: **BALIHAI** ("Bali Ha'i"). The title of

"Thanks, ___!" OBAMA

Whatever their politics, constructors must have a high approval rating of Obama, thanks to the felicitous arrangement of letters in his name. The likes of **IKE** (himself a [Likable prez?], who also appears as **DDE**) and JFK aside, Obama is likely the president clues campaign for most often.

Yet some clues for **OBAMA** solicit another write-in candidate, as Yaakov Bendavid did when he stumped for [Michelle Robinson, now]. Other propositions for solvers to decide on include these:

- ☐ Start to care?
- ☐ Clinton rival
- ☐ Clinton and Carter were in his Cabinet
- ☐ President whose initials "stink"
- ☐ President whose initials were also his dog's name

- ☐ He said, "What Washington needs is adult supervision."
- ☐ U.S. president whose mother's first name was Stanley
- ☐ President whose first name means "one who is blessed"
- ☐ Only president whose surname is more than 50 percent vowels
- ☐ "I have to admit, I'm not the strappy young Muslim socialist that I used to be" speaker

SASHA and **MALIA** are tough enough to differentiate in a grid since they're each [One of the Obamas] whose five-letter names feature a pair of identically placed A's. But when **SASHA** appeared as [One of a White House couple until 2017], solvers could only sigh and say to the constructor: Thanks, Zhouquin Burnikel.

the ["There Is Nothin' Like a Dame" follower] refers to an unreachable island on the horizon, based on the island of **OPA** in Vanuatu. ([Dame ___] **EDNA** is another inimitable Dame follower of note.)

While not quite unreachable, for **EONS** there were precious few ways to reach those two useful answers in the title: **BALI** was often a [Romantic island] or [Neighbor of Java] and **HAI** was almost inevitably ["Bali ___"].

Slowly, **BALI** has become more interesting to visit: Now it's also an [Island known for its meditation retreats], [Island with a Hindu majority], and even a [Big name in bras] (though the company has been around since 1927 and is currently owned by **HANES**).

OPA [___-Locka, Fla.], [Shout at a Greek wedding], [Gramps, to Günter]

EDNA [Novelist Ferber who wrote "Giant"], [Poet ___ St. Vincent Millay], [Irish novelist O'Brien], ["Hairspray" mom], [___ Krabappel, teacher on "The Simpsons"]

EONS [Time to evolve?], [Long stretches?], [Many periods]

HANES [Brief name?], [Jockey rival], [Name associated with boxers]

NOM (*as the French for name,* "*nom*") [Jean, for one], [You go by one in Québec], [French handle?], *or as the English "lolspeak" nom* [Munch, in modern slang]

ATHOS [Fictional swordsman], [Friend of Aramis], [One of a literary trio]

CATS [Boppers], [Some Persians], [Meowsical?], [Half a downpour?]

NENE [Hawaii's only native goose], [Double birdie?], [___ crossing (Hawaiian road sign)], ["Real Housewife" Leakes who appeared on "Celebrity Apprentice"], [Child in chile]

MEME [Lolcats, e.g.], [Web spreadable], [Something that gets passed around a lot], ["Thanks, Obama," for one]

NAENAE [Viral dance of 2015], [Dance craze inspired by the show "Martin"]

NOMS [Eating sounds], [Delicious food, in modern slang], [Jules and Jim, e.g.]

LUAU [Waikiki wingding], [Poi party], [Occasion for a roast], [Gathering of lei people?]

TARO [Tuber type], [Root in Polynesian cuisine], [Starchy plant], [Hawaiian staple], [___ cake (dim sum specialty)], [Bubble tea flavor], [Root for Hawaiians?]

POI [Luau dish], [Hawaiian staple], [Dish cooked in an underground oven]

HAI is now a satisfactory answer for [Yes, in Yokohama], [OK in Okinawa], and even ["O ___" (greeting on many lolcat memes)].

Something similar has happened with **NOM**: For decades, it was almost exclusively [___ de plume] or [___ de guerre]. Now it's nominated in all sorts of ways: Clues like [Nice moniker?] and [Nancy, in Nancy], which mention French cities, are joined by others that might namedrop [Marcel Marceau, e.g.] or [Athos, Porthos, or Aramis]. (**ATHOS** often solos as [A Musketeer].) But just as **NOM** started to receive attention as a [Chance at an Oscar, for short] (short for "nomination"), it went viral as the [LOLcat's sound].

Regrettably, Hawaii's many feral **CATS** are blamed for going **NOMNOMNOM**—a [LOLcat-eating-a-cheezburger noise], as constructor Matt Jones clued it—on local birds like the **NENE**, the [State bird of Hawaii]. **SADFACE** [:(].

Because of its habitat, the [Hawaiian goose], or **NENE** ("nene," "nēnē, or "ne-ne") is the [Aloha State bird], but since *nene* means [Baby, in Barcelona], it can also be seen as [New Mexican]. Found only in Hawaii, the nene evolved to have less webbing between its toes—helpful for walking over dry, rugged lava fields, but leaving it susceptible to certain nonnative predators. "Nene" is not pronounced like **MEME**, but like **NAENAE**.

Thanks to that fad, **NAE**, which was long the [Lassie's refusal] equating to ["Fat chance, laddie"] (discussed in chapter 3) is now [When repeated, a hip-hop dance].

While the dance craze has died down (at least outside of puzzles), the **NENE** is making a comeback: Down to just 30 birds in 1952, conservation efforts have helped boost their population to 2,500. Nevertheless, it remains the [Rarest state bird] and the world's rarest goose.

Speaking of **NOMS**, the **LUAU** is the [Hawaiian shindig] that's part [Pig-out party?], part [Beach ball?]. It takes its name from *lu'au*, the leaves of the **TARO** plant, whose root is the [Poi source] used to prepare squid or chicken and served in countless crosswords.

That other [Polynesian staple] of puzzles, **POI**, is a [Slightly fermented baked dish] eaten like all [Fare at a luau]: as [Finger food?].

In fact, the [Taro root paste] is a [Dish classified as one-, two-, or three-finger in terms of consistency].

A clue for **LEI** like [Hula hoop?] could also have solvers putting a finger to their lips as they try to put a finger on the [Island ring?] that moonlights as a [Hawaiian band?]. And when it's said that [It'll ring your neck], they're not kidding, as roundabout clues for **LEI** like [String of islands?] and [One that's HI-strung?] could also ring true for **UKE**. And while **LEI** can string solvers along as [Leaves in a hot state?], the clue can also brew up **TEA** (to be served in chapter 10).

UKE [Mandolin kin], [Wahine's strings], [It might be picked for a song]

OKAY Corral
Oklahoma, Oral Hygiene, and Nabokov's [Pretty Good] Novels

A [Neat] clue for **OKAY** is ["Fine by me"], but an editor might [Greenlight] one like [Sound], delaying solvers until they finally ["Got it!"]. Even so, they still might wonder ["What the hell"]?

OKAY ["Capisce?"], [So-so], [Allow], [C-worthy], ["If you say so"], ["I guess that makes sense..."] *(See also chapter 1)*

In 2014, Stanley Newman prolixly saw the [Copacetic] term as a [Word that can be a noun, verb, adjective, adverb, or interjection]. That's [Not too shabby]!

There's no disputing that **ENID**, [Oklahoma's "Wheat Capital"], is [An OK city]. Though when they see that last clue, crossword solvers in that **OKLA** city of 50,000 probably say **OKAYOKAY**, ["Enough already"]. (Puzzles have so far refrained from referencing the 500-person town of Okay, OK, named in 1919 to honor its local manufacturer, O.K. Trucks.)

OKLA [Sooner St.], [Short musical?], [Enid's home]

ENID also appears as the [Oklahoma city named for a Tennyson character], referencing [Geraint's wife], the famously patient [Lady of Arthurian legend]. For a name meaning "spirit," "soul," or "life," it's a shame it's shared by two children's authors whose legacies are tarnished by their antisemitism: Enid [Bagnold, the writer] of the 1935 children's classic *National Velvet*, and Enid [Blyton who created the "Noddy" series].

Oral Roberts University is about 100 miles west of Enid, in **TULSA**. Often squeezed to **ORU**, the school was founded by the aptly named televangelist **ORAL** Roberts. Students there surely excel at the [Kind of test whose answers can't be erased], but there's no word on how good they'd be at crosswords.

Two hours north of ORU is **ADA**, the [Oklahoma city] in [Boise's county]. As an acronym, **ADA** can be another tooth pick: It can be the [Org. with an oral fixation?], the American Dental Association, though today it's more often accessible as the [Civil rights legis. of 1990], the Americans with Disabilities Act.

Add another **ADA** or two to the list: Lord Byron's daughter, the 19th-century mathematician Ada [Lovelace, of early computing]— whose name endures as a [Coding language named after the creator of the first computer program]—and the [Nabokov title heroine] from *Ada, or Ardor: A Family Chronicle*. That's a lot of **ADAS**, even excluding [Some prosecutors, for short] ("ADAs," "assistant district attorneys").

Nabokov was likely aware of his contribution to crosswordese, as he felt such **ARDOR** for crosswords that he helped popularize them in Russia. Indeed, he loved word games, puns, and puzzles of all sorts and worked them into many of his novels—though it was specifically **LOLITA** [About whom Nabokov said, "She was like the composition of a beautiful puzzle—its composition and its solution at the same time."].

OTOE and **OTO** are used interchangeably for the [Great Plains tribe] or its members, the [Speakers of Chiwere], a Siouan language. Their name for the Platte River, *Ñí Brásage* (literally, "flat water") became "Nebraska." Besides being the [Palindromic Indian], **OTO**

is an [Ear opening] as the [Ear prefix] "oto-." But listen up: A four-letter [Plains native] can double as either **OTOE** or **CREE**.

OLE, as "olé," is a [Two-syllable cheer] that's a [Cry to a toreador]. Nearer to home, the answer works as a monosyllabic solution to [Like the Opry?] and [Oxford Miss?] (as in "Ole Miss," nickname of the University of Mississippi).

Combine **OTO** and **OLE** to get the [" Laurence of Arabia" star Peter] **OTOOLE**, whose wife, Siân Phillips, appeared in the 1969 adaptation of Nabokov's novel, *Laughter in the Dark*. Belying its title, the film was hardly a **HOOT**. **OTOH** ("on the other hand"), critics tended to like it.

CREE [Saskatchewan native], [Native Canadian], [Largest First Nations group]

OLE [World Cup cry], [Flamenco shout], [Cheer for a matador], ["Rah!"], ["Bravo!"], [Spanish root word?], [Fan belt?]

HOOT [Small amount], [Darn], [Riot], [Stadium sound]

OTOH [Texter's "Then again..."], [However brief?], [Texting alternative?]

Tour Utah by UTE
[Beehive State people] and Places

After perplexity and triumph, **UTAH** is likely the most common state to appear in puzzles, at least in its entirety. Yes, the [Beehive State] will keep solvers busy—[Its motto is "Industry"], after all—as they try to wrap their heads around which [One of the Four Corner states] is a [Hexagonal state], a [Young state] (thanks to Brigham), and a [Jazz club site?] (thanks to the NBA team).

A **UTAHN** judge may have been more suspicious of the defendants' story in *My Cousin Vinny*: Why would they head to **UCLA** for school and not the University of Utah if they were, in fact, two Utes?

When not referring to a [Salt Lake City collegian], **UTE** could be a "getaway" car, like a [4 × 4] as a [Sport ___] utility vehicle.

Originally, a **UTE** was a [Western Amerind] or their language. The [Great Basin people] are a [Tribe with a state named after it], but it's not their own name for themselves. The **AMERIND UTES** called themselves *núuuchi-u* ("the people").

UTES are called [Trojan foes] because the Utah collegians sometimes play **USC**. But it's thought that both "Ute" and "Utah" derived from the name the **UTES**' [Apache foes] used for them, meaning "those higher up," or "mountain top diggers," which the Spanish

UTAHN [Jazz fan?]

UCLA [The Bruins of the NCAA.], [Pac-12 team], [Arthur Ashe's alma mater], [USC rival]

UTE [Pac-12 athlete], [Beehive State Indian], [Western tribe], [Colorado native], [Explorer or Navigator, briefly]

AMERIND (from "American Indian") [Ute or Cree], [Crow, for one], [Delaware or Missouri]

USC as "University of Southern California," [The Trojans of the NCAA], [Trojans' home], or as "University of South Carolina," [NCAA's Gamecocks]

took up and recorded as *Yuta*. In a way, the Utes had as much say in Utah's name as bees had in calling it the **BEEHIVE** State.

Forty miles outside of **SLC** ("Salt Lake City," home of **LDS**, the Church of "Latter Day Saints"), students in **PROVO** attend **BYU**, [Mitt Romney's alma mater, for short]. Romney succeeded another BYU **GRAD**, **ORRIN** [Hatch in the Senate], not to be confused with the [City on Utah Lake], **OREM**.

LEHI, another [City on Utah Lake], is named not for [Where Samson slew the Philistines] but for a [Prophet in the Book of Mormon]. Sip some **NEHI** and then zip up to **ALTA**, the [Aptly named ski town in Utah] since *alta* is Spanish for "high."

MOAB is a [Utah city near Arches National Park] named for the [Land where Moses died]. It's just south of a petroglyph site called **SEGO** Canyon, itself named for the [Western lily] that lined its walls and became [Utah's state flower]. Unlike the state, the name of the lily does come from a word the Utes used. In fact, they and other people indigenous to the area used the [Edible lily] for porridge.

IDA Never Thought of That!
Mining Rich Answers from the [Gem St.]

The rich deposits of **OPAL**, **JADE**, **TOPAZ**, and **AGATE** have made Idaho the Gem State, but digging through clues for **IDA** reveal it as much more than just a [Potato source: Abbr.].

Speaking of spud states, [Mount ___] **IDA** is the [Site of the mountain cave where Zeus was reared]. [Crete's highest mountain] shares its name with another important [Mount in Greek myth], a [Mountain near ancient Troy]. So [Either of two peaks in Greek myth] might emerge more fully formed as **MTIDA**.

From the head of Zeus (or rather Jupiter) sprang **IDA** Minerva Tarbell's middle name. Tarbell's life likely would have pleased the goddess of wisdom, especially as they both famously supported trade, strategy, and, in a sense, defensive warfare. The 1904 book by [Tarbell of the muckraker movement], *The History of the Standard Oil Company*, is still celebrated for contributing to Standard

Oil's dissolution and the formation of the **FTC** ("Federal Trade Commission").

Tarbell, remembered also for her 1912 book, *The Business of Being a Woman,* is less often recalled in puzzles than her contemporary, another pioneer in journalism, **IDA** [___ B. Wells]. Born enslaved, Wells fought tirelessly as a leading suffragist and civil rights pioneer, authoring the influential pamphlet *Southern Horrors: Lynch Law in All Its Phases* and co-founding the NAACP.

Wells went unmentioned in *Times* clues for **IDA** until 1994, but times have changed—or at least the *Times* has: Of the answer's 14 appearances in the paper's puzzle in 2020, Wells was the Ida **IDED** ("IDed," "identified") six times.

Two other women named **IDA**, though rarely alluded to in clues, could well have also written about being in business as women.

- A contemporary of Tarbell and Wells, ballerina and impresaria **IDA** Rubinstein was a standout at the Ballets Russes before launching her own company, becoming the [Ballerina Rubinstein who commissioned Ravel's "Boléro"]. Despite its name, the Ballet Russes was a touring company based in Paris and never performed in either place that's [Moscow's location: Abbr.]: **IDA** or **RUS**.

- The trailblazing mid-20th-century actor, writer, director, and producer **IDA** [Lupino of "High Sierra"] had a brilliant half-century career in film that's hard to match in quality or quantity. Her fame is evident from a 1995 *Times* clue: [Miss Lupino]. When she died later that year, her **OBIT** in the paper made much more than [Passing mention?] of the "earthy, intelligent movie actress who created a luminous gallery of worldly wise villainesses, gangster's molls and hand-wringing neurotics."

It's apt then that **IDA** probably derives from the Germanic *id,* meaning "work" or "labor." The **IDS** we associate with **FREUD** point to the Latin *id* ("it," as seen in *id est,* discussed in chapter 1). Of course, when arriving at a party with either of these **IDS**, the Germanic or the Freudian, it's best that [They're checked at the door].

IDEA [Bean sprout?], [Noodle concoction?], [Head light?], [Piece of mind?], [What's produced upstairs?]

The man who gave Idaho its name was a piece of work himself. A prospector posing as an elected official, he suggested "Idaho," claiming it meant "Gem of the Mountain." He eventually admitted he made up the **IDEA**, basing it on the name of a girl named Ida. Still, you've got to admit: <u>**IDA**</u> yields a mountain of gems.

[Get a lode of this!]
<u>ORE</u> Something in That Vein

TATER [Spud], [Home run, slangily], [Four-bagger], [Idaho, e.g.]

TOT [Add (up)], [Small fry], [Little squirt]

ORE [Mine find], [Smelter input], [Source of iron], [Bauxite, e.g.], [Valuable rock], [Metal resource], [Metal container], [Deposit of a sort], [___-Ida (French fry producer named for the contiguous states where it operates)]

GEM [Beauty], [Something cut by a lapidary], [It has its setting], [Peach]

OIL [Kind of change], [De-squeak], [Lucky strike?], [It can be crude], [A little squirt?]

AURA [Mystique], [Atmosphere], [Vibe], [Psychic's reading material?], [Something about you]

KRONE [Danish dough?], [Norwegian money]

KRONA [Capital of Sweden?], [Capital of Iceland?]

LODE [Bank deposit?], [Rock group], [Silver streak?], [Big deposit], [Mother ___]

A "final word" on <u>**IDA**</u>: It also appears as [Half a frozen potato brand], Ore-Ida, in clues like [Ore-___]. The **TATER** to Ida's **TOT**, **ORE** similarly gets cooked up as [Half a frozen foods brand] or [___-Ida].

ORE is malleable enough to be both a [Heavy metal rock band?] and [Iron man's quest]—which in this case is [A miner matter?]. And even if the [Gold band?] is [Stuff of mine]—if [You can dig it], you too can claim [Mine! All mine!]

You can probably also dig how many of the same clues can work for **GEM**, **OIL**, or **ORE**. Yeah, [It can be hard to process], especially when it's [Molybdenite, for molybdenum] and [It's searched for in a rush].

Clues can also strike [Pay dirt] for <u>**ORE**</u> as a [Vein pursuit], [Vein glory?], [Seamy stuff], and [Nickel in a pocket?], all referring to places whence [It can be picked].

Along the same lines, a **VEIN** can be [Silver streak?] or [Strike zone] besides the [Thin blue line] that's a [Way to a man's heart?].

Though retaining its golden <u>**AURA**</u> from the original Latin, **ORE** is markedly less precious as "øre" ([1/100 of a krone] in Denmark and Norway) or as "öre" (the same [Fraction of a krona] in Sweden). In either **KRONE** or **KRONA**, the singular <u>**ORE**</u> doubles as the plural, piled in pockets as [Some Scandinavian coins].

A <u>**LODE**</u> is an [Ore source] that's a particularly [Rich supply]. Like a [Vein], a lode courses underground, connecting it to the obsolete definition of "lode"—meaning "way" or "path"—still shining as "lodestar."

An **ADIT** is a [Mine entrance], from the Latin *aditus* ("entrance"). The Latin unearths the meaning, combining "coming" and "going": from *ad-* ("to") and *itus* ("going"), revealing its connection to that [Old Roman way], **ITER**. **ADIT** was once frequently entered cross-wordese, but everyone had it with its obscurity, so puzzles have pretty much given the [Shaft's end] the shaft.

The same can't be said for **ASSAY**. Clues tend to [Appraise] it as [Analyze, as ore], but it may [Test one's metal?] as a not very easy [Chemistry exam?] that could lead to a [Mineralogist's job].

Perhaps we can't all discern **GOLD** from **FOOLSGOLD**, but prospectors for answers are often tested on the difference between a **CARAT**, which is a [Gem weight unit], and a **KARAT**, the [Gold purity measure]. If they fail, they get the **STICK**—which is to say they get **STUCK**.

ASSAY [Purity test], [Lab test], [Composition test], [Test], [Test for gold content, say]

GOLD [Au], [500,000-selling, as an album], [Klondike bar ingredient?], [Rush order], [Standard material?], [Rumpelstiltskin's output]

FOOLSGOLD [Pyrite], [Forty-niner's offensive material?], [FeS2, commonly]

CARAT [Gem weight unit], [200 milligrams], [A little over three grains], [100 points, to a jeweler], [A point is a division of one], [Solitaire unit]

KARAT [Unit of purity], [Gold standard], [One of 24 for pure gold], [K, at Kay]

STICK [Linger], [Manual], [Not automatic]

STUCK [Lodged], [Fast], [Nonplussed]

Chapter 4 Puzzle: "Way to Go!"

ACROSS

1 Catch on
4 Glug some grog, maybe
10 With 1-Across, harsh reply to the driver's request that may prove prophetic
14 Carpenter's scraping tool
15 Big band leader Tommy
16 Cooking sub in a tub
17 *1 in California, for one
19 "Giant" writer Ferber
20 October option that beats a trick
21 Lagers whose bottles once came with blue ribbons around them
23 Simba's feathered advisor
25 CC on an email, say
28 Shark preserved in formaldehyde, e.g.
29 Here, to Pierre
30 *The Autobahn in Germany, for one
32 Sneaks made by the company once known as Blue Ribbon Sports
35 L.A. area
36 Delete
39 Powdered wigs
43 Words before "the mill," "the place," or "bad luck"
45 Titular love interest played by Renée Zellweger in a Jim Carrey comedy

46 *Means of entering 1 in California or the Autobahn in Germany
51 TV's "Science Guy"
52 Parts of some wings around the collar?
53 In Disney's "Winnie the Pooh," he says "If it is a good morning, which I doubt."
54 Cracked open, as a door or window
55 Sloppy sort of bed
57 Former NPR host Hansen
59 Where the beef was an apple?
60 Driver's request
65 Laughlin who went from "Full House" to the big house
66 "The Real Slim Shady" rapper
67 Quibble to pick
68 With 1-Across, harsh reply to the driver's request that might be good advice
69 They're juiced
70 Car feature that will do each of the starred answers in order to provide 60-Across

DOWN

1 Driver's need to go from E to F?
2 Summer hours in Orlando
3 Sauce on a gyro
4 ___ fixe
5 That's the spirit!
6 Cosmetic injections in fellows' faces
7 School inits. in Terra Haute
8 Throw some chips in the pot
9 Small end of a telescope
10 Leopold's co-defendant in 1920s crime
11 "A rolling stone gathers no moss," e.g.
12 Popular Nissan
13 Like socks warmed by a campfire
18 ___ TV, cable network airing many reality shows
22 Comedian Aziz
23 Fans' mag
24 Drug to drop
26 Roman goddess of plenty
27 It helps set the scene
31 Speak drunkenly
33 Raison d'___
34 Drunk as a skunk
37 Like Andre Agassi when he won the 1994 US Open
38 Redcoat supporter
40 "Community" star who's a licensed physician
41 Ireland's best-selling New Age artist
42 Prognosticator

44 ___ fighter (term used by Allied pilots for a UFO in WWII)
46 Grandma in Panama
47 It's usually worn by someone who's naked
48 Something with just one shutter
49 Woman's name derived from "Charles"
50 Winter weather windshield solvent
54 Singer DiFranco
56 Have ___ (glug grog on the sly, maybe)
58 They offer pay back?
61 "If you ask me," in a text
62 Mr. Van Winkle
63 A little bite from a salty dog, or a little swig of a salty dog
64 Namesakes of James and Charles, in Monopoly

Chapter 5

AROUND the World
in 80 Ways [Or so]

It may have been a coincidence that the first crossword appeared in a paper called *The World*, but it was no coincidence that the *Times*'s first crossword appeared as America entered World War II. As the paper brought news of the war **HOME**, it added the crossword as a useful, diversionary escape. Yet the world seeped into the grid, often in the form of geography. Though less familiar to Americans now, those answers still dot the grid. As it turns out, the escape crosswords offer is not from the world, but into it.

So let's tour **EUR**—which I hear is [Where It.'s at]—and explore the Middle East while we're **ATIT**. (After all, crosswords are probably the cheapest [Way to go?].)

Oh, and just in case anyone starts feeling homesick, we'll stop for wine and Starbucks along the way. **AMERICANO**, anyone?

HOME [Diamond plate], [Heart's place], [Last word of "The Wizard of Oz"]

EUR [Port. is part of it], [Where It. is], [UK locale], [Asian leader?]

ATIT [Working hard], [Arguing]

AMERICANO [Espresso with hot water], [Yanqi], [One of the turiste in Roma], [Cocktail with sweet vermouth], [First drink ever ordered by James Bond]

[Wild bunch?]
French Rivers Seeded as FLOWERS

MAL [Ill, in Lille], [Not bien], [Start to practice?], [Start to adjust?]

MAL can mean [Evil, to Yvonne]—as in Charles Baudelaire's *Les Fleurs du Mal* (literally, "The Flowers of Evil")—or "unwell" as in *mal de mer* ("sea-sickness"). The [Bad: Prefix] in English ("mal-") may seem a [Bad way to start] this section, but it's an [Adroit introduction] for some French answers that appear [Wrong at the start?].

LILY [Easter bloom], [Valley girl?], [Kind of pad]

LIS [Lille lily], [French bloom], [Sue Grafton's "___ for Lawless"]

FRANCE [Author Anatole], [Nice place?], [Tours site]

The French word for **LILY** sprouts from the clue [Fleur-de-___] **LIS**, (literally, "flower of the lily"), the gold heraldic symbol associated with the royal arms of **FRANCE**.

Yet the flower depicted in the fleur-de-lis is not a **LILY**, but a stylized iris: a plant native not to France but North America, though it goes by the same name in English and French. Very likely, the symbol's name was influenced both by the lily's popularity and its resemblance to the irises found by the [French-Belgian border river] called the **LYS** (or Leie, to the Dutch).

LYS [Lille lily], [River at Ghent]

Indeed, the symbol associated with France is also rendered as the fleur-de-lys. So [Fleur-de-___] might blossom into either **LIS** or **LYS**.

LIS and **LYS** make sense as [French flower], but less clear is how the constructor Chet Currier delivered the same clue—[French flower]—for the **OISE**, a [Seine tributary]. To arrive at the answer, solvers had to read "French flower" as "French flow-er"—only then could they say "Oh, **ISEE**." In this context, when **LYS** answers the clue [French flower], it might refer to either the *lys* or the Lys. (While *lys* and Lys are homonymous—i.e., they have different meanings but are pronounced and spelled the same—"flower" and "flower" are heteronymous: They have different meanings and pronunciations but are spelled identically.)

OISE [River of northern France], [French river or department], [Van Gogh's "L'Église d'Auvers-sur-___"]

ISEE ["Gotcha"], [Neutral response from a therapist], ["Mm-hmm, ..."], [[Nodding]]

These five-letter French "flowers" are worth differentiating:

SEINE [Left Bank river], [Paris divider], [Net with sinkers]

- It's mucky work wading through [Flower of Paris] or [Creator of banks in Paris?] to seize the **SEINE**. But as a seine is also a [Fishing net] used in trawling, it might be snagged as a [Catcher in the Rhine?].

- Following a [Rhône tributary] can put one on the path of the **ISERE** (Isère) or the **SAONE** (Saône).
- The **RHONE** (Rhône), which passes through and is the [Primary outflow of Lake Geneva], continues west to **LYON**, where it's fed by the Saône. From there, the **RHONE** [River painted by van Gogh] one starry night curves south past **ARLES**—another [Setting for many van Gogh paintings]—to the Mediterranean.
- River cruises travel [France's longest river], the **LOIRE**, though [Tours can be seen on it] also because it bisects the city of **TOURS** before emptying into the Bay of Biscay near Nantes.

Turning our attention back to the northern tip of the country, in the lowlands near Lille we can see two of the most infamous examples of crosswordese geography:

- **YPRES** is a small [French/Belgian river] but better known as the [Belgian city sometimes mispronounced "Wipers"] (correctly more like "EE-prə"). It was decimated as a [WWI battle site] in 1914, 1915, and 1917.
- The **YSER** is another [French/Belgian river] and a [1914 battle site]. In 1914, the Belgians opened the sluices along this larger [Belgian river to the North Sea] to flood the region, successfully thwarting the advancing Germans. Puzzles have historically overflowed with the river—hitting a high-water mark of 16 appearances in *Times* grids in 1993—though Shortz has managed to **STEM** the tide.

LILLE, [Charles de Gaulle's birthplace], lies to the south, on the French side of the Lys. The similarity between "Lys" and "Lille" is just a coincidence: While the **ROOT** of "lily" can be dug up in an old Egyptian word for flower, "Lille" springs from the Old French *l'Isle* ("the Island").

Just as English has mostly deserted "isle" for "island," French has moved from *isle* to *île*. All this island-hopping is great for puzzles. **ISLE** beguiles with wiles like [Key], [Cay], [Dot on a map], or

ISERE [Grenoble's river], [French Alps river]

SAONE [River to Lyon], [River of eastern France]

RHONE [French wine valley], [Avignon's river], [River through Lyon], [River with its source in a Swiss glacier], [Some Swiss banks?]

LYON [City on the Rhone], [French city historically known for its silk]

ARLES [City on the Rhone], [Provence city], [Where van Gogh lost his ear]

LOIRE [French wine valley], [Tours divider], [River of Orleans]

TOURS [Balzac's birthplace], [Does gigs], [Military stints], [Navy hitches], [Plays around?]

STEM [Academic acronym], [Arise (from)], [Check], [Marijuana discard], [Bush supporter?]

ROOT [Ginger, e.g.], [Two, for four], [Part of an underground network?], [Hair piece?]

[Bikini, e.g.]. One wonders if John Donne, who wrote ["No man is an ___"] *isle*, considered that [Man is one].

ILE [Elba, to Napoleon], [French vacation spot], [Project completion?], [Infant's rear?]

While **ILE** may work literally as a [Text addition] in English, the French makes it a [L'eau land] (*eau* being "water") or a [Key for Debussy?].

KEY [Anthem author], [Opener], [+ and = share one], [Board member?], [Answer sheet], [Enter or Delete, e.g.], [E or G., e.g.], [Entrance requirement, often], [Islet]

The **KEY** to getting that last clue's answer on your [Answer sheet] is to see the "key" as an [Islet] in Florida, like [West, for one].

But use care as you approach a three-letter [Islet]: In the Caribbean, it's called a **CAY**. And Donne would have known that any such [Isle] in the Thames is termed an **AIT**. Archived under A with **ADIT**

CAY [Low sandy island], [Coral island]

as arch-crosswordese increasingly absent, **AIT** ain't quite done, but

AIT [River islet], [British isle], [Part of the conjugation for "avoir"]

it's been tamed and largely cast away.

The Spanish **ISLA** is land like [Cuba, por ejemplo], *o* (Spanish for "or") [Trinidad o Tobago].

ISLA [Madonna's "La___ Bonita"], [Actress Fisher], [Mallorca, e.g.]

The French **LAC** is a [Body of eau] like [Ontario or Supérieur] or [Fond du ___, Wisc.]. Alternately, **LAC** can cause a sticky situation as a [Sealing wax ingredient] made of an [Insect's resinous secretion] collected from trees. So it's both botanically and etymologically the [Basis for shellac] (literally, to "shell with lac").

Shelled and then some, the [Historic town on the Vire] in Normandy, **STLO**, was a [Town almost destroyed in the D-Day invasion]. The title of a postwar article by Samuel Beckett established Saint-Lô as [France's so-called "Capital of the Ruins"]. Another post-war work by Beckett established **GODOT** as a [Title character not requiring an actor], a [Show no-show], or [What some waiters never see?].

[Track Down] a Nantes-er
Verne, Bly, and How to FIND Nemo and Dory

ISSUE [Printing], [Release], [Offspring], [Time piece?]

PIXAR [Company Steve Jobs once owned] *(note that a fruit can be the answer of this clue's eye)*

FILMS [Shoots], [Flicks], [Thin coats]

Alongside [Henry IV's Edict of ___] **NANTES** in 1598, the city's other famous **ISSUE** was its 1828 son, ["From the Earth to the Moon" writer] Jules **VERNE**, who, like **PIXAR**, could be [Nemo's creator]. Verne's pioneering **SCIFI** stories, besides taking up plenty of [Space on a bookshelf?], have birthed spinoffs and **FILMS**, untold [Future works?], many crossword answers, and even real-life imitators.

For instance, Verne inspired an intrepid venture by the [Pioneering journalist Nellie] **BLY**. Bly had already made a name for herself as the [Nellie who wrote "Ten Days in a Mad-House"], for which she feigned insanity to witness the deplorable conditions inside an insane asylum. As a follow-up, she took to the skies in a daring stunt emulating Phileas **FOGG**, Verne's [Fictional circumnavigor] as the ["Around the World in 80 Days" protagonist].

Despite her **STOPS**—which included literally dropping in on Verne in his adopted hometown of **AMIENS** (and presumably sharing some wine [Somme place]) and later buying a **PET** monkey when alone in Singapore—she completed the circumnavigation in just 72 days, setting a world record and turning **BLY** into a [Real-life Fogg].

STOPS [Stations], [Local listings], [Knocks off]

PET [Favorite], [Darling], [Bad mood], [Lady, but not the Tramp], [___name], [Boo, e.g.], [You name it]

The four-letter name of the [Verne hero] in *Twenty Thousand Leagues Under the Sea*, Captain **NEMO**, is Latin for "no one." No one worked, in a way, for Odysseus, who said his name was *Outis* ("Nobody" in Ancient Greek), to outwit the Cyclops Polyphemus.

Verne's and Homer's heroes are joined by the [Disney clown fish] as ones who can quote Emily Dickinson in saying, "I'm Nobody! Who are you?" To whom [Winsor McCay's "Little" one], the eponymous 20th-century classic comic character from *Little Nemo in Slumberland*, could reply, "I'm Nobody too!"

In one 2005 puzzle, constructor Lynn Lempel built a puzzle whose themers were **UNEMOTIONAL**, **MNEMONICDEVICES**, and **OPPORTUNEMOMENT**. Of course, in searching for those answers, solvers were also **FINDINGNEMO**.

UNEMOTIONAL [Not laughing or crying]

MNEMONICDEVICES ["Every good boy does fine" and others]

OPPORTUNEMOMENT [Best time to act]

The name of [Nemo's forgetful friend], **DORY**, lacks a rich literary legacy, but as a type of [Flat-bottomed boat] that's a [Small fishing vessel], it's useful in finding fish. A dory could even find a dory, as the name also refers to several types of fish. One is the **ROSY** dory, befitting the [Optimistic] nature of the Pixar character whose forgetfulness makes her believe things are generally [Hunky-___] **DORY**. Yet Disney's Dory doesn't really resemble a dory, but rather a blue **TANG**: a name that might have suited her better as [Pep], [Brio], [Zip] and [Zest].

TANG [Piquancy], [Fervor], [Punch], [Gusto], [Oomph], [Bite, so to speak]

At any rate, it all goes around in fate-y ways as another type of fish, the John Dory, was described in *An Antarctic Mystery*, written by no one other than Jules Verne.

Aare You Eger to Detect a Strange ODER?

Swiss and [German River] Names

BERN [Capital of Switzerland], [Alpine capital], [Capital founded in 1191], [Second-most populous Swiss canton, after Zurich]

KYIV [Ukraine's capital, to Ukrainians]

OSLO [Norway's biggest city], [Nobel Institute city], [World capital on a fjord], [1952 Winter Olympics host], [Capital at the center of Czechoslovakia?]

EURO [Continental currency], [100-cent unit], [French bread?], [Disney leader?], [Capital of Latvia?], [What has made some people miss the mark?], [French bread?], [Tip of Italy?]

FRANC [Old French bread?], [Part of a Swiss roll?], [Davos currency], [Former French capital], [Mali money]

RHINE [Locale of some Swiss banks], [Basel's river], [Cologne's rive], [Bonn's river], [Lorelei's river], [Where to find Swiss banks?], [Main outlet]

RUHR [Region in western Germany]

ESSEN [German steel city], [German city in the Ruhr valley]. [European city whose name means "eat"]

The four-letter [Swiss river to the Rhine], the **AARE**, occasionally loses a quarter of its length and appears as the **AAR**. Following its meager beginnings as an [Alpine stream], the Aare gains currency to become a [Swiss bank depositor?]. But Aare might also be a spendthrift, since it runs quickly through the [Swiss capital], **BERN**—which itself grows to **BERNE** as the [Swiss capital, to French speakers].

A clue like [Capital of Europe] can really cause solvers to feel the burn, since other four-letter contenders are **KYIV** (Russians call the [Capital of the Dnieper] **KIEV**), **OSLO**, and two answers seen earlier: **RIGA** and **ROME**. Joining that last answer as another four-letter [Capital of Italy] is **EURO**.

While many Swiss shops accept the Euro, the coin of the realm of the cantons remains the Swiss **FRANC**. Even if [It no longer circulates around the Seine], it's still [Liechtenstein's currency] and a [Common African monetary unit].

Like the Aare (which feeds it) and the Rhône, the **RHINE** originates in the Swiss Alps. Eventually, it bathes its namesake [German wine valley] with the [Eau de Cologne] before its dissolution as a [North Sea feeder].

With its two "ars," it's apt that the **RUHR** follows the Aare's lead as another [River to the Rhine]. Its name also refers to [Germany's largest urban area], the Ruhr Valley, the coal and industrial area that's home to **ESSEN**.

Flowing out of the former Czechoslovakia are the writings of Karel Čapek, whose [1921 sci-fi play], **RUR** (*R.U.R.*, an acronym for words translating to "Rossum's Universal Robots"), was the [Play that introduced the word "robot"].

Čapek credited his brother Josef with creating the term **ROBOT**, derived from the Czech *robota*, referring to the forced labor done by a **SERF**. "Serf" is grounded in the Latin *servus*, which still serves as a root in many English words. With puzzles liberated from **ESNE**, **SERF** is the [One doing the lord's work?] in crosswords now, though it shares the title of puzzledom's [Drudge] with **PEON**. Then again, even a crossword constructor probably feels like a [Worker who probably isn't paid enough]—to say nothing of those doing the solving.

ROBOT [Unpaid worker], [Man of steel?], [Metal worker?], [Many an Amazon "worker"], [Bomb squad member]

SERF [Drudge], [Manor occupant of yore], [Peon], [One making a feudal effort?], [Underclassman?]

PEON [Serf], [Lowly worker], [Grunt], [Low hand?]

[Down] the BLUE Danube
Eastern Europe and an Imre Who's [Dirty, in a way]

The southern **GER** city of **ULM** is famous as [Einstein's birthplace], but another European giant continually springs from just outside the town: the **DANUBE**, [Europe's second-longest river]. Tributaries of [Vienna's river] include the Inn River, making it [Inn's end].

Travelers following the Danube **OST** (*ost*, German for "east") **AUS** (*aus*, German for "out of") *Deutschland*, will enter the nation that's [Mozart's birthplace: Abbr.], not the nation [Where some things are really hopping?: Abbr.].

Further along its route, the Danube divides Slovakia from Hungary. In the cruciverse, 20th-century Hungarian history is a tale of two men named **IMRE**, a name whose possible connections to words like "bravery" or "home" are worth bearing in mind:

GER [Tongue of Jung: Abbr.]

DANUBE [Black Sea feeder], [It flows through four capitals], [European river through 10 countries], [Strauss subject], ["Blue" flower?]

OST [East: Ger.], [East, in Essen], [East of Germany?], [Where die Sonne rises]

AUS [Out of: Ger], [It. borders it]

- **IMRE** Nagy was prime minister of Hungary from 1953 to 1955, and again for two weeks following the Hungarian Revolution of 1956 (until the Soviets invaded, crushed the revolution, arrested Nagy, and eventually executed him). His bold opposition to the Soviets once earned him clues like [Hungarian hero ___ Nagy], but two revelations prove him unworthy of such acclaim. The "[Hungarian patriot Nagy]" had in fact joined the Soviet NKVD prior to WWII and denounced over 200 Hungarians, leading to their imprisonment and the deaths of at least 12. He also played a pivotal role in expelling an estimated 250,000 German speakers from Hungary—including many German Jews who'd survived the Holocaust—60,000 of whom are believed to have died as a result. So today his typical crossword bio is [Nagy of Hungarian history].

- Then there's **IMRE** Kertész: In celebrated novels like *Fatelessness*, the [2002 Literature Nobelist Kertész] described his seizure by Hungarian police at age 14 in 1944 and his subsequent experiences at Auschwitz and Buchenwald.

SLAV [Czech or Pole], [Pomeranian or Dalmatian], [John Paul II, for one]

CROAT [Zagreb resident], [Dalmatian, for one], [Tennis's Goran Ivanisevic, e.g.]

SERB [Belgrade native], [Tennis's Novak Djokovic, by birth], [Tesla, e.g.], [Certain Slav]

SSR [Lat. or Lith., once], [Map abbr. until 1991], [Georgia, once: Abbr.], [Old Russian letters?], [Red letters?]

ODESA and ODESSA [Major Ukrainian port known as the "Pearl of the Black Sea"]

TEX [It's between La. and NM], [Apt name for a Dallas cowboy?], [Handle on the range?], [Gore follower?]

URAL [Russian river], [Russian range], [Territory east of Ukraine on a Risk board], [River through southern Russia], [River through Kazakhstan]

ARAL [Name seen on the Kazakh/Uzbek border], [Sea whose Wikipedia article is written in the past tense], [Former sea that's now part desert]

Further downriver, the Danube separates **SLAV** from Slav: **CROAT** from **SERB**. Finally, it flows by Moldova and Ukraine— each of which was an **SSR**, [Cold War initials] for "Soviet Socialist Republic"—as it reaches the Black Sea.

The Danube reaches the Black Sea just southwest of **ODESA** [Where the Potemkin Steps are]—or were. Previously known as the Primorsky Stairs, they were renamed during the Soviet era to commemorate the 1917 mutiny dramatized in Sergei Eisenstein's classic film, *The Battleship Potemkin*. Following Ukraine's independence in 1991, the Primorsky name was restored. The city's Russian name, **ODESSA**, was taken by the [Texas oil city], probably because the **TEX** town's flatlands were thought to resemble Ukraine's very [Plain], [Treeless tract], or **STEPPE**.

To the east, the **VOLGA** is [Europe's longest river], but it's a mere streamlet in crosswords compared to another [Russian river to the Caspian], the **URAL**, the [Third longest river in Europe, after the Volga and Danube]. Its name, like its waters, originates in Russia's **URAL** [___ Mountains], likely quarried from an old word for "stone belt."

The Ural's brother in harms—at least for many crossword beginners—is the **ARAL** Sea, Kazakhstan's famously [Disappearing sea]. The Soviets' extensive irrigation system diverted its waters, reducing it to several small lakes with a total volume of just a tenth of the original. The [Name of what was once the world's second-largest saltwater lake] and fourth largest lake overall means "archipelago," linguistic remains of the [Sea once home to 1,100 islands]. Further evidence abides in the expanse that's replaced it, the Aralkum Desert (*kum* is "sand" in Turkic)—and the large ships now seen on "Aral Sea" tours stand afloat in its sand, anchored in the exposed seabed. Even though puzzles continue to anchor **ARAL** quite regularly in the grid, it's less frequent than it once was, making it a [Fading sea name] of puzzles too.

[Pisa party?]
ITALIAN Destinations and It.'s Wine

The **TIBER** river is a [View from Vatican City] in **ROMA**, [La Città Eterna]. Tourists also flock to [San ___] **REMO**, the Italian Riviera destination just across the border from **NICE**.

The name of the slanted **FONT** style called **ITAL** for short honors the homeland of its inventor, the Renaissance-era printer Aldo Pio Manuzio. For inpiration, Aldo might have taken the **ARNO** to the [Italian city you might be "leaning" toward visiting], **PISA**. The structure with a nearly four-degree tilt makes the [Birthplace of Galileo] a [City with a famous bell tower].

But don't let a four-letter [Leaning column] give you the wrong idea: It could just be another **OPED**. *(See page 35 for more along those lines.)*

The Italian town with the most famous bell tower in puzzles—and American literature—is **ATRI**, the [Abruzzi bell town] famous as [Longfellow's bell town] in "The Bell of Atri," published in *Tales of a Wayside Inn*. The poem's last line seems apt: "And this shall make, in every Christian clime / The Bell of Atri famous for all time." Or "crossword" clime, at least.

The [Piedmont wine town] of **ASTI** hails from the eponymous [Italian wine region] renowned for its [Italian bubbly], Asti Spumante. The Italian *spumante* is a generic term for any "sparkling wine."

Asti is associated with the **TURIN**-based company founded in the mid-19th century by businessman Alessandro **MARTINI** and

ROMA [Gypsy people], [Oblong tomato], [Capital of Italia]

NICE [Riviera resort], [Christmas list heading?], [Easy mate?], [Slow partner?], [Like guys who finish last?]

FONT [Times, e.g.], [Courier, e.g.], [Century, for one], [Word choice?]

ITAL [Stressed type: Abbr.], [Not this type?: Abbr.], [Right-leaning: Abbr.]

ARNO [Florence's river], [Tuscan River]

PISA [Site to see a listing], [Tuscany tourist city]

TURIN [First capital of the kingdom of Italy], [Locale shrouded in mystery?]

MARTINI ["The only American invention as perfect as a sonnet," per H. L. Mencken]

PRAT [Rear end], [Something to fall back on?], [Kind of fall], [Nitwit, to a Brit]

CAB [Hotel waiter?], [Rainy day rarity], [One getting hailed on Broadway?]

ZIN [Fruity red wine, familiarly], [Red from Cali]

PINOT [Wine grape], [Champagne grape], [Red option]

UBER [Mobile app?], [Company whose business is picking up?],

WINE [Press release?], [Spirits in the cellar?], [Mass consumption?]

vintner Luigi Rossi. In the 1970s, Martini & Rossi—which may have influenced the naming of the cocktail that's a [Bond holding?]—bought the competing vermouth company, Noilly Prat, also named for its mid-19th-century founders. After too many martinis, anyone may be found on their **PRAT**.

Safest, then, to just call for a **CAB**: the one that's hailed as a [Hack], not the [Certain red wine, to connoisseurs]. A cab is also a [Semi-essential part?], referring to the driver's compartment of a semi-truck (as discussed *at length* in chapter 4).

In the mood for something else? Try any of the following, which all work as a [Cab alternative]: **ZIN**, **PINOT**, **UBER**, or **LYFT**.

There's a Greek vintage to the [Prefix meaning "wine"], **OENO**: It's the name of the [Greek goddess who could turn water into wine], and part of the name of Paris's wife, Oenone (literally, "**WINE** woman"), whom he jilted for Helen.

[Where one may place a tall order?]: STARBUCKS Pour-Overs to Pore Over

Coffee talk typically heard in Starbucks has filtered from the **CAFE**—a [Spot of tea] to find [Joe in Paris]—into the grid, even if the names don't quite add up:

☐ **TALL**: This [Ironically, small Starbucks size] is a [Kind of order] that's [Hard to believe].

☐ **VENTI**: The word for [Large, at Starbucks] is the [Italian 20]—which works perfectly as a hot [20-ounce coffee size]—yet a Venti Cold tops out at 24 fl. oz.

☐ **TRENTA**: This [Jumbo size at Starbucks] is literally a [Ridiculous Starbucks size], as the term

meaning [Thirty, in Turin] is a 31-fl.oz. pour in Starbucks.

In Starbucks' defense, *venti* and *trenta* also work in Italian as plurals, respectively used for "twenties" and "thirties." So, like a barista who's "twenty-ish," a drink's size may be "*venti*" if it's somewhere in the twenties.

Another [Tall order?] uses [Canvas for modern art?] to order a **LATTE**, a drink the color of perhaps crosswords' favorite hue, **ECRU**, the [Cream alternative] that gets heady as [Tiss-hue?], [Nude cousin?], or [Buff relative].

Oenone was an **OREAD**—a [Mountain nymph] who accompanied Artemis on her hunts—the most famous of whom was **ECHO**. "Oeno"—as seen in "oenophile"—echoes with **VINO**, not **WINO**.

[Places to call] to Make Rial Money
Middle East and African PORTS

The **RIAL** is a [Mideast currency] used as [Iranian currency], [Yemeni capital], and [Omani money]. From the Spanish *real* ("royal"), like the "**TREX**" it traces to the Latin **REX**, Latin for "king."

The [Arabian sultanate] and [Yemen neighbor] **OMAN** is often called [Muscat's land], referring to the **OMANI** capital city.

The [Algerian port] of **ORAN** (Berber for "lion") was the [Setting of "The Plague"] and the [Escape route city in "Casablanca"]. **NEMEA** is an [Ancient Greek valley] with its own leonine connections, as the [Setting of Hercules' first labor], [Where Hercules slew the lion].

Once the principal port of the [Oman neighbor] **YEMEN**, **MOCHA** became a [Coffee shop order] and then a [Shade of brown], all colored by the somewhat chocolaty [Arabian coffee] from the Moka bean native to the region and exported from the [Eponymous Yemeni seaport]. Modern mochas are made by adding chocolate to coffee, and now the [Main port of Yemen] is **ADEN**, which is serving as the temporary seat of the **YEMENI** government.

Four five-letter answers work for [African capital]:

- **SANAA** (or **SANA**): Inhabited for 2,500 years, the old city in [Yemen's capital] is a [UNESCO World Heritage Site on the Arabian Peninsula].
- **RABAT**: The [Capital of Morocco] since the nation's independence in 1955, it's the [African capital where Berber is spoken] as an official language alongside Arabic.
- **DAKAR**: [Senegal's capital] and largest city, located on the Atlantic, is the [Westernmost city on the African mainland].

ECHO [Oread in love with her own voice], [Agree with], [Second], [Amazon speaker], [Wave back?], [Return some calls?], [Off-the-wall answer?], [Bounce off the wall], ["Art is a delayed___": Santayana]

VINO [Chianti, in Chianti], [Veritas provider?], [Italian port?]

WINO [Lush], [One who might hail a cab?], [Grape nut?], [Port authority?]

TREX [Small-arms runner of years past?], [Sue in Chicago's Field Museum, e.g.]

REX [Latin king?], [Good name for a tow truck driver?]

OMANI [Saudi neighbor], [Rial spender], [Certain Arabian]

YEMEN [Aden's land], [Saudi Arabia neighbor], [Country where camel jumping is a sport]

ADEN [Mideast's Gulf of ___], [City where, according to legend, Cain and Abel are buried]

YEMENI [Saudi neighbor], [Arabian Peninsula native]

SANAA and **SANA** [World capital at 7,200 feet elevation], [Arabian peninsula capital], [Yemen's largest city]

- **TUNIS**: This [Arab capital] might be clued as an [African capital, lake, or gulf], since clues refrain from giving the answer away by mentioning Tunisia. The city is located on the west end of the lake; about 10 miles to the east, Carthage—now a wealthy suburb—abuts the gulf.

The [Largest city in Nigeria], **LAGOS** was an [African capital until 1991] and stands as [Africa's most populous city (21+ million)], so like a set of **LEGOS**, it has many [Blocks that interlock].

SADR [___ City, Iraq] is a Baghdad suburb whose original name, Al-Thawra, was changed to Saddam City by Saddam Hussein, who nevertheless allowed the district of a million Iraqis to collapse into disrepair. In the skies, Sadr (Arabic for "chest") is an apt name for the [Star in Cygnus] found at the intersection of the Northern Cross. Since 2003, the district has been called Sadr City to honor Sadeq al-Sadr, a **SHIA** ("partisan" in Arabic) cleric who openly defied Hussein.

It wasn't until 2019 that the *Times* broke its fast and first observed the [Holiday marking the end of Ramadan], **EID**, also known as Eid-al-Fitr ("Festival of Breaking the Fast"). Unsurprisingly fast, puzzles embraced the [Festival, in Arabic].

The [Mideast acronym] **OPEC** ("Organization of the Petroleum Exporting Countries") is an [International grp. founded in Baghdad in 1960] but based in Vienna since 1965, making it a [Europe-based grp. with no European members]. The current 13-member **BLOC** includes not only the likes of **IRAN** and **IRAQ** but Angola, Equatorial Guinea, and Venezuela.

The [Old Mideast inits.] **UAR** stand for "United Arab Republic." Formed in 1958, the [Short-lived Egypt-Syria fed.] led by Egypt's Gamal Nasser ended following the Syrian **COUP** in 1961. Egypt remained its only member until 1971, when it recouped the name "Egypt" for itself under Anwar **SADAT**.

SHIA [Second-largest branch of Islam], [Muslim minority], [Like the majority of Iraqis and Bahrainis], [Actor LaBeouf]

OPEC [Crude group?], [Grp. that knows the drill?], [Well-funded grp.], [Grp. whose members have reserves]

BLOC [Alliance], [Interest group], [United nations?], [League of nations], [Group], [Cartel]

IRAN [Neighbor of Turkey], ["Argo" setting], [Nation on the Gulf of Oman], [Shiraz locale], [Country that borders three "-stans"]

IRAQ [Neighbor of Turkey], ["The Hurt Locker" setting], [Modern-day home of where the biblical Abraham was born], [Where the Noah's Ark story is thought to have occurred, today], [Modern home of the ancient king Gilgamesh]

UAR [Former Mideast grp.]

COUP [Masterstroke], [Major success], [Upset with the government?], [Happy feat?]

SADAT [Begin's negotiating partner for peace], [1978 Nobel sharer], [Egyptian nobelman?]

Like OPEC, the **UAE** are [Mideast inits.] for an [Oil-rich fed.] The United Arab Emirates formed when six emirates, each with its own **EMIR**, confederated the day after Britain ended its administration of the area in 1971. A seventh emirate joined in 1972.

The UAE's capital is **ABU** [___ Dhabi]: literally, "Father of Gazelle," as *abu* is ["Father of," in Arabic]. The name harkens to a story told about a hunting party pursuing a gazelle on behalf of a sheik. During the chase, the hunters found an **OASIS**. The sheik decided to found a city there, and it's been ruled ever since by the fathers and sons of his dynasty, the house of Nahyan.

ABU is also familiar as [Aladdin's kleptomaniac sidekick], yet it takes a more dignified lead in Abu [___-Bakr (Muhammad's father-in-law)], who also served as Muhammad's advisor and successor.

Many names throughout the Middle East include the partner of *abu*, **IBN**—[Arabic for "son of"]—or its linguistic brother, **BEN**, [Hebrew for "son"].

Both words are **SEMITIC**, describing the [Language family that includes Arabic and Hebrew] and Aramaic and Maltese, as well as their speakers: [Arab, e.g.]. It can also be used for those [Like Jesus or Ashley Tisdale], both being [Jewish] (at least on their mothers' side).

DAR [___ es Salaam], Tanzania's largest city, is literally, "Place of Peace." **SHALOM**, like **SALAAM**, is a six-letter word for [Peace in the Middle East]. A salaam is also a [Long, deep bow].

DAR doubles as the acronym for the [Lineage-based women's org.], the "Daughters of the American Revolution." The historically conservative, [Historically inclined grp.] puts a lot of stock in bloodlines. Tougher clues are likely [To give: Sp.] less of a darn where *dar* comes from.

UAE [Neighbor of Oman: Abbr.], [Home of the Burj Khalifa, for short], [Country that has no rivers: Abbr.]

EMIR [Mideast VIP], [Eastern leader], [Commander, in Arabic], [Weighty Kuwaiti?], [Sheik's peer?]

OASIS [Haven], [Green spot], [Where to get a date?], [Spring for a drink?], [Break ground?]

IBN [Arabic name part], [Scottish : Mac :: Arabic : ___]

BEN [Jerry's partner], [Big thing in London?], [Him that's a Hur?]

DAR [Patriotic org. since 1890], [Flag-waving org.], ["God, home, and country" org.], [To give: Sp.]

SHALOM [Mideast peace talk?]

SALAAM [Arabic "peace"], [Big bow], [Respectful greeting]

Ooh, That [1962 Paul Anka hit]
ESOBESO and a Touch More Spanish

Crosswords love to point out the Spanish words for "that," "those," "this," and "these," each of which has two forms, depending on the gender of what's being described.

Grammatically, modifying words like these are known as "determiners," yet puzzles often eschew obvious clues—like [Those niñas] for **ESAS**—and leave it to solvers to determine which gender is intended. So a clue like [Those, in Toledo] might be **ESAS** or **ESOS**, essentially turning the grid into something of a gender reveal party.

Like a hug paired with a kiss, **ESO** often appears as ["___ Beso," Paul Anka hit], in which the **BESO** in question means [Kiss, in Spanish], just as you guessed so. Knowing that term adds a nice touch to another famous song title, Cole Porter's ["You'd ___ Nice to Come Home To"].

ESAS [Those muchachas]

ESOS [Those caballeros]

ESO ["___ es!" ("That's right!": Sp.], ["___ Beso"]

BESO [Show of amor], [Don Juan's kiss], [X, maybe, in Spanish]

ESTA [___ noche (tonight: Sp.)], [Spanish 101 verb], [Part of the Spanish conjugation of "to be"], [Are in Argentina], ["Como ___ usted?"]

ESTO ["Qué es ___ ("What's this?": Sp.)], ["___ perpetua" (Idaho's motto)], *See under Latin chapter 1*

ESTAS [Form of the Spanish for "to be"], ["Como ___?"]

Answer	Gender-ambivalent clues
ESA (f) and **ESO** (m)	[What that is, in Tijuana]
ESAS (f) and **ESOS** (m)	[Those, to Jose], [Just those of Juan's things?]
ESTA (f) and **ESTO** (m)	[It is, in Spain]
ESTAS (f) and **ESTOS** (m)	[These, in Cádiz], [These, overseas]

[Spanish interrogative]
QUE ["___ es eso?"] and the "Que" in "Que Sera, Sera"?

QUE [What's what in Mexico?]

QUE appears both north of the border as the [Can. province] south of it as *qué*, [Juan's "what"]. So it's capable of provoking a ["Huh?" from Jose] trying to figure out what—or who—is a [N.Y. neighbor]. But that's a quibbling concern compared to **QUE** [___ pasa?] in Doris Day's signature song from Hitchcock's *The Man Who Knew Too Much*, **QUE** ["___ Sera, Sera"].

SERA [Flu fighters], [Shot contents], [Bug zappers?]

PRESQUE [Almost, to Alain]

CHE [That, in Italian], [Michael on "SNL"], [Castro comrade], [Revolutionary icon], [Antonio Banderas, in "Evita"]

SERA, as *será*, can be the future of the Spanish *ser* ("to be"), making it [Will be in Spain?]. However, [Day's "will be"] can't be *será*, as the lyric doesn't make grammatical sense in Spanish.

As *sera*, the "**SERA**" Day serenaded audiences with night after night could mean [Evening in Venice], but *que* is not an Italian word. (However, it is **PRESQUE** the word "**CHE**," which is [What's what in Italy?].)

While the *que* could seem French or Latin, only a man who knows too much might know the phrase **QUESERASERA** ("Que sera, sera") turns out, of all things, to be English: an idiom meaning [What will be, will be] that predates even its use in Marlowe's *Doctor Faustus* 400 years ago. But its very appearance in that play might offer a new reading of the clue [Resigned response to tragedy].

Slightly more recognizable English helps inject puzzles with **SERA** as the plural for "serum," prescribed as [Hospital fluids], [Blood parts], or as Paula Ganache archly cast it, [Shot putters' needs?]—a clue that could put solvers to a [Shot-putter's activity]: **HEAVING**.

Considering all that, it's probably best to agree that whatever **SERA** ["Will be," in a Doris Day song] ["Will be," in a Doris Day song].

[Where El Niño Comes From]
More Essential SPANISH

Several other **SPANISH** words with meanings in other languages have become standards in crosswords.

COSA could be [Pedro's thing] or [Thing, for Italians], as in the [Cosa ___] **NOSTRA** ("our thing"), the autonym of the Sicilian mafia. Another big Sicilian thing is the [Tallest active volcano in Europe], Mount **ETNA**, the [Mount whose name means, literally, "I burn"], not to be confused with its namesake **AETNA**, the towering [Insurance giant acquired by CVS in 2018].

An **HORA** is [Part of un día], from the Latin *hōra* for "hour." Typically spinning counterclockwise is the Jewish [Dance done to "Hava Nagila"], whose name likely derives from the Greek *chorós*, for "dance."

One need not take Spanish for a [Month in Madrid] to know **MES** is an [Año part], or possess much French to see it as the [French possessive]. And **DIA** should be clear as [Day: Sp.]. But did you know **ENERO**, [El primer mes], is crosswords' favorite part of an **ANO**? ["I'll take that as ___"] "a no."

SPANISH [Language in which "foot" is "pie"], [Canary tongue]

COSA [It's a thing in Mexico]

ETNA [European smoker]

HORA [What often includes a chairlift?], [Dance around?], [Wedding ring?]

MES [Mayo, for one], [Julio is one], [My: Fr.]

DIA [Bit of Mayo?], [A day in Spain], [Domingo, e.g]

ANO *as "año"* [Year, in Spain], *as "ano"* [Year in Portugal], *as "an o"* [What makes God good?], *as "a no"* [So that's ___"]

Then again, ["Quién ___?"] **SABE** (Spanish for "Who knows?"). Probably not [Kemo ___] Sabe, as the nickname for the Lone Ranger likely derives not from Spanish but the Ojibwe *giimoozaabi* ("he who peeks"). Conversely, it's the Native American character **TONTO**—the [TV character who said "Help always come when people fight for right"]—whose name is [Spanish for "foolish"].

UNA is the indefinite [Spanish article] or identical [Italian article]. Indefinite may be the operative word, as clues like [Article in El Mundo] make it harder than it should be to get an [A in Spanish].

She's ABROAD [Overseas]
Foreign Feminine Pronouns

DONNA, the [Woman's name that means "woman" in Italian], derives from the Latin *domus*, "home." Its Portuguese paronym—a word sharing the same root as another—is **DONA**, a [Lady of Lisbon], the feminine counterpart of *dono*. As *doña*, the same answer works as the title equivalent to [Lady of Spain], related to the Spanish "sir," **DON**.

A **SRTA** (*Srta.*, short for *señorita*) is a [Mex. miss], but something **SORTA** funny can happen to a **SRA** (*Sra.*, short for *señora*), a [Spanish Mrs.], when a puzzle answer calls her a *doña*. Since puzzles dispense with accents, when *doña* arrives as an answer, she must **DOFF** the **TILDE** she usually dons. Reduced to **DONA**, *doña* the "Lady of Spain" is indistinguishable from *dona*, the Spanish "donut." It **KINDA** even transforms her spouse, as a **DONUT** is a [Coffee mate?].

The [Portuguese greeting] **OLA** (*olá*) is a [Rio hello]. Over the border, it's also a [Wave] in Spain—but the sort made by the sea. As the [Slangy suffix] "-ola," it's more of an [Informal ending].

However, **ALO** (*aló*) is another [Greeting in Rio], being a common [Phone greeting in Central America] equivalent to **HOLA**. Solvers burned by such double dealings will find a [Soother] in **ALOE**, which is such a [Very useful plant in puzzles]—[It might save your skin].

TONTO [Fictional Potawatomi tribesman], [Johnny Depp role of 2013], [Jay Silverheels's TV role], [His horse was named Scout], [Scout leader?]

UNA [A, in Acapulco], [Juan's one], [One, in Italy], [Article in "La Repubblica"]

DONNA [Prima ___], [Disco legend Summer], [Summer's first]

DON [Put on], [Underworld boss], [Teacher at Oxford], [King of the ring?], [Nod backward?], [Family man?], [Soprano's role?]

SRTA [Mex. Miss], [Dora the Explorer, e.g.: Abbr.], [One available in Mexico]

SORTA and **KINDA** [Ish], [In a way]

SRA [Title: Sp.], [Title for Eva Perón: Abbr.]

DOFF [Remove, as a hat], [Flip one's lid?], [Tip]

TILDE [High mark in Spanish class?], [El Niño wave?], [Piña colada garnish?]

OLA [Suffix with "pay"], [Pay stub?], [Motor add-on?], [Schnozz tip?], [Gran finale?], [Crap ending?]

HOLA ["Yo"], [Chihuahua greeting]

ALOE [Soothing succulent], [Eos product], [Burn rubber?], [It's a relief], [Health food store phone greeting?]

The pronoun **ELA** means [She, in Portuguese], perhaps even someone tall and tan and young and lovely, being the [The girl from Ipanema?], as constructor Bill Thompson lyrically clued it.

The [Spanish "she"], **ELLA** is the [Spanish feminine pronoun] used for a *doña*—or for a *dona*, for that matter. But more often it headlines as the [First name of the First Lady of Song], Ella Fitzgerald, as Nancy A. Corbett denoted it in de-lovely clue [Scatter?].

SCAT clues may show some [Jazzy style] when pitched as an [Order to go]. It can also be seen as a [Tracker's clue] suggesting which way a hunter should go depending on where an animal decided to go. The scat of **GAME** shouldn't be mistaken for the game of **SKAT**, a three-player [Trick-taking game played with 32 cards]; doing so would be an [Activity in which people are not playing with a full deck].

Puzzles themselves play a tricky game when they clue **ELLA** as [She: Italian], referring to an archaic, literary usage. Usually, though, the pronoun **ESSA** is [What she is in Italian]—but that answer has cards up its sleeves too, as it's [It: It.] (as in "it" in Italian).

But that's not quite it for "it" in Italian, as [It, in Italy] is also **ESSO**. Fortunately, the answer usually fills in as Esso, the [Old US gas brand] whose name hints at the conglomerate that once operated it, <u>S</u>tandard <u>O</u>il. In 1972, Exxon nixed the Esso brand in the US, but Exxon's Tiger Marts remain vestiges of Esso's old motto, "Put a tiger in your tank." Esso is still [ExxonMobil abroad], especially as a [Canadian fill-up choice]; but domestically it's primarily a crossword fill-in choice.

A [Lady friend in Italy] is an **AMICA**, which isn't far from **AMOCO**, another [Classic roadside brand] whose name abbreviates a prior iteration: <u>Am</u>erican <u>O</u>il <u>Co</u>mpany. Amoco became another [Bygone gas brand] when [It merged with BP in 1998]. But after BP's **BADPR** surrounding its Deep Horizon Spill, it rebranded some stations under the Amoco name.

ELLE, the [French "she"] and [French "her"], is more often read as the [Vogue rival]. **LUI** works in two fashions as a [Match for elle]: first as [French for "him"] and [He, in Paris], and second as the [French men's magazine]. So it's a pretty [Nice pronoun].

SCAT ["Shoo!"], [Ignore the lyrics?], [Improvise with numbers?], [Moving word?], ["Zip-a-dee-doo-dah," e.g.]

GAME [Hunter's quarry], [Kind of preserve], [Willing], [Operation, e.g.], [Clue is one], [Uno, for one]

ESSA [Pronoun for Florence in Venice, say]

ESSO [He, in Italian], [Past gas?]

AMOCO [BP brand], [Gas brand with a torch in its logo], [Classic gas brand with a red, white, blue, and black logo]

BADPR [Celebrity mug shot, typically], [Spinning concern]

ELLE [Fashion issue?], [Women's issue?], [She: Fr.], [That girl in France], ["Legally Blonde" role], [How she looks in Paris?], [Notre Dame, e.g.], ["W" competitor]

LUI [That guy, to Guy]

REI [Gear chain?]

ICEAX [Good pick for a mountaineer?], [Scaling tool]

COOP [Kind of board], [Fowl territory?], [Shut (up)], [Cheep joint?]

REI used to hail the [King, in Portugal] but the reigning reference now is to the [Big name in camping gear], the store whose letters head "Recreational Equipment, Inc." The retailer formed in 1938 in Seattle when a married couple, fans of mountaineering but not wild about having to import an **ICEAX** from Austria, founded it as a **COOP**.

[This is the way]... Or Is It?
TAO, Tze, and Tsar

LAO [People with a language of the same name], [Language spoken along the Mekong], [Language in which "puzzle" is "pid sa"]

TZU [Lao-___], [Sun ___, "The Art of War" philosopher], [Shih ___ (dog)]

TZE [Lao-___], [Chinese philosopher Mo-___]

TSE [Lao-___], [K'ung Fu-___ (Confucius)], [China's Mao___-tung], ["The Waste Land" author's monogram], [Brand of cashmere pronounced "say"]

SIZZLED [Was very exciting, informally]

PIZZASTONES [What some pies may be baked on]

PIZZA [Cheesy choice?], [Box lunch, perhaps], [Subject of a all made during the Super Bowl?]

CZAR [Pre-Communist Russian ruler], [Nicholas I or II], [Drug___], [Industry magnate], [Kingpin], [Titan]

TSAR [Old Russian ruler], [Peter or Paul, but not Mary], [The first Fabergé egg was created for one], [Terrible title?]

Taoism's founder, **LAO** [___-tzu], shares his name with a [Language akin to Thai] that's mostly monosyllabic. Though typically seen as "Lao-tzu" in clues, his name can also be spelled **TZU** in clues, it is slightly more likely to arrive in answers as **TZE**, though both options are far outnumbered by a third possibility, **TSE**. (Puzzles tend to choose **TSU** through the [Houston sch.], Texas Southern University, or the [Nashville sch.], Tennessee State University.)

Among many other references, **TSE** can also spell the name of a Cyrillic letter used in many Asian and Eastern European alphabets. Constructor Jem Burch, a student of Russian and linguistics, included **TSE** as the [First letter of "tsar" in Russian] in a grid whose **PUZZLEBOXES**–clued as [Confounding contraptions], not parts of a crossword–**SIZZLED** with zees, as in **PIZZASTONES**. That's a neat trick, as the "tse" is used for "zee" in the Russian versions of words like "**PIZZA**," which is spelled with two tses.

Like the back-half of Lao-Tzu's name, the spelling of the [Title that comes from Caesar] more often appears one way when part of a clue–**CZAR** (which as an answer can is used in non-Russian senses)–yet as an answer tends to wreak havoc by rearing its head in another way: **TSAR**. It's enough for solvers to agree with constructors Priyanka Sethy and Matthew Stock (not to mention Tevye the Dairyman): ["May God bless and keep the ___ . . . far away from us!"].

But it's **TAO** that is one of the cruciverse's biggest imports from [Way overseas]. Literally meaning [The way], it's true that knowing

[Process of nature by which all things change]: Clues for __TAO__

- ☐ Spiritual path
- ☐ Cosmic order
- ☐ Eastern "way"
- ☐ Chinese "path"
- ☐ Confucian path
- ☐ Way overseas?

- ☐ Chinese principle
- ☐ Way out in China?
- ☐ "I Ching" concept
- ☐ The so-called "path of virtue"
- ☐ Principle behind yin and yang

- ☐ "Natural order of the universe"
- ☐ "That was Zen, this is ___" (philosophy pun)
- ☐ "The ___ of Pooh"

the answer makes puzzles [Literally, "way"] easier to solve. But it's the clues for the [All-encompassing concept] that can represent a [Path to enlightenment].

The [Confucian principle] is enigmatic as an [Indescribable religious ideal], iconic as crosswords' [Eastern "way"], and ironic as the ["Eternally nameless" thing] so frequently named in the grid.

In the __TAO__ ["___ Te Ching"], Lao-Tzu describes the [Metaphysical concept] as if referring to the crossword clue and answer together: [What Lao-tze said "is hidden but always present"]. And elsewhere, in musing on the [Underlying principle of the universe], he seems to nail the underlying principle of the cruciverse: ["The wonder of all things," per some translations of Lao Tzu].

__TAO__ [Chinese "path"], [Indescribably religious ideal], [The natural order of the universe], [Principle behind yin and yang], [Virtuous conduct, in Confucianism], ["The ___ of Pooh," 1982 best seller], [Terence who's known as the "Mozart of Mathematics"], ["That was Zen, this is ___" (philosophy pun)]

Chapter 5 Puzzle: "Spill the Beans!"

ACROSS

1 Billiards technique to get the cue ball to spin back after it hits another ball

9 NYSE alternative

15 More than a third of Indonesians

16 Beethoven's third symphony

17 *Hokey dance move?

19 Where to find a tiny hammer and anvil

20 Priest's vestment

21 Windy City commuter rail system: Abbr.

22 *Helen Hayes and Katharine Hepburn in film, e.g.

27 Always, in poetry

28 Small-size batteries

29 Udon alternative

30 They, in Italy

31 Way to get sleepy after looking at a time piece

34 Long-legged waders

36 *Kitchen counter?

38 Ones in a nativity scene?

41 Hazardous construction material

45 N.Y.C.'s Madison and Lexington

46 Tone on a phone

47 ___ generis (of its own kind)

48 Korean automaker that started as a bicycle parts manufacturer

49 *1861 incident that nearly caused war between the United States and the United Kingdom

53 Get into a pretzel?

54 Apple mobile platform

55 Animals: Suffix

56 In "Moby-Dick" they're English—but in the starred answers they're 15-Across, so to speak

63 Posts someone's personal info online maliciously

64 It's often a-pealing

65 Handel opera about Agamemnon's son

66 Car whose logo is a symbol of Neptune

DOWN

1 Vinyl spinners

2 Go, team, go!

3 "Selma" director DuVernay

4 React to an alarm clock

5 "Slammin' Sammy" of golf

6 Misses with means

7 "East" of Eder

8 It's often hot when it's cold and cold when it's hot

9 Harper Lee's first name

10 Most residents of Bharain, Riyadh, and Dubai

11 Cry

12 Bishop's realm

13 Most sharp, as an angle or pain

14 Residents of Bharain, but not Riyadh or Dubai

18 Dalai ___, title for Tenzin Gyatso

22 "Blergh!"

23 Sun stream

24 Nile nipper

25 Send to a bitter end

26 Say neither yea or nay

30 Slips up

32 Sounds of one hazzing a cheezburger

33 Eggs, scientifically

34 Decorates vividly

35 Word with willikers

37 "The wolf ___ the door"

38 Manages with what's available

39 Pilot

40 Butcher's cleaver

42 Org. that has security down pat

43 Say yes to l'adresse?

44 Word before "three bags full"

46 Antonym of ancestor: Abbr.

49 Whence Tenzin Gyatso lives in exile

50 Jazz saxophonist Charlie whose last name is a synonym of 4-Down

51 Have an iron in the fire?

52 Speaker setting in a car radio

57 Drs.' orders
58 Dutch carrier whose name travels between J and N
59 Aussie pop star who sang "Cheap Thrills"
60 Time period
61 Go from this to thhhhhhiiiiisssssssss, in music: Abbr.
62 Tre + tre

Chapter 6

ROCKOUT with Music
Crosswords [Crank up the amp to 11 and go wild]

Crosswords—and cruciverbalists in general—might be the world's greatest **DJS**. Sure, crossword types aren't typically thought of as [Party people], but consider this: They're [Mix makers], [Masters of spin?], and [They play at work]. Heck, they'll be [CD players], [LP spinners], [AM or FM workers]—whatever letters you've got.

DJS [Record holders?], [Singles players?], [Mixers found at some bars]

Crosswords could certainly claim to love every kind of **MUSIC**. You'll find so much [Noted work] on their playlist that [You may need a staff to write it] all down.

MUSIC [Something to face?], [Staff stuff], [Rest area?], [The Bard's "food of love"], [Some strains], [What's the score?], [It usually has a key], [Work done to scale], [Country, e.g.], [Genesis creation?]

But like people who claim to love all genres of music, when pressed, puzzles admit some preferences. For instance, they're unlikely to tune into **LITE** FM, as the idea of "easy" listening probably doesn't appeal, especially if it means [Less filling].

And while any crossword will probably find moments to play some classical stuff, jazz it up, and get funky, they probably prefer **ROCK**. Not only do they have plenty of answers to [Wear, and look great doing it], as constructor Herre Schouwerwou put it, but they like to [Shake up] the language, [Swing alternative] ways to consider words, and add a [Little ___] [Contemporary sound] to their [Firm foundation].

ROCK [Big ring stone, slang-ily], [Sling missile], [Seesaw], [AC/DC output]

<u>ODE</u>, How I Solve Thee
Dedicated Lines to [Dedicated lines]

From the Ancient Greek ōidé ("song" or "legend"), the **ODE** is cross-word's [Laudatory poem].

ODEA [Ancient Greek theaters], [Classic concert chambers], [Ancient halls]

Millenia before **ODE** ever led ["___ to Our Ocean" (Amanda Gorman poem)] or ["___ to a Nightingale" (John Keats)], and long before even the time [Ben Johnson wrote one to himself], odes were sung in [Outdoor theaters] called **ODEA**, a word whose singular form, "**ODEON**," also appears cracked in two as ["___ Grecian Urn"].

ODEON [Ancient arts venue], [Movie palace], [Classic theater name], [Nickel finish?]

Clues pointing to <u>ODE</u> themselves are a bit **ODIC**—in fact all clues are—in that they act [Like many works with "To" in their titles], sometimes even managing to be a bit [Lyrical].

ODIC [Pertaining to odes], [Exaltedly poetic], [Keatsian or Pindaric]

ODIST [One offering lines of credit], [Certain foot specialist]

If you'll oblige me, I'd like to play **ODIST**, a [Tribute writer of sorts] to the answer and some of its sundry clues. After all, even if I'm not wild about the answers **ODS** and **ODED**, I'm wild about odes, and no one has ever [Had too much] of them. Until now maybe . . .

ODS (as in "overdoses") [Some E.R. cases]

ODED (as in "overdosed") [Took too much, briefly]

"[Salute in stanzas]: An Ode to **<u>ODE</u>**"

O, ode, I say, as [O might open it],
Here's fodder folded into your tip jar,
a [Tribute that may be urned?]

So ideal your [Poetic form],
No wonder your clues' [Inspired lines]
Expose your charms like a [Model's midriff?]

Even as they seem to lie in support,
suggesting a similarly sized [Uplifting piece]
Or that you're over one's head, as [Elevated lines];
By contrast, this is mere [Promotional writing?],
Pointing out, like a palmist tracing [Love lines],
The relatively apparent: that you're [Psalm's cousin],
And you [Work with feet].

So, long-ohed ode, this o'er-stuffed oddity
for your [Dedicated work]
In puzzles, these [Kind words of a sort],
And I mean it—my [Words of honor?]—
Since who but you could offer the [Glowing piece?]
Anointing "anode" so poetic [An ending?]

Grids' Block Rockin' BEATS
Rock Bands, [Heartthrobs], and [Hits]

ABBA: The name of the [Swedish supergroup] is an acronym of the first names of the ["Fernando" singers]. Meaning "dad" in Aramaic and Hebrew, *abba* is a [Biblical "father"], raising a new meaning in the clue ["Mamma Mia!" pop group]. As a Hebrew name, it names the mid-century [Israeli statesman Abba ___] **EBAN**.

Poets might like **ABBA**, as it's the [Pop group whose name is also a rhyme scheme], but perhaps less so when it's the ["I Do, I Do, I Do, I Do, I Do" group]. That grouping of words more closely resembles another [Basic verse option], the **ABAB** rhyme scheme.

ACDC: The Young brothers are an electric [Power couple?], particularly as the ["Thunderstruck" band]. To fans in Australia, they're "Acca Dacca," making their name [Flexible, in a way].

The [Bee ___] **GEES** aren't named after the "Brothers **GIBB**"— [Bandmate Barry, Maurice, or Robin]—but for the shared initials of

EBAN [Israel's foreign minister during the Six-Day War], [Meir contemporary], [Abba not known for singing]

ACDC (as "AC/DC" for "alternating current/direct current" or the band) ["Back in Black" rockers], [Hard rock band formed by Malcolm and Angus Young], ["High Voltage" was their first album, ha ha],[Current choice], [Choice of juice?], [Young brothers' band]

GEES [Turns right], [Baffled expressions]

GATES [Bill worth billions], [Track lineup], [Passes through a wall?]

Barry Gibb, promoter Bill Goode, and Bill **GATES**. (No, not the billionaire [Bill in Washington?], but a disc jockey in Australia.)

DEVO: The name of the surrealist, new wave ["Whip It" band] highlights their assertion that humanity is <u>devo</u>lving, a message very much in concert with "Weird Al" Yankovic's homage, "**DARE** to be Stupid." Contrarily, Devo's name displays shrewdness, riffing slyly off "divo," the less-heard male form of "diva."

DARE [Alternative to truth?]

ELO ["Evil Woman" band], ["Xanadu" band], [Band with the record for most Top 40 hits without ever having a #1 single]

ELO: Electric Light Orchestra is the British ["Don't Bring Me Down" grp., 1979], which is a tune whose title chess players might quote, referring to their rankings according to the Elo [Chess rating system].

FYI [Cluing-in letters], [Letters accompanying a tip]

GMS [Chess VIPs], [Baseball VIPs], [Chevys, e.g.]

FYI, an Elo rating of 1979 almost qualifies as "Expert" in chess, but falls 500 points short of the bar for **GMS** (as in "Grand Masters," not "General Managers" or "General Motors").

PROF [Campus VIP], [Classy sort?]

ORG [Part of NATO: Abbr.], [Dot follower], [AA or AAA]

Devised in 1960 by the physics **PROF** Arpad Elo, the rating system is also used by the **NSA**: not the [Org.? What org.?] in DC or the [Letters for friends with benefits] ("no strings attached"), but the **ORG** for fans of stringing letters together, the National **SCRABBLE** Association.

SCRABBLE [Torture over a rack?], [Where "TWELVE" is worth 12], [Where you might get a word in edgewise]

UFO [Night light?], [Pie in the sky?], [Vehicle without local plates?]

PENTAGON [World's largest office building], [Brass building?]

FOO [___ Fighters]: The name of the band fronted by Dave Grohl, refers to US and UK WWII pilots' term for a **UFO**, currently called UAP ("unexplained aerial phenomena") by the **PENTAGON**, but not crosswords. Postwar scientists seriously investigated **FOO** fighters before declaring ["Aw, nuts!"], the floating lights were more likely St. Elmo's Fire than aliens.

ETS ["Star Trek" extras?], [Short aliens?], [Saucer users, in brief?], [Mars rovers, in brief?], [Superman and others, for short], [And many times in France?], [& & &, in France]

HOMME [French man]

ETS ("extraterrestrials") might not land immediately as [Down-to-earth types?]. And to arrive at [French connections], solvers may need to make contact with [Travelers from afar, for short], like Parisians, to recognize *ets* as French "ands." Perhaps they could call **HOMME**. No wonder it's so tough: As the initialism for "Educational Testing Service," **ETS** is also the [AP exam company] behind the **SAT** ("Scholastic Aptitude Test") and the **GRE** ("Graduate Record Examinations"). Of course, even scarier ET initials—at least for felines—belong

SAT [Posed], [Parked it], [Gained a lap?], [Couldn't stand any more?], [Was not off one's rocker?], [Hurdle for a H.S. senior, maybe]

GRE [Test for coll. seniors], [Hurdle for an MA pursuer], [Test for a future PhD], [Sr.'s test]

to the [Cat-eating 1980s TV character] **ALF**, whose name stood for "alien life form."

Aside from singles, [Most bands' first releases] are **EPS** ("extended play" records). [Pre-album albums, briefly], they run under 25 minutes, making them [Brief albums, briefly] compared to the more popular sellers and answer, **LPS** ("long playing" records).

Both **EPS** and **LPS** qualify as a [Groovy collection?], [Some wax], and [Contents of some sleeves], even if **EPS** can refer to **CDS**.

In all of popular music, there's one album that stands out in crosswords' record collection:

AJA is the eight-minute title track on the [1977 double-platinum album by Steely Dan]. The song's lyrics are addressed to someone or something called "Aja," sought for some reason: love, solace, or pleasure, it's not clear. A band member claimed it was based on a Korean woman by that name, but details are scant. "Aja aja fighting" is a Korean call of encouragement, comparable to "Go get 'em!" So "Aja aja fighting!" to anyone trying to solve the riddle behind (or on the cover of) the [Record that's the same forward and back]. Heck, may we all find **AJA**—or whatever it is we're searching for.

ALF [TV ET], [TV character who went to high school for 122 years], [Cat fancier from Melmac]

LPS [33 1/3 r.p.m. records], [In 2020, they outsold CDs for the first time since 1986]

CDS [Burnable items], [Lasers read them from the inside out], [Bank offerings, in brief], [S&L offerings], [IRA options]

It Sounds Better in MONO
Mononymous Musicians
with a Hit [Single-track] or Two

ENYA, [Ireland's best-selling solo artist], is played most often as the ["Orinoco Flow" singer]. Despite being a [Four-time Grammy winner for Best New Age Album], she might not approve of clues like [One-named New Age singer], having disavowed that genre label for her music. Instead, she insists her genre is "Enya." The **ORINOCO** might prefer to be just another [Venezuelan river], but gets singled out as a [Noted piranha habitat].

The Nigerian-English artist **SADE** was the ["Smooth Operator" singer, 1985] who adopted her stage name from her middle name, Folasade, meaning "honor confers a crown" in the Yoruba language. Sade's name resembles one belonging to a notoriously un-smooth

MONO ["The kissing disease"], [Single], [MSG component?], [One to start?], [Maniacal leader?]

ENYA [One-named Irish singer], [Grammy winner who sometimes sings in Gaelic], ["A Day Without Rain" singer], [Musical artist known as the "Queen of the New Age"]

SADE [One-named Nigerian singer], ["The Sweetest Taboo" singer, 1985], [One-named singer awarded a CBE in 2017], [Marquis de ___]

operator: the renowned writer, libertine, rapist, and pedophile Marquis de Sade, who can be clued somewhat sadistically as [Donatien Alphonse Francois de ___].

Dr. **DRE** is the ["Black-ish father"], [Dr. who can't write prescriptions], and [Rap mogul of the highest degree?] born Andre Young. Though the man behind [Beats by ___] **DRE** is near the top of charts in crosswords when bereft of his title, as **DRDRE** he's beat out by **DRNO** as the cruciverse's preferred **DOC**.

The ["One Mic" rapper] with a one-word name, **NAS** was born Nasir bin Olu Dara Jones. Not only do his lyrics rhyme, but his records do too: He's the ["Illmatic" rapper] and ["Stillmatic" rapper"], the [Rapper with the 1999 #1 album "I Am..."], and the [Rapper with the 2003 hit "I Can"]. His name has an echo too, thanks to country-rap star **LIL** [___ Nas X].

The [Wee] [Rap epithet] **LIL** is the [Start of many rapper names], as in [Rap's ___ Kim], ["Turn Down for What" rapper ___ Jon], and ["Tha Carter" rapper ___ Wayne]. Note that the last clue features **THA** [Everyday article in rap titles] also seen in the **JLO** album, *J to Tha L-O! The Remixes.*

The ["Gangnam Style" rapper] and [K-pop superstar] **PSY** styled himself as the [Freud subj.] because it connoted "**PSYCHO**." Let's not even [Start to analyze?] it further.

SIA is the Australian [Singer with the 2016 #1 hit "Cheap Thrills"]. Constructors hope the ["Chandelier" singer, 2014] will have a long career. Decades ago, the answer **SIA** would come up via [N.M. Indian], an obsolete rendering of the name of the Zia people, so puzzles had to say "**SEEYA**" to that reference. Clearly, they'd rather see Sia produce a popular **ENCORE** album than have to say **ADIEU** again.

ENCORE [Again]?

The Beatles Meet a Meter Meta and Write a Meta Rita, Rita Moreno, Anita, Moor, Eno, Merino, Marino, Ono, Ohno, More Eno, Some Emo, and [More!]

Since they [Like the Beatles], fans of the **FAB** [___ Four] may know **STU** Sutcliffe as the [Beatles' bassist before Paul] who helped form and name the band before changing tracks to pursue life as a painter. Still, they may need a crossword to pick out the irony: As constructor Will Nediger depicted it, Stu is an [Artless nickname?].

Sutcliffe never appeared on a Beatles record, unless one counts his appearance on the cover of **SGT** [___ Pepper]. It's said McCartney wrote that album's "Lovely **RITA**" upon receiving a parking **TKT** from a traffic cop named Meta Davies. So although he'd met a Meta, he wrote a Rita.

Not only do "Meta" and "Rita" have the same ring, they both mean "pearl"—each derived from a form of Margaret (Margareta or Margarita). As the English word or prefix, **META** can be [Cleverly self-referential] [Like this clue], or, as Caitlin Reid cleverly referenced it, [In and of itself?].

RITA [Moreno of "West Side Story"] got the "O" of her **EGOT**, the [Acronym for the four major entertainment awards], for playing **ANITA** in the Broadway musical.

The surname "Moreno" means "dark-haired" in Spanish. It's rooted in *moro-*, meaning "**MOOR**"—as in [Othello, for one]—and *-eno*, a suffix for "coming from," the same way "**JALAPENO**" means "from Jalapa." Though they may sound related, the name of the [Fine wool], **MERINO**, means "**OVINE**" in Spanish, and the last name of the [Legendary Dolphin] Dan **MARINO** is, aptly enough, Italian for "nautical."

That positions the quarterback closer to the [Name whose Japanese symbols mean "ocean child"], **YOKO** [___ Ono]. It's logical that the shorter part of her name, **ONO**, appears more often in puzzles, but it's also fitting, as *Ono* means "small field" in Japanese.

FAB [Old-style dope?]

STU [Queue after R], [R-V connection], [VW predecessors?], [Good name for a cook?], [Good name for a flight attendant], [Guy found running through the alphabet] *(See the introduction for further study)*

SGT [Cpl.'s Superior], [NCO], [PD rank], [Pepper, e.g.]

RITA [Meter maid of song], [Former US poet laureate Dove], [Journalist Skeeter in the Harry Potter books], [Lime-A-___ (alcoholic beverage)]

TKT [B'way buy], [Sta. purchase], [It gets you in the house: Abbr.]

META [Parent company of Facebook], [WhatsApp owner], [Modern lead-in to "verse"], [Like casting Michael Keaton in "Birdman" as an actor who used to play a superhero], [Physical leader?]

ANITA [Hill on the Hill, once], [Santa follower?], [___ Bath (prank call name)]

MOOR [Anchor], [Secure], [Tie up], [Make fast], [Heath], ["Wuthering Heights" setting], [Heath for Heathcliff], [Peaty tract], [Wasteland]

JALAPENO [Heat source?]

OVINE [Like Bo Peep's flock], [Sheepish?], [Dolly-esque, say]

MARINO [Dan or San], [First quarterback to exceed 5,000 passing yards in a season]

The [Japanese-born conceptual artist] lent her name to the Plastic **ONO** Band, which she and John Lennon formed in 1968. When the two wed the next year, she lent it again: Lennon changed his middle name from Winston, filling the heart of [John ___ Lennon]. In 1975, [Sean Lennon's mom] and dad both contributed to the name of their sonorous son, the musician and producer [Sean ___ Lennon]. In 1980, Sean's parents teamed up to produce their fifth and final record together, so **ONO** and **LENNON** are each a ["Double Fantasy" figure].

ONO also figures as an answer for a [Cry of horror, quaintly] ("O, no!"), or the [Hawaiian mackerel], also called **WAHOO**. So the same fish can elicit ["Yippee!"] or "Yikes!"

Natives of the Aloha State may use **ONO** to mean [Six, in Hawaiian], or, as 'ono, "delicious." So, presented in the order conforming to Hawaiian grammar, Yoko Ono can cook up 'ono ono ono, or "six delicious fish."

Considering the small field of ways **ONO** appears in puzzles—indeed, at least "six"—calling it merely a ["Double Fantasy" figure] seems to sell the little answer short.

The short track [Speed skater Apolo] Anton **OHNO** may have had competitors saying ["Good heavens!"] whenever they heard who was about to step **ONTO** the ice, but attentive solvers are [Not fooled by] his name. They know that **APOLO** is merely an [Olympian's first name that sounds like another Olympian's name], while **APOLLO** is the [Son of Zeus]—and also the [Renowned Harlem venue] where Ono and Lennon performed in 1979.

"Apolo" was **APROPOS** for the pro who started races [On point]. Ohno's father chose it by adding "lo!" to the Ancient Greek apó ("away from"), [Fitting] them together to form something like "Look out! Steer clear of this one!"

Apó links up with gê (the root behind "Gaia" and "geography") to form **APOGEE** (literally, "from earth"), the [Highest point in an orbit]. In puzzles, **APO** ("Army Post Office") is a [Mil. Address], making the [Private address?] [How to address a sgt.?].

Ohno won four golds in the 2002 Olympics and later won *Dancing with the* **STARS** (an answer that can also skate by as [Dallas icemen] or do a "pole" dance as [State representatives]). Fellow Olympic gold-medal skater Kristi Yamaguchi won *Stars* too, and without a single **AXEL** or **LUTZ** in her program (both of which qualify as a [Cold feat?] that sounds accidental as [Spin out on the ice?]).

After Sonja **HENIE** retired, the former Norwegian [Winter Olympics athlete at 11 (1924)] and [Skating gold medalist of 1928, 1932, and 1936] became a [Skater on the Hollywood Walk of Fame]. **SONJA** remained [Henie on ice], skating in movies like *Thin Ice* and *Iceland*. It was nice she had [Something to fall back on?], besides her **HEINIE**.

STARS [Stage draws], [Isn't supporting?], [Us people?], [People people?], [Sky lights]

AXEL [Jump with 1.5 turns], [Eddie, as a Beverly Hills cop], [Jump on the ice], [Move named for the 19th-century skater Paulsen]

LUTZ [Skating leap with one full rotation], [Eponymous skater Alois___]

SONJA [Actress Sohn of "The Wire"], [Figure skater Henie], [Hollywood's Henie]

HEINIE [Bum], [Bottom], [Rear]

Apollo: Atmospherics and Soundtracks and other albums by the cruciverse's [Musician Brian] **ENO** so moved astronomer Marc Buie that in 2019 he made the ["Music for Airports" composer] a new sort of "rock" star by naming an asteroid after him.

That honor came just months after **ENO** was inducted into the Rock and Roll Hall of Fame as a [Roxy Music co-founder]. But by then, crosswords had **CITED**, **SIGHTED**, and **SITED ENO** for decades as a [Brian of rock].

After all, Eno also produced albums like Talking Heads' *Fear of Music*, U2's *The Joshua Tree*, and *Q: Are We Not Men? A: We Are Devo!* Oh, and he co-wrote "Heroes" with David **BOWIE**. Amid all that, the [Art-rocker Brian] **ENO** emerged, releasing several critically acclaimed solo albums.

But these days [Rock's Brian] is more often seen (and heard) as [Ambient musician Brian]. [The musician who coined the term "ambient music"] is literally an [Ambient composer of note]: He's the [Composer of "The Microsoft Sound," which, ironically he wrote on a Mac].

CITED [Referenced], [Named], [Pointed to], [Commended], [Gave a ticket], [Made an example of]

SIGHTED [Espied], [Saw], [Aimed], [Not blind]

SITED [Positioned], [Put in place], [Located], [Set]

BOWIE ["Space Oddity" singer], [Kind of knife], [Knife handle?], [___ State (Arkansas nickname)] *(because the knife originated there)*

Who's the Biggest LOSER? [MISFIT] Names Shrunk Down to Size

A **NAME**, like a [Finger], need not be long to [Point out] [Somebody]. In fact, a "monicker" already holds a "Nickname" inside. Several answers crosswords [Call] on often are shortened forms of what would otherwise be too much for a grid to [Handle].

Comparing what a [Big shot] had on their [Birth certificate info] to what they [Designate] as [Something to drop] when they pick [Something to go by] professionally, the top five "losers" of crosswords are listed below.

5. Andre Romelle Young › **DRE** (18%)
4. Eithne Pádraigín Ní Bhraonáin › **ENYA** (15%)
3. Sia Kate Isobelle Furler › **SIA** (14%)
2. Salvador Domingo Felipe Jacinto Dalí Doménech › **DALI** (10%)
1. Lawrence Tureaud › **T** (7%)

YEAH, [OK], ["I know"]: The [Mohawked man of "The A-Team"], [Onetime bodyguard of Muhammad Ali and Michael Jackson], and [Noted pitier of fools] is **MRT** in puzzles, but **T** has on very rare occasions been an answer in crosswords that have bent the rules, even when delineated as [___-Square]. So it's possible. Please direct any complaints to Mr. T in person.

ENO [Playwright Will who wrote "The Realistic Joneses"], [William who invented the crosswalk, or composer Brian], [William Phelps___ (creator of modern-day traffic laws)], [Stop sign inventor William],["Here Come the Warm Jets" musician], [Self-described non-musician], [One day I'll write a puzzle that doesn't include this Roxy Music co-founder], [Brian who scored the soundtrack to "The Lovely Bones"], [Brian who is a rare example of someone whose prominence in crosswords is commensurate with his actual prominence], [Brian who said "It's not the destination that matters. It's the change of scene."]

A nifty clue from an old Inkwell puzzle once even called him a [Composer of crosswords?], which seems especially apt since **ENO** has described himself a [Composer of music "as ignorable as it is interesting"], words that could be applied to many answers in this book. (In this instance, in a way he even helped compose that crossword clue).

And since his birth name qualifies him as the [Rock producer Brian Peter George St. Jean le Baptiste de la Salle ___] **ENO**, by winnowing it down to eight letters, he really is a [Minimalist composer Brian].

As a producer, perhaps he couldn't help remixing what remained, as he's [Musician Brian who used the anagrams "Ben Arion" and "Ben O'Rian" as pseudonyms]. That tracks for the [Musician who said "For the world to be interesting, you have to be manipulating it all the time"]–and for the [Musician who started the Obscure Records label].

That's enough about [Brian ___] **ENO**, but in the spirit of what's "as ignorable as it is interesting," Eno's brother, Roger, is himself an [Ambient music pioneer], so a clue like [Big name in ambient music] can apply to either Eno. In fact, before [Ambient composer Roger] embarked on his own solo career, the siblings with the [Ambient surname] paired up to make the *Apollo* album mentioned earlier. So the title could reference the album's unmistakable spaciness, the god of music, and Greek myths' most famous brothers. Oddly enough, while the Enos made [Mood music?] and [Kind of rock], those clues are set down for their last name's near twin: **EMO**, the [Angsty music genre] that's an [Offshoot of punk].

EMO [Like a broody teen, maybe], [Goth relative], [Broody music genre], [Post-punk genre], [___-pop (genre for Billie Eilish)], [___-rap (music subgenre)], [Genre for Fall Out Boy], [Genre for My Chemical Romance], [Jimmy Eat World music genre]

Big ACTS to Follow
More Musical Monikers Taken
When One [Isn't oneself]

Whether or not they love him tender, solvers should know [Elvis's middle name] was **ARON**. His parents picked the [Graceland name] likely in honor of one of their friends and in tribute to Elvis's would-be identical twin brother, Jesse Garon, delivered stillborn. [The King's middle name] also belongs to another twin brother: the ["East of Eden" son] who's a sibling to Caleb.

ACTS [Is decisive?], [Is directed], [Isn't naturally], [Makes a move], [Makes a scene?], [Works with a part?], [Luke book]

The Anglicized name of Saint **ELVIS** isn't quite the [Oft-cited sighting] as his namesake, ["The King"]. But the sixth-century Irish saint also known as Ailbe of **EMLY** is still alive in puzzles, at least when performing as the [Little girl in "David Copperfield"].

[Singer James or Jones] both went by **ETTA**. The ["Don't Go to Strangers" singer Jones] was and remains less popularly celebrated than the ["At Last" singer James], but is certainly no less well-regarded in jazz circles. [Jazz singer James] is jammed into puzzles more often than [Jazz singer Jones] and has the "betta" story regarding the [First name in jazz]: Born Jamesetta Hawkins, James was discovered at age 14 by the "Godfather of Rhythm and Blues," Johnny Otis, who advised her to divide her original first name and transpose it.

ETTA ["___ Is Betta Than Evvah!" (1976 album)], [James played by Beyoncé in a 2008 biopic], [___ Candy, best friend of Wonder Woman]

[Johnny, "King of Rock and Roll"] **OTIS** also shares his name with
several other R&B and soul singers: [Redding dubbed "The King of
Soul"], [Williams of the Temptations], and [The Knights' Day].

[Elevator pioneer] Elisha **OTIS** was the [Inventor who had his
ups and downs?]. [He gave us a lift] in a huge way, as his "safety
elevator"—which uses locking side rails to prevent the car from
crashing if a cable snaps—opened the door to skyscrapers. His
eponymous company is still a big [Name in escalators and moving
walkways], but it was his first name, **ELISHA**, that may have foretold
his rise, arising from the [Wonder-working biblical prophet] whose
miracles included raising a boy from the grave.

The 1960s [Folk singer Phil] **OCHS** who was the [Phil who
described himself as a "singing journalist"] really did have a [Big
name in publishing] as the [Name in several generations of "New
York Times" publishers]. First belonging to [Newspaper publisher
Adolph], who bought the paper for $75,000 in 1896, **OCHS** returned
to the masthead from 1963 to 1997 as [Punch Sulzberger's middle
name]; most recently it was found on the nameplate of Adolph's
great-grandson, the ["New York Times" publisher Arthur ___ Sulzberger Jr.] from 1992 to 2018.

It was the first [Adolph who coined the motto "All the News
That's Fit to Print"]. Phil was unrelated to the *Times's* **OCHS** but
titled his debut record *All the News That's Fit to Sing*. Considering the
preponderance of Greek letter names in its puzzles, some might see
the *Times* crossword as "All the Nus That's Fit to Hint."

IGGY [Pop of rock] was born with the decidedly less snappy name
of James Newell Osterberg Jr., later restyling himself as [Pop's ___
Pop] in reference to his high school band, the Iguanas. Like [Pop's
Pop], when the Australian rapper Iggy [Azalea with the 2014 #1 hit
"Fancy"] (née Amethyst Amelia Kelly) fancied a new identity, she
adopted a pet name, pairing her childhood pup, Iggy, with the flow-
ery name of her childhood street.

AXL [Rose of Guns N' Roses] followed Pop's precedent more
closely. William Bruce Rose Jr. was so happy whenever he [Rose
on stage] with his high school band, AXL, that he took his friends'
advice and took the name himself.

YMA [Sumac of Peru] named herself after *ima shumaq*, Quechua for "how wonderful," befitting the sound of the [Sumac whose voice covered five octaves]. Stretching from low baritone past soprano, it helped make the [Sumac with wide range] one of the biggest stars in so-called exotica music in the 1950s and '60s.

In the **COEN** brothers' 1998 film *The Big Lebowski*, Sumac's song "Ataypura" plays in the background as "The **DUDE**" offers a [Stoner's greeting] at the kinky [Kind of ranch] where the **EROTICA** producer, Jackie Treehorn, **RESIDES**. So, like The Dude, Yma Sumac [Abides].

[Singer India.___] **ARIE**, born India Arie Simpson, was given the toponym "India" to honor Gandhi and "Arie" for its airy sound. Aptly, *arie* is German for "aria," making it a [German opera highlight]. Yet **LIZZO** is the ["I put the sing in single" singer].

As a man's name from the Hebrew for "lion," **ARIE** is the [First name in auto racing] thanks to "The Flying Dutchman," Arie Luyendyk, who indubitably is prouder of his two Indianapolis 500 wins than of leading all drivers in current crossword mentions. Making up ground on his pop, though, is the Dutch-American [Racer and "Bachelor" star ___ Luyendyk Jr.], who previously placed second in both *The Bachelorette* and the **INDY** Light Series. Perhaps father and son could each be imagined as an Indy.Arie.

ARIES is a particularly appropriate sign for racecar drivers, and not just because [It's a sign] of a [Bold, impatient type, astrologically] and [A natural leader, supposedly]. It's also the [The first astrological sign], a [Bygone Dodge] and ["The Ram"].

COEN [Filmdom family name], [Joel or Ethan]

DUDE [Bro], ["I'm impressed, man!"], ["I can't believe you just did that!"]

EROTICA [Blue books?], [A nice word for dirt?], [Bedtime stories]

ARIE ["Voyage to India" Grammy winner's middle name], [Bachelor who dumped and then married Lauren]

LIZZO ["Rumors" singer] (née Melissa Viviane Jefferson)

INDY [___ 500], [May race, familiarly], [Race place], [Dr. Jones, familiarly]

ARIES [First of twelve], [First sign], [A fire sign], [Northern constellation], [Sign of April Fools' Day?], [Sign of spring]

Staging ARIA
And a [Number of operas?]

Sophisticated amusements themselves, crosswords frequently visit the opera, especially if it means taking in an **ARIA**, the term for a [Song sung solo].

Heir to the Ancient Greek aḗr ("air"), **ARIA** still floats in from overseas as [Italian for "air"], where it's used in many of the ways found in English, including as a synonym for "song." That explains

ARIA ["Summertime," e.g.], ["Aida" highlight], ["O mio babbino caro," e.g.], [Fine tune?], [Piece of Glass?], [Soliloquy relative]

[Air on stage], just as another synonym scores it as a [Number for one] or a [Number that's often in Italian]—even if the latter puts on foreign airs.

A [Diva's big moment], an **ARIA** can also provide constructors a chance for their own [Star turn]. Clues like [Met number], [Met score], and [Piece at the Met] might send solvers afield, while others get stood up at [Single's bars?].

There, the **BAR** is the [Impediment], alluding not to a [Dive, maybe] but to the [Musical measure] found in a staff. Then again, when not the synonym for **STAVE**—the [Set of lines on which musical notes are written]—a **STAFF** could work as [Bar personnel?].

DIVE can double for "divas" as an alternative plural, but clues don't sink so low. The unusual pluralization is an Italian import, where **DIVA** first performed in Latin. [Literally, "goddess"], it derives like "divine" from *deus*. A [Goddess of song] like [Beyoncé, e.g.] can take "diva" as a compliment, but she played a fierce [Hard-to-please type] in the [2009 Beyoncé hit single] that aptly reached the charts of the Australian Recording Industry Association, better known as ARIA.

OPUS, which shares its root with the fertility and earth goddess covered in chapter 2, Ops, was first used as the [Latin for "work"] and continues to be similarly employed in Italian. Like a "diva," it can be a real [Piece of work] in English, especially since it has two plurals: "opuses" and "opera." As an **OPUS** is often a [Numbered musical composition] such as [67, for Beethoven's Fifth], both **OPUSES** and **OPERA** fill in for [Numbered works].

Generally, though, **OPERA** performs in its more familiar singular role, even if it does so in less than opaque ways, like [Where glasses may be raised?] or as a [Glass piece], the latter eyeing the composer of ["Einstein on the Beach," e.g.].

Like **ARIA**, **OPERA** is crosswords' fourth most-popular answer at its letter length, but neither its common status in the cruciverse nor its working-class start can completely diminish its refined reputation. So in the tradition set when [The Marx Brothers spent a night there], clues might take a dig at **OPERA** by re-airing old one-liners:

BAR [Milky Way unit], [Object from Mars?], [Lush surroundings], [Sauce location?], [A room with a draft?], [Tender spot?]

STAVE [Ward (off)], [Barrel part], [Song verse], [Word used in place of "chapter" in "A Christmas Carol"]

STAFF [Noted lines?], [Chorus lines?], [A flat place?], [Support group?]

DIVE [Low bar?], [Act like a loon?], [Go by the board?], [Go in over one's head?], [x3, a suborder?], [Ring fix?], [Low joint]

DIVA [Maria Callas or Mariah Carey], [Agent's handful, say], [Many an exploding star]

OPUS [Work], [Work for an orchestra?], [Work with a number], [Any work of art], [Sonata, e.g.], [Composition]

OPERA [Word with space or soap], [Literally, "works"], [Works in the music business?], [House work?], [Phantom's haunt?]

- ["___ is when a guy gets stabbed in the back and, instead of bleeding, he sings": Ed Gardner]
- ["___ in English is, in the main, just about as sensible as baseball in Italian": H.L. Mencken]
- ["No good ___ plot can be sensible": W.H. Auden]
- ["How wonderful ___ would be if there were no singers": Rossini]
- ["In ___, there is always too much singing": Debussy]

If crosswords invite you to the opera, you'll probably see **AIDA**. The Giuseppe Verdi [Opera set in Egypt] about the eponymous [Verdi heroine] has been a [New York Met performance 1,000+ times] since 1886, and the *New York Times* has been roughly keeping pace since debuting it as an answer in 1942. Knowing it's the only four-letter [Verdi opera] can free up the answer, but it can't free the [Nubian heroine of opera]. Spoiler alert: [Its final scene is set in a tomb.]

AIDA [Verdi princess], [Elton John musical], [It's set in Egypt], [It premiered in 1871], [It debuts in Cairo], [Radames's beloved], ["O patria mia" singer]

Considered by many the greatest opera composer, **VERDI** is the [One who made many Shakespeare characters sing?] in operas like *Falstaff* and **OTELLO**, featuring the [Verdi villain] **IAGO**, who also hatches as a [Shakespearian schemer] and ["Aladdin" parrot].

VERDI ["Rigoletto" composer], ["La Traviata" composer], [Opera giant]

ERI, a [Form of the Italian "to be"], rings through opera houses and crossword grids as the word starting the title and lyrics of Verdi's aria **ERI** ["___ tu"] ("It Was You,") from *Un ballo in maschera* (*A Masked Ball*). In the song, the **HERO**, having discovered his wife's got the hots for his **BRAH**, sings of his decision to spare her life but (uncool, ["Dude!"]) kill his **BFF**, making him a real [Pal until the end, for short]. The hero's anguish is evident in that first line: "It was you who tainted that soul, the delight of my soul . . ."

OTELLO [Classic opera set in Cyprus], ["Ave Maria" opera], [1887 La Scala debut]

IAGO ["Otello" baritone], [Emilia's husband], [Casio's rival], ["I am not what I am" speaker], [Villain who says "What you know, you know"], [Shakespearean villain who says "Virtue? a fig!"], [Literary character who says "I will wear my heart upon my sleeve"], [Shakespearean role with more lines than the title character]

The title of that aria, if not its sentiments, resembles that of another song: the Spanish band Mocedades' 1974 American top 10 hit, "**ERES** *Tú*" ("It's You").

HERO [Subway fare?], [Long lunch?], [Lead]

MILAN may be a city of endings, as it's [Where to see "The Last Supper"] and a [Setting for much of "A Farewell to Arms"], but its opera house, La **SCALA**, [Literally, "the Stairway"], was known for its openings. Giacomo Puccini hoped his **TOSCA** would debut there under the baton of his pal Arturo Toscanini (whose last name just

BRAH [Male buddy, in slang]

BFF [Pal 4 life]

ERES [You are, in Spain]

TOSCA [Classic opera in which every leading character dies]

happens to start with the first name of the [Puccini title heroine]). But *Tosca* was a political [Opera set in 1800 Rome] and Puccini's publisher insisted that it be an [Opera that premiered in Rome in 1900]. So like [Floria ___, Puccini title role], Puccini was subject to Roman politics beyond his control.

Easy Money: DOREMI
Clues Pitched as [Monetary notes?]

SOLTI [Conductor Georg whose name consists of two musical notes], [Student of Bartók]

SOL [Lead-in to la], [G, in the key of C], [Sun, in Ibiza], [World's biggest star?], [Star closer than Alpha Centauri], [What astronomers call a day on Mars], [Roman god often depicted with a radiant crown], [G], [G-string?]

EROICA [Beethoven homage to Napoleon], [Vienna premier of 1805], [What some consider to be the first Romantic symphony]

DREI [Eins + zwei], [Teutonic trio], [Cologne crowd?]

NOTE [Piece of a piece], [Addition to the staff?], [Do, say], [A or E, but not I, O, or U], [A, E, or IOU], [A, B, or C]

SCALE [Step on it], [It might reveal what you lost], [Plate of fish?], [Run from a pianist]

LONGI ["Aye," phonetically], [Nice vowel source?], [Hi-fi sound?], [Eli has it; Ellie doesn't]

SHORTI ["It" starts with it], [Hip sound], [Igloo feature?], [Second of six?], [One of an "inquisitive" foursome?']

TWAS [Start of a Christmas poem], [First word of "Jabberwocky"], ["___ brillig..."], [It was in the past?], [What's before the night before Christmas]

The conducting style of the [Longtime leader of the Chicago Symphony Orchestra], [Conductor Sir Georg] **SOLTI** earned him a record 31 Grammys. Solti's rehearsing style, meanwhile, earned him the nickname "The Screaming Skull." But it was the musical syllables of "Solti" that earned him the clue [Longtime maestro with a "noted" name].

SOL might not resound as a [Fifth of eight], but it's literally stuck in solvers' heads when it's a [Note that's "needle pulling thread" in the song "Do-Re-Mi"]. As the [Fifth tone], it might be [Beethoven's Fifth?] (Another number heard in the Alps makes [Beethoven's Third]—which usually cues the **EROICA**—count for **DREI**.)

SOL also rises as "Sol," [Our sun], named for the [Roman sun god], from an ancient root that likely enlightened the names of his German/Norse counterpart Sól (whose name we herald each Sunday), and the Greek analog, Helios, as well as the *sol* that's the [Spanish sun] and the French *soleil*.

As the only [Solfège syllable] not two letters long—"solfège" being the popular music education method named after its fifth and fourth notes—**SOL** is the [Longest note?] and thus the only **NOTE** of the **SCALE** crosswords can sing singly.

One such too-tiny note, tone sometimes pipes up as the [Scale notes] **TIS**, but typically trades in its **LONGI** for a **SHORTI** to make the [Quaint contraction]. **TIS** ["___ a pity"], but at least [It is fancy], as [It's in poetry?] and [It's in a carol?], being [The season opener?]. Despite all this, it can be difficult to appreciate ['Twas in the present?]. **TWAS** [Had been in puzzles] many times before appearing

["__ not to be"]. On other occasions, solvers saw ["__ nothing"] to worry about.

DOREMI is relatively clear as a [Lyric for the Jackson 5, Woody Guthrie, or Julie Andrews], but even perfect pitch might not be useful in identifying [Upscale trio?], [Steps on a scale], or [Folding money]. The last capitalizes on "do-re-mi" as a dated alternative to [Moolah] akin to [Simoleons], [Mazuma], and [Kale, lettuce, and cabbage?].

The **IDIOM** works off the "dough" made by the first note. Which reminds me: What do kids use to buy Broadway tickets? Their Play-Doh.

IDIOM [Challenge for a language learner], [Hit the nail on the head, e.g.], [In a pickle or in a jam]

[Fun thing on a string]
A Guide to How to Play like YOYO Ma

Italian terms used as musical directions are often clued with hints denoting their milieu. So **LENTO** and **LARGO**–both of which mean [Slowly]–can be arrived at faster as [Slowly, in music], [Slow, to Solti], or [Slow in scoring?]. Similarly, **RIT** (an abbreviation of "ritardando") is usually [Slowing down, on a score: Abbr.].

Jimmy Buffet might play **LARGO** even when playing fast. Whatever the pace, count on it being in a [Florida Key], and that its lyrics will provide an [Indication not to rush].

Puzzles play **ADUE** (*a due,*) a bit dully when they duly clue it literally as [For two, in music].

ADUE [Together, in music], [Scored together?]

ATEMPO (*a tempo*) is used for "on time" or "in time" in everyday Italian) and to [Resume the previous speed, in music]. **ARCO**, Italian for "bow," arrives as [With the bow, on a score]—as opposed to *pizzicato*, or plucked. Or clues might direct a cellist to the nearest ARCO, a [West Coast gas brand] affiliated with Marathon and BP. Despite operating in the Northwest, its name arrives from a merger creating the Atlantic Richfield Company. After filling up, proceed *a tempo* to rehearsal.

ARCO [It's a gas], [Taking a bow at the symphony?]

BREVE ("brief" in Italian) can refer to either a [Double whole note] or the ˘ accent that's a [Pronunciation mark] seen mostly in

BREVE [Two whole notes, essentially]

ALLA [___ breve (2/2 time)], ["...and to ___ a good night!"]

dictionaries as a [Mark over an unstressed syllable]. It pops up in music and puzzles as **ALLA** [___ breve] (*alla breve,* "according to the breve") to indicate "cut time." The Italian *alla,* à la the French, can also mean [In the style of], as in [Mozart's Rondo ___ Turca], or the [Italian menu word] cut from [Penne ___ vodka]. Or it may be "at the," as in [Teatro ___ Scala].

LUTHIER [Maker of stringed instruments]

AMATI [Italian known for pulling strings?]

The **LUTHIER** Nicola **AMATI** was [Stradivari's teacher], and his name is used as a noun for any [Fine fiddle] he fashioned. The same clue can auction off the [Pricey strings] Amati's student made, a **STRAD**.

[Violin virtuoso Leopold] **AUER** had a Strad, short for Stradivarius. Auer, like Amati, is also remembered as a master teacher, counting among his students the legendary violinist Jascha Heifetz and the [Many-time Grammy-winning cellist], **YOYOMA**, who is a [Virtuoso taking a bow before a performance?] (If something doesn't sound right about that clue, try reading the "bow" as the stick, not the bend).

[Consonant] Ones
Bachs in Boxes and HARMONIC Anton-nyms

The most noted name of classical music belongs to the **BACHS**, the [Musical family] which included [JS and CPE], plus JC, JCF, and WF, to name a few. (In case you're like, **WTF**: That's Johann Sebastian and his sons Carl Philip Emanuel, Johann Christian, Johann Christoph Friederich, and Wilhelm Friedmann.)

WTF ["___ with Marc Maron" (popular podcast)]

[On the double] let's add **PDQ** [___ Bach ("Fanfare for the Common Cold" composer)]. If [Straightaway] something about the composer's name or composition feels a little funny—perhaps even sickly—it should, as they refer to [J. S. Bach's fictional descendant], a "lost son" of JS invented by Peter Schickele. Besides his Bach **PARODIES**—which appear on records like the 1990 Best Comedy Album Grammy-winner, *1712 Overture and Other Musical Assaults* (whose title track appears on the first [LP half], I add as an **ASIDE**)

PDQ (*"pretty damned quick"*) [ASAP], ["Stat!"], [By yesterday]

PARODIES [PDQ Bach's "Sanka Cantata" and such], [Mad pieces]

ASIDE [Digression], [Tangent line?], [In the wings], [Hamlet's first line, e.g.], *or* ["Penny Lane," not "Strawberry Fields Forever"] (*as "A-side"*)

Schickele's other symphonic creation is the tromboon, a hybrid of the trombone and the **BASSOON**.

BASSOON [Big wind], [One of the reeds], [The grand-father, in "Peter and the Wolf"]

But back to **BACH**—the actual and original, [Johann Sebastian ___]. Bach was a [Mass producer] as the composer of his *Mass in B minor*, but also as the most prolific of the great composers, scoring over 1,000 pieces. He was also prodigiously productive in bed, being the [Composer with 20 children]—or 21 if you count PDQ.

BACH ["Goldberg Variations" composer], [Baroque master], [Fugue master], [Canon creator]

(True, two children were twins, but roughly, that's another **SCORE** of scores, or times he was able to [Really get his groove on?]—a clue that refers to "score" meaning to [Scratch], but works for [Get lucky]—to credit his "body of work." [Get the point?])

SCORE [20], [One of a Lincoln quartet?], [XX], [50-50, maybe], [Get home safe?], [Ballpark figure], [Make a good point], [Note book], [Noted script], [Manage to get, informally], ["Jackpot!"]

Of course, it's not just the quantity but the quality of his output that makes **BACH**, like Beethoven and Brahms, [One of the Three B's] of classical music. Such notoriety led Brad Wilber to award him [A B].

Be that as it may, in crosswords it's **ANTON** who scores an A in composition. Actually, the answer can refer to any of the many Antons of classical music: the [Austrian composer Bruckner], [Austrian composer Webern], [Czech composer Dvořák], [Russian composer Arensky], and [Russian pianist-composer Rubinstein].

ANTON [Writer Chekov], [Singer-actress Susan], [___Chigurh, villain in "No Country for Old Men"]

"**ANTON**" doesn't have musical roots; the consonance of the final *-ton* and "tone" is **PHONETIC** coincidence.

PHONETIC [Spoken], [Soundbased], [Like the spelling "kuh-zin" for "cousin," e.g.]

But the Ancient Greek root, *tónos* ("stretching" or "tension") is echoed in the English "**TONE**," either as the [Pitch] made by a stretched string or meaning to [Firm (up), as muscles]. Thus, a **TONIC** is a [Restorative] [Pick-me-up].

TONE [Shade], [Pitch], [Mood], [Step on a scale], [Scrambled note?], [Pitch in a NOTE?]

Along the same lines, *tónos* underscores the English "**TUNE**." Perhaps that weight of history is why, as constructor Nancy Solomon raised it, [It's hard for some people to carry].

TONIC [C in a C scale, e.g.], [Coke, as originally touted]

"**TONY**" inherits its [Upscale], [Stylish] meaning from "tone" too. The name of the [Broadway honor], though, honors Antoinette "Tony" Perry, co-founder of the American Theater Wing. Winning a [Player's trophy] for, say, portraying the ["West Side Story" role] would be cool, or in modern slang that also equates excellence with tension and firmness: "tight."

TUNE [Pull some strings?], [Fix a flat?], [Do a grand job?], [Adjust uprights?]

TONY [Props for a Broadway play?], [Soprano who's unlikely to sing?]

[Asian music source] and Norwegian Wood

SITAR, Tabla, Raga, Ravi, and Oboe

The **SITAR** is a much-[Fretted instrument], but it can be a surprisingly helpful instrument for reaching other answers. If its name is somewhat unusual in the West, it may sound strange in India too: [Its name means "three strings" but it can have up to 21]. The constructor David Alfred Bywaters stretched it in a way befitting his own name, archly pointing out that [It notably has two bridges]. It can be a far-flung, forgotten member of the family as [Banjo's cousin]. And it's probably not the [Sound of the '60s] most folks think of first.

Yet, setting the sitar as an answer aside for a second, when it's plucked for use within a clue, "sitar" is as distinctive as its sound. Of the 50 times or so "sitar," "sitars," or "sitarist" has appeared in a clue in the *Times* in the Shortz Era, it has only led to three answers:

Twice it clued **TABLA**, the [Small Indian drum] that's a [Relative of bongos] and [Sitar accompaniment] in and out of crosswords.

Eleven times it led to **RAGAS** or **RAGA**, the structured but improvisational [Backbone of Indian classical music] whose name refers to the form's intent to "color" listeners' minds. The nature and cultural significance of the [Music played on a sitar]—often stirring, complicated pieces overlaid on traditional forms and lasting over an hour—is frequently belied by clues like [Bit of Indian music] that can seem willfully disinterested or disparaging. But then a clue like [Jam ingredient from India] comes along and preserves one's faith in the cruciverse.

The other 39 occasions "sitar" played a part in a clue, it helped pluck **RAVI** [Shankar with a sitar]. Born Robindro Shaunkor Chowdhury, he went by the Sanskrit rendering, Ravindra Shankar, until shortening his first name to Ravi, another name for Surya, the [Hindu sun god], meaning "sun."

Though their names don't suggest it, Shankar was [Norah Jones's father]: She adopted her mother's maiden name following her parents' separation. The [Beatles' friend Shankar] was also [George's sitar teacher]. Shankar's raga heavily influenced the sound of "Norwegian Wood," even if the song's title doesn't suggest that connection either. In a way that does suggest a connection, **JOHN** Coltrane honored his good friend Shankar (and involuntarily infuriated crossword solvers) by naming his son, another [Jazz saxophonist Coltrane], with the four-letter name **RAVI**.

Ultimately, "sitar," "tabla," "raga," and "Ravi" are each such a ["Help!" mate] in clues pointing to the others that they're crosswords' subcontinental equivalent of John, Paul, George, and **RINGO**. (You could even think of each one as a [Starr of a foursome], almost.

Two years after "Norwegian Wood," the Beatles reached for a woodwind, playing "Penny Lane" with the puzzle's favorite instrument, the **OBOE**. The [Double reed woodwind] that's an [Instrument featured in "I Got You Babe"] has got its own sonorous partner with a *cher* name: the oboe [___ d'amore], which is slightly larger than an oboe and a bit shorter than another close relative, the cor anglais.

The [Wind from the French for "high wood"] has a winding etymology. It was once called the [Hautboy], taken from its French name, *hautbois* (*haut* being "high" and *bois* "wood" or "woodwind"). Playing by ear, the Italians heard *hautbois* and transcribed it as **OBOE**; English picked it up from there. Crosswords have their own ideas about what to call it:

- High wind
- Black wind
- Slight wind?
- Wind in a pit
- Slender reed
- Wind in the reeds
- Wind up on stage?
- The duck in *Peter and the Wolf*

- Member of a pit crew?
- Nash's "ill wind that no one blows good"
- It's "reeds are a pain / And the fingering's insane," per Ogden Nash
- Instrument whose name sounds like a rebuke of Obama's dog

Chapter 6 Puzzle: "Wait!" (a Sunday-size puzzle)

ACROSS

1 Rapper whose debut album was "Purrr!"
8 Public square
13 ___-wop
16 Knight's title
19 Make way
20 Move the tomatoes to the top, say
21 Japanese self-defense method
23 "I thought I could handle this puzzle but..."
25 Take down the wrong path
26 Farrow and Hamm
27 1981 Grammy co-winner for Album of the Year
28 "Rumble in the Jungle" fighter
30 Words before "I now pronounce you"
31 Commotion
33 "These answers will be easier..."
38 Breaks a law
42 Govt. security
43 Lament
44 Reciprocal
45 Street rep
46 Self-learning machines: Abbr.
47 Letter addenda: Abbr.
50 Bygone Korean automaker
51 Folk singer Joan
52 "Drawing a blank now, but..."
55 Like errands still on a list

57 Filthy stuff
58 Jazz pianist Earl Hines's nickname
59 Nice response
63 It gets its own bin at the airport
65 Nair alternative
66 "I was going to quit this but..."
69 Non-naan bread
70 "Banana Hammock"
71 Film buffs
72 Bring forth
74 "Macbeth" witches, e.g.
75 Hardly a house of cards
76 "I know the answer's got to be..."
78 "Everything Is Illuminated" author
79 Big number that inspired a search engine's name
84 Long, long time
85 Fire
86 Word heard with a gavel thump
87 Risky undertaking
88 FedEx alternative
89 "The Jetsons" character
91 Some extra action at the casino
92 With 107-Across: "Hey, I finished it--..."
97 Concorde, e.g.
98 Longest Spanish river
99 Co-star of Betty and Estelle
100 Brazilian greeting

101 Boats like Noah's
104 Your four pals for this puzzle?
107 See 92-Across
113 Polite request from the curious
114 Police, in slang
115 Question to a pet or poker player
116 Sends a personal message to, on Twitter
117 Put on
118 Rises dramatically
119 "And if I got some letter wrong along the way, you know what:..."

DOWN

1 Imbiber's hwy. offense
2 Ottawa's prov.
3 Leon Black portrayer on "Curb Your Enthusiasm"
4 Jai___
5 Soft drink
6 Athletes often tear them, for short
7 Way into Shea, once: Abbr.
8 Likely (to)
9 Citrus plant
10 ___ Dhabi (Mideast land)
11 "High School Musical" star Efron
12 Fright-filled
13 Dance track
14 Nice response?
15 IHOP beverages
16 Kind of pad
17 Sculptor Noguchi
18 Less polite

22 Former Apple software bundle
24 Sounds of surprise
29 Fib
31 Very eager
32 Good name for a waitress at a greasy spoon?
33 Tiny
34 Spanish version of "Agnes"
35 Stylish, in the '60s
36 Chi-town daily
37 Joseph, in Arabic
39 Man's name that's a homonym of 63-Down
40 Provoke, as a feeling
41 1992 Democratic presidential candidate Paul
45 Easter treat
46 Central Pennsylvania town
47 Copyright's cousin
48 What a villain might hatch
49 Plays roller derby
51 Kind of algebra or web search
52 Like wisdom teeth that smart
53 Crafter of stringed instruments
54 ¿Dónde están los___?
56 Playful ocean mammal
57 Took a load off
59 Gibson of "Fast & Furious" movies
60 West African-derived religion similar to Obeah

61 Pumpkin spice time
62 In a ___ (very fast)
63 John to King John
64 Promised
67 Merchandise: Abbr.
68 The beginning
73 ___ Sketch (drawing toy)
75 Round trip for one?
77 Concert venue
78 Golfer's warning
80 Gambling parlor, for short
81 Wrong conclusion?
82 Crumbs
83 "___ we forget"
86 Home of the house of Cards?
87 Big shot
88 Garment worn by Gandhi
89 Downed a sub?
90 Flagpoles
91 Annihilate
92 Site hypochondriacs should avoid
93 Letter-shaped girder
94 Please return them to the upright position
95 "A Doll's House" playwright Henrik
96 Furry figures in Times Square
101 'Rule, Britannia' composer Thomas
102 Laugh-a-minute
103 "Felicity" star Russell
105 Take it for a trip
106 Fair hiring letters
108 Annual Carnaval locale
109 Fertility clinic cells
110 Chick-___-A
111 Christen, as a knight
112 Office no.

Chapter 7

SPORTS
The Puzzle [Shows] Team Spirit

Like [Fly-fishing, for one], [Quidditch, e.g.], and [Chess or poker, technically], it can be hard to think of crosswords as a **SPORT**. But a puzzle is sort of a sport, at least in the sense that [One can take a joke]. Hopefully a solver is too, or else a crossword will seem less a [Whimsical pursuit] than something looking to [Squash, e.g.] a [Fella] like a [Cricket, for one] and leave him [Hurling, e.g.] on the field.

SPORT [Golf or polo], [Kind of shirt], [Big spender or tipper], [Alternative to Rover or Rex], [Don]

Despite what folks say, the brain's not muscle—in fact, it's the fattiest organ. Still, it's fun to slosh the old skull jelly around, [Curling, for one] answer, [Hunting or fishing] for others.

Think of this chapter, then, as a [Field test?] of those answers to [Have on] hand so that when puzzles do throw a curve, you can knock it over the [Fencing, e.g.].

Because remember, ["Buddy boy"], it's a stretch to think of crosswords as a sport. It's only a word [Game].

DIAMONDS in the Rough
[Baseball fields] Answers
and Makes Questionable Calls

DIAMONDS [Tigers habitats], [Where flies get swatted?]

BAT [Animal that symbolizes good fortune in Chinese culture], [Fly-by night?], [Something to do at home?], [Athletic club?], [Club for swingers], [Card holding?]

OUTS [Excuses], [Loopholes], [What flies usually become]

MLB [Org. for the A's and O's], [Org. for Tigers, but not Lions or Bears], [Org. with Card games]

BASE [It might be stolen in full view], [Runner's place], [Place to lead a private life?], [Two, for binary arithmetic]

FIRST [Historic event], [Who's there], [Low grade?]

PLATE [Part of the earth's crust], [Auto ID], [Strike location]

LITHO [Print type, briefly], [Stone: pref.], [Graphic opening?]

Returning home, in a way, to the shape of Arthur Wynne's original Word-Cross grid, modern clues about baseball can flash a "diamond." A **BAT** is a [Diamond club], **OUTS** are [Diamond data] and the **MLB** ("Major League Baseball") is a [Diamond org.].

Similarly, a **BASE** is a [Diamond bag]; the "bag" harkens to the use of canvas pillows as bases like **FIRST**, a [Diamond corner].

Back then, an actual [Dish] or **PLATE** served as what's now a [Five-sided home?], as seen in a classic Currier and Ives **LITHO**. The Ancient Greek for "stone," *lithos*, provides a [Rocky start] for "lithography," another plate-based activity.

Befitting a [Ballpark figure], an **UMP** can be tough to reckon with, appearing to be a rock appraiser as [Diamond arbiter] or a crossword arbiter as [Grid official]. Crosswords even challenge solvers to play [Judge at home] and [Call] an **UMP** out on a curveball like:

- Bag man?
- Fair judge?
- Home body
- Maker of calls
- Man in black?
- Person behind a strike?
- One working from home?
- One who's critical at first

- One using foul language?
- First, second, or third person
- Person who might call you out?
- One who might err on the safe side?
- Person who regularly cleans his plate?

TAGGED [Touched by an Angel?]

Perhaps the answer was **TAGGED** best by constructor Harvey **ESTES** (good crossword surname!–see chapter 4 for more on that Colorado [___ Park] place) in a *Wall Street Journal* puzzle, when he gamely judged the authority of an **UMP** as [The power behind the thrown?].

Who's [Not a team player?]: **REF** (and Often **UMP**)

Sometimes cited as [Bartlett's] or [OED, e.g.], **REF** is more often the [Ump kin] who's somehow both a [Game warden?] and a [Lion's zebra], a [Bowl monitor] and a [Blow monitor]. Here are some of the choice words for the [Hated card dealer], including some that could equally apply to either [Game official], a **REF** or an **UMP**:

REF only

- ☐ Flag bearer
- ☐ Ring leader?
- ☐ Round figure?
- ☐ Call the shots?
- ☐ Whistle blower?
- ☐ One in a corner?
- ☐ One in the middle of a fight
- ☐ One tweeting about football?
- ☐ One who puts his hands together over his head for safety's sake?

REF and **UMP**

- ☐ Play critic?
- ☐ Fault caller
- ☐ Short zebra?
- ☐ Tennis official
- ☐ Field worker?
- ☐ Field marshal?
- ☐ One who cries foul?
- ☐ One often accused of blindness
- ☐ One who works while others play?
- ☐ One to whom you might say "Boo!"

Get a Load of ALOU

The Rojas Brothers' [Baseball family name] with [Jesus in the outfield]?

ALOU is a [Big name in the diamond business?] thanks to [Baseball's Felipe, Matty, Jesús, or Moises].

In 1958, [Baseball's Felipe] Rojas **ALOU** was the first of the family to **SHOW** up—and the first Dominican to regularly play—in **THESHOW** ("The Show," a nickname like "the **BIGS**" for the [Majors]). Following his excellent 17-year career, he became the first Dominican-born manager. He proved a much better than [Fair] manager as a Montreal **EXPO**: acquiring pitcher Pedro Martinez in an international [Trade event] and being named the National League Manager of the Year.

SHOW [Evince], [Air], [Come in third], [Lose one's place?], [It's just a little out of place?], [Program], [Oxygen element?], [Tell's partner?]

THESHOW [A good thing to steal]

EXPO [Big show], [Major show], [Big name in dry-erase markers], [1967 Montreal event], [Member of a former ball club from Montreal]

ERROR [Foul-up], [Fluff], [Diamond flaw], [Goof], [Miss, e.g.], [Slip], [Trial partner?]

SIN [Sloth, e.g.], [Vice principle], [Clerical error?], [Original idea?], [It "exists when one goes against one's conscience," per Pope Francis]

CIN [The Reds, on scoreboards], [Bengals, on scoreboards], [Red letters?]

BROS [Surfer dudes, e.g.], [Sibs... or Sigs, maybe], [Marx and Wright: Abbr.]

TRES [Uno y dos], [Spanish crowd?], [101 word in both Spanish and French], [Very, in Vichy], [Very French?], [Oh so]

ERR [Goof], [Go the wrong way], [Display one's humanity, in a way]

TRINITY [Christian supergroup?], [First A-bomb test]

JESUS [Christmas delivery], [One with more than two billion followers], [Pacifist with canons?]

Speaking of trading big names, the name on his jersey should have read Rojas, but the scout who discovered him made an **ERROR**, more of a [Bad call] than a **SIN** (an answer constructor Kate Hawkins didn't overlook as [Missing letters in "transgre-s-o-," appropriately]). In fact, the mistake led to another "bad call," as the name used in lieu of "Rojas" started being misread aloud as "a-Lou" instead of "a-Low." Had Rojas not allowed himself to be renamed Alou, it might have been more appropriate for him to sign with **CIN**, as his rightful name is likely related to **ROJO**, [Red: Sp].

In 1960, Felipe was joined on the Giants by his brother—the future [1966 NL batting champ Matty] **ALOU**. In 1963, Jesús Alou became team -[Mates] with his **BROS** too. Toward the end of a game near the end of the season, the **TRES** *hermanos* Rojas—all having adopted the last name "Alou"—became the first and only all-brother outfield, making **ALOU** every [Outfielders' name]. Unlike that scout years earlier, they did not **ERR**—no batter even gave them a shot to [Drop the ball].

Though he was the least accomplished hitter of the **TRINITY**, it's understandable why **JESUS** is the [Miracle worker?] of crosswords. He makes **ALOU** sound divine as [Baseball's Jesus] or sacrilegious as [Slugging Jesus]. And he helps create an exclamation potentially useful when beholding the *Christ the Redeemer* statue towering over Rio: "[Giant Jesus]!"

Add to the lineup Felipe's nephew—pitcher Mel Rojas—and Felipe's sons—manager Luis Rojas and the outstanding [Outfielder Moises] **ALOU**—and the [Dominican baseball-playing family] endures as a [Noted diamond dynasty].

Crosswords' HALL of Fame
A [Clue locale perhaps]

HALL [Long way?], [Long way for a runner?], [Place on the Clue game board that is inexplicably called a room], [College building], [Rice building], [Where there may be a mess?]

Only about 1 percent of Major League's more than 22,000 players are in Cooperstown's Hall of Fame. Fortunately for solvers, the odds of a player receiving a **HALLPASS** (once gamely clued as [Toilet paper?]) to crosswords' "Hall of Frequent Answers" are even slimmer.

Alous aside, most players from bygone eras need to get into Cooperstown before puzzles permit them entry, and "Hall-of-Famer" or "in Cooperstown" often appear in their clues. Such nods to players' feats on the **FIELD** can double as **HINTS** to solvers lacking the **KEN**, say, of [Baseball historian Burns] or ["Jeopardy" genius Jennings].

The list that follows will include some of crosswords' biggest hitters but **OMIT** those whose fame endures. **SORRYNOTSORRY**, Ty **COBB**: You were too good for your own good, in this respect, at least.

While their fame may have faded, these players (listed with their years active) belong in every solver's Hall of Familiar.

- **TRIS** Speaker (1907–28): The center fielder's career numbers rank him first all-time in doubles, fifth in hits, and sixth in batting average. Equally adept defensively, his glove was known as "Where triples go to die." Speaker went on to become a manager, but somewhere along the line the epithet became associated with both Willie Mays and a star player Speaker managed, Shoeless Joe Jackson, as it is in the film *Field of Dreams*.
- **EDD** [Roush of the Reds] (1913–31): A contemporary of Speaker's in center field, he possessed an unmatched arm and a literally great bat: It weighed 48 **OZS** or three **LBS**, while bats today are usually 33 oz., 35 at most. Fully named Edd J. Roush, he and his twin brother, Fred J. Roush, had the same middle initial: J.
- [Polo Grounds great Mel] **OTT** (1926–47): The [First NL player to hit 500 home runs] was only 5'9", a fact which earned him the sobriquet ["The Little Giant"]. That's also apt for his name, considering its propensity to drop into puzzles and cause trouble. In *Field of Dreams* the **GIANT** can be seen following Shoeless Joe out of the cornstalks.

    Even when solvers can write **OTT** quickly in the grid, it's nothing compared to what ["Master Melvin"] could do. Aided by the brevity of his full name, he could sign 500 autographs per hour. He once quipped, "Every time I sign a ball, and there must have been thousands, I thank my luck that I wasn't born

FIELD [One to grow on?], [Park place?], [Trip leader?]

HINTS [Help for those at sea?], [Some people can't take them], ["It has one syllable" and "Its fourth letter is T"]

KEN [Understanding], [Grasp], [Either of Baseball's Griffey Sr. or Jr.], [Teen who's had 40+ jobs], [He's a doll]

OMIT [Drop], [Opposite of stet], [Forget a line?], [Not to mention?]

SORRYNOTSORRY [Sarcastic apology], ["Deal with it"], ["Oops, accidentally picked out Parcheesi at Toys 'R' Us #___"?]

COBB [One of the first five inductees at Cooperstown], [Baseball's "Georgia Peach"], [Kind of salad]

TRIS [Cleveland's Speaker], [Mr. Speaker], [Speaker of note], [Push-up targets, for short] *(TRI out other answers in chapter 2)*

EDD [Rousch of Cooperstown], [TV announcer Hall whose credits include "The Tonight Show"], [Announcer Hall], [Teacher's advanced deg.]

OZS [1.5 in a jigger: Abbr.], [Birth announcement abbr.], [Small wts.]

LBS [Press letters?], [Reduced weight?], [Ozs. and ozs.]

OTT [Mel who hit 511 home runs], [Legendary Giant], [Giant among Giants], [Giant of old], [Baseball's "Master Melvin"], [Subject of Durocher's "Nice guys finish last" sentiment]

GIANT [Yankee killer?]

Coveleski or Wambsganss or Peckinpaugh." Once Ott retired, sportswriters continued to jot **OTT** for Ottawa's NHL team, [The Senators, on sports tickers].

ENOS [Slugger Slaughter], [Slaughter in the Hall], [Cardinals' "Country"], [Slaughter with a club], [Slaughter on the field?] *(For more on ENOS, see chapter 2)*

- **ENOS** "Country" Slaughter (1938–59): Somewhat belying his name, Slaughter was known less for his power than for his contact hitting and hustle. He ran hard to first even when he walked, and famously helped St. Louis win the 1946 World Series with his "Mad Dash" home. A Cardinals right fielder for most of his career, Slaughter picked up his original nickname, "Country Boy," as a minor leaguer in Ohio. If he stood out as a hayseed there, imagine him as a Yankee in New York, where he ended his career.

- The [Negro leagues star Buck] **ONEIL** (1937–48): The first baseman for the Kansas City Monarchs was a three-time All Star in the Negro leagues, winning a batting title and a championship along the way. He'd go on to become an outstanding manager for his old team, a scout for the Chicago Cubs (notably signing

ERNIE [Hall-of-Famer Banks a.k.a. "Mr. Cub], [Naïvely optimistic Muppet], [Banks of Chicago]

ERNIE Banks) and Major League Baseball's first Black coach.

To baseball's discredit, O'Neil was never given a chance to manage in the Majors, and it wasn't until 2022, six years after his passing, that he was finally inducted into the Hall of Fame. Nevertheless, he was a great lifelong emissary and historian of the game, contributing his vast experience,

BASEBALL [Game of tag?]

insights, and remarkable stories to Ken Burns's **BASEBALL** documentary. Considering that he continued to ceaselessly advocate for the Negro leagues, its players, and the sport itself until the end of his life, O'Neil's career could well be listed as 1937–2006.

GIL [Hodges of the Dodgers], [Jazz pianist Evans], [Buck Rogers portrayer Gerard], [Fisherman's name?]

- **GIL** Hodges: (1943–63): The [Old Dodger great Hodges] was another posthumous 2022 inductee, and like O'Neil, he sacrificed two seasons to serve in WWII. During the 1950s, he was considered the best first baseman in baseball, thanks in large part to his huge hands. In fact, his fellow [Teammate of

REESE [Eponymous candy man], [Piece maker?]

Robinson], Pee Wee **REESE**, said Hodges didn't need a **MITT**

MITT [Diamond accessory?], [Fly trap?], [Paw]

to play the field, but used one because it was the fashion. After retiring, Hodges, like O'Neil, managed a championship team, leading the 1969 "Miracle" or "Amazin'" **METS**. Hodges died at just 47, but like Speaker and Ott, who'd preceded him by a generation or two, he was given a reprise in *Field of Dreams*.

METS ["Amazin'" team]. [Queens favorites?]

Though not in Cooperstown, three **EXMET** players are often given reprieve, a pass issued by crosswords likely in part because New Yorkers would know them. Together, round out this imagined "Crossville Nine":

EXMET *("ex-Met")* [Strawberry, e.g.]

Hodges's 1969 ["Miracle Mets" center fielder Tommie] **AGEE**, remembered for an outstanding catch in Game 3 of that World Series, occasionally pinch hits for the [Writer James]. The Mets brought the title back to **SHEA** Stadium in 1986 with the help of pitcher **RON** [Darling of baseball].

AGEE [Tommie of the Amazin' Mets], *(See also chapter 1)*

SHEA [Where the Mets once met], [Flushing site?]

Crosswords have plenty of options to play **RON**, and Darling can likely name most if not all of them, being a devoted crossword solver. In a 2013 interview for the *Times*, he said that after breakfast on Sundays, "**DESSERT** for me is the *New York Times* crossword puzzle . . . I'm probably an hour or half-hour guy with the puzzle—not in Bill Clinton's elite category, but not too bad."

RON [Friend of Harry and Hermione], [Howard of Hollywood], [Howard or Paul], [1989 Gold Glove winner Darling], ["Anchorman" anchorman], [Tarzan player Ely]

DESSERT [Course shunned by losers], [Order that's rarely followed?]

In the 1988 **NLCS** ("National League Championship Series"), Darling faced another elite pitcher, **OREL** [Hershiser of the Dodgers], who won the Cy Young Award that year. Later he'd become [Hershiser of the Mets] and then [Hurler-turned-sportscaster Hershiser]. "Orel" is also a [Russian oblast or its capital], a [City whose name means "eagle" in Russian] which was [Ivan Turgenev's birthplace].

NLCS [MLB semifinal], [Pennant race inits.], [It was first won by the NY Mets in 1969]

DARLING ["Peter Pan" surname]

DARLING is now a color commentator for his [Dear] old team at **CITI** [___ Field] and for **ESPN**. Likewise, Hershiser covers games for the Dodgers, and used to work at the channel that gives the **ESPY** [Award for a great play]. Looking down, they could [Make out] the [Spot] on the mound where they once vied to become **CHAMPS**, while each [Works on a bit?] about the game at hand. But since Shea was demolished in 2009, that vision can only exist in [Fields: Fr.] of dreams.

CITI [Bank opening?], [Field opening?], ["The ___ Never Sleeps" (bank slogan)], [Bank that "never sleeps"]

ESPN [Postgame shower?], [Play station?], [Game show network?]

ESPY [Behold], [Frequent Award for Tiger Woods], [Arthur Ashe Courage Award, e.g.], [Best Driver, for one], [Play honor]

CHAMPS [Up sides?], [Belt holders]

If Shea did reappear by some [Unexplained phenomena], it would be a [Dubious gift]; suggesting many fans miss it is an **ESP** [Debatable claim].

ESP *(as "esp.")* [Particularly: Abbr.], *(as "ESP")* [Telepathic letters], [Medium strength?], [Reading ability?], [Sixth of five?], *(as "Esp.")* [Lengua de Mex.]

[Common ___] ERA
Crosswords' [Big time] Answer

ERA [It's amazing if it's under 2], [It goes up with a HR], [#MeToo___], [Victorian, e.g.], [Cenozoic or Mesozoic], [Obama ___], [Follower of Bush or Gore], [Cheer competitor], [Tide rival], [Prime time?], [Period piece] *(See also part one)*

A [Hall of Fame stat] that's in a league of its own is **ERA**. **ERA** could also be called crosswords' most valuable **PLAYER** since it's both the most frequently [Cast member] of puzzles' lexicon and because, like a [Thespian], it can act in many ways. So while it's a [Key participant] in puzzles, it can often take a [Pickup artist] to discover its name.

ERA (as ERA, "earned run average") is a [Stat for which lower is better] or something [Mean pitchers try to keep low], because as an average, it literally "means" the number of runs a pitcher allows per nine innings. An "ace" is a star pitcher, so [An ace has a low one]. Baseball fans know [A good one is under 3.00] and can at least guess the answer from [Ruth's was 2.28] (ranking 17th all-time), if

BABE [Pig pic], [Sweets], [Honey], [Woods denizen?], [Toots]

they recall that the **BABE** started as a [Knockout] pitcher. After moving to the outfield, Ruth went nine years before pitching again, so his ERA remained the same for an **ERA** (here as "era"). Even for pitchers with complicated wind-ups, nine years is an incredibly [Long stretch?].

Unrelated to the [Ballpark fig.], baseball offers three contexts for **ERA** in the sense of a [Memorable time]:

- [Baseball's dead-ball ___] era, spanning from roughly 1900 to 1919, when home runs and scoring dropped
- [Baseball's steroid ___] era, roughly the 1990s and early 2000s, when home run numbers soared due to **PED** use (as in "performance enhancing drug," the [Banned steroid, e.g.]; not "ped" as in [Walker, briefly], though walks rose during that time too)
- [New ___ (official cap maker of Major League Baseball)], founded in Buffalo in 1920, which was indeed the [Dawn of a new ___] **ERA**: both for baseball—as the start of the "live-ball era"—and for the country, marking the start of the [Roaring Twenties, say] and [Prohibition, e.g.]

ERA seems to rival a [Notable time] when it's a [Century 21 competitor]. The second clue refers to the redundantly named corporation, ERA Real Estate (here short for "Electronic Realty Associates"). In this sense, it's reiterated in crosswords as a [Big name in real estate], even at only three letters long. The conglomerate that owns the firm, Realogy Holdings Corp., must know it's making itself redundant: After all, the term they invented, "Realogy," suggests "the study of realty." If they've been **LOGY** about changing the brand because they appreciate the free advertising in puzzles, that would be a "study of reality."

LOGY [Sluggish], [Half-awake]

The sad reality about **ERA**—as the initialism for the Equal Rights Amendment, which would outlaw gender discrimination—is that the [Change to the Constitution first proposed in 1921, for short] still isn't a reality. [Today], [As you read this clue], groups like **NOW** ("National Organization for Women"), the [Feminist org. since 1966], want it passed [Like, immediately]—or more accurately, [By yesterday]. The only questions about the amendment they might have are ["WHEN DO WE WANT IT?"] and ["What are you waiting for?"].

NOW [In], [In style], [Here's partner], ["Chop chop"], [ERA proponent], [Word said before "then," oxymoronically]

Like the [Pitcher's stat] and the [Women's org.], the **ERA** that's a [Bold alternative] as a [Popular laundry detergent] appears in print as "ERA," not "E.R.A." So although [It may contain three periods], the clue [Part of B.C.E.] only refers to [A little bit of history]—the last part of "before the Common Era."

Without mentioning [All alternative] ways **ERA** can be clued, here are some examples of how this old answer gets loaded into puzzles to come out looking new:

- Day
- Long division?
- Span of attention?
- Historic time piece?
- Therapy center?
- Time of one's life, maybe

With so many ways to [Gaslight ___] **ERA**, solvers may well sigh and agree with David Steinberg and Barry C. Silk, who suggested [A simpler one may be recalled].

To make matters of time and space worse, having entered **ERA** for a [Long time], it may take a solver [Quite a while] to realize the answer is **EON**. The two share many clues that, in the [Long run?], can frustrate solvers [Big time], time and again. Fortunately, easier puzzles may nudge the solver toward **EON** through some [Hyperbolic wait time] like [Lo-o-ng time], [Ages and ages], [1,000,000,000 years], [Seemingly for-ev-er], [Eternity], or even [Forever and a day].

EON [Length of time spent on hold, it often seems], [Now we're in the Phanerozoic one], [Time period, or an anagram for one?], [End of lunch?], [Long time between dates?], [S_c_ _d (time in time)], [It's a stretch]

Baseball CARD Abbrs.
Clues with [Wit], But Solvers
[Wag] Their Fingers

Like scoreboards and sports tickers, crosswords rely so heavily on abbreviations for baseball team names that they can start to resemble the backs of baseball **CARDS**. Such shorthand seems fair game, since they're common enough outside of the grid for solvers to say [I'll play these], especially when the clues are [Witty ones]. But [Jokers and aces] are different things, and even sharp clues can't save answers essentially nonexistent outside of puzzles from being [Things to cut]. Constructors feel likewise, yet sometimes still rely on such [Shaky house-building materials?] to keep their grids intact.

CARDS [Missouri team, for short], [Mo. pros], [Jokesters], [What's the big deal], [Hand makeup], [House-building material?]

For instance, solvers across the cruciverse agree: **ALER** ("American Leaguer") and **NLER** ("National Leaguer") are just bad answers. Not only are these shortenings found nigh exclusively in crosswords, but the terms they abbreviate aren't common either. The best constructors can do is try to make the clue amusing, cluing **ALER** as [A, e.g.], [A or O], or [Ray or Jay] and **NLER** as [Nat or Phil]. But these clues hardly make the answers themselves any less obnoxious. Like players with little to contribute, these answers, and their even more shabbily constructed **PLURALS**—**ALERS** and **NLERS**, should be sent to the **SHOWERS** and retired for good.

ALER [Angel, e.g.], [Oriole or Jay], [Blue Jay but not Cardinal, for short]

NLER [Card, e.g.], [Red, for one], [Phil, for one], [Giant, e.g., briefly], [Brave, for instance], [What an A is not], [Modern-day Pirate, e.g.]

PLURALS [Cats and dogs]

ALERS [A and O, but not E, I or U]

NLERS [Giants of the sports page]

SHOWERS [Windups for some pitchers] *(i.e., pitchers taken out of games get "sent to the showers")*

STL [Card display?], [Card's place], [Mo. town]

By comparison, the following broadcast of abbreviations is aired with the full written consent of the answering body:

STL may turn up as the St. Louis [Cardinals on scoreboards] or [Card letters], but don't lay your cards down too fast: The last two (and any others mentioning "Cards") also suit **ARI**, arising from the homonymous NFL squad, the Arizona Cardinals.

Baseball's Arizona Diamondbacks can box **ARI** into [D-backs, in box scores], but puzzles tend to tune in more to [NPR host Shapiro], [MSNBC host Melber], and [Singer Grande, to fans]. Thanks to them, puzzles are finally taking their leave of **ARI** [Ben Canaan, hero of "Exodus"], whose full name means "Lion of God, son of the Promised Land." But there's no escaping the ["Exodus" author] who himself is a literary lion, being the [Literary Leon] **URIS**.

NAT often gets dressed up as a [DC pro], but the Nationals are Canadian by birth: The Montreal Expo franchise quit Quebec in 2004, making a [DC player] essentially an [Expo, today].

SOX is a gamy plural, mostly found playing Scrabble or at the ballpark—or in crosswords. It's typically available in two options— [White ___] and [Red ___]. Puzzles prefer visiting **CHI** over **BOS**, where things can get muddy: The **BOSOX** play at **FENWAY** Park in the Fenway neighborhood, itself named for The Fenway (an old parkway designed by Central Park architect Frederick Law Olmstead), the name ultimately anchored in the area's historic topography: a **FEN**, or [Swampland]. Infelicitous enough as a ball field site, a **FEN** presents a real [Quagmire] when grounded in a grid, as nearly all its clues can have solvers entering a **BOG**.

So it can be said that [Hall-of-Fame third baseman Wade] **BOGGS** was a natural fit when he joined the Red Sox in 1982. Yet a decade later, he packed his bags and moved to the Bronx, where he won a ring with the Yankees. But he moved on to the Tampa Bay **RAYS** before the **YANKS**—who really are [Big jerks], according to many Sox fans—won the championship three times in a row, so Boggs wasn't a part of the three-**PEAT**. True, all that [Bog buildup] used for [Fen fuel] was a [Turf] act to follow! But that just comes with the territory when you wade through bogs, for **PETES** sake!

URIS [Author Leon], ["Exodus" novelist], ["The Haj" author], ["Battle Cry" author] *(i.e., pitchers taken out of games get "sent to the showers")*, ["Trinity" novelist], ["Topaz" author Leon], ["QB VIII" author], ["Mila 18" author" Leon], [Leon on many spines]

NAT [Insurrectionist Turner], [Singer Cole], [Entomologist's first name?], [One stealing in DC?]

SOX [Either of the World Series winners of 2004 and '05], [Either of two A's rivals], [Short hose?]

CHI [___-Town] *(See chapter 1)*

BOS [Derek and Diddley], [Jackson and Hopkins], [2011 Stanley Cup winners]

BOSOX [Noted curse breakers?]

FENWAY [Park with one red seat]

FEN and **BOG** [Marsh], [Mire], [Wetland], [Where cranberries grow], [Peat's place]

RAYS [Tanners], [You may catch them on a boat, in two different ways]

YANKS [Sox foes], [Rebs' foes]

PEAT [Mulching material], [Scotch flavorer], [Fire fuel in whiskey production], [Dried fuel], [Fertilizer source], [Everglades deposit], [Flammable moss], [Marsh matter], [It's in the bog]

PETES [Seeger and Sampras], [Whose sake?], ["___ a Pizza" (punnily titled children's book)], [Rose and others] *(as in the former player banned from baseball, but not puzzles)*

Where Cross-Checking Will Land You in the Box
The **NHL** as [Orr's org.]

NHL [Goal-oriented org.], [Sharks' and Jets' org.], [Flames shoot in it: Abbr.], [Blues group?], [Devils' advocate: Abbr.]

The **NHL** can elicit shouts of "Shoot!" with its [Wild grp.] of clues, deflecting solvers' attempts on goal with traps like [Toronto and Ottawa are in it, for short], [Penguins' home?: Abbr.], [Senators', org.], or constructor Hal Moore's slapshot, [Grp. that frowns upon illegal checks].

ORR [Hockey great Bobby], [Boston Bruins legend], [Bobby on ice], [Bobby who won eight Norris Trophies (and is in NORRIS TROPHIES)], ["Catch-22" character described as "a warm-hearted, simple-minded gnome"]

As far as crosswords are concerned, the **NHL** is basically [Orr's old org.]. The ['60s-'70s Bruin Bobby] **ORR**, the [Three-time N.H.L. M.V.P.] Hall-of-Famer known as ["Bobby Hockey"], is equally prolific in puzzles. His jersey makes him [Notable #4 on the ice], observed by constructors Peter A. Collins and Bruce Haight as the [Hockey great whose jersey number rhymed with his name].

YETI [Legendary mountain climber], [Subject of a blurry photo, maybe], [Subject of a onetime Nepali hunting license [true fact!]]

Though a Bruin, as a [Legendary iceman] **ORR** can look less like a bear than a [Himalayan humanoid], the **YETI**, another [Fabulous creature], [Elusive legend], and [Figure that's unbelievable?] in its own right. Yet I digress . . .

PTS [Qt. halves], [N, E, W, and S], [Two for a basket: Abbr.], [A trilogy has three: Abbr.], [Max. 3,3333,360, in Pac-Man], [Spread makeup: Abbr.]

Orr holds the record for **PTS** (point of order: those "pts." are [Score amts.], not [The eight in a gal.]) by a defenseman. The **BRUIN** shares his name with a **FLYER** who's another "crash-prone" member of a line of defense, Joseph Heller's Captain **ORR**, the ["Catch-22" character who "hasn't got brains enough to be unhappy"].

BRUIN [Bear], [UCLA athlete], [Beantown skater], [Bobby Orr, notably]

FLYER [Aviator], [Philadelpia hockey player], [Circular]

The fictional Orr's more offensive squad-mate was the infamous ["Catch-22" profiteer], the profligate First Lieutenant **MILO** Minderbinder—whose first name is [Venus's home].

MILO [Venus de ___], [Whence Venus?], ["The Phantom Tollbooth" protagonist], [Ventimiglia of "This Is Us"], [Actor O'Shea], [Heller's Minderbinder]

COURT [Bar room?], [Try for a mate?], [Place to press a suit?], [Jazz gig setting?], [Match box?]

Puzzles [Try to win] at COURT
Basketball Proves Cagey, but Tennis Says Lets

WNBA ("Women's National Basketball Association") [Org. for those with Dream jobs?], [Sun bloc?], [The Sun and Mercury are in it: Abbr.]

Thanks to their teams, the **WNBA** is the [Home of the Sun, Storm, and Sky], setting it similarly to that other [Hoop grp.] and [Professional bouncers' org.] seen as the [Suns' org.], the **NBA**.

NBA ("National Basketball Association") [Pelicans' home, for short], [Jazz grp.], [Org. with a travel ban?]

A third [Court org.], the former **ABA** ("American Basketball Association"), was [Dr. J's first pro league]. More often, though, the answer is clued according to another acronym, the "American Bar Association," an [Org. with suits and cases]. So both **ABA** orgs suit up as [Court inits.]—and either might form a [Defense grp.?].

A **CAGER** is a [Basketball player, in old slang], though it can appear to moonlight as [Jazz player?] if it shoots hoops in Utah. "Cager" recalls the sport's beginnings, when 12-foot-tall wire mesh fencing was used to protect the crowd—giving a whole new meaning to "defense." Suiting the grid's **CAGY** look and **CAGEY** clues, crosswords still embrace the term "cager," though less often as an answer than in clues like [Cleveland cager] for **CAV**, a cavalier form of "Cavalier." In a clue where it receives an [Alley-___] **OOP** pass from a Dallas nickname, [Big D cager] scores for **MAV**, a maverick form of "Maverick" (after the eponymous 19th-century Texas rancher who didn't brand his cattle).

Two other groups branded as a [Court org.] are the **USTA**, "United States Tennis Association," and the **ATP**, "Association of Tennis Professionals"—both of which also appear as [Racketeer's org.?] and [Singles group?].

A few other tennis answers are often served with spin: **DEUCE** refers to a [Court tie] of [Forty all]. But careful, [It may be wild], as in: [It comes between ads]. Solvers wondering, "What the [Dickens]?" need to spot that the word for a [Two-spot] in poker is also the tennis [Score before ad in or ad out].

ADIN ("ad in," for "advantage in") can be a [Pre-service announcement?] of the [Score after deuce], or—much less directly—[What results from an ace and a deuce]. Like **LOVE** and **LET**, it's a common [Court cry].

LOVE gets you [Zero] in tennis, a clue that may cause ["A temporary insanity," per Ambrose Bierce]. Unlike tennis, it's ["A game that two can play and both win": Eva Gabor].

In soccer, **NIL** is [Love by another name]; fortunately, a shootout can end the [Pointlessness?] of continuing to [Zip around the field?]. Teams scoring nil may feel as blue as **ANIL**, a [Deep blue dye].

ABA [Judicial ratings grp.], [Noted org. with a brief history?], [Case worker's org.?], [Practice grp.?]

CAGER [Baller, in old lingo], [Hoopster], [Any Raptor]

CAGY and **CAGEY** [Shrewd], [Evasive], [Cautious]

CAV [Ohio pro athlete, informally], [University of Virginia athlete]

OOP [End of an alley in the lane?]

MAV [Dallas pro], [NBA nickname]

USTA [Ashe stadium org.], [Org. where love means nothing?], [Org. for the Williams sisters]

ATP [Sports org. hidden in "great play"], [Org. for Nadal or Federer]

DEUCE [Devil], [Ad preceder?], [Curveball, in slang]

LOVE ["<3<3<3" sentiment], ["A madness most discreet," per Romeo], ["A smoke made with the fume of sighs," to Romeo], ["Friendship that has caught fire," per Ann Landers], ["Like the measles, ___ is most dangerous when it comes late in life": Lord Byron]

ANIL [Source of indigo], ["Slumdog Millionaire" co-star ___ Kapoor]

LET [Tennis serve that nicks the net], [Tennis redo], [Do-over], [Pig tail?]

BORG [Wimbledon champ, 1976–80], ["Star Trek" villains]

GRAF [Winner of 22 Grand Slam singles titles, second-most in the Open Era], [Agassi's 2001 bride]

ILIE [Nastase with a racket], [Arthur lost to him at the 1972 US Open], [Bjorn beat him in the 1976 Wimbledon finals], ["Nasty" Nastase]

At Wimbledon, [Imperfect service] leads to a [Call to reserve] even if [It's not your fault]. Off the court, **LET** is nimble enough to [Allow] [Grant] to [Rent out] his place while on [Leave].

["Off the Court" author] and [1975 Wimbledon winner] Arthur **ASHE** is such a regular sight in puzzles, the ['60s–'70s tennis great Arthur] qualifies as simply a [Tennis name] or [Court star]—permitting "Arthur" to take leave of his own clue. The clues also give a shot at either title to challengers like Bjorn **BORG**, Steffi **GRAF**, and **ILIE** Nastase. [Court name] works likewise, except it can also refer to *the* Arthur **ASHE**: the eponymous [US Open stadium] alluded to ingeniously in another clue: [Queens' Arthur court?].

Crosswords' ACE [___ in the hole]

Wow, an **ACE** can have *two* values in blackjack? Don't make crosswords laugh. Puzzles can top that in a single [Crackerjack] clue by puzzle [Whiz] Erik Agard, the crossword editor at *USA Today*, who carded it as a [Term in tennis, golf, and baseball, all with different meanings]. To break that down, it's a [Server's wish] on clay courts, a [Hole in one] on the links, and a [Star pitcher] at the ballpark. And that clue is no [One-hit wonder]: [Pro] constructors continually find new, backhanded, [Virtuoso] ways to [Put something past?] solvers and prove themselves a [Top card].

- ☐ A card?
- ☐ Big heart?
- ☐ Suit bottom
- ☐ King topper
- ☐ One in play?
- ☐ Hole dweller?
- ☐ Big heart
- ☐ Valuable diamond
- ☐ So-called bullet
- ☐ One in Vegas, maybe?
- ☐ Part of the upper deck?

- ☐ Breeze through
- ☐ Nail
- ☐ Crush
- ☐ Ringer
- ☐ Big pitcher
- ☐ Top gun
- ☐ Shooting star?
- ☐ Big shot in the sky
- ☐ Dogfight participant
- ☐ Snoopy, in his dreams
- ☐ Rickenbacker or von Richthofen

- ☐ Course rarity
- ☐ Rare driving result
- ☐ Peak service?
- ☐ Serve well-done?
- ☐ Point of no return?
- ☐ Missile from Venus?
- ☐ Result of rapid service?
- ☐ Nickname for a pal
- ☐ Big name in wrappers
- ☐ Word made out of vitamins

But **ASHE** is beloved for reasons beyond his tennis skills. As an advocate for AIDS awareness, Haitian refugees, and urban healthcare, [He was named 1992's Sportsman of the Year, despite retiring from tennis 12 years earlier]. [Courtly Arthur] passed away in 1993, but is remembered each year at the US Open through Arthur Ashe Kids Day, and—in a small way—through clues like [Activist and tennis legend Arthur].

ASHE [Arthur who ruled the court?], [First winner of the US Open], [World's largest tennis stadium, familiarly], [1985 Tennis Hall of Fame inductee], ["Days of Grace" memoirist], ["A Hard Road to Glory: A History of the African American Athlete" author Arthur]

The [Giant first name] of Puzzles

Grid Irony and Gridiron-y ELI

The most frequent name in crosswords is **ELI**, one of the top-10 answers during the Shortz Era. Solvers with only a passing knowledge of football may be thrown by [QB Manning], more familiar with Peyton than his little brother, the [Manning of the New York Giants]. Both **QBS** won two Super Bowl rings, but Peyton was the greater success on the field. Yet **ELI** is crossword's [Giant Manning].

An earlier **ELI** elevated in puzzles was a [Biblical high priest] whose name, befitting his position, is "ascent" or "high" in Hebrew. And yet when he learned the Philistines had captured the Ark of the Covenant, the [Teacher of Samuel] fell down, broke his neck, and died.

Perhaps with his last breath, the [Biblical judge] said something sounding like his own name, as **ELI** can also mean ["My God!" in Hebrew], as in "Eli, Eli," a Holocaust resistance song and unofficial anthem of Israel. Similarly, it's the Aramaic ["My God!," as cried by Jesus] from the crucifix: *Eli, Eli, lama sabachthani* ("My God, my God, why have you forsaken me?").

Any ["Y" wearer] will recognize **ELI** as the [Ivy League nickname] for the [New Haven collegian], comparable to **YALIE**. Named for the British merchant Elihu **YALE**, the [Brown alternative] is [Where Bill met Hillary]. **ELIS** may sing as [Whiffenpoofs, e.g.], or study the

ELI [Actor Wallach], [Pharmacist Lilly], [Clockmaker Terry], [Inventor Whitney], [First name in gins?], [The "E" of the REO Speed Wagon], [Gin name?], ["Hostel" director Roth], [Samuel Alito, Clarence Thomas or Sonia Sotomayor, schoolwise]

QBS [Play directors, briefly], [Snap targets, for short], [Passers, briefly], [Ones going for hikes, for short?]

YALIE [Bush or Kerry], [Bulldog], ["Baa! Baa! Baa!" singer]

YALE [Lock inventor Linus], [Master of locks], [Harvard rival], [Schlage rival], [It's a lock], [The Bulldogs], [Elis' school], [Bowl site]

ELIS [Skull and Bones members], [Jodie Foster and Meryl Streep, collegiately]

[Ancient Greek land that hosted the Olympics]. Either way, as constructor Lucy Gardner sagely saw them, they're [Y's guys?].

When it was published in 1901, Yale's unofficial, ebullient fight song, "Boola **BOOLA**" made plenty of **MOOLA**, topping national sheet-music sales charts. Yet not even its writer could say how he came up with the title "word." While echoing lyrics in other songs popular at the time, perhaps "boola" struck a chord chiming with "bulldog" and "bow wow." A dozen years later, Cole Porter wrote Yale's official fight song, "Bulldog," which opens just as one might expect (unless expecting Cole Porter-level lyrics): "Bulldog! Bulldog! Bow, wow, wow, Eli Yale," which *maybe* makes more sense?

ELHI—even if it's just [K–12] and skips a lot of school as "Elementary through High"—is an even more academic answer. **ETON** is another precollege answer. Since its founding in 1440, Eton has produced a [Kind of collar] and a [Kind of jacket] donned by bookish sorts like George Orwell, Aldous Huxley, and James **BOND**—perhaps because Ian Fleming studied there. And it's the villain Captain Hook's school—perhaps because J. M. Barrie didn't.

Have a [Driving passion?]
For That Sinking Feeling, Try GOLF

GOLF may be ["A good walk spoiled," per Twain], but Jacob Stulberg made a good word dazzle when he clued **PGA** (Professional Golf Association), an [Org. whose members may be putting on a show?]. (**SYNC** the answer by letting "putting" sink in.) Doug Peterson holed **PGA** beautifully from the rough [A major?]. (Here the "PGA" isn't the organization but the PGA Championship, one of the four men's competitions known collectively as the majors).

PGA and **LPGA** tend to pop up as a [Tour grp.], or slightly camouflaged as a [Green org.?]. **PAR** is a [Golf course standard], but [It's not unusual] to find this [Average] [Golf goal] disguised as [Something to shoot for]. Other potential hazards for these three popular answers include the following:

PGA or LPGA		
Links org.	Swingers' grp.	Org. monitoring eagles?
Masters org.	Iron workers' org.?	Org. involving course work?
Fringe grp.?	Club club, for short	Course overseer, for short
Drivers' org.?	Its members often pitch	Open organization, for short
Couples' grp.	Org. with aces and chips	Org. whose members are teed off?
Club circuit?	Sports org. with pitching	Org. whose website has a lot of links?

PAR		
Equality	Duffer's delight	Standard for the course
Go for it	What's expected	Recover from a bad stroke?
72, often	Green yardstick	When it's broken, that's good
The usual	It's hard to shoot	One of nine numbers on a card
Links figure	Get a 3 on a 2, e.g.	What one will never be, in golf
Hole number	3, 4, or 5, usually	What drivers try not to go over
Course guide?	An eagle beats it	2, 3, or 4, usually in miniature golf
4 is a high one	It's to be expected	Score between a birdie and a bogey
6 is a rare one	You may feel below it	Value which for Apple stock is $0.00001

[Golf great Sam] **SNEAD** was the [Winner of a record 82 PGA Tour events]. The oddest, in which he bested 14 women in a battle-of-the-sexes tournament, makes him the [Only man ever to win an LPGA Tour Tournament, (1962)]. Snead was called [Slammin' Sammy] long before [Baseball's "Slammin' Sammy"] **SOSA** was born.

Snead aside, the top LPGA name might belong to the [Golf great Lorena] **OCHOA**. The Mexican-born Hall-of-Famer had held the top ranking on the tour for three years straight when she retired in 2010. "Lorena," the Spanish "Lauren," branches from the Latin for the **LAUREL** tree.

A Japanese golfer in the World Hall of Fame, **ISAO AOKI**, was also awarded a laurel at birth: His given name, *aoki* (literally, "blue tree") refers to the Japanese laurel. The American Mark **OMEARA** ("O'Meara") made a [Mark on a golf course] twice in 1998, winning two majors to become the PGA Player of the Year. "O'Meara" doesn't

SOSA [Slugger Sammy], [Sammy with 609 homers], [McGwire's 1998 rival]

LAUREL [Source of bay leaves], [Bay tree], [Poet's honor], [Branch of the Olympics?], [Hardy companion?]

ISAO [Golf's Aoki]

AOKI [PGA's Isao]

OMEARA [Mark in the World Golf Hall of Fame]

mean "laurel," but there's no reason to feel let down—it's thought to have roots in "merriment" and "mead."

Crosswords' perennial Player of the Year is the [South African golfing great], [Swinging Ernie] **ELS**. His 6'3" frame and smooth swing made him [Golf's "Big Easy"], and he's golf's big easy answer when appearing as [Golfer Ernie].

But **ELS**, befitting [Right-angle shapes] or [House wings], tend to get bent in puzzles. As a [Trio in Valhalla?], they're [Loopy cursive letters]. As [Above-ground trains] in Chicago, they're [Loop loopers]. And that's hardly the [End of all?] the ways they throw solvers for a loop.

When it Doesn't Come [The Big Easy] Way: [Logical tips?] for ELS		
Lines up?	Cars over the road	LLL
High ways?	Lines around Chicago?	Roll back?
High rollers	They're caught in Chicago	Dull couple?
Old N.Y.C. lines	Many characters in "Kill Bill"	Yellow belly?
C.T.A. transports	Higher forms of transportation	Llama heads?
Cab alternatives	Trains seen at the end of tunnels?	These run high
Chicago bearers?	Shapes made by thumbs and index fingers	Volleyball quartet?

"ALI Ali Boxin' -G!"
["The Greatest"] Answer?

ALI [Stand-up comic Wong], [__Baba], ["Aladdin" prince], [Mahershala of "Moonlight"], [HBO's __G]

KOD [Put down on canvas?], [Floored], [Decked]

SONOFA ["Why you little..."], ["What in the...!"]

If not "the greatest" answer in terms of frequency, the [Ring master?] Muhammad **ALI** rates pretty high. And well he should, considering that—like the Hebrew cognate belonging to another giant athlete of the cruciverse, **ELI**—the Arabic **ALI** is a [Name meaning "high"].

Solvers looking to pull the answer down may find themselves laid out flat, **KOD** ("K.O.'d," as in knocked out) by clues that float like another line and sting like a **SONOFA** b—.

- 1960s slugger
- Noted ring leader
- Foreman's superior
- Louisville slugger?
- Lord of the ring?

- Remodeled Clay?
- Well-known jabber?
- Big name in flooring?
- Clay, transformed?
- 🥊 🦋 🐝

If that last clue caught you flat-footed, it might help knowing it came from a puzzle by Brian Kulman called "The Emoji Movie," which solvers discovered used emoji trios as clues to condense the plots of 16 films. So it's technically not Muhammad Ali that's the answer, but the 2001 [Will Smith biopic], *Ali*.

ALI also stands in for Muhammad Ali's prizefighter daughter, [Laila of the ring]. Another pair of seeming relatives, the [Son-in-law of Muhammad] and [Cousin of Muhammad], refer to the same man: Ali ibn Abi Talib was both.

Last and (let's face it) least, there's **ALI** [___ G (Sasha Baron Cohen's rapper character)], who's more apt to show up in full as the barely intelligible **ALIG** ("Ali G"), the ["Interviewer" who asked Kobe Bryant how many springs are in a basketball].

Solvers floored by that or any of the clues for **ALI** might heed the advice of the [Athlete who said "Silence is golden when you can't think of a good answer"]. Or just answer with a 🥊.

ALIG [Cohen character], [Character who interviewed Newt Gingrich], [TV interviewer who called astronaut "Buzz" Aldrin "Buzz Lightyear"]

Chapter 7 Puzzle: "Hit Me!"

ACROSS

1 Something used for buttering up?
5 "Skyfall" singer
10 He wrote a lot of notes
14 Successfully serve some punch
15 Sea red?
16 Pool shade?
17 49, 50-50, and 51
18 Lead-off and clean-up hitters?
20 Palindromic double platinum Steely Dan album
21 Taunt
22 Another name
23 Home team, to fans?
27 Talk nonsense
28 Bee follower
29 Mo. town?
32 Spielberg or Soderbergh
35 Way to stand
36 "The Lion King" daughter
37 Basemen?
40 He's always itching for a fight
41 Online answer page
42 Amusement park wheels
43 Stadium shout
44 Member of Attila's horde
45 ___ Tin Tin (old TV dog)
46 Grounds crew chief?
52 Front or rear car parts
55 One who knew there'd be a rain delay

56 Strike
57 Trades—e.g., from 29-Across to 64-Across—or what this puzzle does four times
60 Pak in the World Golf Hall of Fame
61 &&&
62 Japanese massage practice
63 Morris or Hyman who opened a deli in New York in 1888
64 Something held for those who don't like it
65 He really dotted his i's
66 Flushing Stadium that's an anagram of 1-Across

DOWN

1 Dulcé of the "The Daily Show"
2 Pilgrim to Mecca
3 Like the bald eagle and blue whale, once
4 Spots on the field?
5 Words before "faith" or "God"
6 "There she was, just a-walkin' down the street, singin' ___..."
7 Wear away
8 Certain Southeast Asian
9 Certain North-Poler
10 Big dos
11 Here, in 12-Down
12 Olympic gold medalist in baseball in 1992, 1996, and 2004

13 Rudolf ___, early 20th century amateur horticulturiast interested in avocados
19 Oscar-winning actress Blanchett
21 "Look for yourself!"
24 Hangover locales?
25 Purple drupe
26 Mark down as clearance, perhaps
29 It's Northern California's fault
30 Initialism before a text synopsis
31 It's often least
32 Guess
33 By way of, briefly
34 Dullsville
35 With 10-Across, "composer" of "Fanfare for the Common Cold"
36 Finnish tech giant
38 Jaguar's canine?
39 Transform
44 "Boo!"
46 Ashton Kutcher's "That '70s Show" role
47 One way to walk
48 Salad items
49 "Li'l Abner" teacher Hawkins, namesake of ladies'-choice dances
50 Ball spinning about 1,000 m.p.h.
51 Portmanteau for conveying happiness with a look
52 First one to be ejected for acting smart?

53 TV's "warrior princess"
54 Grey with more orange in it?
58 Day at the gym?
59 Boardroom bigwig
60 Music genre name imitative of its guitar sound

Chapter 8

ANIMALS
Crosswords' Most [Fabled characters?]

Any cruciverbalist can tell you, crossword grids display a certain **ANIMAL** magnetism. In this chapter, we'll visit [Cats and dogs], [Things in farms], and some really [Wild ones] representing the weirdest, funniest looking [Critters] to have ever roamed (or haunted) the earth. (Relax, okapi, coati, and kudu—I refer only to your spelling.) Toss in some [Cat and mouse] clues, and things can really get hairy.

As for crosswords' spirit animal, it's hard to say. The [Sponge, for one], makes a good candidate, or maybe the [Muppets drummer]. Either way, we've got [A kingdom] to explore and a [Wrangler's charge] ahead.

So grab your **HAT**—it's time to go on safari.

HAT ["The Cat in the ___"], [Beaver, for one], [Porkpie, e.g.], [Rabbit's place, maybe], [It may be cocked], [Deerstalker, e.g.], [All ___ and no cattle]

221

ELAND
Where the Deer and the Elk Could Play,
But Not the [African Antelope]

In 1994, Cathy Allis constructed a crossword containing no vowels but "E," which she cleverly entitled "Eland." Its namesake was an animal of great renown in crosswords, the **ELAND**, a [Serengeti grazer]. The name of the [Dik-dik's cousin] roamed to England by way of the Dutch word for "elk."

Ironically, the "A" in **ELAND** precluded the [Spiral-horned antelope] from being a [Safari sighting] in its own puzzle. **ANT**, **ASS**, **PUG**, and **YAK**, were not offered an **EVITE** ("e-vite") either. To put it another way, they were *évité*, or [Shunned: Fr.].

(Then again, perhaps they just couldn't find the right "Eland." There's one hiding in Iceland, Ireland, Cleveland, and two places that can even evoke a crossword grid: Graceland and Wasteland.)

The eland's **ILK**, the **ELK**, met the spelling criteria but might not have been wanted, as [They're game] to behave like a [Horny forest creature]. Then again, even if they act like a [Member of a benevolent order], they're apt to be [Cougar prey], especially when one is a [Male that might be in a rut?].

RUT might seem like a [Bad thing to be in], but it refers to the term for certain mammals' mating season. So what's a [Daily grind] to some might be a ram's [Groove] [When ewe are in the mood].

The cruciverse's famed [Farm female], the ubiquitous **EWE**, was (or were, as it's also an alternative plural to **EWES**) also weirdly **AWOL** from "Eland." Similarly, while **URN** couldn't earn its way in, it would have been the perfect [Vessel] as a **EWER**.

While solvers were much more likely to encounter crosswords' [Decorative pitcher], the **EWER**, years back, the [Wide-mouthed jug] still turns up as a fairly [Common still-life subject] in puzzles. Skewered as a [Pitcher that can't throw], it sounds like a [Pour thing], but the [Big-mouthed one that can hold its wine?] also retains its pride, being [One with a stiff upper lip?].

At least "Eland" was not bereft of **EFTS**. An **EFT** (as "eft") is an [Immature salamander] but can also be (as "EFT," "electronic funds transfer") a [Direct deposit, for short]. Either way, an **EFT** can mature and multiply in a bank.

Before we depart Eland, we better drop in on puzzles' dear **DEER**, **ENA**, who is unfamiliar family to many solvers as [Bambi's aunt]. Ena's last name is totally unknown, so let's call her Ena **DOE**. (Using the other [Anonymous last name], **ROE**, for her would seem sort of fishy.) If Bambi had an uncle, he would have been a **HART**, a [Doe's mate] or [Rogers's partner, in song]—even if he often arrives [Stag].

DEER [A buck or two?], [Does as a group?], [Fast-moving game?]

ENA [Disney doe], [Actress Hartman]

DOE [Mommy deerest?], [Where the buck stops?], [Female caribou], [Female kangaroo], [Female koala], [Female squirrel or rabbit], [Female kid], [Figure in many suits], [John no one knows]

ROE [Caviar], [Preschool group?], [Norma McCorvey's alias in a famous court case], [Output from a bass]

HART [Male deer], ["The Lady is a Tramp" lyricist]

It Ain't Me, Babe,
It Ain't <u>MAA</u> Ewe're Looking for
[What the goatherd herd?]

It can be difficult to know what gets to enter the kingdom of crosswords, as puzzles don't differentiate the sheep from the goats, at least by their sounds. Only **MAA** can be called to summon the old [Ewe in the movie "Babe"], but in most other respects, either [Sheepish remark], **MAA** or **BAA**, can be a **MEWL** or **PULE** from a goat or sheep.

Encountering clues for **MAA** or **BAA**, solvers can insert an "AA" battery in the back and test how they work to get the answer to start. Eventually, the "M" or "B" will appear through a cross, the lamb's sound will be identified, and there'll be much rejoicing at the revelation of the word.

With utterly sheer genius, Matt Gaffney did a little Dr. Dolittle impression by translating **BAA** as the ovine for ["I am a sheep"].

MEWL and **PULE** [Whimper], [Act the crybaby]

Pretty [Hairy animals]
Fuzzy MAMMALS to Get the Warm Fuzzies Over

FAUNA [Flora's friend], [Regional wildlife]

FAWN [Babe in the woods], [Young buck], [Forest issue]

IBEX [Bearded mountain climber], [Alpine goat], [Goat with recurved horns], [Animal also called a steinbock]

FAUN [Half-man/half-goat], [Pan, for one], [Mythical spirit], [Forest flautist]

GNU [Serengeti grazer], [Animal in a herd], [Stampede member in "The Lion King"], [Prey for a lion] *(See part one for more on this [White bearded Kenyan])*

ZEBRA [Ref], [Maned creature], ["I finally got around to reading the dictionary. Turns out the ___ did it": Steven Wright]

SILENTG [Paradigm feature]

Other **FAUNA** crosswords **FAWN** over includes the **IBEX**, a [Wild goat] different from the wilder but only-half-as-[Goatlike creature], the **FAUN**.

The ibex shares its "mane" facial feature with that infamous [Bearded beast] of the cruciverse, the **GNU**, also known as the [Wildebeest], which by now should be familiar [African game]. Despite their pint-size names, gnus are huge, weighing 350 to 550 pounds. They're well suited for puzzles' vertical lines, as they often graze among **ZEBRA**, who can alert them to predators.

Nevertheless, they're common prey in grids. The silent "G" makes **GNU** a [Fresh-sounding antelope], though paradoxically it's also an [Animal that doesn't have a sound coming out of its head?]. To add to the irony, the word "gnu" is quite old, originating in southwestern Africa and mimicking the grunting sound that comes out of the animal's mouth.

In fact, it's actually English speakers who have made the antelope sound new; its original name is likely either *t'gnu* or *!nu*. Whether unable to find a satisfactory English-seeming transliteration for *t'gnu*—or simply stymied by the alveolar click at the head of *!nu*—English decided to give it the **SILENTG** treatment.

That gee is audible when part of **GNU** ("GNU"), the computer [Operating system that's "not Unix"]. GNU is a recursive acronym (i.e., it reflects on itself—which, in a twist, is more like the horns of an ibex than a gnu) for "GNU's Not Unix!" So maybe the question's not "What's gnu?" but "What's **UNIX**?" The answer, in brief, is an [Early operating system] that, as an [MS-DOS alternative], formed the basis for Mac's **OSX**. (So we really are on **SAFARI**.)

The **ORYX** is another [Serengeti roamer]. The four species of [Large African antelope] include the [Gemsbok], making the other oryx (or "oryxes") each a [Gemsbok's cousin]. "Oryx" might track to the Ancient Greek for "dig," as some dig shallow holes to rest and cool in. So oryx must dig filling holes in a grid (itself a cool spot for solitary downtime).

KUDOS to solvers who ken **KUDU**—yet another [Large antelope]—as [Eland kin].

Speaking of kin, the endangered **OKAPI** is a [Giraffe's cousin]. But when described as a [Striped African creature], solvers are likely to enter another five-letter answer before exclaiming something like "okapi!" Okapi are renowned for using their 18-inch tongues to clean their ears and eyes, but good luck making it a [Safari sight]; it was so long before any Westerner laid eyes on one that the [Rain forest ruminant] became known as the ["African unicorn"].

To **SPOT** one, head to an [Ocelot's spot]—a **ZOO**. Solvers doing so in Oaxaca will be *o*-so-happy to know **OSO**, [Spanish for "bear"], and **OSA**, a [Spanish she-bear].

There'll be little need to translate **LOBO**, used in puzzles to refer to the common [Timber wolf], though probably clued more accurately as the endangered [Gray wolf], also known as the Mexican wolf. Or for one gray wolf in particular: the eponymous "Lobo the King of Currumpow," the 1898 story by Ernest Thompson **SETON** relating his attempt to trap Lobo, who with his pack would [Attack] (as "set on") livestock. The heartrending account would inspire a young boy named David Attenborough and a 1963 live-action Disney film.

A **STOAT** can also be called an **ERMINE**, but especially in winter, when the stoat's coat turns white, making a [Luxurious fur]. The less-valued **VOLE** is a [Mouse lookalike] that's a [Cousin of a lemming]—a clue that involuntarily sounds insulting.

UNIX [Windows alternative]

OSX [Yosemite platform], [One of a number of big computers?]

SAFARI [Mac browser], [Chrome alternative], [It's Swahili for "journey"], [Place to watch the big game?]

ORYX [Straight-horned Saharan antelope], [Margaret Atwood's "___ and Crake"]

KUDOS [Praise], [Acclaim], [Glory], [Thumbs up], ["Great job!"]

KUDU [Spiral-horned antelope], [Striped antelope], [Beast hunted by Hemingway in "Green Hills of Africa"]

SPOT [Descry], [Espy], [Primer dog], [Dog tag?], [Tea serving?], [Advance], [Pip], [Ad], [Gym request], [Bit of trouble], [Bane for Lady Macbeth], [Bind]

ZOO [Hippo campus], [Ram home?]

OSO [One in un zoológico]

OSA [Mexican mama bear]

LOBO [Wolf], [Spanish wolf], [Wolf out west], [University of Mexico mascot]

STOAT [Short-tailed weasel], [Mink kin], [Source of brown fur], [Brown ermine]

ERMINE [Status symbol in many Elizabeth I portraits]

COATI [South American animal also known as a "hog-nosed coon"], [Kinkajou's cousin]

The comfy-sounding **COATI** pops up almost invariably along the lines of [Relative of a racoon]. Its name refers to its long, flexible snout, meaning "belt-nose" in the Brazilian language, Tupi.

TAPIR [Much smaller relative of the rhinoceros], [Animal with a trunk], [Mammal with four toes on its front feet and three on the back]

But puzzles' nosiest animal is the **TAPIR**, as clues often point to his peculiar proboscis, as in [Animal with a prehensile snout]. Known as the *mo* in China and *baku* in Japan, the tapir shares its name in both countries with a similar, mythical, dream-eating chimera made from the scraps leftover when other animals were created. In Japan, children summon the *baku* to eat their nightmares, but they mustn't do so too often, or the *baku* will feed on their good dreams as well, leaving the child soulless. Combined with the actual animal's propensity to bite when provoked, it's probably for the best that puzzles don't tap **TAPIR** as an answer too often.

MALAGASY [Madagascar resident], [Madagascar language]

AYEAYE [Roger's cousin]

The stuff of nightmares to many, a **MALAGASY** is the **AYEAYE**, a [Nocturnal lemur] with an eye-catching elongated finger on each hand. Superstition holds that aye-ayes sneak into homes at night and use their eerily long digits to slit sleepers' throats. So if ever awakened by such a lemur, the safest response is "Aye aye," ["Yes, Captain!"], ["Whatever you say"]. On the main, the same applies: Just say ["Sí, sí," at sea"].

LEMUR [Ring-tailed primate]

In English, **LEMUR** has a similar tale, the word housing the soul of the Latin *lemurēs* ("spirits of the dead"), referring to the primates' nocturnal habits and ghost-like faces.

BLACKBIRDS Singing in the Dread of Night
[Crows], Rooks, Ravens, the Roc, and Big Bird

ROC [Sinbad's bird], [Bird of myth], [Hip-hop's ___-A-Fella Records]

BAKU only rarely slips into puzzles, and then in reference to the [Capital of Azerbaijan]. That likely makes **ROC** the most legendary answer in the cruciverse. The giant [Mythical bird in the "Arabian Nights"] looms as large in puzzles as it supposedly did in the sky: [One carried Sinbad to safety], and it famously fed not on dreams but on elephants. Today it feasts on novice crossword solvers, but that's a small price to pay for getting to see the **ROC** as [Big bird].

"Roc" reflects the same Persian root as **ROOK**, the [Chess piece whose name is derived from the Persian for "chariot"]. A sneaky rook can steal a chess game, but the homonymous bird, also called a Eurasian crow, has it beat. The rook's crafty and thieving ways have made its name synonymous with [Swindle] and [Fleece]. In turn, "rookie" arose because a greenhorn can be easily tricked.

The **CROW** are [People also known as the Apsáalooke]: literally, "children of the large-beaked bird," which the French rendered as "people of the crow." Despite adopting the name Crow, many in the tribe believe the "large-beaked bird" refers to another legendary flyer, the Thunderbird.

The **CROW** that's a [Caws cause] is another story. Like its close relative the rook, the crow is associated with thieving and villainy, as evidenced in the Latin **ADAGE** *Corvus oculum corvi non eruit* ("A crow will not pull out another's crow's eye"). In other words: There's honor among thieves. On the high seas, it's the "pirate code." In the mafia, it's **OMERTA** (*omertà*). In either, it's a [Code of silence].

As it happens, rooks, crows, and ravens have some capacity to **TALK**, speaking to why the **EDGAR** with the [Literary monogram] **EAP** chose the **RAVEN** to haunt his poem. The constructor Mel Taub once sized up **POE** as the [Writer whose work describes him to a T].

A **CROW** is even given to [Boast] or [Brag], as might anyone who got to play the part of [The bird in Hitchcock's "The Birds"]—let alone a [Participant in a murder]. Crows are so deathly that even when they **CAW**, they **CROAK**.

Somewhere between a caw and a croak is a crow's **CRAW**. Also known as a [Bird's crop], it helps break food down, though for humans it can be a [Sticking point] when clued as [Bird food holder] or [Food crop?].

So for a crow, a **CROP** is both a place to store what it eats, and what it eats before storing it.

But that's **CROWS** and rooks for you, up to their old crookery in the **ROOKERY**.

ROOK [Orthogonally moving piece], [Part of a king's guard], [Castle], [Starting piece on a1 or h8, say], [Figure in a corner]

CROW [Native American tribe of Montana], [Caws cause], [Plains Indian], [Prying tool], [Rub it in]

ADAGE [Saying], ["Birds of a feather flock together," e.g.], [Oft-repeated words], *(See also MAXIM in chapter 1, and how clues for either might seek another five-letter [Saw], AXIOM)*

OMERTA [Code broken by rats], [Rule against singing]

TALK [Sing under pressure?], [Cheap commodity?], [Converse], [Yak]

EDGAR [Annual literary award], [Mystery prize]

RAVEN [Lustrous black], [Baltimore footballer], [One-word bird?]

POE [Pioneer of detective fiction], [He once wrote "I became insane, with long intervals of horrible sanity"], [Who wrote "All that we see or seem / Is but a dream within a dream"]

CAW [Field call], [Cornfield cry]

CROAK [Kick the bucket], [Raven's remark], [Pass on]

CRAW [Esophageal pouch], [Gullet]

CROP [Field's yield], [Jockey's whip], [Downsize?]

CROWS [Toots one's own horn]

ROOKERY [Breeding ground for birds]

BLACKBIRDS Singing in the Bread Take Flight

Magpies and [Nursery-rhyme pie filler]

MAGPIE [Crow cousin], [Black-and-white bird], [Trinket stealer], [Mischievous bird]

Even compared to its fellow corvids—the family of birds that include the crow, raven, and rook—the **MAGPIE** is a [Noisy bird], its name long a synonym for [Chatterbox].

Also known for its scavenging, stealing, and collecting of trinkets, it would make a perfect mascot for crosswords.

The magpie was first simply known as a "pie," from the coincidentally PIE ("Proto-Indo-European") root word *pe-*, meaning "pointed." The *pe-* part could refer to the magpie's tail or its **NEB**, as it does in woodpecker.

NEB [Bird's beak], [S. Dak. neighbor], [Pen tip], [Tip]

MAG ["O," "Us," or "GQ"], ["Time," e.g., in brief]

The "**MAG**" part was added later, referring to magpies' noisiness or senselessness. In the Middle Ages, "mag" was used colloquially to refer to an overly talkative woman, itself derived from "Margaret," a chauvinist term used in the same way. It's hard to know how Margaret Farrar felt the few times she ran **MAG** as [Chatterbox] or [Chatter: Colloq.], but perhaps she took special pleasure in editing the 1954 puzzle that clued **MARGARET** as a [Princess who does crosswords].

MARGARET [Windsor princess], [Shakespearean queen], [Lady Thatcher]

PIED [Multicolored], [Varicolored], [Motley], or [Blotchy, in a way], [Like a noted piper], [___-a-terre]

Magpies may be notorious thieves of shiny objects, but they've given English some fetching new words in return. Their black-and-white coloring inspired **PIED** and its synonym, "piebald." **BALD** in this sense isn't [Hairless] but reflects its earlier usage, "white," especially referring to animals' heads, [Like some eagles] and horses.

BALD [Completely bare], [Like Sir Ben Kingsley], [Lacking tread], [Topless?], [Unlocked?]

PICA [Type of type]

And as they were thought to eat anything, magpies' Latin name, *pica*, is used in English for the compulsion to consume nonfood substances. **PICA** is also a [Typesetting unit], a measurement equal to [12 points] or [One-sixth of an inch], originating from a 15th-century Church of England book known as the *pica* or pye book: The tight, black type on its white pages resembled the magpie's markings.

PIE [Three Stooges missile], [Filling dessert?], [Shoeless cobbler?]

The magpie even helped cook up **PIE**, perhaps because its habit of bringing sundry items back to its nest resembled the way various ingredients were assembled into pies. (It could be said the word came full circle when pies flew again, thanks to **MOE** and the Stooges.)

And, yes, the birds were baked into more than just the name: Eating crow pie was an unpleasant reality for Europeans of little means in the Middle Ages. In middle-class homes and inns, enormous, foot-tall free-"standing" pies contained a veritable edible menagerie enjoyed piecemeal over many days. To keep it fresh, its insides were extracted by the handful and the crust then patched back together.

A **RECIPE** from 1450 lists "beef, beef suet, capons, hens, both mallard and teal ducks, rabbits, woodcocks and large birds such as herons and storks, plus beef marrow, hard-cooked egg yolks, dates, raisins and prunes." **UMM** ["..."], ["Er-r..."] **YUM**?

Those able to indulge in frivolities would sometimes bake birds into a pie as a **LARK**. A 1549 Italian cookbook included a recipe for "pies so that birds may be alive in them and fly out when it is cut up." **CUTUP**, indeed!

Puzzling BIRDS
Merl(e), Ern(e), & Other Rarae
Double-Parked on the Grid's <u>AVES</u>

The **MERL**, though not a Corvid, is yet another [Blackbird] common in nature and crosswords. It's also spelled **MERLE**, a name that carries a tune as Merle [Haggard with 38 #1 country hits]. Haggard's highpoint was his 1969 anti-hippie, anti-drug tune, "Okie from Muskogee," using **OKIE** as a [Sooner State resident], not a [Depression-era migrant].

Haggard eventually changed his tune about **POT**, became a regular **USER**, and said he regretted writing the song. Coming out [Against] what he was [Against from the start?], Haggard's **ANTI**-anti-pot stance amounted to no small change. But small change is an **ANTE** [Pot grower].

A haggard can be a **HAWK** caught as an adult and used for hunting, which might account for "haggard" as [Looking exhausted]. Thus "Merle Haggard" takes down two birds with one **STONER**.

MOE [Slap-happy sort?], [Curly poker?], [AKA Morris (Koffman)]

RECIPE ["Eye of newt" may be part of it]

YUM [Indication of good taste?], [Brand that owns Taco Bell, KFC, and Pizza Hut], ["I can really taste the rosemary!"]

LARK [Bird symbolizing daybreak], [Escapade]

CUTUP [Dice, say] (or as "cut-up") [Prankster], [Laugh-a-minute sort], [Wild card?]

MERL [Old world blackbird], [European blackbird], [European thrush], [Jazz keyboardist Saunders who played with the Grateful Dead]

MERLE [Blackbird], ["Sixteen Tons" songwriter Travis]

POT [Baking ingredient?], [Cabinet member?], [Poker prize], [Kitty], [Ante body?]

USER [Addict], [Account creator, maybe?], [Fee payer, often], [One with a password, maybe], [The "U" in UX], [Employer]

ANTI ["Nay" sayer], [Con], ["Freeze" tag?], ["No" body], [Body opening?], [Climactic opening?], [Beginning to matter?], [Lock opener?], [Against from the start], [Not even semipro?], [Pro fighter?]

ANTE [Pay to play], [Feed the kitty], [Stud fee?], [Chip in a chip], [Part of a.m.]

HAWK [Atlanta cager], [Peddle], [Pro-war sort], [Dove's foe]

STONER [One living the high life?], [Type that can't stay off the grass?], [Biblical punisher], [High-minded sort?]

The double-avian name makes Merle Haggard a **RARAAVIS** (*rara avis*, literally, a "rare bird"), but he's not quite [One of a kind] in that respect. **RARA** might be [Hard to find in Latin?], but **AVIS** is found in old country-and-western singer Merle Travis's last name. So his name also contains two **AVES**, which is [Birds, scientifically speaking], as the plural of *avis*.

AVIS [Hertz rival], [Dollar competitor], [Alamo rival?]

AVES [Birds], [Flying class?], [High class], [Streets: abbr.], [DC's New York and Pennsylvania], [Greetings of old]

REGAL [Uncommon?]
(See also AVE in chapter 4)

But no merl, merle, or Merle will ever match the *rara avis* of puzzledom, the **REGAL** Merl Reagle, regarded by many as the greatest crossword constructor ever. For over three decades, his fresh and playful Sunday puzzles ran in scores of papers.

Readers may recall Reagle's "Gridlock" puzzle, discussed in chapter 4. Viewers of the crossword documentary *Wordplay* may remember him creating the film's featured puzzle, with its ingenious puns on its own milieu, like **CROSSWORDS** ("cross swords"), which ran in the *Times* on May 31, 2005.

CROSSSWORDS
[Duel (with)]

Reagle and Will Shortz would pair up again, delighting crossword-loving *Simpsons* fans by making cameos in "Homer and Lisa Exchange Cross Words," a crossover episode inspired by the doc.

"Merl Reagle" is yet another name nesting two aves. Living up to his name and reputation, Reagle himself called **MERL** a [Puzzling bird], a clue that refers to the crosswordese bird of puzzledom, but is hard not to also see as slyly self-referential (but endearingly so, seeming to suggest a "strange bird" as well as a puzzle-building Merl).

DIRECT [As the crow flies]

Other constructors have found more **DIRECT** ways to give **MERL** the Reagle treatment, regaling him in clues like [Cruciverablist legend Reagle].

MERLIN [Magician of Arthurian legend], [Arthur's boyhood advisor], [Small falcon]

ERNE and **ERN** [Coastal flier], [Sea bird], [Coastal predator], [Shore bird], [Eagle of many puzzles], [Cousin of a kite], [Large bird]

But through his clue associating the bird with puzzles, Merl—that semi-**MERLIN**—was up to yet another trick. Solvers may have thought of **CROW** or **ROOK**, since they solve puzzles. More likely, a clue for a four-letter answer to something like [Crossword bird] would have had most veteran solvers' thoughts flying toward **ERNE**, the [White-tailed sea eagle] mostly seen as a [Sea eagle]. The [Fish-eating raptor] earned its name from the same root as "eagle" and earned its status as a predator in grids largely through the help of its alternate spelling, **ERN**.

Today, **ERNE** has all but vanished; it **ALIT** nine times in 1995, yet only once from 2017 to 2021. **ERN** is fairing a bit better, hailed either as the bird or the [Suffix with north or south]. Maybe it's just more manageable since [It follows directions]. More indirectly, erne returns, in a way, through **ARNE**, a Scandinavian name that, like Arnold, means "eagle."

As a nest for hawks and erns, the grid could be an **AERIE**, crosswords' common yet lofty term for a raptor's [High nest]. In something of a [Cliff hangar?], constructor Tony Orbach laid it as a [Place for a bald-headed baby?]. But since becoming an [American Eagle intimate apparel brand] (spelled with letters from "<u>A</u>merican <u>E</u>agle linge<u>rie</u>"), there's a new sense to clues like [Where the eagle has landed?] and [Top spot?]. If the label continues to fly off the rack, no doubt this new **AERIE** will itself become the [Takeoff point for many a flight] of fancy.

ERN [Southwest terminal], [East ender]

ALIT [Touched down], [Landed]

ARNE [Obama education secretary Duncan], [Composer Thomas], ["Rule Britannia" composer], ["A-Hunting We Will Go" composer]

AERIE [Eagle's home], [Cliffside nest], [Lofty abode], [Digs up?], [Victoria's Secret competitor]

Get [Duck down] Pat
as Word [Quilt filler]
Tern, Teal, EIDER, Skua, Auk, and Dodo

It may sound crazy, but it pays to be birdbrained in crosswords—even if clues can make even the most knowledgeable birders feel like they're playing some game called Duck, Duck, Guess.

Add a "T" to turn "ern" to "**TERN**," any of several species of [Shore flier] related to the **GULL**. The Arctic tern might (with tongue-in-beak) be termed "bipolar," making a yearly, 57,000-mile circuit between the Antarctic and Arctic. In return for their trouble, they enjoy two summers per year and more daylight than any other animal.

Trade the "R" of "tern" for an "A" and reveal "**TEAL**," any of several small, freshwater dabbling ducks. The telltale streaks on a teal's

TERN [Fork-tailed bird], [Beach bird], [Migratory seabird]

GULL [Scavenger on the beach], [Con man's victim], [Coastal predator], [Hoodwink]

TEAL [Pond swimmer], [Duck or one of its colors]

SHADE [Tangerine or peach], [Where the sun don't shine?], [Insults, when thrown]

AQUA [Water color], [Shade at the beach], [Lead-in to culture]

CYAN [Ink cartridge filler], [Blue hue], [Shade used by printers], [The "C" of the CMYK model]

LITTORAL [Of the seashore]

DAB [Dance move where you duck your head and stick out your arm], [Smidgeon]

EIDER [Duck down], [Duck for cover?], or [Where to get down]

SKUA [Antarctic flier], [Arctic bird]

SEMODNILAP [Reversible word]

AUK [Arctic bird, that, despite its name, swims quite gracefully]

ACK ["Oy!"], [Cry of disgust], [Remark from Cathy, in the comics], [Comic cry of disgust]

SORRY [Pathetic], ["My bad!"], ["Not my problem!"]

BYRD [Late West Virginia senator Robert], [Robert ___, longest serving senator in US history (51 years)], [Polar explorer], [Explorer Richard who made the first flight over the South Pole] *(That part of his bio is not diputed)*

NORTHPOLE [Starting point for an annual flight], [Its only direction is S], [Alaska city with a Santa Claus Lane], [Alaska city getting much December mail], [Canada's postal code H0H 0H0]

head and wings gave the **SHADE** its name. But as a [Blue-green] shade, it's hard to tell **TEAL** from **AQUA** and **CYAN**.

Ducks **DABBLE**—that is, [Splash], dip, or wet their heads in water to feed—earning them the name "duck" after the verb. The **LITTORAL** definition of **DABBLE** in water then spread to the verb meaning to [Do something superficially].

Sometimes just a little "dab'll" do ya. **DAB**, as in a [Dollop], connects to "dabble," but was probably influenced by **DAP**, a dab of old onomatopoeia meaning to [Skip over water, as stones] or to [Bob, as bait]. But the eventual use of **DAP** for [Fist-bump] is thought to have inspired the use of **DAB** for the [Modern dance move]. "Dap" is probably owed a dap for that.

EIDER are three species of handsome Arctic [Sea duck] prized for their eiderdown, the fine feathers plucked by females from their breasts to insulate their nests. Tearing "eiderdown" only produces more of the same as "eider" and "down." So **EIDER** can be either [Duck] or [Down].

Larger species of the **SKUA**, a fearsome, [Gull-like predator], feast on puffins and gulls, while smaller sorts pick off lemmings. Another four-letter [Arctic seabird] and [Polar bird], it can also eat up solvers who think they see a **TERN** or **ERNE**.

Flip the bird—that is, turn "skua" backward—and get "auks." That makes it a **SEMORDNILAP**—a word that's another word backward, as "semordnilap" is for "palindromes." (As such, it's a word you might find easier to spell if you turn around.)

Originally, **AUK** might have been made by echoing the cry of the flightless great auk, a sound lost to the ages when the last of these [Arctic diver] birds was clubbed to death in 1844. **ACK**, **SORRY** for the downer.

Fortunately, smaller species of **AUK** like the dovekie and guillemot survive and might have been a [Bird that Byrd might have seen], referring to Richard **BYRD**, the [Disputed North Pole visitor]. Byrd is a [Polar-izing figure?], as many doubt he really reached the **NORTHPOLE**. But even if his [High point?] wasn't quite [How high you can go?], it's not the [End of the world?]: There's no disputing he was an Arctic Byrd who made an Arctic turn.

232   PART TWO: CROSSWORDESE

Emulating EMUS
[Certain ratites]

Four species of the flightless group of birds called ratites rate high in puzzles, even if they're earthbound. While ratites like the ostrich and cassowary are (by crossword standards) too large to regularly pen in a grid, puzzles can't resist their relatives, the **RHEA**, **EMU**, **KIWI**, and **MOA**, each of which is an [Ostrich's cousin] and a [Cassowary's kin]. Freed of gravity, they take flight in the **TWOD** ("two-D," "two-Dimensional") grid, soaring as if [On a plane, for short]. The moa has even been brought back from the [Depthless, for short] abyss of extinction.

The **EMU** might be hard to chase down as a [Noted six foot runner], but it's hard to miss as a [70-pound bird]. Despite running 30 mph, it's [Prey for a dingo] since [It'll never get off the ground]. While most birds' incubation duties are shared between parents, only male emus have the honor, a trait shared by the rhea, cassowary, and all but one species of kiwi.

A **KIWI** is a [Chicken-size flightless bird] and by far the [Smallest ratite bird]. The [Bird whose name is the same as its call] was first called that by the Maori; now any [New Zealand native] is called by that sound. The adorable [Apteryx autralis] first appeared as a national symbol on soldiers' uniforms in the late 19th century. The bird-land bond solidified through a theronym (a brand derived from an animal's name): Kiwi Shoe Polish, which became popular with soldiers during **WWI**. Ironically, the polish is a product of Australia; it was named "Kiwi" to honor the birthplace of its inventor's wife.

Similarly, **KIWI** that's a [Fuzzy berry] is in fact native to China. Arriving in New Zealand in 1904, the so-called [Chinese gooseberry] became popular when Allied Forces discovered it during **WWII**. The **KIWI** call the [Fruit named for a bird] "kiwifruit" to strengthen its ties to their land and differentiate it from the walking kinds of kiwis and Kiwis.

The **MOA**, a 12-foot-tall [Feathered 500-pounder of old], is an [Extinct cousin of the kiwi] likely more closely related to non-ratites.

RHEA [Bird with three toes], [It can't take wing], ["Better Call Saul" Emmy nominee Seehorn] *(See chapter 2 for more on [Hera's anagrammatic mother])*

EMU [Big bird], [Outback speedster], [Creature whose male incubates the eggs, during which it won't eat, drink or defecate for 50+ days], [Outback steakhouse meat?], [It'll never fly], [LiMu___: bird in Liberty Mutual TV], [___War (conflict that saw large flocks of birds outlast armed Australian forces)]

KIWI [Bird that lays a one-pound egg], [Egg-shaped fruit], [Flightless New Zealander], [Bird whose males incubate the eggs], [Male hatching eggs]

TWOD [Lacking depth, informally]

WWI [It ended Nov. 11]

WWII [V-J Day ended it]

For millennia, the moa's only predator was the Roc-like, enormous Haast's eagle, which may have also preyed on humans. The **MAORI** arrived in New Zealand in 1300 and over the next century hunted down every last Haast's eagle and moa. Only the moa's name survives to tell the tale, but "moa"—Maori for "fowl"—usually refers to chicken. Today, it's the emu that's fair game for dinner, though it's considered red meat.

MAORI [Native Kiwi], [About 15% of New Zealanders]

The Dog STAYS in the Picture
Who [Is a good dog, in a way?]

TOTO [Barker in a basket], [1930s film dog], [Miss Gulch biter], [Curtain puller of film]

Pup quiz: Was **TOTO** male or female? You're right, either way. The [Fictional terrier] was male, but the [Film terrier] who "played" him was female. Here's another head scratcher: Which dog played the role of Toto: Terry or Toto? You're right again! The role made Terry the terrier so famous that Terry's name was subsequently changed to Toto. So the "which" really did get the little dog too. (Of course, what I really want to know is: Did changing the terrier's name actually make Toto any less Terrier?)

TOTO also inspired the name of the [Band with the 1983 #1 hit "Africa"] (TOTO) according to the band itself. Nevertheless, it's said the band stuck with the name because "toto" can mean [Completely, after "in"]. It's unclear why L. Frank **BAUM** chose "Toto," though perhaps it had to do with being "**INTOW**" ("in tow").

BAUM [The wizard of Oz?]

INTOW [Following close behind], [Along for the ride], [Tagging along], [Behind]

GALE [Air force], [This really blows]

LAIR [Den], [Animal house], [Pride's place?], [Thieves' hideout], [Retreat]

Dorothy **GALE** was aptly named, and Bert **LAHR**'s last name totally fit the [Lionized actor?], as its near homophone, **LAIR**, makes a good [Place for a cowardly lion?].

Puzzles' all-time favorite four-lettered [Tinseltown terrier] was the [1930s film canine] **ASTA**, who was sniffed out by constructor Robert H. Wolfe as the [1930s film star with notable facial hair]. The least hairy clue is ["The Thin Man" dog], referencing the first of a series of films in which Myrna **LOY** was also a [Frequent Powell co-star]. The [Dog star] also played the [Fictional schnauzer] "Mr. Smith" in the screwball comedy *The Awful Truth*, in which Cary

ASTA [Star with a tail], [Hollywood pooch], [The Charleses' pet], [Repeated film role for Skippy], [Four-legged William Powell co-star]

Grant mistakenly calls him by his real name, Skippy—which was just the paw-full truth.

Asta was later paw-trayed—okay, stopping now—in a way by Uggie in the 2011 film **THEARTIST** (*The Artist*), a movie once artfully screened in a French-pun themed puzzle as [Expert at brewing oolong in Orléans?].

Solvers left wondering ["What ___?"] needed to notice the above answer used [Not just any old] **THE** to [Fill-in-___-blank], but specifically the "the" that's *thé*, the [Alternative to café]. [An alternative] way to clue it would be as an [All-time connector], as "the" can (at least sometimes) connect the words in "all-the-time."

THE [On-line connection], [Useful article], [A cousin?], [Start of 19 John Grisham titles]

"Asta" may have been the [Logical start?] for **ASTRO**, ["The Jetsons" dog]. An Astro (or **STRO**, for short) can refer to a [Houston pro] ballplayer whose stadium features a **DOME**, a [Capitol idea?] even if [It may be retracted].

ASTRO [Introduction to physics?], [Houston ballplayer], [Pirate battler, at times]

STRO [Houston pro, informally], [Minute Maid Park player, for short]

NANA, the ["Peter Pan" dog], is the Saint Bernard who acts as nurse to J. M. Barrie's [Darling girl], **WENDY**, and her brothers. Barrie noted that Nana "will probably be played by a boy, if one clever enough can be found, and must never be on two legs except on those rare occasions when an ordinary nurse would be on four." Presumably, Barrie's doubts about boys' aptitude were well founded, as Nana was originally played by a grown man in a dog suit.

NANA [Mom's mom], [Tot minder], [Dog in "Finding Neverland"], [Sha follower], [Gram alternative]

WENDY [Darling of literature], [Fast food eponym]

[F.D.R.'s dog] was a Scottie named **FALA**, in honor of Murray the infamous Outlaw of Falahill, one of the president's ancestors. A popular little **FELLA**, Fala received fan mail and starred in a short film shot from his dog's-eye view. Fetched fairly regularly in puzzles for a long time, Fala disappeared from the *Times* puzzle in 2015, finally turning up again in 2020. (See, kids, we told you he was just off the grid somewhere upstate!)

FALA [1940s White House dog], [Beginning of a seasonal refrain]

FELLA [Chap], [Buster]

Chapter 8 Puzzle: "You Dirty Bird!"

ACROSS

1. Mama of the Mamas and the Papas
5. State bird of Minnesota
15. Have __ to pick
16. Board game mascot once known as Rich Uncle Pennybags
17. Country singer Kramer of "One Tree Hill"
18. Rows between boats?
19. Doesn't Lyft
21. Poet's contraction
22. Endangered bird whose name is Maori for "parrot"
29. Stone of the Family Stone
30. Mexican Grill chain whose name is Spanish for "marinades"
31. Old Italian money
33. "There it is!"
34. "Take that!" sound
35. Galapagos seabird known in part for its mating dance
41. Tailless cat
42. Where Helen of Troy was from
43. Type of load on the road
44. .3, compared to .5 and 1, in pens
46. Test site in Tempe
49. Clucker associated with a town 20 miles south of London
52. Not your grandfather's, e.g.
53. More of a wallflower
54. Prohibition movement
61. Not __ many words
62. Happen upon
63. "And others," in a bibliography
64. Small orange and brown reedling
65. Type of language used in this puzzle?

DOWN

1. They're born on the bayou
2. Girl's name that's spelled like something Adam and Eve had
3. Strong and lean, like triathlete
4. HBO rival that aired "The Pillars of the Earth"
5. There's about 90 of them in a yard: Abbr.
6. Home planet of Mindy's mate in an old sitcom
7. Roman year of an Odyssey?
8. Rita who won an Oscar for "West Side Story"
9. Taking a prescription
10. Reason not to solve this puzzle in pen?
11. Audiophile's collection
12. Cry of delight
13. Cry of encouragement
14. Where Helen of Troy is from?: Abbr.
20. __ Tranquility (lunar area)
23. "To God" in Italian, as after "Grazie"
24. 2008 Summer and 2014 Winter Olympian Jones, who lived "down" to her name more as a bobsledder than as a hurdler
25. Diminishing
26. "The First Phone Call from Heaven" author Mitch
27. A G of grams?
28. Certain Semite
32. "__, My Daughter," biography by Mitch Winehouse
33. Annoying one
35. Mini Cooper maker
36. Put down
37. Erase
38. Bill that rises with AC (or DC) use
39. "Gossip, girl!"
40. "__it art?" (question asked of paintings done by an elephant)
44. Former Beyoncé alter ego Sasha
45. Like thoughts that don't turn out to be anything?
46. Comparable with
47. Big lever, to Beaver?
48. Pull some toilet paper
50. Work some dough
51. Bigshot in a longhouse
54. Initials for getting the job done, though not when in used by a frozen yogurt chain

55 Want ad abbr.
56 Sport where athletes get their butts kicked: Abbr.
57 Apiece
58 Opposite of "Way!"
59 CBS forensic drama
60 Letters set in stone?

Chapter 9

HOLLYWOOD Squares
Crosswords Go to [The movies],
Watch Old TV, and Binge
on Video Games and Comics

When referencing an [Old camera need] like a **FILM** actor only recalled through a [Thin haze], clues may [Shoot] off some [Canon fodder?], making the answer hard to [Picture].

Puzzles are like screwball comedies wrapped up as caper movies. Hijinx ensue as rogue characters acting as [Crack] detectives try to [Untangle a mystery]. Despite being at cross-purposes, answers team up and **SOLVE** the case—if ultimately thanks to some audience participation. (So just [Do what you're doing]!)

So even if you prefer to solve the puzzle on paper, let's [Vet] some answers that might appear (or [Hide]) on **SCREEN**.

SCREEN [Sift], [Basketball play], [Bug barrier], [One getting the picture], [Present for viewing… or prevent from being viewed]

I'm Not an Answer,
I Just PLAY One in Crosswords
Actors Who Might Create [Drama]

You can forget author Edgar Rice Burroughs or any stars of the many movie adaptations; crosswords' favorite ["Tarzan" portrayer] is ["Tarzan" actor Ron] **ELY**. Ely's 1966–68 **TARZAN** could really be described as a [Noted swinger], as the series cut out the role of **JANE**, potentially making an open-ended question out of ["Me Tarzan, you ___"].

When not in a loincloth, **ELY** can be the [English cathedral city] located on the Isle of Ely, a swampy region near Cambridge that's an inland fenland whose name is thought to mean "island of eels." No wonder Tarzan swung from vines.

ESAI [Morales of "NYPD Blue"] continues to appear in crossword syndication through a clue that doesn't issue a TV guide: [Actor Morales].

ODAMAE ("Oda Mae") Brown was [Whoopi's "Ghost" role]. At one point, Oda **MAE** says, "You can't just blurt it out like that!"—which could be a response to seeing **ODA** clued as a [Harem room] or [Concubine's chamber], or to any number of quotes from **MAE-WEST** (Mae West).

["V" for Vendetta" actor Stephen] **REA** was nominated for an Oscar in 1992 when he was [Stephen of "The Crying Game"], playing an **IRA** ("Irish Republican Army") member consumed by guilt over the death of a British soldier. Whether that guilt constitutes [Mens ___] **REA** (*mens rea*, being Latin for "guilty mind"), the standard test of criminal liability, would be up to a judge.

ISSARAE ("Issa Rae"), the ["Insecure" star], has quickly secured a starring role in puzzles. Born Jo-**ISSA** Rae Diop, her first name combines those of her grandmothers, Joyce and Isseu.

RAE was long primarily clued as ["Norma ___" (Sally Field film)], which edged out [Arctic explorer John] and [Charlotte of "The Facts of Life"]. [Singer Carly ___ Jepson] briefly grabbed the throne, but now it's Issa's.

ELY [Ron who plays Tarzan]

TARZAN [Title character of 100+ films since 1918], [Vine connoisseur?]

JANE [Calamity out West?]

ESAI [Morales of "Criminal Minds"]

MAE [Fannie ___], [Wild West?], [___ Jemison, first Black woman in space]

ODA [___ Mae (Whoopi's role in "Ghost"], [Certain ladies' room]

MAEWEST ["Sex is an emotion in motion" speaker], [She said "I used to be Snow White, but I drifted"], [Who said "It's not the men in your life that counts, it's the life in your men"], [Who said "I'll try anything once, twice if I like it, three times to make sure"]

IRA [Militant org. in a 1994 peace agreement] *or as "individual retirement account"* [Savings plan, briefly], [1040 abbr.], [S&L offering], [Shelter for the future?], *or as Ira* [Glass of "This American Life"], [Glass on the air], ["Rosemary's Baby" novelist Levin], [Good name for an investor]

ISSA [Actress Rae of "The Lovebirds"]

RAE [Actress/comedian Issa], [Woman's name that's a part of the body backward]

Admittedly, the fight to control the continent of Essos in *Game of Thrones* is a more compelling tale. **NED** is the head [Stark family member on "Game of Thrones"] and father of **JON** [Snow on television], **SANSA**, **ARYA**, and **ROBB**.

Robb's wife, Talisa, is played by **OONA**, the [Chaplin granddaughter named for her grandmother], who herself was [Eugene O'Neill's daughter] and Charlie [Chaplin's last wife].

Talkin' TOLKIEN
The [Giant of Fantasy] and Lord of the Square

ENT (for "ear, nose, and throat" doctor) sounds as otherworldly as [Otolaryngologist, familiarly] or [Adenoidectomy specialist, for short], but other-wordly, it's truly fantastical as the [Tree-like creature of Middle-earth]. It's one of several answers originating in **LOTR** (*Lord of the Rings*), the J. R. R. [Tolkien trilogy, for short], whose epic length might lead one to declare **TLDR** ("too long; didn't read").

Tolkien double-dipped into Old English: He took little *ent* ("giant") for his race of towering tree-trolls, and *orcneas* (used in *Beowulf* to describe a no-good, [Goblinlike creature]) for **ORC**, ["The Lord of the Rings" baddie]. (*Orcneas* also gives us **ORCA**, which constructor Joe DiPietro once spouted as a [Swimmer with big calves].)

The upshot is that a three-letter [Tolkien creature] can be either **ENT** or **ORC**, a conundrum compounded by another ["The Lord of the Rings" figure]: the **ELF**, which is hardly a [Little help?]!

[Gaming device]
Video Games Puzzles Play to CONSOLE,
[Comfort or cheer]

The [Microsoft console] **XBOX** [___ 360] that works as a [Halo platform] is angelic to crossword constructors too. That's because its spelling makes it a double "X" word, so it **XES** or [Checks] the box as a useful answer.

NED [Pulitzer Prize–winning composer Rorem], [Guy in a Devine comedy?], [Nancy Drew's boyfriend] *(See part one for clues imported from Flanders)*

JON [Stewart in the "Wordplay" documentary]

SANSA [___ Stark, role for which Sophie Turner was Emmy-nominated]

ARYA [Name of the girl on "Game of Thrones" who said "A girl has no name"]

ROBB [Eldest Stark son on "Game of Thrones"]

ENT [Tolkien tree-being], [Creatures such as Treebeard], [Sinusitis-treating doc]

TLDR [Short response to a long post]

ORC [Dungeons & Dragons foe], [Elf's evil counterpart], ["World of Warcraft" warrior]

ORCA [Apex predator of the sea], [School bully?], [Black-and-white cruiser?], [Boat in "Jaws"], [One in a pod]

ELF [A little cobbler?], [Seasonal worker?], [Pole worker?]

XES [Deletes, with "out"], [Check alternatives]

XWORD [Type of puzzle], [What you're solving, informally]

Of course, in another way every answer in an **XWORD** (short for "crossword") is some "X word" to be found in order to fill in "X" number of boxes.

All that might help explain why Microsoft thought it could sell an **XBOX** game tied to the TV program *Merv Griffin's Crosswords*. But the show was soon canceled, **EXED** (as in [Crossed out] or [Deleted] from the schedule), and attempts to find an audience for the game [Struck out]. In the end, many an **EXEC** at both projects was probably ticked off by not being a better [Fortune reader, maybe].

EXEC [Biz bigwig], [V.P., e.g.], [Suit]

WII [Xbox competitor]

PWN [Utterly defeat, to gamers], [Totally wreck, as a noob]

NOOB [Beginner, in modern lingo], [Novice gamer], [One getting pwned in online gaming]

The name of the **WII**, the 2006 [Nintendo console], is wee: perfect for working out in puzzles to get [___ Fit]. Nevertheless, its weird look can **PWN** a **NOOB**.

NES [Old gaming inits.], [Duck Hunt console, for short], [Super Mario Bros. platform]

The **NES**, or Nintendo Entertainment System (*Nintendō*, perhaps meaning "luck of heaven"), was an [8-bit system, briefly] released in 1985, then updated in the 1990s as the 16-bit Super NES.

EPIC [Grander than grand], [Way cool], [___ fail (disaster in slang)]

EPIC and **SAGA** ["Iliad, e.g."], [The Lord of the Rings", e.g.], [It's a long story]

In 1946, Irving Bromberg helped start a company called "Service Games," which distributed slot machines across the Pacific for service members to play. The company eventually became **SEGA**, meaning Bromberg can also be called a [Big name in video games] and a [Creator of Genesis]—although the latter clue makes it sound like a much more **EPIC** **SAGA**.

ATARI [Arcade pioneer], [Console pioneer], [Asteroids company], [Missile Command maker]

The [Pong creator] **ATARI** had its genesis in 1971, when it created *Computer Space*, the first arcade video game. At the time, the company went by the decidedly less crossword-friendly **SYZYGY** Engineering. In 1972 the company took the Japanese term *atari*, used in the game Go for pieces that may be captured on the next move.

SYZYGY [Eclipse cause], [Alignment of three celestial bodies], [Highest-scoring Scrabble word that doesn't use A, E, I, O, or U]

[Top-tier] Family Ties
Crosswords' ALIST: Astin, Addams, and Arnaz

SEAN [Penn name], [One of the Lennons], [John, abroad]

DUKE [Nukem of video games], [Wayne nickname], [Bo or Luke of Hazzard County], [First name in jazz]

SEAN Astin, the son of Patty **DUKE**, is known for his roles in *The Lord of the Rings, Rudy, Stranger Things*, and *The Goonies*. His adoptive father, John Astin, played Gomez on the 1960s TV series, *The Addams Family*—a role later filled by **RAUL** [Julia of Hollywood].

Sean's brother, Mackenzie Astin, portrayed Andy Moffett in the 1980s sitcom *The Facts of Life*.

That makes **ASTIN** the [John who played Gomez], [Sean of "Rudy"], [Mackenzie of "Facts of Life"], [His wife was a Duke], [Duke's ex], and [Duke's son]. That's a large line of credit.

Puzzles' most popular member of the **ADDAMS** family is the hirsute [Classic TV cousin] **ITT**. In one episode, Gomez asks Itt what's underneath his hair, to which Itt responds with his usual gibberish, which Gomez translates for the audience: "**ROOTS**." So while he may be an **ITTY** Itt, don't mishear the description: He's the brainy one.

Robyn Weintraub, a constructor who always has a fresh fact to tease out, clued **ITT** as [Cousin ___ acacia (fuzzy evergreen named for a TV character)]. While I love random strands of info in puzzles, other solvers may side with another clue in that puzzle: ["Don't test me"]—**IMINNOMOOD** ("I'm in no mood").

Created for the sitcom, Itt didn't appear in Charles "Chas" Addams's original *New Yorker* comics about the family. Nor were the magazine's pages ever graced with the most famous creation of the [Old "New Yorker" cartoonist William] **STEIG: SHREK**. It was in his 1990 kids' book that Steig introduced the world to the **OGRE** whose name means "terror" in Yiddish. ("Ogre," meanwhile, traces back to the monstrous roots of "orc.") Similarly, "**TOTORO**" turns up from the Japanese *Torōru*, for "troll."

The musician who's an [Apple with keys] shares her name with the ogress with the key to Shrek's heart, **FIONA**—from the Irish *fionn*, "fair" or "blond"—who was voiced by the actor often seen as [Cameron on camera], Cameron **DIAZ**.

DESI Arnaz shared his name with his son, the [Ball boy?] Desi Arnaz Jr. (who also has an Astin association, as he was once Patty Duke's lover). Both his parents shared their names with their daughter, Lucie Désirée Arnaz, making **DESI** [Lucie's father], [Lucie's brother], and [Lucy's husband or son]—either way, [Lucy's love]. That's enough to make a lot of people dizzy.

ADDAMS [Wednesday, e.g.]

ITT ["Ooky" TV relative]

ROOTS [Cheers (for)], [Hair pieces?]

ITTY [Wee], [Minute, informally] *(See ITSY part one for ITTY, another [Teeny] clues)*

SHREK [Donkey's mate]

OGRE [Grimm heavy?], [Meanie]

TOTORO ["My Neighbor ___," acclaimed animated film from Hayao Miyazaki], [Neighbor in a Studio Ghibli film]

FIONA ["Criminal" singer Apple], [Apple on an iPod maybe]

DESI [South Asian living abroad], [Having South Asian roots] *(as "Desi," borrowed from Hindustani)*

Stranger (Little) Things
<u>ROZ</u> [Chast of cartoons] and Puzzledom

The name most often drawn from the *New Yorker*'s funny (or funny-**ISH**) pages—or rather from cartoons appearing periodically in the periodical's pages—is <u>ROZ</u> Chast, the hilarious (no -ish about it) cartoonist.

ART is a [Notoriously hard thing to define], as constructor Julie Bérubé sketched it. But there's no question that Chast has made an art—and a career—out of sharing the wonder, frustration, and joy she finds in corners of the world others take for granted. It's no surprise, then, that her work often embraces strange bits of language (be they real or imagined)—and that she's a devoted crossword solver.

"Seeing my name in a crossword is definitely **SURREAL**," Chast assured me, emphasizing the last word. "I love crosswords (and acrostics and diagramless and Spelling Bee and all the 'variety' puzzles), though I hate sudoku and I don't even get what Ken Ken is. But words . . . yeah. Compulsive, compelling. So to be doing a puzzle and then see my name is a dreamlike feeling."

Asked about another frequently-appearing name, she added, "I love Brian Eno. *Music for Airports* was one of my favorite albums long, long ago. I often think of 'ignorable as it is interesting.' Such a thought-provoking (notice how I did not say 'interesting') concept."

Chast's logophilia was on display even in her first *New Yorker* cartoon in 1978, "Little Things," an <u>OLIO</u> of 10 drawings of doodads and doodles labeled with the likes of "sood," "hackeb," "tiv," "bie," and "enker." These words weren't just notoriously hard to define, but impossible. She'd made them up.

Or maybe she hadn't, as the names Chast gave two of her "little things" had appeared as answers in *Times* puzzles the previous few years: **TIV** must have tied solvers in knots as a [Nigerian tongue] and **BIE** likely seemed out of reach as a [Tech. school degree]. Could these bits of extremely rare (and since abandoned) crosswordese have gotten stuck in Chast's head?

Chast said she "Had no idea about that (tiv and bie). That is very strange. One thing I *did* learn was that people in the sound departments of the movie biz started calling a certain sound-measuring device a 'spo,' because it resembled the 'spo' in another cartoon."

So, purposefully or not, Chast has become crosswordese, appreciated crosswordese, drawn crosswordese, and if a clue like "Sound-measuring device" is ever answered by "SPO," she'll have invented crosswordese too.

For all that, Chast knows what it's like when nonsense piles up in a grid. In "Answers to Last Week's Puzzle: A Toughie," she presented a moment familiar to so many solvers. At least all the across answers look plausible.

[Contents of el Prado]
Modern ARTE and the End of the Line

[Dadaist Jean] **ARP** makes **DADA**—a term purposely coined to sound like a [Bit of baby talk]—almost echo itself again, as [Arp's art].

ARTE, Spanish for "art," might be hard to decipher as [It might be abstracto] (*abstracto* is Spanish for "abstract," both coming from Latin meaning "draw away from") as [Works in Madrid?].

ERTE ("Erté") was the name taken by Romain de Tirtoff, the [Art deco artist] famous for his many *Harper's Bazaar* covers. "Erté" is the phonetic spelling of his initials in French.

ERNST takes on a surreal quality as [Young partner?], but the really surreal answer is the German [Max at the MoMA].

Though buyers can't seem to go wrong investing in a [Spanish surrealist], solvers can: The answer may be **DALI** (Savador Dalí) or **MIRO** (Joan Miró).

Pablo **PICASSO** gets twisted into a [Cubist before Rubik], referring to **ERNO RUBIK**, the latter half of which, at least, can be solved fairly easily as [Cube dude].

GESSO is frequently found—though unseen—in art, put down as an [Undercoat of an oil painting] and [Undercoat used in sculpture]. Since four of its letters—the G, E, S, and S—are common endings for other answers, it also serves as a sort of undercoat in grids, often found along the bottom row or the farthest-right column.

Many previously discussed answers like <u>SSN</u>, <u>SST</u>, <u>ESS</u>, and their plurals do that job for puzzles too. Though less frequent, answers like **LOESS** (pronounced "less") and **ESSENE** essentially serve the same function. So I like to think of each of these answers as a "gesso," because they mirror that answer's function in grids and echo the sound of a constructor's answer when reflecting if the answer's worth using. Some more familiar words are used the same way, but cloaked in ways that make them just as hard to detect:

ESTATE [A lot of wealth?], [Dead giveaway?]

TSETSE [Fly around the equator?], [Flying transmitter]

TRESS [Rapunzel feature], [Hair piece]
SERENE [Cool as a cucumber]

As seen in that last clue, the words **ASA** ("as a") are a [Simile's center], and often the missing ingredient in the same cucumber sandwich: [Cool ___ cucumber]. Coincidentally, **ASA** (as "Asa") is the first name of [Botanist Gray], who studied but failed to fathom how cucumber plants create their curling tendrils.

This [Thick-brick filling] may seem out of place in this section, but there's some artistry to it—especially when filling the answer in **ASA** [Pretty picture connector].

ASA [___reminder], [___whole], [Cool-cucumber center?], [Flat pancake filling?], [Nutty-fruitcake center]

Strip Tease
More COMIC [Multi-square entertainment]

The "Father of the American Cartoon," the political [Cartoonist Thomas] **NAST** blisteringly evoked Tammany Hall and Boss **TWEED**, which was hardly [Academic material?] at the time. Nast is also remembered for creating the **GOP** elephant and the enduring image of Santa.

["Popeye" cartoonist E.C. ___] **SEGAR** gave puzzles much to laugh over through his [Yam user?] **POPEYE**, the [Toothpick Olive?] **OYL**, and their foundling, **SWEE** [___' Pea] ("Swee' Pea").

Still, the [Royal son of the comics] is Prince **ARN**, scion of the eponymous hero *Prince Valiant*, which has followed a continuous plot since Hal Foster created it in 1937.

NAST [Media magnate Conde___], [Cartoonist who popularized Uncle Sam]

GOP [Herd of elephants?], [Bush league?], [Red letters]

SEGAR [Elzie___, Popeye's creator], [Wimpy's creator]

OYL Olive with a little salt?], [Tune with an uncle Lubry Kent]

SWEE [Pea opener in toons?]

ARN [Palmer, to pals], [Prince Valiant's boy]

No Mere [December temp]: SANTA Clauses Seen Year-Round

Hoer?	Year-end temp	Present-day hero?
Pole star?	Grinch disguise	One with a small work force?
Nick name?	Team manager	Traveler who carries his own bag
Dancer's boss?	Cupid's master?	One who flies south in the winter?

KETT [Etta of old comics]

STRIP [Take off?], [Lose a suit?]

ABNER [Capp lad], ["Li'l___"], [Daisy Mae's love, in the funnies], [Doubleday of baseball lore]

SADIE ["Sexy" lady in a Beatles song], [Actress Sink of "Stranger Things"]

NOV [National Adoption Mo.], [Guy Fawkes Day mo.]

GURU [Expert], [Whiz], [Maven], [Teacher sitting crossed-legged, maybe], [Wise guy]

MIA [Hamm of soccer], as "MIA" for Miami [The Heat, on scoreboards], as "MIA" for "missing in action" [Unaccounted for, for short], [Honoree on the third Friday of September], and as the Italian "mia," meaning "my" ["O patria___" ("Aida" aria)]

SARGE [Base boss], [Looie's underling]

OTTO ["Beetle Bailey dog], [Comics canine], [Palindromic guy], [Germany's Von Bismarck], [Director Preminger], [___Octavius ("Spider-Man" villain Doc Ock's "real" name)] (See part one for uno otro OTTO)

EIN [German "a"], [German article], [Article in "Der Spiegel"]

SEI [Thrice due]

HEEL ["Follow"], [No-goodnik], [Lab instruction?]

SNERT [Hägar the Horrible's dog]

SNOOPY [Prying]

[Toon flapper Etta] **KETT** was the main character in Paul Robinson's **STRIP** bearing her name. From 1925 to 1974, Kett and her friends were presented as paradigms of "typical" (i.e., white, middle class, suburban, Protestant) high school life, perhaps explaining why the fashionable teen is no longer in fashion.

[Krazy ___] **KAT**, the titular feline star of George Herriman's 1913–44 cartoon, has remained somewhat popular, even if less so in crosswords than the ["2 Broke Girls" actress Dennings] and the broken-off piece of a [Kit ___ bar].

[Cartoonist Al] **CAPP** created the critically acclaimed, satirical strip starring Li'l **ABNER** Yokel. Clues like [Dogpatch denizen] refer to the fictional Appalachian small-town home of Capp's crew. The clue could also work for **SADIE** [Hawkins of "Li'l Abner"] who, to find herself a husband, created Sadie [___ Hawkins Day], still celebrated by high school dancers each **NOV**. The Beatles' tune about a certain sexy Sadie was originally titled "Maharishi," its lyrics wondering why the **GURU** allegedly hit on **MIA** Farrow. ["Mama ___!]"

[Beetle Bailey's superior] in Mort Walker's comic was **SARGE**, short for Sgt. Snorkel, whose protective pooch was named **OTTO**. Of the many Ottos in puzzles, the [German artist Dix] is summarily the most impressive: In Italy, [Due + sei] is **OTTO** and across the Alps, [Twice cinq] makes **DIX**. Put them together and Otto Dix was 18 his whole life, or maybe 810.

Either way, [One, to Otto] would've been the German **EIN**. On the flip side, [Six, in Italy] is **SEI**, an answer once rolled out as [Die on one side of Italy?].

Before adopting Sarge's **OTTO** for a four-letter [Cartoon dog], consider **ODIE**, a much more popular [Comics pooch]. Cartoonist [Jim Davis's drooler] might be hard to recognize when [He wears a yellow coat and pants]. In fact, though dismissed as a [Dimwitted dog of comics], Trenton Charlson boxed him in a brainy way as the [Comics character who once, surprisingly, solved a sudoku puzzle].

Others that **HEEL** to the clue of [Cartoon dog] include **SNERT**, **ASTRO**, **DILBERT**, and **SNOOPY**, the [Brown beagle?]. That last clue must've left some solvers [Curious] until they considered his owner's last name.

Finally, in a *Garfield* role-reversal, there's **REN**, the clever cartoon chihuahua pal of the truly simpleminded Stimpy, a **MANX** [Cat o' no tails?]. The two friends seemed to merge when Robert W. Harris had solvers chasing their own tails by cluing **GATO** as a [Chihuahua cat].

REN [Stimpy's TV pal], [Rap's MC___] *(See chapter 10)*

GATO [Feline: Sp.], [León relative]

["What Hump?" speaker]
IGOR (or Is It Ygor): First Names of Horror

[One with a pretty strong hunch] might guess the ["Young Frankenstein" assistant] as **IGOR**, but it could also be **INGA**, referring to the part played by **TERI GARR**. (Not to be confused with **GAR**, which sounds like a horror show as [Slender fish].)

Those thinking Igor is also the ["Son of Frankenstein" aide] or the [Lab assistant in a 1939 film] will need aid themselves, as that eager helper was **YGOR**, played by **BELA** [Lugosi of horror films].

In Hungarian, **BELA** means "heart," as in "guts," things needed when watching the work of this [First name in horror]—or even solving that clue, as it can also be **BRAM** [Stoker who wrote "Dracula"]. As a form of Abraham, "Bram" means "father of many," which might account for all the knockoffs made about the infamous **COUNT**.

Those not up for a Bela flick can go hear **BELA** [Fleck of the Flecktones]. Born Bela Anton Leoš Fleck, the [Banjoist Fleck] took his names' calling to heart, having been named after the Hungarian composer **BELA** [Bartók], the Austrian composer Anton Webern, and Czech composer Leoš Janaćek.

Still others answering to a [First name in horror] are the director **WES**—that's the [Director Craven], not the [Director Anderson]— the old film actor **LON** [Chaney of silents], star of *The Phantom of the Opera* and *The Hunchback of Notre Dame*, and his son, **LON** [Chaney Jr. of "Son of Dracula"].

Fortunately, the **LON** that's [Basketball coach Kruger] only sounds nightmarish.

IGOR ["Rite of Spring composer Stravinsky], [Stravinsky's first?], ["Prince___" (Borodin opera)], [2019 #1 album for Tyler, the Creator], [Marty Feldman's role in "Young Frankenstein"]

INGA [Actress Swenson of "Benson"]

TERI [Actress Garr], [Actress Hatcher], [Actress Polo]

GARR [Teri of "Tootsie"], [Teri of "Mr. Mom"]

GAR [Needle-nosed fish]

YGOR [Bela Lugosi's role in "The Son of Frankenstein"]

BRAM [Stoker of fear?]

COUNT [Matter], [Go from 0 to 60, e.g.?]

WES [Craven one?], [Jazz guitarist Montgomery], [Basketball Hall-of-Famer Unseld], [NBA coach___Unseld Jr.]

LON [Cheney of chillers], [Colleague of Bela and Boris], [Either Chaney]

GOMER [Inept sort], ["___ Pyle, USMC"]

PYLE [TV marine], [Nabors role], [Ernie ___, Pulitzer-winning journalist of WWII]

OPIE [Ron Howard role], [Mayberry moppet], [Bee's charge]

BEE [Garden worker?], [Low-tech drone?], [Meet for a spell?], [Competition in which the winner always gets the last word?], [Social], (See also BEES in chapter 1)

OTIS [Mayberry town drunk] (See also chapter 6)

SOT [Bar fixture], [Juicer]

PAGO [Half of the Samoan capital]

SAMOA ["Survivor" locale in the South Pacific], [Coconut-covered cookie], [Where lava-lava skirts are worn], [Where Apia is found], [Home of Pago Pago], [Apia is its capital], [Pago Pago is its capital]

RHETT [Scarlett suitor], [Butler of fiction], [Role for Clark], [Ashley's rival], [He didn't give a damn]

TARA [Scarlett's home], [Skater Lipinski]

LEIGH [Shower scene star]

OSCAR [You can get one for a song?], [Trash-talker on daytime TV?], [Crowe's feat?], [Prize that, surprisingly, contains a large amount of tin]

ELIA ["East of Eden" director Kazan], ["On the Waterfront" director Kazan], ["A Letter to ___," 2010 documentary co-directed by Martin Scorsese], ["Essays of ___"], [Lamb, by another name], [Princess Martell of "Game of Thrones"]

A PYLE of Goobers, a [Gomer of Mayberry], and Other Answers to Give a Damn About
"The Andy Griffith Show" and "Gone with the Wind"

The use of **GOMER** for a [Yokel] traces to *The Andy Griffith Show*'s Gomer **PYLE**. But the use of the name of [Gomer's cousin], **GOOBER**, for [Yokel] sprouted from its use for [Peanut, in Dixie], rooted in *nguba*, several African languages' word for the legume.

Still, the memorable peanut of that sitcom was [Sherriff Taylor's boy], **OPIE**, a [Bee relative] thanks to his aunt. Aunt **BEE** may have had the name of the [Bud drinker?], but the actual [Mayberry sot] was **OTIS** Campbell—a **SOT** being [One who can't pass the bar?].

Crosswords' apiarist-in-residence is **ULEE**, [The beekeeper in a 1997 film] and [Peter Fonda title role] in *Ulee's Gold*. **APIAN** is a [Bee-fitting description?], but **APIA** is the answer fitting [Capital of Samoa]. (Not to be confused with **PAGO** Pago, the capital of American Samoa—except when answering some clues for **SAMOA**.)

RHETT [Butler of "Gone with the Wind"] appears often enough in clues like [Butler of film] and [Butler in a romance] to seem like crosswords' valet. Clark Gable's character even makes the [Fictional plantation] of **TARA** [Butler's quarters?]. "Rhett" stems from the Dutch word for advice, a name he mostly lived up to—at least until Scarlett asked, "Where shall I go? What should I do?"

Gable's fellow ["Gone with the Wind" star], Vivien **LEIGH**, won her first **OSCAR** for playing Scarlett. Switching from red to white whine, she would win her second as Blanche DuBois in *A Streetcar Named Desire*, directed by **ELIA** [___ Kazan]. While crosswords no doubt respect his achievements, when they want his name named, the clue [Director Kazan] tends to suffice. Elia is also a famous literary alias as [Charles Lamb's pen name], used in the title of the writer's oft-cited collection, *Essays of Elia*.

May the FORCE Be with Us
Attempting to [Pry open] "Star Wars" Names

As George Lucas has often been unforthcoming or made contradictory claims about the origin stories of his **STARWARS** characters' names, much of this section constitutes conjecture, not **CANON**. That said, some connections have been verified over the years, and others seem too clear to be coincidental. Ultimately it may not matter much; like the movie franchise itself, probing these names from a galaxy far, far away can reveal much about our world, even if—or because—so much of both is built on old myths.

STARWARS [Solo vehicle?]

CANON [Officially accepted works], [What fan fiction is not]

Anakin "ANI" Skywalker

Darth Vader's real name was almost certainly influenced by the English director Ken Annakin, though Lucas's publicist has denied it. And **DARTH** sure sounds like "death," but Lucas says he chose it for being **AKIN** to "dark." While **VADER** evokes "invader" or suggests Darth Vader started as "dark water," Lucas says he chose it for its connection to father (*vater* is German for "father"). That's plausible, though many doubt the writer had worked out the family tree when he named his villain.

That Lucas also went to high school with a boy named Gary Vader only muddies the water further. Crosswords long housed **ANI** as the ani, a [Black bird] that's a [Tropical cuckoo]—so little Ani could've been a little cuckoo from the start. But Lucas's big idea for the name probably came through "Anakim" (a race of giants mentioned in Genesis). And "Skywalker" is another name for Loki, the Norse trickster god.

ANI [Darth, as a boy], ["Star Wars" nickname], [Singer DiFranco], [What's far from fair?], [Mississippi cheerleaders ask for it a lot]

DARTH [Sith Lord's title], ["Star Wars" title]

AKIN [Similar (to)], [In the same family]

VADER [Heavy breather at the movies]

ARTOO DETOO ("Artoo-Detoo" or "R2-D2")

In a story that's widely accepted, while making *American Graffiti*, Lucas overheard his sound editor request some audio by referring to it as "R2, D2," short for "Reel 2, Dialog Track 2." Another little "R2" unit in puzzles is **ARETOO**, who bickers with **AMNOT** over which is a [Playground retort].

ARTOO [__-Detoo], [Threepio's pal], [Sci-fi beeper]

DETOO [Artoo-__], ["Star Wars" surname?]

ARETOO and **AMNOT** [Schoolyard comeback]

ATAT

The "All Terrain Armored Transport" was visually inspired by an extinct hornless rhinoceros known as *Paraceratherium* that likely stood 20 feet tall—about a third the height of an AT-AT. It's shortened name mimics the gunfire sound [Rat-___] **ATAT** ("rat-a-tat").

ATAT [Massive walker in "The Empire Strikes Back"], [Rat tail?]

DROID

In her 1952 story "Robots of the World! Arise!," American science-fiction writer Mari Wolf coined "droid" from "android," itself built from the Greek *andr-* ("man") and *-oid* ("having the likeness of"). Twenty-five years later, Lucasfilm trademarked "droid," so Verizon Wireless pays the studio to use it.

DROID [C-3PO], for one], [Sci-fi extra], [iPhone rival]

ENDOR

The Bible's book of Joshua tells of the city of Endor, whose name may be connected to "eye" and "generation." Saul consults the Witch of Endor, a **SEER**, on the eve of a battle against the Philistines. She tells him he'll die the next day. Saul is only wounded in the Israelites' loss, but falls on his sword after the battle.

ENDOR [Forest moon inhabited by Ewoks], [Biblical witch's place]

SEER [Forward-looking sort?], [One who has a ball at work]

EWOK

The Ewoks were named after the Miwok people native to Northern California, particularly to the forest near Lucas's Skywalker Ranch where the Endor scenes were filmed.

EWOK ["Star Wars" critter], [Creature of Endor]

HAN Solo

Han is a form of Johan, John, and Hans. (The German suffix *-el* forms diminutives, making Hansel and Gretel pass for Littlejohn and baby Maggie). Han also smacks of "hand," as in "handy" and "handsome"—a pair that have historically shared usages for "good-looking," "apt," or "clever"—making it an apt, clever first name for Han **SOLO**, the [Go it alone], [Stag] character who takes many a [Star turn]. Nevertheless, as crosswords point out, he's the ["Star Wars" pilot who, despite his name, flies with a co-pilot].

Around 1900, the famous German horse *der Kluge Hans* ("Clever Hans") was thought capable of answering math equations by

HAN [Flying Solo?], [Solo in space], [River or dynasty name], [China's largest ethnic group]

SOLO [Aria, usually], [2018 sci-fi prequel], [Helpless?], [Play by yourself?]

stomping answers; it turned out he was able to judge from his owner's face when he'd arrived at the right answer. Clever, indeed— though ultimately not very handy, being **SANS**—or [Lacking, in Le Mans]—in the hands department.

SANS [Without], [Lacking], [Minus], [Word in many font names], [___souci (carefree)]

JABBA the HUTT

Jabba Desilijic Tiure speaks Huttese, a tongue based on the **INCAN** language Quechua. He does seem to jabber, and he's the size of a hut, which is welcome as the rest of his name seems so inscrutable. There is a striking sonic similarity, though, between Desilijic and **DESI** [Lydic of "The Daily Show"]. Don't try to tell us that's just a coincidence too, George!

JABBA [Fat blob of film]

HUTT [Jabba's race]

INCAN [Early Peruvian], [Like Machu Picchu], [Quechua-speaking], [Like Atahualpa], [Like the sun god Inti]

JEDI

As a child, Lucas read the sci-fi novels of **BURROUGHS**—as in [Edgar Rice ___, creator of Tarzan], not the ["Naked Lunch" author] William—in which men of rank were addressed as *Jed* or *Jeddak*. The Japanese *jidai* means "era" or "period," as seen in the *jidai-geki* (period dramas) of Japanese director **AKIRA** [Kurosawa who directed "Ran"] and whom Lucas has cited as influential.

JEDI [Wise one], [Sci-fi knight], [Forceful one?]

Landonis "LANDO" Calrissian

Landonis might bridge "land on" and **ADONIS**, used for any [Hunk], or specifically [Aphrodite's mortal lover]. The **LANDO** [___'Lakes: dairy company] ("Land O'Lakes") name lands since it was founded in **MINN**, the [Land of 10,000 Lakes: Abbr.].

LANDO [Role for Billy Dee], [Pal of Han]

LEIA [Han's hon], [Princess with a twin], [Carrie character]

DOS [Uno + uno], [Hair arrangements], [Beehives and buns], [Bobs and weaves], [Parties], [Some advice]

Princess LEIA Organa

Whether it's her do with its **DOS** ("*dos*," as in [Two in Toledo]) **BUNS** or her metal **BIKINI**—the latter perhaps giving her "buns of steel"— puzzles just love Leia. Her name is similar to the biblical matriarch **LEAH**, connected with softness and weeping. In Old English, *leah* meant "woodland" or "meadow," which became crosswords' much-loved English word **LEA**, a [Meadow]. So Leia is a natural match for her adoptive last name, Organa.

BUNS [Place for a pat?], [Cheeks], [Dog holders]

BIKINI [Spare clothes?]

LEAH [Jacob's first wife], [Two-time Emmy winner Remini]

LEA [Pasture], [Grassy field]

FRO [To's partner], [Way to sway], [Back again], [Not to], [__-yo], [Big do], ['60s do], [Do with a pick, maybe]

CAAN [James who played Sonny Corleone], [Co-star of Ferrell in 2003's "Elf"]

UPDO [Prom coif], [Beehive, for one], [High style]

LUKE [Gospel writer], [Patron saint of surgeons], [Book that's the source of the phrase "Physician, heal thyself"]

While he didn't sport one as Lando, Billy Dee Williams did grow a **FRO** for his role in the 1971 made-for-TV movie, *Brian's Song*, which also starred [Actor James] **CAAN**. A fro may seem like an **UPDO**, but that term is reserved for the kind of [Coif that might use pins and spray].

LUKE Skywalker

The biblical Gospel of Luke tells the story of the Prodigal Son, conversion to Christianity might be seen as a model for the boy who comes to believe in the Force. Besides retaining a twinkle of the Greek *leukos* ("light"), Luke is the English form of the Latin name "Lucas," tracing back to "Lucius," or "bright one."

As his last name is a term for the Norse god, Leia's brother is basically Luke Loki. So it's probably for the good that he's "Luke S."

OBI [What secures a kimono], [Kabuki sash], [Accessory that might have a netsuke attached], [It's a wrap], [Band of geishas?], [Tie that binds]

COMICCON [Where Vulcans congregate?]

WAN [Pale], [Ashen], [Pallid]

ALEC [Smart __], [One of the Baldwin brothers], [One of the literary Waughs]

OBI-WAN "Ben" Kenobi

Obi-Wan was inspired by a character from Kurosawa's *The Hidden Fortress*, so much so that Lucas wanted the actor from the Kurosawa film to play the role. An **OBI** is the [Kimono sash] of the cruciverse and the term for the [Martial artist's belt] conventionally seen at **COMICCON** ("Comic Con") around the waist of many a wannabe Obi-Wan Kenobi—whose name is bound at either end by "obi." **WAN** suggests whiteness and agedness, and "ken" can be knowledge. So both his portrayers' first names have been apt: **EWAN** McGregor's is very wan and **ALEC** Guinness had the [Name for a wise guy?].

PADME ["Star Wars" queen]

AMI [Brest friend], [Nice friend?], [Self-reflective question]

AMIE [Catherine, to Jules et Jim], [Gallic gal pal], [Guy's gal], [Nice dear?], [Honey found in Dijon?], [Friend of Nancy?]

DALE [Hollow], [Glen], [Depression]

PADME Amidala

Befitting the wise and loving queen who is associated with flowers, Padme is Sanskrit for "lotus flower," and Amidala echoes "amygdala," the part of the brain that processes memory, emotional responses, and decision-making. **AMI** and **AMIE** work for a [French friend], though only **AMIE** is the one that sounds like a [Gaul friend?]. *Dala*, Old English for "valley," gave English **DALE**, connecting Amidala with her daughter, Leia.

Kylo REN

The son of Han Solo and Princess Leia first spurned his parents by renouncing his original name, Ben Solo, meaning "Son of Solo." *Ky* and *ren* are ancient Egyptian for "other" and "soul," respectively, so an "Other Soul" might surround the small part of his true self hinted at by the "-lo" from "Solo." That he sort of resembles a villain out of a **REN** [___ Faire (event with jousting, for short)] is surely beside the point.

REN [Last name in "Star Wars"], [Knights of ___ ("Star Wars" order)]

SITH

Sith is obsolete English, used variously for "after," "during," and "before" (in the first sense, often part of "sith than," meaning "after that," which has since contracted to form [Since, once]). It was also used for "next in succession" and "continuously from then on"; a "journey," "way to go," or a "lifelong path" like a pilgrimage; and "misfortune" or "trouble." Add to all this Sith's serpentine, sinister sibilence, and it doesn't sound good—unless you're a bad guy.

SITH [Jedi foes], [Group on the dark side of the Force]

YODA

"To know" this is, as the Hebrew root Y-D-H seen in *yeda* ("knowledge") and *ani yodea* ("I know"). "Warrior" means this, as the Sanskrit *yodha*. The Sanskrit **YOGA**, [Literally, Sanskrit for "joining"], the character's name and spryness also suggests. The [Home stretch?] of our [Meditation exercise] to [Kind of master] *Star Wars* answers— even if at times [It's a bit of a stretch] and in the end [It's all just posturing]—this concludes.

YODA ["Star Wars" sage], [Noted character with object-subject-verb syntax], ["Star Wars" character who could have written this clue?]

YOGA [Activity with a lotus position], [Kind of pants], [Poses in a studio?], [Class for posers?]

Chapter 9 Puzzle: "Big-Screen TV Set"

ACROSS

1 Old Blue Eyes
8 Multilayered dish
15 Scarily lifelike
16 Like a mournful poem
17 Least likely to be saved?
18 Diminutive jabber
19 Goldfinger?
20 Word with sidewalk or trapeze
22 Dells, e.g.
23 Response to "Less filling" in old beer ads
27 ___fond farewell
30 Sorta
31 Make a boo-boo
32 Comic Kumail
34 Button-ups that aren't button-downs
36 With airs of Ares
37 Judge proper
39 Goodyear's home in Ohio
40 Like some rye and raisins
42 One to one, for one
43 Strain
44 Mannerly fellow
45 Reveled
49 Home to the world's busiest airport: Abbr.
52 Kubrick film based on a Nabokov novel
53 Kazantzakis character
55 Horn of Africa nation
58 Certain something
60 Brand name taken from "Pocket Monsters"
61 London area terrorized by Jack the Ripper

62 Boom boxes
63 Places for answers—or, with three from this puzzle, whence celebs asked for answers

DOWN

1 Get to go "Huh?"
2 Kind of column
3 Anything goes
4 Met highlight
5 Golfers' needs
6 Dorm mentors: Abbr.
7 Church area
8 Omitted
9 Take a side
10 Observe, in the Bible
11 Uneasy feeling
12 Bit of work?
13 Slangy refusal
14 Take the stage
21 Curtail
23 Greek earth goddess
24 One hardly needing a kick in the pants
25 Half of six
26 Formerly, formerly
28 A fan of
29 Bottled spirit?
32 T'Challa's ex-lover in "Black Panther"
33 German shepherds
34 Brazilian soccer superstar
35 Black cat, to some
36 "I can't___" (modern jokey admission)
38 Advantage
41 Get out the door
43 "Later"

46 Change one letter in 7-Down?
47 Eydie with Grammys
48 Uses up, with out
50 Steak cut
51 Fats for cooking
53 Pitts of Hollywood
54 Bi- quadrupled
55 Some vinyl, briefly
56 "Baloney!"
57 Presidential nickname
59 Online answer page?

Chapter 10

FOOD
[Chow] Down and Across

By now, we've [Filled up on] a lot of answers.

We [Sampled from the smorgasbord] of crosswordese in part one, [Had ham] in chapter 1, [Did some consuming] in chapter 2, [Made it through crunch time] and [Had a date] with mussels in chapter 3, [Got into a jam?] in chapter 4, [Broke a fast] in chapter 5, [Partook of a buffet] (okay, Buffet) in chapter 6, [Enjoyed a club] or two in chapter 7, [Had a little lamb], [Had wings] that [Stuffed a pie hole], and [Went to Wendy's] in chapter 8, and finally [Became full of it] (make that ITT) in chapter 9.

But as we've almost [Finished the course?], it's high time we actually **ATE** some real food.

ATE [Took in a poor boy?], [Was in a mess?], [Had a cod piece?], [Took a leek?], [Gave peas a chance?]

[All-you-can-___] EAT
And Puzzles' Atë Something Funny

Many of the clues we've seen for **ATE** have corollaries for **EAT**. But these two frequent answers can be prepared in such a large variety of ways that there's plenty more to **EAT**.

ATE can be an [Alien attachment], an unearthly reference to the suffix"-ate" likely to alienate some solvers. Truly, it's worthy of the [Goddess of mischief] herself, which is fitting, as she too is the nearly unidentifiable, troublesome daughter of Zeus and Eris, Atë.

As the goddess of infatuation, folly, strife, and ruin, Ate was understandably the object of constructors' infatuation for ages. But her days of cooking solvers' goose seem over: After Maleska invoked her 50 times in his last decade at the *Times*, Shortz hasn't summoned her once in the 450 occasions he clued **ATE**.

Perhaps that's just deserts for the [Goddess banished from Olympus] whose antics often [Took down a hero] who [Took the bait]. Yeah, she was [Corrosive]. One could even say that after constructors and editors [Had] for so long [Feasted on] her name, they [Got fed up], [Dug in] and [Tucked it away]. Basically, she was [Absolutely killed, in drag slang].

In a delicious curiosity, **ATE** has appeared as both [Had a little brat?] and as [Eris's brat], the latter referring to her mother, the goddess of discord. No wonder the answer gave solvers indigestion. At any rate, editors seem to have finally said, [Thanks, but I already__"] have better options.

How Puzzles [Dig in] to EAT

Have	Take in	"Mangia"	Have a cow	Throw back a fish?
Down	Use up	Not fast	Have a date	Put away the dishes?
Lunch	Get down	Wolf, say	Have breasts	Stuff in a muffin, say?
Snack	Put down	Fill the bill?	Take sides, say	Follow your gut instinct?
Graze	Wear down	Sink a sub?	Get into a stew?	Word between two dogs
Erode	Have some	Dinner order?	"You're too skinny!"	Engage in some capers?

Then again, puzzles may one day hanker for foreign food again, deciding it's time they switched course and [Took in some takeout, say].

When You Feel Like a [Zombie or flaming volcano]
Time for a DRINK

It's always 5-Across somewhere, so let's have an **APERITIF**. If you'll **RUE** gin tomorrow, it "currantly" makes sense to have **KIR**, which combines white wine and **CASSIS**. *Cassis*, borrowed from the French, is likely rooted in the Hebrew word for the cassia tree, though the berry used actually comes from the black currant tree. Kir, once called "blanc-cassis," is now named for the former mayor of Dijon, Félix Kir, who popularized the drink after World War II while promoting the twinning—or "sister cities"—movement to delegates visiting him in Burgundy. Aptly, the drink unifies two ingredients found in the region. **DIJON** does the same: combining brown mustard seeds with white wine.

IPA ("India pale ale") is a more popular [Draft pick] and [Hip thing to sip] in puzzles and pubs.

ALE has always been a regular, seen as [Stout, maybe], [Ginger ___], [Brown ___], or a [Blonde you might pick up at the bar?]. But good luck: It can be a [Bitter pull to swallow] since it often resembles its potential twin, **IPA**.

Crosswords toast **OAST** as a [Brewery kiln] or [Hops-drying oven], making the [Old brewery feature] a little-known remedy for those in search of a [Drying out spot].

As for drinks with **ICE**, the **MAITAI** ("mai tai") is crosswords' favorite order. The [Rum cocktail] is the [Drink that gets its name from the Tahitian word for "good"]. But the grid appreciates the drink most as an [Umbrella holder, perhaps].

Other times is seems crosswords can't hold their liquor very well, usually drinking only half of a **MAI** [___ tai]. The answer sometimes

APERITIF [Appetite stimulant], [What gin might be], [Cordial]

RUE [Stew over, say], [Paris street], [The French way?]

KIR [White wine aperitif]

CASSIS [Black currant liqueur], [Type of brandy], [Hercule Poirot's favorite drink]

DIJON [Mustard with wine], Bread spread], [Where René cuts the mustard]

IPA [It has a head and hops], [Inits. at a bar]

ALE [Bath suds?], [Draft pick?], [Hopped-up drink?], [IPA ingredient?]

ICE [Chill], [Cool], [Cinch], [Have in the bag], [Bump off], ["Rocks"], [Diamonds], [Decorate], [It's cleared for takeoff]

looks like the [Shortest month in Paris?], or even how Spanish speakers might see it as the month that's [French mayo?] ("*mai*" being the French equivalent of the Spanish month of *mayo*). Such clues might be easier to see after [Half a drink] than before one.

[Slippery sort]
<u>EEL</u> Electrifies the Grid

<u>EEL</u> [It may be charged in water], [Long Japanese meal], [___Pie Island (artist commune on the Thames)], [It might have an electric organ?], [Lithe swimmer], [Marine migrator], [Long-distance swimmer?], [Shrieking fish in "The Princess Bride"]

No mere [Meal for a seal], crosswords' favorite food is <u>EEL</u>, so it should be no surprise puzzles serve it up in all sorts of ways, often cooking recipes sourced from across the globe.

In Japanese cuisine, it can appear as [Anago or unagi] or a [Popular Japanese pizza topping]. In Spain, the [Glass ___] eel—an eel that's early in its life cycle, so-named because it's transparent—ranks among the most expensive foods, costing up to 1,000 euros per kilogram. And [It may be smoked] in Holland, Sweden, or in England, where it's also a [Fish often jellied].

True, Americans who consider the critter an [Icky ichthyoid] may find the thought of enjoying jellied eel a contrived concept, even an [Elusive one]. But for many Brits, conjuring a savory concoction of congealed, condensed confit of [Conger]—perhaps with some vinegar condiment—is easy. Perhaps as easy as [___ pie (old British dish)].

When crosswords have a mind to do so, they can really make the [Paragon of slipperiness] [One that's hard to get ahold of]. Constructor Tom McCoy coyly clued it as the [Cause of a shocking Amazon charge?]. And constructor Mike Selinker—whose very name is rather suggestive of a [Serpentine swimmer]—pitched it as [Part of a wriggly field].

(For those wondering, about the sixth clue in the box, to "spitchcock" is to split and spread flat for cooking.)

But the [Fish often grilled with sweet soy sauce] was perhaps most sweetly prepared when constructors Natan Last and Andy Kravis teamed up with a crossword class from the Jewish Association Serving the Aging to suggest [That's a moray!].

It's a well-known fact that [It has electric organs], making it a [Zapping biter]: a fitting description for an animal that's a [Cousin of a wrymouth].

Most beginner solvers find it **EELY**, or [Hard to grasp, say], that they might need to know that an **ELVER** is a [Young eel] slightly more mature than a glass eel, or that a **GRIG** is a [Small eel]. But eels are so common that somewhere along the line, every crossword solver has [Sniggled]—the precise term for having hunted for eels, or **EELED**—to qualify as an **EELER**, regardless of whether they've been a [Pot user, maybe].

EELER [Sniggler], [Angler with a pot]

INDIA [Where shampoo was invented], [Country with 28 states], [First country to discover water on the moon]

INDIA [___ ink]
Puzzles Slip Into a [Sari state?]

INDIAN [Like many attendees of the Bangalore Queer Film Festival]

Though the **INDIAN** mottled eel is in fact found in the West Indies, there are plenty of answers from India that slip solvers up. For instance, [Indian flatbread] seems simple enough to discern as the staple of Indian and crossword cuisine, **NAAN**, a word from the Persian for "bread." But about 20 percent of the times [Indian flatbread] is on the menu, they're serving **ROTI**. And sometimes the former is spelled **NAN**, which also clicks for crosswords' favorite photographer, Nan Goldin, whose name is short for Nancy.

Wash it down with a cup of **CHAI** or try some **ASSAM**, the [Black tea from India] named for the [Tea-growing area of the Himalayas].

NAAN [Leavened flatbread]

ROTI [Unleavened bread], [Bread whose name derives from the Sanskrit for "bread"]

NAN [Photographer Goldin], [Mum's mum], [Gram alternative], [Bread also called khamiri]

CHAI [Hindi for "tea"], [Hebrew word for "life"]

ASSAM [Silk center of India], [Indian state known for its tea]

LHASA [Tibet's "Forbidden City"], [Sacred city in Buddhism]

APSO [Tail of a dog?]

LASSI [Yogurt-based Indian drink]

LASSO [Dogie catcher], [Stock holder?], [Ring around the collar?]

LASSIE [TV collie], [Dog star?], [Hot dog, once]

LASS [Glasgow gal], [Plaid-clad miss], [Colleen]

RAITA [Indian yogurt dip with vegetables]

RIATA [Lasso], [Rodeo rope]

AGRA [Noted mausoleum site], [City that's home to three UNESCO World Heritage Sites]

AGGRO [Belligerent, slangily]

AGRO [Farming prefix]

GOA [India's smallest state]

RAJA and RAJAH [Indian prince], [King, in Hindi], [Indian chief]

RANI [Indian princess], [Hindu queen], [Eastern royal]

SARI [Rani's raiment], [Red wedding garment, perhaps], [Dress that the historian Ṛta Kapur Chishti called the "magical unstitched garment"]

ZSA [When doubled, a Gabor sister], [Eva's half sister?]

TOQUE [Chef's hat], [Pizza maker's topping], [Child's headgear] (think Julia)

FIX [Pickle], [Jam], [Kettle of fish], [Candy binge, to a sugar junky]

SPRAT [Lover of lean cuisine?]

NOFAT [Really lean], [Skim]

Across India's northern border soars Tibet's [Capital at 12,000 feet], **LHASA**, whose name means "place of the gods." The name of its native dog, the Lhasa **APSO**, might translate to "barking guard of the place of the gods." Further east, the **SHIH** [___-Tzu] means "lion dog" in Mandarin.

The difference may be clear between a glass of **LASSI** and a length of **LASSO**, though solvers not at home on the range might mistake a **DOGIE**, a [Motherless calf], for a little **LASSIE**, who takes her name from a [Miss], or **LASS**. Alas, things can easily go awry if solvers try to corral a steer with a **RAITA** instead of a **RIATA**.

The [Indian tourist mecca] **AGRA** is the [Site of the "crown of palaces"], referring to the main draw of the [Taj Mahal city]. It's okay if you get a little **AGGRO** trying to reach the rice-growing **AGRO** communities far south in **GOA**, as the state is also an [Indian tourist destination] famous for its beaches on the Arabian Sea. Besides, ["We all ___ a little mad sometimes": Norman Bates].

A **RAJA** (or **RAJAH**) may pick up a [Sticky roll] wrapped in **SARAN**. But if an [Indian princess], or **RANI**, decides on a [Delhi wrap], [It's a wrap] that she's picking out a **SARI**. There are over 80 ways to wear a sari, but apparently none of them suited the Hungarian-American actress **ZSA** Zsa Gabor, as Sári was [Zsa Zsa Gabor's real given name]. Yet the name was apt for the Gabor and the garment, as "Sári," like "Sarah," derives from the name of the Biblical matriarch whose name means "princess" or "woman of high rank" in biblical Hebrew.

[Try to take it lightly?]
A Strict DIET of Crosswordese

Crosswords are keen to take up a **TOQUE** and **FIX** up their favorite meal. But ultimately it's up to solvers to [Scrape] up the ingredients and [Make, as a sandwich] something of it.

If indeed [Jack ___] **SPRAT**, that famous [Dieter of nursery rhymes], ate **NOFAT** ("no fat"), he would have been wise to stay clear of crosswords, as they often contain **OLEO**, or [Margarine].

To cover up their reliance on spreading [Some pats] of **OLEO** in so many grids, puzzles try to disguise what they [Stick in the fridge] as just about anything, so long as solvers can't believe it's not [Butter substitute]: [Bread stick], [Spread in a tub?], [Yellow sub?], even a [Little pat on your buns?]. Perhaps it's best to come clean, as one clue did, and admit it's so useful in getting other answers to set in grids that it's [Puzzle lube].

SUET, the [Fat used in mincemeat], wouldn't suit Mr. Sprat either. Instead, give Jack fruit, even if it's **UGLI**, like [Jamaican tangelo]. The [Wrinkly fruit] is a [Citrus hybrid] of the tangerine and either the grapefruit or its principal ancestor, the pomelo—hence the portmanteau "tangelo." He might even break a fast with **SLOE**, the [Sharply sour fruit] that can be complementary. The [Fruit also called blackthorn] has such a rich, purple-blue hue that sloe ["___-eyed"] describes someone with deep, dark eyes.

SUET [Tallow source], [Haggis ingredient], [Bird feeder fill], [It's for the birds]

SLOE [Gin flavoring], [Cousin of a plum]

Puzzles' [Potted plant?]
Get [Kind of cozy] with TEA

While [Some like it hot] might cast a **DOG**, **SPA**, or **TUB**, puzzles are usually requesting the [Coffee alternative], **TEA**, the [Sri Lanka export] that crosswords prefer as a [Party drink] even over the mai tai. So if you show up to a [Genteel affair] at casa del crosswords, be forewarned that although it was [Marijuana, in older slang], the [Pot leaves] puzzles pass around offer a mellower sort of [Social] [High ___]:

DOG [Track], [Frank], [Tail], [Pluto, for one], [Animal for which the Canary Islands are named], [Boxer that can lick anyone?], [Greyhound, e.g.]

SPA [Retreat], [Body shop?], [Place for sweaters?], [Therein lies the rub!], [Bath, for one]

TUB [It has a certain ring to it], [Clunker at sea], [Clunky dory?], [What's behind the curtain?], [Spot for a male threesome?]

- It's in the bag
- Bagged leaves?
- Drink from a bag?
- Leaves for a drink?
- Leaves in hot water?
- Hot spot?
- Four spot?
- Break fluid?

- Leaves before paying the check?
- London spot?
- Time in London?
- Wimbledon service?
- Gossip
- It was once harbored in Boston?

[Fishy Business]
A SUSHIBAR Scene

"**I** get no respect!," shouted **TAI**, a [Sea bream, in a sushi bar]. "Here I am, a [Red snapper, in a sushi restaurant], and crosswords continue to treat me violently, thinking my full name must be Tai [___ chi (martial art)]. They like to joke that I'm a [Chi preceder], trying to get people to call me **PHI**, the Greek letter—but I'm me!

"Worse, when I'm in a crossword," **TAI** continued, "it's almost always as [Mai ___]. Do I look that sweet to you?" Indeed, Tai was so red and ready to snap, no one dared mention he could also be clued as the [Unhip "clueless" girl].

POKE [Give the finger to?]

POKE, a [Slow sort, informally] agreed. "Yeah. Just once, I'd like to [Give a pointer?] to some of these rude puzzles when they [Elbow] solvers with a pun, or [Prod] them to call me an old bag: I'm not just a [Place for a pig]! I'm a [Raw fish dish]. If I had the energy, I'd give them a [Finger jab], or maybe use a chop [Stick]. It'd be [___ fun]!"

This time, no one had the heart to [Extend (out)] a [Gentle reminder] that **POKE** really didn't belong at the sushi bar, being a [Hawaiian raw fish salad] whose name means "to slice."

AHI [Bigeye or yellowfin, at a sushi bar], [Kona catch, maybe], [Fish in a poke bowl]

"What really rubs me raw," said **AHI**, a [Yellowfin tuna], "is how I'm called a [Rarely served fish] when I'm [Popular sashimi tuna]! Even if it's true that I'm traditionally a [Hawaiian delicacy] now used as a [Marketing term for some sushi], [Poke fish] like me enough and I become one [Raw tuna]. I have my pride! And I just don't like how crosswords talk about us!"

["Me neither"], said the [Japanese seaweed], **NORI**, "I'm more than an [Edible algae]! I'm an [Onigiri need]!"

Some of the other **SUSHI** yelled their agreement, sick of looking like pretzels and beer nuts as just another [Bar food]. Or else crusty old [Dinner rolls?]. Or worse yet, [Fluke roll-ups?]!

Just then, a piping-hot [Japanese bowlful] piped in with, "Gimme a break! **UDON** know how good you have it. They call me a [Thick noodle]! They're the ones with thick noodles. And then I get piled in with [Japanese buckwheat noodle], **SOBA**. Look how much browner and grainier he is!"

Honestly, it was a little hard to tell the difference. And nobody was about to point out to Udon that in fact he was the denser of the two.

"I'm so incredibly delicious, I can't imagine why I'm treated so bad," said **UNI**, the [Sea urchin at the bento bar], who wasn't given to being prickly when out of his shell. "Until Americans [Start to form] a better idea of sushi names, they'll still think I'm just [College to a Brit]. Like some place where they might catch [Mono-]. Not that I mind being a [Sex leader], mind you. But if they took a culinary [Introduction to sex?], maybe they'd learn that when they eat me, they're enjoying my sex organs, sometimes called my gonads or corals." The other patrons sipped their drinks and tried not to think of uni's private issues, especially his [Corn opening?].

"And here I am," said **RAMEN**, "thinking I'm a [Popular college course]!" He chugged a huge **ASAHI**, crushed the can from [Japan's largest beer brand] against the **EDGE** of his bowl cut, and belched so the whole place smelled like his Japanese brew.

EDGE [Lip], [Upper hand], [Leg up], [Nose out], [Fringe] [Little lead], [Skirt]

BENTO sat quietly under a light in his snappy hat, keeping things to himself, trying to clearly compartmentalize everyone's tastes. "It's true," he ventured gingerly, "for me, being called a [Lunch box] can sometimes feel demeaning, but it's also kind of funny. Just like being a [Square meal] can seem like compliment or an insult. Still, I'd think crosswords could include me more often. After all, I am a [Box lunch]. Come to think of it, I'm essentially the crossword puzzle of food, a little of this, a little of tha—"

"Hey, look, there's a fungus among us," Ramen shouted, motioning to the underappreciated [Stringy white mushroom with a small cap] floating into the izakaya. **ENOKI** just stewed, unable to think of a [Ramen topping]. He knew it didn't matter; he understood they were just jealous of how often he appeared in crosswords. Was it his fault that puzzles seemed to [Fancy mushrooms] like him?

So he just went to the bar and ordered something hot to drink from **TOFU**, the bartender and chef. Tofu was big and useful but not very sharp. He could stand for hours like a [Brick in the organics section] of the market, and he was something of a [Block in the kitchen]. He poured Enoki an enormous bowl of [Chunks in miso soup].

"Yo, **SOY**," Enoki screamed, so heated that he used Tofu's birth name, "You [Dim sum dip]! I don't want this [Much of miso]!" He nearly blew his little cap.

"Oh, you want a lot less?" Tofu asked, truly dumbfounded. "Or maybe you'd prefer a [Latte option] more?"

"No! Not coffee or **MISO**," Enoki seethed. "Is your [Bean paste]?" The bar was stunned: No one had ever been so [Course with tofu]. After a few deep exhales, the mushroom cooled down. "Listen," Enoki said, "Just give me a [Tokyo tipple]. You know, a [Drink in a little cup]. A traditional [Japanese quaff]. A nice [Honshu drink] served hot, ["For goodness' ___] **SAKE**!"

The bartender took back the miso and replaced it with a shot glass of steaming **KIRIN**, a [Beer from Honshu].

This was definitely not okey-dokey with Enoki, but feeling too limp to **EKE** out even a meek **EEK**, he drank it anyway. And as he did, he pulled out his book and read a short story called "The Square Egg," written by **SAKI**, a [Contemporary of O. Henry]. "Hey, everyone," Enoki called out, "come here! You have to see this. Someone wrote a story about our buddy, Tamagoyaki!"

TAI came over and looked at Enoki's book sadly, thinking about how long it had been since Tamagoyaki, a type of Japanese omelette, first came to America, how he still hadn't been in a puzzle, and how maybe he never would be. He sighed and realized being called [Half a drink] was better than never being called at all.

PAVLOVA and Out

An [Immortal name in ballet] and Desserts

The Russian [Ballet legend Anna] **PAVLOVA** is best remembered as the originator of *The Dying Swan*, a four-minute solo piece. But to those with a sweet tooth, her name may be a piece of cake: the [Meringue-based dessert named for a ballerina]. Invented in New Zealand or Australia in the 1920s at the time Pavlova became the [First ballerina to tour around the world], the crisp-crusted cake covered with cream and fruit is surprisingly easy to prepare and remains a point of national pride in those countries, where it is still popular, particularly in **YULE** (that is, **NOEL**) celebrations.

English took "meringue" from the French; the word's earlier history is impossible to unscramble. However, it's believed that Dominican merengue music may have borrowed the term in the mid-19th century, inspired either by the sound of an **EGG** being whipped, or by whipped eggs' airy quality. The same might be true of méringue, another form of dance music cooked up concurrently in Haiti that set the stage for the familiar Latin dance.

In ballet, a **JETE** (*jeté*) is a [Jump from one foot to the other] and a **PLIE** (*plié*) is a [French dip?]. If dancers crack up thinking of that clue while performing the smooth, continuous bending of the knees [Movement that's French for "bent"], it's a double *plié*, as the French is also used colloquially to describe being bent over in laughter, the equivalent of being "in stitches."

PAS (as "P.A.s," "public address systems") might sound strange as [Hearing aids?]. And it can be hard to pin down (as *pas*, the French negative) when it's [Not in France]. But those meanings are sidestepped by the other French *pas*, meaning [Step], that's part of ballet's linguistic repertoire pointed to a *pas* [___ de deux] (literally, "step of two," as it's a "dance for two"). Hopefully such a duet has fewer [Faux ___] pas than many daytime talk shows, which use paternity tests to ascertain real or faux pas. Of course, watching just a few minutes of those [Stage setups, for short] for determining [Dads] can make viewers plead, "[No mas!]"

Before saying **TATA**, we should check out the **TUTU**, an [Outfit for Pavlova] typically made of **TULLE**. Like "meringue," "tutu" too traveled to English from French, where it may have grown out of *cucu*, a bit of **BEBE** (*bébé*) babble for a **DERRIERE**. *Cucu* is built by doubling **CUL**, a more "mature" term for a [French bottom] that's also used in cul [___-de-lampe] (literally "bottom of the lamp"), the triangular typographic ornament used to show readers that they've come to **THEEND**.

YULE [Christmas season], [Jolly time], [Noel], [Kind of tide], [Log time]

NOEL [Yuletide], [Christmas carol]. [Holiday song]. [Winter air?], [Seasonal strain?], [Present time in Paris?], [Coward from England]

EGG [Spur (on)], [Early bird?], [Baby carrier?], [Beat it!]

JETE [Dance term literally meaning "thrown"], [Barre hop?]

PLIE [Dip in "Swan Lake"?]

PAS [Not for moi?], [Old men], [Step up to the barre?]

TATA ["Cheerio!"], ["Peace!"], [Parting word], [Line out the door?]

TULLE [Veil material], [Fine netting]

BEBE [French newborn], [Tony winner Neuwirth], [New Mexican?]

DERRIERE [Can], [Bum], [Seat], [Behind in French class?], [Nice behind?]

CUL [___-de-sac], [Parisian posterior]

THEEND [Famous last words], [Credits preceder], ["That's all, folks"]

Chapter 10 Puzzle: (Themeless)

ACROSS

1 Ideate
9 Attired
15 1815 win for the British and Dutch
16 1998 Masters and British Open winner Mark
17 Literary defense
18 Not change at any rate?
19 Field without leather
20 Donald and Daffy, e.g.
21 Follower of "someone" or "something"
22 Author Gay
23 "Me too"
27 Big battery
29 Eswatini neighbor
32 Hat edge
36 2016 doc about a NYT section
37 Spew
38 Small amount
39 Jeer
40 Looking youthful
42 "Don't make such ___!"
44 "Shoot!"
45 Pilloried
48 Wide spaces
51 Line-___(listed individually)
52 Inopportune
57 "Dish!"
58 The Duck's theme, in Prokofiev's "Peter and the Wolf" is one
59 Feral
60 Their tongues have never been pulled
61 Wide open, say
62 Life, e.g.

DOWN

1 Part of a test at a pharmacy
2 Sobriquet for Haydn
3 "Believe ___ not"
4 Start to commute?
5 Bosom buddy, more currently
6 Scummy
7 They may need girding
8 Enhanced interrogations?
9 What some grills resemble
10 Like Tom Ripley
11 Effect of events on memories
12 Winner of a 1978 Supreme Court affirmative action case
13 Great Lakes Indians
14 "___ Macabre"
23 Eros, to Romans
24 Buckwheat noodle
25 Comic Ansari
26 Grounds for some spring balls?
28 Alternatives to glasses
30 Asea
31 Factory seconds: Abbr.
33 Sway
34 Couple
35 Like a Mafioso
41 Spends the least time running, say
43 "Dig what I'm saying?"
45 Raise, on eBay
46 Do penance
47 Hill count in Roma

49 "Who's Afraid of Virginia Woolf?" playwright
50 Given away, as one's cover
53 "___ for real?"
54 Styx, for Pluto
55 Certain util.
56 One pill a day, perhaps

ANSWER KEYS

Part One Mini Puzzle:
"Play...D'oh!!!"
Page 31

A	B	E		J	A	Y
P	E	A		U	K	E
B	A	R	T	M	A	N
		L	I	B		
S	Z	Y	S	L	A	K
T	A	O		E	P	I
U	P	N		S	U	M

A	S	S		C	R	A	M	P	S		F	S	U
L	E	O		R	E	G	A	L	E		R	I	M
E	X	T		O	C	E	L	O	T		O	L	A
	Y	O	U	C	A	N	T	T	H	I	N	K	
T	E	S	H		P	T	A	S		A	T	T	A
S	L	A	N	G				G	M	A	I	L	
O	F	Y	O	U	R	T	R	O	U	B	L	E	S
			L	O	V	E	Y	A					
	W	H	I	L	E	S	O	L	V	I	N	G	
Z	O	O	M	S				A	L	A	R	M	
A	R	G	O		G	M	A	J		L	M	A	O
P	E	W		B	I	O	M	E	S		E	Y	E
		A	C	R	O	S	S	W	O	R	D		
M	A	R	G	A	R	E	T	F	A	R	R	A	R
A	N	T	I		N	Y	E	R		S	O	D	A
C	D	S		O	S	L	O			P	J	S	

Part One Puzzle:
"Puzzle Power!"
Page 48

272

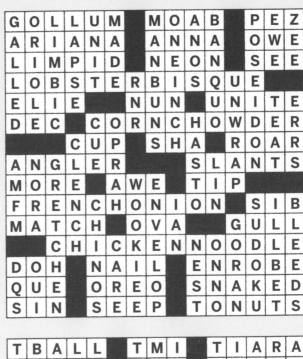

Chapter 1 Puzzle:
"Super Salad"
Page 78

G	O	L	L	U	M		M	O	A	B		P	E	Z
A	R	I	A	N	A		A	N	N	A		O	W	E
L	I	M	P	I	D		N	E	O	N		S	E	E
L	O	B	S	T	E	R	B	I	S	Q	U	E		
E	L	I	E			N	U	N		U	N	I	T	E
D	E	C		C	O	R	N	C	H	O	W	D	E	R
			C	U	P		S	H	A		R	O	A	R
A	N	G	L	E	R			S	L	A	N	T	S	
M	O	R	E		A	W	E		T	I	P			
F	R	E	N	C	H	O	N	I	O	N		S	I	B
M	A	T	C	H		O	V	A		G	U	L	L	
	C	H	I	C	K	E	N	N	O	O	D	L	E	
D	O	H		N	A	I	L		E	N	R	O	B	E
Q	U	E		O	R	E	O		S	N	A	K	E	D
S	I	N		S	E	E	P		T	O	N	U	T	S

T	B	A	L	L		T	M	I		T	I	A	R	A
H	A	N	O	I		W	A	D		R	O	L	E	X
C	H	I	C	K	F	I	L	A		A	N	I	M	E
			K	E	R	R	I		O	C	T			
D	O	T		W	A	L	K	E	R	E	V	A	N	S
I	C	H	T	H	Y	S		R	A	Y		L	E	A
S	E	E	S	A			T	I	L		L	O	U	
B	A	C	K	T	O	T	H	E	B	A	S	I	C	S
A	N	O		Z	O	E			T	O	S	E	A	
R	I	P		U	Z	O		A	R	T	S	O	N	G
S	C	A	N	D	I	N	A	V	I	A		N	E	E
			O	D	E		N	E	C	C	O			
J	D	A	T	E		S	N	E	A	K	S	O	U	T
O	R	D	E	R		N	I	N		A	L	A	R	M
N	E	E	D	S		L	E	O		D	O	R	I	C

Chapter 2 Puzzle:
"A Real Kick in the Rear!"
Page 102

Chapter 3 Puzzle:
"Is That 'Z' as in 'Zoos'?"
Page 118

Chapter 4 Puzzle:
"Way to Go!"
Page 150

Chapter 5 Puzzle:
"Spill the Beans!"
Page 172

Chapter 5 Puzzle grid:

D	R	A	W	S	H	O	T		N	A	S	D	A	Q
J	A	V	A	N	E	S	E		E	R	O	I	C	A
S	H	A	K	E	I	T	A	L	L	A	B	O	U	T
			E	A	R			A	L	B		C	T	A
G	R	A	N	D	E	D	A	M	E	S		E	E	R
A	A	S		S	O	B	A			E	S	S	I	
H	Y	P	N	O	S	I	S		E	G	R	E	T	S
		O	V	E	N	T	I	M	E	R				
M	A	M	M	A	S		A	S	B	E	S	T	O	S
A	V	E	S		D	I	A	L		S	U	I		
K	I	A		T	R	E	N	T	A	F	F	A	I	R
E	A	T		I	O	S		Z	O	A				
S	T	A	R	B	U	C	K	S	O	R	D	E	R	S
D	O	X	X	E	S		L	I	N	G	E	R	I	E
O	R	E	S	T	E		M	A	S	E	R	A	T	I

Chapter 6 Puzzle grid:

D	O	J	A	C	A	T		P	L	A	Z	A		D	O	O		S	I	R
U	N	B	L	O	C	K		R	E	B	A	G		J	U	J	I	T	S	U
I	T	S	A	L	L	T	O	O	M	U	C	H		M	I	S	L	E	A	D
	M	I	A	S		O	N	O		A	L	I			I	N	M	E		
A	D	O			W	H	E	N	I	M	S	I	X	T	Y	F	O	U	R	
V	I	O	L	A	T	E	S		T	N	O	T	E		R	U	E			
I	N	V	E	R	S	E		C	R	E	D		A	I	S		P	S	S	
D	A	E	W	O	O		B	A	E	Z		I	L	L	B	E	B	A	C	K
		U	N	D	O	N	E		S	M	U	T		F	A	T	H	A		
T	H	A	T	S	G	O	O	D		L	A	P	T	O	P		N	E	E	T
Y	O	U	R	E	A	L	L	Y	G	O	T	A	H	O	L	D	O	N	M	E
R	O	T	I		S	P	E	E	D	O		C	I	N	E	A	S	T	E	S
E	D	U	C	E		H	A	G	S		S	T	E	A	D	Y				
S	O	M	E	T	H	I	N	G		F	O	E	R		G	O	O	G	O	L
E	O	N		C	A	N		S	O	L	D		V	E	N	T	U	R	E	
		D	H	L		A	S	T	R	O		S	I	D	E	B	E	T	S	
W	I	T	H	A	L	I	T	T	L	E	H	E	L	P			S	S	T	
E	B	R	O		B	E	A		O	L	A		A	R	K	S				
B	E	A	T	L	E	S		F	R	O	M	M	Y	F	R	I	E	N	D	S
M	A	Y	I	S	E	E		F	I	V	E	O		I	N	O	R	O	U	T
D	M	S		D	O	N		S	O	A	R	S		L	E	T	I	T	B	E

Chapter 6 Puzzle:
"Wait!"
Page 196

```
S H E A   A D E L E   B A C H
L A N D   C O R A L   A Q U A
O D D S   T W O O F C L U B S
A J A   G O A D     A L I A S
N I N E O F H E A R T S
  G A S       C E E   S T L
S T E V E N   P A T   N A L A
T H R E E O F D I A M O N D S
A R E S   F A Q   G O K A R T
B U D   H U N     R I N
    K I N G O F S P A D E S
A X L E S   N O A H   R A M
D E A L S A C A R D   S E R I
A N D S   R E I K I   K A T Z
M A Y O   M O R S E   A S H E
```

```
C A S S   C O M M O N L O O N
A N I T   M R M O N O P O L Y
J A N A   S K I R M I S H E S
U B E R S     E E N
N E W Z E A L A N D K A K A
S L Y   A D O B O S   L I R A
    V O I L A   B L A M
B L U E F O O T E D B O O B Y
M A N X   I L I U M
W I D E   F I N E S T   A S U
  D O R K I N G C H I C K E N
    N E W     S H I E R
T E M P E R A N C E   I N S O
C O M E A C R O S S   E T A L
B E A R D E D T I T   F O W L
```

S	I	N	A	T	R	A		L	A	S	A	G	N	A
T	O	O	R	E	A	L		E	L	E	G	I	A	C
U	N	HOL	I	E	S	T		F	LYW	E	I	G	H	T
M	I	D	A	S			A	R	T	I	S	T		
P	C	S			G	R	E	A	T	T	A	S	T	E
		B	I	D	A		I	S	H			E	R	R
	N	A	N	J	I	A	N	I		P	O	L	O	S
M	A	R	T	I	A	L		D	E	E	M	F	I	T
A	K	R	O	N		S	E	E	D	L	E	S	S	
T	I	E		T	A	X		G	E	N	T			
H	A	D	A	G	OOD	T	I	M	E			A	T	L
	L	O	L	I	T	A		Z	O	R	B	A		
E	R	I	T	R	E	A		X	F	A	C	T	O	R
P	O	K	E	M	O	N		E	A	S	T	E	N	D
S	T	E	R	E	O	S		S	Q	U	A	R	E	S

S	P	I	T	B	A	L	L		G	A	R	B	E	D
W	A	T	E	R	L	O	O		O	M	E	A	R	A
A	P	O	L	O	G	I	A		L	O	C	K	I	N
B	A	R	E	H	A	N	D		D	R	A	K	E	S
		E	L	S	E			T	A	L	E	S	E	
A	S	A	M	I		D	C	E	L	L				
M	O	Z	A	M	B	I	Q	U	E		B	R	I	M
O	B	I	T		E	R	U	P	T		I	O	T	A
R	A	Z	Z		F	R	E	S	H	F	A	C	E	D
	A	F	U	S	S			A	S	K	M	E		
B	A	S	H	E	D		T	A	B	S				
I	T	E	M	E	D		I	L	L	T	I	M	E	D
D	O	T	E	L	L		O	B	O	E	S	O	L	O
U	N	T	A	M	E		N	E	W	S	H	O	E	S
P	E	E	L	E	D		S	E	N	T	E	N	C	E

[Giving ___] THANKS
Acknowledgments

An immense and heartfelt [Word of appreciation] is due to the scores of crossword constructors and editors—named in this book or anonymous—whose work fills and sparkles in these pages, particularly to those editing and contributing puzzles in the *Atlantic*, the *Chicago Reader*/Inkwell, the *Chronicle of Higher Education*, CrosSynergy, *Harper's*, the *Los Angeles Times*, *Newsday*, the *New York Sun*, the *New Yorker*, AV Club Xwords, the *Universal Crossword*, *USA Today*, the *Wall Street Journal*, the *Washington Post*, and, of course, the *New York Times*. Truly, this book is a product of their collective genius, and I've often felt less like the author than a magpie collecting others' shiny trinkets.

I regret that space constraints prevented me from attributing each remarkable clue I've presented. And I similarly rue not being able to more than once name and [Give props to] constructors whose clues I time and again came across, and thinking, ["That's just what I needed!"], yoinked. If I had, the preceding pages would have swelled with many more [Salutes, say] to Erik Agard, Patrick Berry, Sam Ezerski, Matt Gaffney, Peter Gordon, Elizabeth C. Gorski, Matt Jones, Natan Last, Will Nediger, Stanley Newman, Brendan Emmett Quigley, Nancy Solomon, and Ben Tausig—to all of whom I'm truly [Much obliged!]. Fortunately, there are ever-growing resources available online, and I encourage readers who've expressed particular [Cheers] for a clue to do some sleuthing for the source and search out additional puzzles by that constructor or the publication that presented it.

When I did name a clue's author, I tried to find its first iteration. Apologies for any misattributions, as surely sometimes earlier instances escaped my notice: ["I owe you one!"]. Many other clues were likely the unheralded work of those esnes of crosswords, the puzzle editors, so let me squarely offer profound [Gratitude] for the work done by the likes of Evan Birnholz, Rich Norris, Mike Shenk, Patti Varol, and especially Will Shortz, as well as their colleagues.

An [Appreciative remark] is also due to those whose contributions to the cruciverse do not explicitly appear in this book, yet have provided such enrichment, joy, and wonder through their labors. Perhaps, in turn, this book will pass along some of that good crossword karma.

For their time, guidance, input, and support, [I'm grateful] especially to Roz Chast, Sarah Goocher, Dean Olsher, Marilyn Reppun, Noah Veltman, April Whitney, and David Steinberg and Jeff Chen (both of whom also authored many clues found in these pages). The author also [Acknowledges as a gift]—specifically in terms of research for this book, but also to the cruciverse in general—the colossal compilation of data at xwordinfo.com, a site co-run by Chen and Jim Horne. Their work is ["Much appreciated!"].

Similarly, this book owes a great debt to several other phenomenal websites. To Deb Amlen and the team at Wordplay, Amy Reynaldo and company at Diary of a Crossword Fiend, and Michael Sharp at Rex Parker Does the New York Times Crossword: Reading your work has taught me so much, and by no means just about crosswords. ["I appreciate it!"]

To my editor, Steve Mockus: Muchas [Gracias] for your great patience, trust, and generosity of spirit, which helped this book grow in so many unexpected ways.

["Merci"] *beaucoup* to Amy Bukszpan, whose curiosity and drive are a daily inspiration. To my mom, Maxine Bukszpan: you inspired my love of language and puzzles—I couldn't overstate my [Expression of gratitude]. Ditto to my dad, Roger Bukszpan, whose continual encouragement was invaluable. Wish you could've seen this.

And to my ever on-point wife, Natalia Boesch: It's only fitting that I've now run out of clues for **THANKS**, as I'm clueless as to how I could ever thank you enough. I'm so glad our paths crossed. Here's to a life of finding answers together.